Syntactic
Typology

Syntactic Typology

Studies in the
Phenomenology
of Language

edited by
Winfred P. Lehmann

UNIVERSITY OF TEXAS PRESS   Austin and London

International Standard Book Number 0-292-77545-8
Library of Congress Catalog Card Number 78-56377
Copyright © 1978 by the University of Texas Press
Printed in the United States of America

Contents

Preface

Language has been viewed by many linguists in the dominant
tradition as a mechanism — in the words of Humboldt, as a
"dead mass" (1836/1968: lxxviii). For de Laguna, "language,
like the tool, is primarily an instrument to be used for
the accomplishment of objective *ends*" (1927/1963: 244).
Investigation of this instrument is then the linguist's
primary task, as the widely influential Bloomfield put it:
"The linguist deals only with the speech-signal" (1933: 32).
And even though the dominant voice of the transformational-
ists departed from a mechanistic to a mentalistic approach,
for it the "generative grammar internalized by someone who
has acquired a language" is a "device" (Chomsky 1964: 915).
Such conceptions represent only a partial understanding of
language. For a more complete understanding, language and
grammar must be viewed in Humboldt's fuller characterization
as a "mass carrying within itself the living germ of a never
ending definability" (1836/1968: lxxvii). To understand
language fully then, we must find means to deal with that
"living germ" as well as with the "dead mass."

This aim has been pursued by a small number of scholars
who are acknowledged among the most brilliant linguists,
Humboldt, Finck, Sapir among them. Besides grammars these
linguists were concerned with rules for the structure of
language. Their approach, in contrast with the descriptive-

historical, is typological, a designation as inadequate as
"descriptive" but equally installed in linguistic study.

Typology, pursued even before Humboldt, has gained in
insights concerning language since his time, as the eight
chapters of this book set out to show. Among these gains is
deeper understanding of Humboldt's paradox that "language is
objectively influential and independent to exactly the extent
it influences in a subjective way and is dependent" (lxxix).
Thus, while language fulfills certain functions, those
functions and the rules of human discourse may also affect
language. The approach to the typological study of language
then does not simply seek out characteristic types but inves-
tigates language for the various roles it fulfills in meeting
human needs for expression as well as communication.

The results of such investigation might be presented in a
philosophical literary essay like Humboldt's, sometimes
identified as the most difficult comment on language. Yet,
to simplify presentation of the approach, specific languages
have been selected here as "consistent"; the bases for such
selection are illustrated with examples. Such languages
provide a key to the understanding of others, including those
labeled inconsistent because of their contrasting structures.
It would, however, be remarkable if any language were completely consistent, inasmuch as languages are always changing,
partly as a result of influence by neighboring languages,
partly as a result of the flux evident in all social conventions. Nonetheless one can point to languages like Japanese
and Turkish which have relatively few inconsistent characteristics, possibly as a result of relative isolation,
possibly for other reasons.

This book has been designed to provide an interpretation
with examples first of consistent languages, and then of

specific points of interest in typological study. For reasons of space the discussion has been restricted almost entirely to syntactic characterization, to the exclusion of semantic and phonological matters. Chapter 1 lists the structures which differ characteristically in languages with VO order as opposed to those with OV; it also sketches the background of the typological approach, and some of its implications.

Chapter 2 gives a detailed account of a highly consistent OV language, illustrating how the structures identified in Chapter 1 may be explored in any language. It also exemplifies how one may demonstrate that a language indeed belongs to a given type, and points out relationships between the occurrences of forms and their functions. Chapter 3 gives an account of a highly consistent VSO language, though without the detail of Chapter 2, for the language selected by the writer was accessible to him only in written texts. Chapter 3 then illustrates some of the problems encountered in the treatment of languages which cannot be studied with the help of native speakers. Chapter 4 deals with the third prominent type, SVO, using English as an example. Since Chapter 2 thoroughly illustrated the regular structures, the discussion of English turns to devices found in language which vary the monotony of rigidly preserved patterns. These devices relate to considerations of function, of discourse, and of style.

The next three chapters explore further implications of a typological approach. Chapter 5 in examining Chinese suggests that lack of inflection affects syntactic patterns. Chapter 6 deals with the relatively infrequent VOS type, exploring its problems and shortcomings from a functional and discourse point of view. Chapter 7 explores ergativity, that is, a patterning which blurs distinctions between S and O by

aligning the objects of transitive verbs with the subjects of
intransitive verbs. As with functional forces and the requirements of discourse, the effects of ergativity lead to richness
in language patterning, so that efforts to find an underlying
system for language may well be questioned. Yet underlying
principles must be involved, as study of the basic structures
of language and of language in change demonstrates. Implications of this view are sketched in the final chapter, which
points out how the typological framework can lead to the understanding of problems as diverse as the dual word order patterning of standard, written German and the development of the
Indo-European languages through five millennia. Concern with
linguistic phenomena accordingly leads to an appreciation of
the "living germ" recognized by Humboldt.

To distinguish the view of language exemplified here from
that which has been dominant in linguistics, language here is
examined as a phenomenon, not as an instrument, not as a
structure centered on a speech-signal, not even as a system
defined by a grammar which is a device. Its "living germ"
regulates it in interesting though restricted ways which
linguists have barely started to explore. When explored
further, such "regulation" may be examined in hierarchies,
as of animacy. Speakers may not introduce markers for nouns
whose functions are obvious; for example, the three items of
Children collect stones have only one interpretation
regardless of their order or their inflection. A language
may economically dispense with means to distinguish animate
from inanimate nouns, or even subjects from objects, dis-
playing in this way hierarchies of elements and categories
while illustrating its "living germ." A logical system, by
contrast, or an artificial language, would apply parallel
distinctive markers to all categories of note.

The internal force may also be evident in similar patterning
for similar processes, such as modification. Whether a modifier
is expressed through an adjective: the lot neighboring this
one, or a genitive: the lot of the neighbors, or a relative
clause: the lot which the neighbors own, similarity of function between the three constructions might well lead toward
similarity of location with regard to the noun which is head
of the construction. Here too a hierarchy exists, but of
constructions, with presumably the relative clause directing
the genitive and adjective. The phenomenon, language, then is
not simply an inert mass but in Humboldt's words (1836/1968:
lxxviii) a "stock of words" and a "system of rules" with
mutual interrelationships, determined in part by the patterning of human discourse.

To account even in part for such a phenomenon, analyses
should deal with its patterning in discourse, with its
presentation of meaning, with its central structure represented in syntactic rules and elements, with the shapes of
its words, and with its sounds. This large task has been
severely restricted here to syntactic structures, for in this
area new insights have recently been made which are central
to fuller accounts. Further, a more complete characterization
of any one language would result in a book at least the size
of this, though it would by no means be a "grammar." As more
is learned about language as a phenomenon, such characterizations may indeed be produced; in contrast with descriptive
grammars or historical grammars they might be viewed as
biographies of a language.

This book grew out of a seminar of the 1976 Linguistic
Institute arranged by the State University of New York at
Oswego, New York. The authors were given the set of patterns
included below in Chapter 1, section 3, with freedom to present

their languages or their topics as they considered most
effective. While minor editorial adjustments have been made,
the authors are then responsible for their own chapters and
no others.

The transcriptions and transliterations of examples cited
in papers are taken directly from sources, from spellings of
informants or representations of investigators; no attempt
has been made to achieve complete accuracy and consistency.

Besides expressing my appreciation to the authors, I would
like to thank especially Carol Justus, director of the institute, and her colleagues at SUNY, Oswego, and in the SUNY
system. Helen-Jo Hewitt saved me a great deal of time by
guiding my efforts on a CRT to combine bibliographical lists
compiled with disparate stylistic practices. I am also grateful to Ruth Lehmann and Theodore Lightner, as well as
students, for comments on earlier versions of these essays,
and to James McCloskey for the Irish and Hundirapola Ratanajot
for the Sinhalese in the first chapter.

W. P. L.

Syntactic Typology

1. The Great Underlying Ground-Plans

Winfred P. Lehmann

1.1. The Bases of Linguistic Typology

Languages, in spite of their outward differences, are formed
by identical principles. This conclusion follows from the
ability of humans to master any natural language, so that a
child learns as native language the language or languages
spoken to it. The ability persists for children and adults;
they may acquire additional languages quite different in
external features from those native to them. And if the new
language is to be used only for simple communication they may
produce an amalgam from languages of different outward
patterning — a so-called pidgin. The outward differences then
are shown to be surface characteristics which may be modified
or eliminated while underlying principles direct the newly
formed language.

Assumption of an underlying similarity among languages is
also supported by the possibility of translating materials of
great complexity, whether literary, scientific, or religious,
from one language into any other. In translation as in the
formation of a pidgin the surface differences are resolved
but a common thread is retained. This underlying structure
makes possible the highly abbreviated languages used by
logicians and mathematicians, whatever their native language.
Movement from one language to another, whether innovative
like the language of poetry, or controlled, like that of

logic, suggests that all human languages are based on common
inward patterns and principles. This book seeks to identify
those common patterns and principles, and to illustrate how
they are manifested in languages of outwardly different
structure.

Students of language have long concerned themselves with
attempts to determine the common features of languages. Early
scholars manifesting such concern, whether philosophers like
Plato (427? - 347 B.C.) and Aristotle (384 - 322 B.C.) or
linguists like Panini (fourth or fifth century B.C.) and
Sibawayhi (eighth century A.D.), were hampered by lack of
information about a broad range of languages. In the last
several centuries, however, steps were taken by philosophers,
notably Leibnitz (1646 - 1716), and by linguists, such as
Adelung (1732 - 1806), to overcome this shortcoming by
assembling materials from many languages with the aim of
determining their essential characteristics. These steps led
to the activity which is the topic of this book: the typology
of languages.

Typology in the broader sense is concerned with the study
and classification of any selected human activities and
products. Rather than concentrate on language, a typologist
might deal with other social phenomena, such as games or
tools — for example, digging implements. The importance of
such study depends on the characteristics selected as central
and the comprehensiveness and quality of the data. Thus the
characterization of a language as guttural is based on
external phenomena; moreover, since these have been
inaccurately observed, the characterization is of little
value. Characteristics used in earlier works, such as that
of Adelung illustrated below, led to inadequate conclusions
because the available data were not yet adequate. Subsequent

linguistic study, notably in the past several decades, has achieved from comprehensive materials in a broad array of languages an understanding of language which permits a well-founded typology of language.

Such a typology is far more than a taxonomy. Taxonomic analysis is constructed on selected external characteristics. The influential taxonomy of plants produced by Linnaeus (1707 - 1778) is based on characteristic physical features such as stamens. A taxonomy of languages might be constructed on classification of characteristic parts of speech, or shapes of words, or kinds of sounds. By contrast with these external characteristics linguistic typology is based on the analysis of patterns and principles which have been identified as central in language, such as the structure of the simple sentence and its constituents, and processes like government, modification, and subordination. Successful typology then requires an accurate understanding of language and its elements.

Human language may be defined as a system of communication conveying meaning by means of speech sounds. Its mechanisms are treated in three distinct though related components: semantic, syntactic, and phonological. Since the semantic component is constructed at least in part in accordance with the outside world, and the phonological in accordance with parameters of speaking and hearing, the syntactic component is the most distinctive of human language. It is also the most significant for linguistic typology.

Typological analysis accordingly takes syntax as the central component. The analysis is based on the structure of the sentence, and on that of its constituents. For example, English and a large group of languages are referred to as SVO (Subject-Verb-Object) languages because the typical structure

of the simple straightforward sentence involves these
essential elements in SVO order, as in:

(1) The children saw the gosling.

The syntactic pattern is taken as more central than
morphological characteristics because it regulates and makes
use of varying forms; saw, the past tense form of see, is less
fundamental for construction of this sentence than is the use
of a verb between its subject and object. The syntactic
pattern is also more significant than the phonological,
regulating phonological processes when conditions are
appropriate; though the chief accent falls on the object
(gosling) in a sentence like this, if one wished to identify
and contrast a particular animal (a tiny gosling), the adjective tiny would receive the chief accent and gosling would
have a different pronunciation from that in sentence (1).
Moreover, fundamental meanings are expressed by the syntax;
since in SVO languages the agent of the action is placed
before the verb, the meaning of the sentence is totally
different if the syntactic order is modified to:

(2) The gosling saw the children.

These and many other characteristics that might be cited
illustrate that the syntactic component is central in
language, and therefore might be expected to provide the
basic criteria for the typology of language.

Among syntactic constructions, that of the verb with regard
to its object is most fundamental. Since two orders of V and
O are possible, there are two types of language, VO like
English, and OV like Turkish. In Turkish, sentence (1)
would be expressed as follows:

(3) Çocuklar   kazı   gördü.
    child-Plural goose-Object see-Past
    'The children saw the goose.'

The distinction between these two basic types of language is
manifested in many constructions which will be identified
and illustrated in the course of this book. Observation of
language patterning and also investigations into control of
language by the brain support the assumption that the verb
is central in human language and that it in combination with
an object is a basic construction.

   The central position of the verb may be demonstrated in
many languages, for the simplest kind of sentence may be made
up solely of a verb. Such sentences are commonly found in
expressions for natural phenomena, such as rain and thunder,
or for feelings, such as anxiety and fear. In Classical Latin,
Greek, and Sanskrit, for example, the English statement of
example (4) is expressed with a simple verb form.

(4) It is raining.

(5) Sanskrit: Varṣati.

(6) Greek: Húei.

(7) Latin: Pluit.

When such sentences consist of more than one word, the
additional word is not the subject. Thus in Japanese the
statement is made with a so-called subjectless sentence
(Kuno 1973: 33).

(8) Japanese: Ame da. (Lit., 'Rain is.')

Comparable verb sentences expressing feelings are extended by
an object, not a subject, in Latin and German.

(9) a. Latin: Miseret. 'It excites pity.'

b. Latin: Eius mē miseret.
            his me excites-pity
            'I pity him.'

c. German: Mich jammert ...
           me   excites-pity
           'I pity ...'

These examples may illustrate that the most basic sentence
type consists of a verb, or a verb plus object — not of a
noun, or a verb plus subject.

Sentences consisting solely of a noun or other element are
abbreviatory. Thus the utterance:

(10) Joan!

in answer to the question:

(11) Who saw the gosling?

is an abbreviation of the more complete sentence:

(12) Joan saw the gosling.

And when used in address a single noun like:

(13) Joan!

is comparable to the object of a construction like:
'I want ...' or 'I want the attention of ...'

The verb is thus the basic constituent of the sentence.
Constructions consisting of a verb plus an object are the
primary constructions made up of more than one constituent.
Every language is accordingly classified as either VO, like
English and the languages of Europe and the Semitic
languages, or OV, like Japanese, Turkish, and the Dravidian
languages of India.

The primacy of the verb in human language is further
exemplified in the control of language by the brain. In the
process of maturing, one of the hemispheres of the brain

becomes dominant in the control of language; for 98 percent
of human speakers this hemisphere is the left. Such laterali-
zation has been investigated in many ways, including simple
binaural experimentation. Probably the most intriguing studies
have been undertaken with speakers having bisected brains
(Gazzaniga 1970). The studies have indicated that while the
right, nondominant hemisphere can manage utterances of nouns,
especially concrete nouns, only the left, dominant hemisphere
can manage the utterance of verbs. Since human language is
intimately connected with specially developed sections of the
left hemisphere which have the unique capability of controlling
verbs as well as the information conveyed through nouns, we
have nonlinguistic evidence to support the linguistically
based conclusion that the verb is the most characteristic
segment of human language. Linguistic typology then must
concern itself centrally with the verb and its constructions.

Other features and constructions of language must be
examined in their relation to the fundamental syntactic
patterns. An array of features presented simply because they
can be discriminated contributes little to our understanding
of language, as may be determined by scanning Adelung's
characterization of Turkish given below. From improved
understanding of the basic characteristics of language we
can now identify its most basic patterns as well as the
processes and devices involved in them.

1.2. Characteristic Processes and Devices of Language

In using language we are compelled to deal with it as a
linear phenomenon both in speaking and in hearing. Disregard-
ing the more complex processes of these two activities, we
may observe here that one process in the use of language
involves the arranging of elements in sequence. This is one

of two fundamental processes: selecting recognized elements
(words) from a large set and arranging them in an accepted
order. These requirements govern the fundamental structure of
language, as examination of sentence (1) illustrates. This
sentence consists of four words: children, gosling, the, saw.
These can be arranged in one of two orders to make a normal,
acceptable sentence in English, the order of sentence (1) or
that of sentence (2). The device known as *arrangement* or
order is the most important process of language. It is
utilized in the phonological and semantic as well as the
syntactic component; make is a different entity from came,
and income is a different entity from come in. Arrangement
owes its significance to the linear structure of language.
Its linearity requires that entities must be arranged in
order.

While arrangement.is most significant, it requires in
language sets of entities subject to various patterning.
Such sets have long been classified and studied as parts of
speech. Among these, verbs and nouns make up the largest and
most important sets. They also play the most important role
in the basic syntactic pattern, for nouns typically fill the
role of object, in this way amplifying the central element —
the verb. The process of filling the positions in any given
sentence is known as *selection*. In producing a sentence such
as The children saw the gosling, saw is selected from the
possible set of English verbs to fill the V position;
children and gosling are selected from the set of nouns to
fill the S and O positions. Selection and arrangement in this
way result from the possibilities available in a linear
communication system.

In a linear sequence of entities two processes are most
prominent: arrangement and selection. Yet because of the

possibilities inherent in the mechanisms used for speech, two
further processes are found in the production of speech:
modification of the selected elements, chiefly their beginning
or their ending though also often the entire element, and
intonation, that is, melodic variation superposed on the
linear unit. Both processes are associated with concentrations
of energy in speech, that is, with distribution of stress or
pitch patterns. For example, when the strongest stress is
placed on the pronoun in the following sentence:

(14) Let ús go!

the pronoun has a full vowel, in contrast with its pronunciation under the following stress placement:

(15) a. Let's gó.

The variation of us results from the process known as
modification.

Modification is associated with differences in meaning and
is accordingly significant — signaling (14) as an exclusive
first person plural (= we but not you are to go) and (15) as
an inclusive (= all of us are to go). Varieties of modification are closely associated with characteristic types of
languages. VSO languages foster modification of initial
elements, OV languages of final elements. But the uses of
modification in language are less central than arrangement
and selection, and accordingly less significant in typology.

Intonation is also less significant, though for a different
reason. Some characteristic patterns, such as final rise of
pitch to indicate uncertainty, are widespread, virtually to
the point of being universal. If, for example, sentence (15)
is uttered with final rising pitch:

(15) b. Let's go↑

the utterance is an expression of surprise or challenge
(= you really mean we should go?). Intonation patterns are
accordingly in great part regulated by general principles,
rather than by the specific principles which lead to a
characterization of language.

As the processes leading to linguistic sequences are
applied, two forces are at work: *control* and *delimitation*.
Control involves the domination of one element by another.
It leads to hierarchization. It has been most widely investigated with regard to verbs controlling nouns, where the force
is traditionally known as *government*. In the central segment
of sentences a governed element is often identified by a
change in form, e.g.:

(16) See them! (< they)

The change in form of the substantive rather than of the verb
reflects the dominance of the verb in this construction.

Another word class involved in government is that of
adpositions, prepositions in VO languages and postpositions
in OV, e.g.:

(17) By them.

The patterns of control in verbs and adpositions are highly
transparent.

More subtle control is found in causative verbs, or in
verbs accompanied by a complement; yet in such patterns the
control is in accordance with the arrangement of verb and
object. In the following English sentences the controlling
verb precedes the controlled.

(18) They caused Henry to resign.

(19) She persuaded Lynn to go.

(20) They told John to negotiate.

The extent of control in such sequences varies; in sentences
(18) and (19) the actions of "resigning" and "going" were
carried out, while in (20) it is not certain that "negotiating"
was carried out. Control or government plays an extensive role
in language, with subtleties that still demand much study.

Delimitation may seem similar to control, yet it operates
differently; the delimiter modifies rather than controls and
is thus subordinate to the element it delimits; when an
extended modifier, essentially an entire clause, is incorporated in a construction, the process is referred to as
embedding. While a controlling element often brings about
change of another element, as illustrated above, a delimiting
element is commonly itself changed to "agree" with the element
it modifies, in this way reflecting its secondary role. The
process is known as *agreement* or *concord*.

A characteristic pattern for modifying nouns is that known
as relativization. In English, relative clauses provide
examples of the changes found in embedding, using who for
animate, generally human, nouns in contrast with which for
inanimates:

(21) The children whom we met ...

(22) The book which I bought ...

Modifiers however are commonly identified simply by their
arrangement rather than by the process of selection. Thus
adjectives in English are placed before nouns, with no
inflection to indicate congruence. Similarly, in Japanese,
relative constructions are identified by their position
before nouns.

While relative constructions are the characteristic
modifiers of nouns, relationships may also be expressed
which are less direct, as illustrated in the following example.

(23) They met Anne at the time that they had fixed.

(24) They knew Betsy at a time when she could hardly sew.

(25) They knew Betsy when she could hardly sew.

The last clause in (24) and (25) is not viewed as a relative
construction but rather as a subordinate clause modifying a
verb, even in (24) where it is adjacent to a noun — hence it
is classified as an adverbial clause. Because conjunctions
commonly take over the role of relating subordinate clauses
to matrix clauses, as in example (25) as opposed to (23),
grammars distinguish sharply between relative and adverbial
clauses.

Adverbial clauses may indicate "agreement" variously with
some element involved in the embedding. Special verb forms,
such as subjunctives, may be used, pronouns may be modified,
and so on, as in example (27).

(26) He said: "I will come."

(27) He said he would come.

If a clause is the object of a verb, it is referred to as
a *complement*. Like adverbial clauses, complements are comparable to relative clauses, as the following examples
illustrate.

(28) They expected the fact that he would arrive.

(29) They expected that he would arrive.

Complements too reflect in various ways the relationship with
the verbs accompanying them.

In the expansion of the central constructions of language,
either OV or VO, government and agreement are primary forces,
as the constructions discussed above and the selected
patterns presented in the following section illustrate.

1.3. Selected Patterns in VO and OV Languages

The typological sketches of selected languages given in subsequent chapters will indicate how comprehensive are the constructions regulated by the basic structure of a language. This section includes a brief number of those constructions which are given here to illustrate the processes discussed above, and to provide concrete examples for some of the patterns listed in section 1.4. For these illustrations Modern Irish and Modern Sinhalese are used. Both are Indo-European languages. Yet in the course of their history they have become strikingly different in structure. Irish is a highly consistent VSO language, Sinhalese a highly consistent OV language.

In examining languages for characteristic typological patterns we distinguish these more clearly for the VO type in the VSO subtype than in the SVO subtype, for in this the subject must be taken into consideration when verbal modifiers are introduced. SVO languages have characteristic constructions like modal auxiliaries, due in part to the placement of the subject before the verb, as will be observed in Chapter 4. In VSO languages, on the other hand, this problem is not met, for in them as in OV languages verbal modifiers can be placed between the V and # (sentence boundary) with no interference from other constituents.

As indicated in section 1.4, typological characteristics will be given in accordance with nine patterns, each with subclasses:

> I. Simple clauses
> II. Nominal modifiers
> III. Verbal modifiers

[IV. Sentence adverbials]*
V. Compound and complex sentences
[VI. Marking]*
[VII. Grammatical processes]*
[VIII. Morphological characteristics]*
[IX. Phonological characteristics]*

From this list it is obvious that complete accounting for these patterns in any language would require an extensive grammar. It is one of the aims of this book to provide guidelines for improved explanatory grammars; yet the examples introduced with this aim must be severely limited in the interest of pedagogical effectiveness. Accordingly, primarily the first three patterns will be illustrated here.

OV — Sinhalese   VSO — Irish

I. Structure of the simple clause

(I.1) Basic sentence pattern: 'John saw the dog.'

Jōn ballavə däkka   Chonaic Seán an madadh.
    dog   saw   saw   the dog

(I.3) Adpositional pattern: 'John saw the dog from the window.'

Jōn janēle iňdəla   Chonaic Seán an madadh
    window from   ón   fhuinneog.
ballavə däkka.   from-the window

(I.4) Constructions with a standard:

(I.4.1) Comparison of inequality: 'The dog is bigger than the cat.'

Balla balələtə vaḍā   Tá an madadh níos mó
      cat-from more   is   bigger

---

*Omitted for reasons of space.

loku y.   ná   an cat.
big is   than

(I.4.2) Name with title: 'Professor Smith/Bāləgē/
        MacGabhann'

Bāləgē Mahācāryatumā   an tOllamh MacGabhann

(I.4.3) Family name with given name: 'John Smith'

Bāləgē Jōn   Seán MacGabhann

(I.4.4) Additive numerals: 'thirteen, seventeen'

daha-tunə, daha-hatə   trí déag, seacht déag
ten   three ten seven   three ten   seven   ten

II. Nominal modifiers:

(II.5) Relative constructions: 'John saw the dog
       that ate the meat.'

Mas kāpu ballavə Jōn   Chonaic Seán an madadh
meat ate

däkka.   a   d'ith an fheoil.
                                 that ate   meat

(II.6) Genitive constructions: 'John saw his
       neighbor's dog.'

Jōn eyāge asalväsiyage   Chonaic Seán madadh a
    his   neighbor's   his
ballavə däkka.   chomharsan.
                                 neighbor's

(II.7) Descriptive adjectives: 'John saw the big dog.'

Jōn taḍi ballavə däkka.   Chonaic Seán an madadh mór.
    big   big

III. Verbal modifiers

(III.11) a. Interrogative expressions: 'Did John see
            the dog?'

Jōn ballavə däkka də?   An   bhfaca Seán an madadh?
            Int.   Int. saw

(III.12) a. Negative expressions: 'John didn't see
         the dog.'

Jōn ballavə däkke nǟ.   Ní   fhaca Seán an madadh.
                Neg   Neg.

(III.11 and 12) b. 'Didn't John see the dog?'

Jōn ballavə däkke   Nach   bhfaca Seán
                             Int.-Neg.
nä-d-də?
Neg.-Int.   an madadh?

                             (cf. Old Irish: in-nad   )
                                             Int.-Neg.

V. Compound and Complex Sentences:

(V.25) Complementation:' Mary told John to feed the dog.' '

Ballaṭə kǟm dennə   Dūirt Máire le Seán
       eat cause   told   to

kiyəla   Mēri   an madadh a chothú.
Complementizer   to provide-for

Jōnṭə kīva.
     told

The process determining the arrangement of the constructions under I is government. The patterns exemplified are
parallel. Just as a verb governs its object, so does an
adposition. It is accordingly understandable that VO languages
include prepositions while OV languages include postpositions.

While the constructions with a standard do not strictly
speaking reflect government, the relationship between a
variable and its standard is comparable to that between a
verb and its object. Thus the comparison of inequality
involves a situation in which a variable is related to a
selected object or standard. In such a comparison the standard
may be an object like a cat or a house and so on. In other
constructions involving a standard, such as names, the same
relationship is taken into consideration: the standard is the

family name, with possible variables selected from titles or
given names. In a VO language, the variable element precedes
the standard, and in an OV language the reverse is true.
Curiously, this sequence also applies to addresses, as in
Japanese before addresses were influenced by international
postal conventions. The name of the largest entity, the state,
was placed first, followed by designations for progressively
smaller units and finally the surname of the addressee. The
order is also observed in other "additive" patterns such as
numerals compounded on the basis of adding, a pattern commonly
used to construct "teen" numerals. In these the lower digit
is given with reference to a specific standard, for example,
3 with regard to 10 = 13.

The patterns regulated by government are relatively few,
yet they make up the principal constructions of the simple
clause.

When the constituents of the simple clause are modified,
the modifications are carried out in accordance with a
fundamental principle for both nominal and verbal elements
(Lehmann 1973a). By this principle, which is given below, the
central sequence, whether VO or OV, must not be interrupted.
Any modifier is then placed between the modified constituent
and the sentence boundary.

$$\# \ Q \ V \ (N^{Obj.}) \ (N^{Mod.}) \ \# \ \rightarrow \ \left\{ \begin{array}{l} \# \ Q \ V \ (N^{Obj.}) \ (N^{Mod.}) \ \# \\ \\ \# \ (N^{Mod.}) \ (N^{Obj.}) \ V \ Q \ \# \end{array} \right\}$$

The symbols used here will be accounted for more fully in
1.8 below. In the grammar on which the principle is based,
$N^{Obj.}$ is used for an object, Q or Qualifier for a verbal
modifier. In accordance with the principle, nominal modifiers

precede nouns in OV languages and follow them in VO languages; verbal modifiers follow verbs in OV languages and precede them in VO languages. The constructions involved include many of the patterns in language.

The basic construction for introducing descriptive modifiers with nominal elements is the relative clause, as noted above. In this construction, two sentences with an equivalent noun or noun phrase are combined, as syntacticians have stated for more than a century. Thus the two sentences given as (30a) and (30b) may be combined if the noun phrase the dog has the same reference.

(30) a. John saw the dog.

b. The dog ate the meat.

c. John saw the dog that ate the meat.

In accordance with the principle the modifying sentence is embedded after its antecedent in VO languages, before it in OV, as illustrated in Irish and Sinhalese (II.5 above). The embedded sentence then is generally reduced, especially through "deletion" of one of the equivalent noun phrases; the results vary in detail from language to language. If the verb in the embedded sentence is the copula (BE), it as well as the equivalent noun phrase is deleted, leaving a descriptive genitive, as in (II.6), or a descriptive adjective, as in (II.7). Other nominal modifiers are not illustrated here, nor are multiple nominal modifiers, such as adjectives plus relative clauses with one noun.

Verbal modifiers affect the entire clause, as might be expected from the role of the verb. Here only two frequent verb-modifying constructions are exemplified, interrogatives and negatives. As in Sinhalese and Irish, these modifiers may be expressed through particles. These particles typically

stand between the verb and sentence boundary, as in the
three sentences of (III.11) and (III.12) above. In SVO
languages, however, other devices are commonly used, such as
auxiliaries in English or shifts of word order in German.

(III.11) c. Sieht Hans den Hund?
         sees John the dog

Further, the verbal modifier may be expressed through
intonation, as in the echo questions of English:

(III.11) d. John sees the dog?

Intonation is the dominant means of expression for declarative
statements (III.10), though some languages also use particles
for it; the particles concerned are then closest to the
sentence boundary. And, as the combined modifiers in the
sentences translating Didn't John see the dog? illustrate,
the expressions for interrogative and negative are generally
placed in this order with regard to the sentence boundary.
Such placement of surface markers reflecting underlying
hierarchy of linguistic elements is remarkable. It is also
troublesome, for it may lead us to overstate how surface
patterns mirror underlying syntactic structures; they may do
so, especially in OV languages, which have strings of
elements marking the verbal modifiers generally arranged in
the order indicated in the section from (III.10) to (III.19).

   Of compound and complex patterns only complement structures (V.25) are exemplified here, largely to illustrate the
comparability of such patterns with single elements. As
noted above, complements can be compared with objects. They
observe the order of objects with regard to their verb, as
the examples indicate. But, like all extended constructions,
they vary in accordance with the type of language, as will
be illustrated in the chapters dealing with individual
languages.

The four groups noted here — I. simple clauses; II. nominal
modifiers; III. verbal modifiers; V. compound and complex
sentences — are those best understood in typological patterning. The grammatical processes listed in VII are becoming
better understood, as a result of recent study. On the other
hand, sentence adverbials (IV) have been largely untouched.

The process of marking (VI) has also been dealt with only
peripherally, with references to study of it in phonological
and stylistic investigations, especially as carried out by
Roman Jakobson. Marking involves various devices from language
to language, such as shifts in the basic clause order,
sentence adverbials, the processes included in VII, and
special intonation patterns, as in the marked variants of
the following sentence.

(31) a. I saw John yesterday.

     b. John I saw yesterday.   (Shift of basic order)

     c. Why, John I saw yesterday.   (Sentence adverb and

                                           shift of basic order)

     d. It was John I saw yesterday. (VII.30. Clefting)

     e. I saw John only yesterday.   (Intonation)

Marking then can be carried out in various ways, so that it
could be treated at length. Here correlation of various
marking devices with language types and subtypes will be of
primary interest.

Grammatical processes also vary in prominence in the
various language types and subtypes. Clefting, for example,
is particularly prominent in SVO languages. Passivization is
prominent in SVO languages, but not at all in OV languages;
it is essentially a tool for achieving topicalization for the
object, and such a tool is unnecessary in OV structures.

Moreover, OV languages are poor in pronouns. As with marking, variation in the use of grammatical processes among the different types will be of major interest here.

Relationships between types and the characteristics included in sections VIII and IX are little known. Yet it has been clear for some time that VSO languages are characterized by prefixation and OV languages by suffixation. Moreover, VSO languages are notable for initial morphophonemic modifications, while OV languages undergo final modification. In general, the structure of clauses has diminishing effect as the device in question is less central. Thus it is difficult to suggest any correlation between the number and kinds of vowels and a given typological structure. Less concrete phonological features, like syllabification or use of suprasegmentals, may however show such correlations. Thus OV languages tend to have simple syllables, of C(C)V structure. Moreover, the effect of phonological processes is "progressive" in OV languages, "anticipatory" in VO. OV languages tend to have vowel harmony and progressive assimilation; VO languages tend to have umlaut and anticipatory assimilation. Yet for such processes to be productive a language must have the requisite structure of words and syllables. Correlations between phonological patterning and language types must then be examined with delicacy.

Such correlations, as well as other characteristic typological patterns and processes, will be better known and described as further languages are investigated for their characteristics. The following section presents in schematic form patterns which are dealt with in the subsequent chapters here, and might well be the basis for examination of any language that is being studied.

1.4. Patterns and Processes

In typological investigations certain patterns and processes
have been identified as characteristic for possible language
types. These are listed here. Some may well be expanded, as
I and (I.4) are here. Others may need amplification, such as
III.A and III.B, expressions for modality, aspect, and tense.
Most have been extensively investigated, though as noted above
others are poorly known, such as IV, sentence adverbials.
Undertakings to illuminate murky areas, such as causative
expressions and topicalizations, have begun to illuminate more
of the patterns and processes (Shibatani, ed. 1976b; Li, ed.
1976). This book has been designed in part to arouse further
such study.

The patterns and processes are as follows.

    I.   Structure of simple clauses

    I.A. Verbal sentences; predicate clause types

    I.B. Nominal sentences; equational clause types

       1. Position of O with regard to V

       2. Position of S with regard to V

       3. Adpositions

       4. Constructions with a standard

       4.1. Comparison of inequality

       4.2. Name with title

       4.3. Family name with given name

       4.4. Additive numerals in the teens

    II. Nominal modifiers

       5. Relative constructions

       6. Genitive constructions

       7. Descriptive adjectives

       8. Limiting adjectives

       9. Numerals

III.   Verbal modifiers
   10. Expressions for declarative
   11. Interrogative expressions
   12. Negative expressions
   13. Middle expressions — reciprocals, reflexives
III.A.   Expressions for modality
   14. Necessitative expressions
   15. Voluntative expressions
III.B.   Expressions for aspect and tense
   16. Perfective expressions
   17. Momentary expressions
   18. Iterative expressions
   19. Causative expressions
   20. Tense
 IV.   Sentence adverbials
  V.   Compound and complex sentences
   21. Coordination; parataxis
   22. Subordination; hypotaxis
   23. Indirect statements and questions; quotatives
   24. Adverbial clauses
   25. Complementation
 VI.   Marking
VII.   Grammatical processes
   26. Pronominalization
   27. Anaphora
   28. Topicalization
   29. Passivization
   30. Clefting
VIII.   Morphological characteristics
VIII.A. Inflection
VIII.B. Derivation

A full account of each of these topics for any language
would lead to a lengthy statement, virtually as extensive as
a grammar. Rather than such an extensive account, the
characteristic patterns of syntax and the processes they
undergo are aimed at here.

1.5. Earlier Typological Studies

It is instructive to compare the criteria used in earlier
typological studies. Two major undertakings have dealt with
the characteristics of individual languages, Adelung's
Mithridates (1806 - 1817) and Müller's *Grundriss* (1876 - 1888).
Adelung's is far more extensive; Müller's undertaking was
limited by his relatively early death, with no collaborator
to continue his work. Subsequently published studies have been
more limited in scope (Finck 1909), or directed at specific
characteristics (Schmidt 1926) or at external accounts of
languages (Meillet and Cohen 1952; Voegelin and Voegelin
1973). Even Müller, in spite of his assertion of progress
beyond Adelung, is more restricted than the *Mithridates*
in concentrating largely on the morphology of selected groups
of languages. Accordingly an excerpt will be given only from
Mithridates, to illustrate earlier typological study. The
excerpt will consist largely of Adelung's characterization of
Turkish, in translation; Turkish citations are given in the
spelling of today, and printing errors have been corrected,
but the text is otherwise maintained.

Adelung's purpose is clearly stated in introductory essays.
The following sentence from one of his prefaces summarizes his
aims: "The most important thing for me was to penetrate into
the inner and outer structure of each language, because only
in this way can the distinctiveness of each and its difference
from all others be recognized" (1806: Vorrede XIV). As will be
noted from his account of Turkish, Adelung pursues these
aims, giving morphological elements or outer structure as in
(7), as well as internal patterning as in (9).

The characteristics are arranged in accordance with the
usual order of grammars, with statements on the phonology
given first, followed by statements on morphology and syntax.
There is no attempt to state the characteristics of Turkish
in reference to a general framework for languages, except in
(1) and (2), which use the languages of Europe as norm,
especially the Germanic. Such concentration on one's own
language and ethnocentricity are unfortunate, but not unknown
even among linguists today. In spite of their shortcomings,
Adelung and his successors are to be commended for identifying
characteristic patterns such as verb-final position (17), the
presence of postpositions (16) and the type of comparison (9).
Since Adelung's insights and shortcomings are readily apparent,
no further commentary will be given here.

Mithridates I.462 - 466:
Character of the Turkish Language

(1) In this language not only is the old Tatar basic
material mixed with Arabic and Persian words, but there is
also much that is Germanic in it, which permits one to
conclude that there was a close relationship of both
peoples, presumably in their first habitations in Central
Asia.
(2) Otherwise it has a very distinctive character, and
only in its substantives and adjectives some similarity
with European languages.

(<u>3</u>) It has also the letters of the Persians, besides
their sound, and in addition still, a nasal, accordingly
in all, 33 letters.

(<u>4</u>) The inflectional and derivational sounds at the ends
of words are very manifold.

(<u>5</u>) The accent most frequently falls on the last syllable,
even in polysyllabic words.

(<u>6</u>) Substantives have no gender, except by meaning. In
order to avoid ambiguity the natural genders are distinguished by special modifying words: <u>karindaş</u> means
'brother' and 'sister'; in order to distinguish them,
<u>er karindaş</u> 'brother', <u>kız karindaş</u> 'sister'. Augmentatives,
diminutives, nouns of action, of place, of time, etc.,
have their own derivational syllables.

(<u>7</u>) The Turk has no article, but on the other hand a
declension with six very definite cases, including the
vocative, in final syllables, which are added to the
plural after it is formed, as well as to the singular.
The plural is always formed with the syllable <u>ler</u>. A dual
the Turk doesn't have. E.g., <u>er</u> 'the man'.

Singular	Nominative	er	Plural	Nom.	erler
	Genitive	erin		Gen.	erlerin
	Dative	ere		Dat.	erlere
	Accusative	eri		Acc.	erleri
	Vocative	Ya er		Voc.	Ya erler
	Ablative	erden		Abl.	erlerden

(<u>8</u>) Adjectives designate neither gender, nor number, nor
case, but are added to substantives like adverbs: <u>güzel er</u>
'a handsome man', <u>güzel erler</u> 'handsome men', <u>güzel
erlerden</u> 'from the handsome men'.

(<u>9</u>) The comparative is either expressed through a preceding ablative: <u>erlerden güzel</u> 'handsomer than the men';
or through the adverbs 'much, very' etc. or also through
a suffixed syllable, <u>güzelrek</u> 'more handsome'. The superlative is paraphrased by a further word.

(<u>10</u>) The pronouns do not designate gender, but are
declined in all six cases. Possessives have the special
characteristic that they at the same time place the
genitive of the personal pronoun in front of the substantive, as if one would say in Latin <u>tui frater tuus</u>, <u>tui
fratrem tuum</u>, <u>tui fratres tuos</u> ('your brother your').

(<u>11</u>) The verb is the most difficult segment of the
Turkish language, because of the quantity of moods and
tenses, and of their special inflections. The Turk has an
indicative, subjunctive, and optative. Of tenses he has a
present, two imperfects, two perfects, a pluperfect, and

four futures, the latter with regard not to time relationships but to inflection. Furthermore, an imperative,
infinitive, participles, and gerunds. The conjugation can
be explained for the most part from the combinations of the
the verb BE with the participle. All infinitives end in
mak or mek. One might believe they were actually phrases
compounded with the word machen 'make': make (a) cut
rather than cut, make love rather than love, especially
since this make disappears completely again in the
remaining conjugation.

(12) The passive is formed by intercalating an l between
the mak or mek of the infinitive, and in all moods and
tenses between the main word and the personal ending:
sevmek 'love', sevilmek 'be loved'; sever 'he loves',
seviler 'he is loved'.

(13) In the use of participles the Turk is like the
European, especially in the fact that he uses them so
often for the formation of his conjugation.

(14) Negation is brought about in the verb through
insertion of m or ma: olmak 'be', olmamak 'not be';
sevmek 'love', sevmemek 'not love', sevdim 'I have loved',
sevmedim 'I have not loved'; and thus in all moods, tenses,
and persons. Here too there is a phrase-analog, which can
be explained by love not make, especially since ma is also
a negative particle in Arabic.

(15) On nouns, negation is expressed through the syllable
siz or suz: korku 'fear', korkusuz 'fearless, unscared'.

(16) Prepositions are postpositions in this language.

(17) Syntax is far more complex than in Semitic or in
the Persian language. Since the Turk has specific cases
in declension, he permits inversions, where frequently the
governing word, as in Latin, stands quite at the end of a
relatively long sentence.

(18) The Turkish language is just as rich in compounds
as the Persian, namely of those that arise through simple
compounding, without inflection: dağ-burunu 'mountain
nose', i.e., 'foothills'; çayır-kuşu 'field-bird', i.e.,
'lark'; arpa-suyu 'barley-water', i.e., 'beer'; buz-at
'ice-horse' (buz 'ice'), i.e., 'a gray horse', frengi-çeşm
'Frank-eye (European-eye)', i.e., 'a pair of glasses'.
Such compounds the Arab cannot make. In order to give a
name for steel, the invention of which he ascribes to the
Europeans, the Arab says hadid afrendschi 'Frankish iron'.
Accordingly he uses the adjective because he cannot, like
the Turk, say 'Frank-iron'; he would then have to say in
the genitive plural 'iron of the Franks'; that however is
no compound.

Adelung's characterization of Turkish may be taken as
representative of his typological approach. The Turkish
statement is shorter than some, longer than others, especially
those for indigenous languages of the Americas and Australia;
these may have been the languages which Müller considered
more fully treated in his *Grundriss*. While it may seem highly
compact, it should also be noted that Adelung included five
hundred languages in his undertaking. Such an aim would be
totally unrealistic today, for we do not have adequate
information on five hundred of the world's languages to
state their patterns and processes in accordance with the
outline given in section 1.4. This shortcoming in linguistic
study can be remedied if students of individual languages
describe them adequately so that descriptions like those
presented in Chapters 2 - 5 are available; such descriptions
could be far more extensive than is possible here.

1.6. Implications of Typological Study
for the Description of Languages

Typological analysis is of fundamental importance in
linguistics because of the framework it provides for the
description, explanation, and understanding of individual
languages. These aims represent the goals of linguistics.
They have been pursued in various ways. Traditional grammars
set out to present languages in accordance with a time-
honored approach based on previous work; in Western
linguistics this work goes back to the Classical grammarians.
The approach is constantly updated, in part with reference
to other traditions, notably the Indian. Jespersen presented
the views of his generation in two influential books:
Language of 1922 and *The Philosophy of Grammar* of 1924.
Bloomfield in his book *Language*, which more than Jespersen's

is in the German tradition, "tried ... to present the
accepted views" of his day (1933: viii). Like their predeces-
sors in Western linguistic theory, both draw only on SVO
languages, thus presenting a seriously flawed treatment of
linguistic theory. One need only examine the treatment of the
comparative by either of these influential scholars to note
their unfortunately restricted views (Jespersen 1924: 244 -
253).

Some linguists have broken more sharply with traditional
grammar, developing linguistic theory in accordance with other
disciplines, notably logic. Hjelmslev and Chomsky are examples.
Yet they too have based their theory on examination of the
languages of Europe, notably English for Chomsky and his
followers. Accordingly a rule as fundamental as that
specifying the structure of the sentence is given as ordered
by Chomsky and as though language is fundamentally SVO in
structure: S → NP Aux VP. Attention to other disciplines has
not therefore led such linguists to a more fundamental understanding of language. In view of the concentration on just
one subtype of language, these linguists also "are deficient
in that they leave unexpressed many of the basic regularities
of the language with which they are concerned" (Chomsky 1965:
5). Linguistic theory will be adequate only when it is based
on study of all types of languages. Since typology sets out
to determine and explicate these, it is fundamental in the
projection of theory as well as in the description of
languages.

If, as is generally held, language is constructed in
accordance with certain fundamental rules, these should be
determined by typological study. When fundamental rules are
proposed and the patterns governed by them, the resultant
view of language may however seem too rigid. Thus the patterns

listed in section 1.4, as well as the additional morphological
and phonological patterns not specifically stated there, may
appear to reflect a view of language as a static product of
an automaton, not the creative instrument of human speakers.
Yet the patterns are governed by only two axioms, and accordingly are not as manifold as a lengthy list may suggest. The
first is that government tends to operate similarly on all
structures in which it is involved in a given language. The
second is that modification also takes place in accordance
with a general principle. In view of the rapidity of language
acquisition by children and in accordance with observed
linguistic phenomena, the assumption of two such axioms is
highly plausible. Moreover, a language may accord with the
ideal scheme, or nearly so. The languages presented in
Chapters 2 and 3 closely approximate ideal types.

Yet there are inconsistencies. A notable inconsistency in
Japanese has to do with the expression for reflexivization in
an OV language. In accordance with the discussion in section
4.3, it should be expressed through suffixes, as it indeed
is in many OV languages. Japanese however uses a substantive,
zibun 'self', also labeled a reflexive pronoun. The constructions in which zibun is used are highly intricate, creating
many problems for grammatical description (see Kuno 1973:
291 - 323). On the basis of these problems one might propose
that zibun is irregular, even foreign to the structure of the
language. We know the history of Japanese adequately to
identify zibun as a borrowing from Chinese. This knowledge
makes us receptive to acceptance of its irregular status and
leads us to seek an explanation for its introduction as well
as to propose the expression for it in the earlier stage of
Japanese (Lehmann 1974b). The Japanese pattern of reflexivization also illustrates the importance of examining languages

with reference to a typological framework. With it we identify problems in the structure and history of languages, and attempt to provide solutions.

Another such problem is the use of VO type relative and subordinate constructions in Turkish, as in:

(32) Dedi   ki   takti yok.   (Jansky 1954: 235)
     he-said that time is-not
     'He said that he had no time.'

In contrast with the expected preposing of embedded clauses in an OV language, these constructions are felt to be foreign; today they are infrequently used, in accordance with puristic tendencies after the Atatürk revolution.

While such examples need little clarification, since Japanese and Turkish are well documented for the last millennium, structures in languages with less data may be recognized and accounted for if these languages are examined in accordance with the typological framework now available. With it we can account for the aberrant comparative patterns like Latin tē maior 'from-you bigger = bigger than you' in the early periods of the Indo-European languages. The comparative is only one of the structures to be treated in this way. Another is the use of adpositions. Even the eminent syntactician Jacob Wackernagel provides only an awkward account of postpositions in the Classical languages, referring to them as "nongenuine prepositions" (1928: 157). An example is Greek dé, in the Phrase Oúlumpon dé 'to Olympus', which is cognate with the English preposition to. Its cognate zu is also preposed in German, and accordingly Wackernagel notes that "the word has developed to a full preposition" (1928: 157). But he does not provide the explanation that such a development would be expected when a language changes from OV to VO structure.

Languages then may not be consistent, not even as consistent
as Japanese with its imported reflexive as one of its very few
non-OV patterns. The reasons for inconsistencies are those
noted for the examples above: (1) diffusion of characteristic
patterns from one language to another, or borrowing, as it
is known in linguistics; (2) internal change, whether from
OV to VO structure, as in most of the Indo-European languages,
or from VO to OV, as in Sinhalese, Chinese, and many languages
of Africa. Until such changes are completely carried out, the
languages in question may be labeled inconsistent.

Identifying languages as either consistent or inconsistent
is not sufficient to account adequately for variant typological forms of language. In a period of a change from one
type to another a language may show both VO and OV patterns,
with neither predominant as they are in inconsistent as well
as consistent languages. Such languages may be referred to as
ambivalent.

One construction has been accounted for through the understanding that ambivalent languages must be recognized, the
so-called absolutes. Absolutes are embedded sentences which
have no formal relationship to the matrix clause, as in the
following ablative absolute from Caesar's *Gallic War* I.6:

(33) Omnibus rēbus   ad   profectiōnem comparātis
     all-Abl. things for departure   provided-Abl.
     'All things having been provided for the departure,

     diem dīcunt.
     day they-name
     they name a day.'

Absolutes can be accounted for by assuming that the language
is so structured that it is unclear whether an embedded
segment should precede or follow, and accordingly it is
unattached. They were prominent in Classical Greek and

Sanskrit as well as Latin, though not in earlier or later
stages of these languages. Later stages of Greek and Latin
came to be SVO, so that embedded elements followed their
head — and accordingly absolutes were no longer in keeping
with the structure of the language and were not used. Until
languages were examined for their typological structure, the
absolute construction was unaccounted for. The explanation
given here at once clarifies it and its abandonment, and
illuminates the kind of language in which absolutes are
found.

The increased understanding of language resulting from
typological investigations is especially important in
accounting for languages with scanty data. If crucial
constructions can be identified, the language may be clarified
more than the amount of data would suggest, even though it was
not consistent. Thus the language of the Mohenjodaro inscrip-
tions is doubtless OV, in view of its suffixation, even
though the texts have not yet been surely interpreted. And
in spite of their confused and scanty texts one might propose
that the Tasmanian dialects were VSO because adjectives and
numerals were placed after nouns. Similarly, hypotheses may
be proposed concerning the structure of the languages of
Anatolia in the second millennium B.C. Hattic with its
multiple prefixes was VSO. Even the presence of conflicting
patterns may permit improved understanding of languages,
especially as our grasp of the relationships between the
various characteristics of language types becomes more
secure. Hittite, for example, with its various OV characteristics inherited from Proto-Indo-European and with VO
characteristics like its sentence-initial clitics, may have
introduced the VO patterns from neighboring languages, much
as Sumerian has. Further studies of these and other languages

will illuminate both their interrelationships and the
patterning of languages in contact with one another.

Typological study accordingly provides guidelines for
identifying characteristic patterns in the study of any
language. These patterns should be accounted for in all
grammatical sketches, as they are in the following chapters.
Moreover, various processes affecting them must be noted and
elucidated. It will not do simply to present conflicting
patterns in specific periods or individual authors, such as
statistics on the number of clauses in which verbs precede
their objects and the number in which they follow their
objects or stand in even more complex relationships. Such
statistics are valueless unless each order is interpreted.
The normal pattern must be identified, and thereupon the
patterns used for marking and other special processes, such
as topicalization. When it is pertinent, the sociolinguistic
situation should also be taken into consideration, as when
speakers of two or more languages are in contact. It is
highly likely, for example, that late Middle English authors
were influenced by French, as in the arrangement of adjectives.
In short, the guidelines provided by typological study
identify not only patterns which must be ascertained, but
also variant forms and the reasons for these. Consistent
languages like the Dravidian or those used as examples here
are indeed found, but more commonly languages have unexpected
constructions, like the preposed adjectives of modern English
in contrast with the postposed position of French and the
other Romance languages. If adequate background materials are
available, such constructions may be accounted for, either by
sociolinguistic or by historical explanations.

Explanations of many patterns of languages are possible

on the basis of typological studies. Such explanations must
be viewed as major tasks of descriptive linguistics.

1.7. Implications of Typological Study
for the History of Languages

Through the identification of aberrant patterns typological
analysis provides perspective for the historical study of
language. English furnishes examples, both in its present
form and earlier. As illustrated in section 1.3, adjectives
should follow nouns in a VO language, as they do in French,
Spanish, and the other Indo-European languages of southern
Europe. From their aberrant position in English one may
propose the hypothesis that English is a language which has
been changing from OV structure to VO structure.

By itself the aberrant position of adjectives would not be
decisive for support of this hypothesis, because adjectives
precede nouns in relatively many SVO languages. But English
had additional OV characteristics in earlier periods. In Old
English, genitives also preceded nouns in 90 percent of their
occurrences. In the millennium between Old English and the
present the order of genitives has gradually been changed so
that today 90 percent of them follow their nouns (Fries 1940:
199 - 208); unless animate nouns are involved, genitives are
generally expressed today with _of_ constructions. The direction of the syntactic change suggests that additional OV
constructions might be expected in Old English. Such constructions are indeed attested, especially in the earliest poetic
texts, such as the _Beowulf_.

Besides the OV order for adjectives and genitives the
Beowulf includes government constructions of the OV pattern.
According to an eminent editor, end-position of the verb
predominates in the _Beowulf_ (Klaeber, ed. 1950: xciv).

Adpositions may follow the element they govern, such as <u>mid</u>
in the line below.

(34) 1625 mægenbyrþenne   þāra þe   hē him mid hæfde
           mighty-burden   that which he him with   had
           '(he rejoiced) in the mighty burden that he
           had with him.'

OV type comparatives also occur, as in *Beowulf* 1850 with the
standard <u>þē</u> preceding the comparative <u>sēlran</u>:

(35) þæt þē   Sǣ-Gēatas   sēlran nǣbban
     that from-you sea-Geats   better not-have
     'that the Geats would not have anyone better than you.'

The breadth of OV constructions in the oldest English texts
then supports the inference based on the change in order of
the genitive that English at an earlier period was strongly
OV in patterning. This conclusion leads to improved understanding of the history of English, permits explanation of
aberrant constructions in its early period, and illuminates
the gradual development of patterns like the passive and
modal auxiliaries.

In addition to these developments many others are clarified.
Some have to do with morphological change. Suffixed inflections, which are characteristic of OV languages, become
fewer and fewer in English. Instead preposed particles are
introduced as grammatical markers. Besides <u>of</u> for genitive
constructions and <u>to</u> for datives, adverbs have been introduced before the standard in comparative constructions; the
variety of particles — <u>as</u>, <u>be</u> (<u>by</u>), <u>nor</u>, <u>or</u>, as well as the
ultimately general <u>than</u> — suggests by itself that a new
pattern was developing. Similar observations may be made for
all the Western Indo-European languages; the patterns listed
in section 1.4 are clarified in the course of their development in these languages by examining them in relation to a
change from OV toward VO structure.

The opposite direction of change can be observed for
Sinhalese, from VO to OV. Like Sanskrit it had developed
toward an ambivalent language around the beginning of our
era, with many SVO characteristics. Thereupon, heavily
influenced by the neighboring Dravidian languages, it changed
to its virtually consistent OV patterning of today. Characteristic patterns of the language of the present were
illustrated above. Further additive numerals are given here,
which in contrast with the forms in Old Sinhalese and
Classical Sanskrit, show the OV order in the teens, with
exceptions explained below.

	Old Sinhalese	Sanskrit		New Sinhalese	
11	ekaḷos	ékādaśa	'1 + 10'	ekaloha	'1 + 10'
13	teḷes	tráyodaśa	'3 + 10'	daha-tunə	'10 + 3'
18	atādaśa	aṣṭādaśa	'8 + 10'	daha-aṭə	'10 + 8'

It is noteworthy that the VO order of Old Sinhalese is
preserved in some numerals of contemporary Sinhalese; like
that for 11 presented here, those for 12 and 15 have not been
modified. The numerals for 11 and 12 are also maintained in
aberrant patterns in the Germanic languages (11, 12 =
'one/two left over/ as opposed to 13 = '3 + 10', etc.). The
numerals for 11 and 12 presumably maintain aberrant patterns
because numeral systems often include them with the set from
1 to 10, and hence would not associate them with the group
to be restructured.

Whatever the reasons for retention of old patterns in some
of the teens, irregular sets, like that of the teen numerals
in contemporary Sinhalese, will in time be used by
historical linguists to reconstruct earlier patterning in
languages by means of methodological principles based on
observations in well-documented languages, even when older

materials are unavailable. Tentative attempts of this kind
have been made in dealing with African and Amerindian
languages attested only today (Givón 1975; Hyman 1975;
Lehmann 1975b).

The use of a typological framework will then permit
explanations for many syntactic, morphological, and phonological phenomena. The analytic procedures and the phenomena
are parallel to those long observed in the study of phonology
and morphology. A small number of irregular forms, for
example, are generally relics of earlier patterns, such as
the plurals of common English nouns like goose : geese,
mouse : mice, and so on. Such irregular forms generally
survive among the frequently used everyday words; it is
assumed that in language acquisition they are mastered as
individual entities rather than as members of a paradigm like
that generally used for English plural formation — book :
book + s. The English plurals with internal change are
survivals of plural formations of a paradigm with high
front vocalic suffix that were once more widespread but have
gradually been replaced by s-plurals. In much the same way a
number of common adjectives are preposed in French rather
than postposed, for example bon 'good', grand 'big', petit
'small'. Their arrangement may be accounted for by viewing
them as relics of the earlier OV order, which had for the
most part been replaced even in Latin.

Investigations using a typological framework in historical
study of well-documented languages will then provide
guidelines for improved understanding of the development of
languages. Among findings which will permit extrapolation
for earlier periods, such as pre - Old English, or for
languages with no earlier materials, such as those of Africa
and the Americas, are conclusions on rate of retention,

periods required for specific shifts, and interrelationships
of changing patterns.

The shifts in English and French lead us to propose
different rates of retention for specific structures. Among
the nominal modifying patterns the rate of retention is
greatest for descriptive adjectives; relative constructions
apparently change position earliest, followed by the genitive
and subsequently the adjective, and eventually limiting
adjectives and adjectival numerals. Such hierarchies of
maintenance must be verified from study of all languages.

Further, if the shift of the English genitive noted in
Fries's study is taken as typical, a millennium may well be
required to carry out changes in one of the nominal modifying
constructions. Such studies must be pursued on changes in
other patterns where data are available, as in Sinhalese.
Another such area — Latin and the Romance languages — can
yield figures on changes from a predominantly suffixing verbal
system to one in which many forms are periphrastic. And
though the situation in the early stages of Latin is not
well documented, the shifts in such constructions as
comparatives (from tē maior 'you-from bigger' to maior quam
tū 'bigger than you') and adpositions may provide data on
the periods involved in carrying out these shifts as well as
the interrelationships between shifts in the various constructions noted in section 1.4.

Interrelationships between changes of patterns have also
been hypothesized on the basis of very little data to the
effect that datives may be among the first patterns to be
shifted in OV languages, when postposed as a kind of afterthought, as in example (37), from Vedic Sanskrit, in
contrast with (36).

(36) 9.105.5   sákheva   sákhye   náryo rucé   bhava
               friend-like to-friend manly for-esteem be
               'Add to esteem like a manly friend to
               his friend.'

(37) 4.37.7   ví no ... patháś citana yáṣṭave
               up for-us paths open   to-sacrifice
               'Open up the paths for us, for sacrificing/
               that we may sacrifice.'

Such placement of the dative, leading toward disruption of the
OV structure, signals a shift in basic word order; it would
be followed in turn by a change in other government constructions as well as in nominal modifying constructions like
relative clauses.

The sequences of shifts, as well as identification of
pertinent patterns, must be confirmed by observations of
further languages and their changes. In its concern with a
wide number of languages, typological study is closely related
to the study of universals, for the processes as well as the
structures examined are identified by relationship to them.

1.8. Typological Study and the Study of Universals

The study of universals has been pursued vigorously in
recent investigations of human behavior and society, not
merely in linguistic study. The most notable event arousing
interest in such investigation of language today was a
conference held in 1961 which led to the subsequent publication of the papers, entitled *Universals of Language,* edited
by Joseph H. Greenberg. The conference was arranged after
circulation of a memorandum by Greenberg, C. E. Osgood, and
J. J. Jenkins which included the following definition:
"Language universals are by their very nature summary statements about characteristics or tendencies shared by all human
speakers" (Greenberg 1966: xv). The definition clearly

resulted from haste. For if only statements applicable to
"all human speakers" were formulated, they would be severely
limited; many of them might well be trivial, for example
that all languages include consonants, words, and sentences.
After the conference the statement was amplified as follows:
"There was general agreement that it was necessary and completely legitimate to include as universals in addition to
statements of the simple type 'all languages have a given
feature x,' likewise implicational relations, universal
frequency distributions, statistically better than chance
correlations, and other logic types ..." (Greenberg 1966:
xii). The study of universals was accordingly broadened to
deal with more than "summary statements about characteristics
or tendencies shared by all human speakers."

The "logic types" comprise matters of great interest to
typological study. If one defines processes like arrangement
and modification as "features," it is indeed of importance
for typological study that "all languages have" them. Features
of major concern, as noted above, are patterns motivated by
others, including those with "statistically better than
chance" correlations. In surveying languages for such
features, typological study has yielded major contributions
to general grammatical theory, for it has made clear the
segment of the grammar which is indeed universal, and has
disclosed guidelines for its patterning.

Among these guidelines is the observation that the basic
patterns in the universal segment of grammar must be
unordered. While one may assume that sentences will contain
verbs and objects, their arrangement is determined not by
universals but by typologically specific rules. One kind of
grammar positing unordered underlying rules has been labeled
case grammar. In such a grammar the sentence rule specifies

a verb, but neither subject nor object. These are subsequently introduced from abstract nominal categories in accordance with the lexical item functioning as verb in a given sentence. The resultant grammar is in keeping with observations about language, and leads to identification of the patterns listed in section 1.4. An initial rule specifies both the propositional constituent of sentences and the modalities or qualifiers expressed in it. Since language permits arrays of two or more sentences, the initial rule in the grammar provides for such construction.

The terminology and notation utilized are of secondary importance, though symbols are best selected which avoid ambiguity. Since the abbreviations V = verb, S = subject, O = object are well installed in typological study, the unambiguuous symbol Σ is chosen to indicate sentence. And since modalities make up only a portion of the qualifying elements of the sentence, the symbol Q, suggested by Seuren, represents these. The universal rules in grammars of any language may then be formulated as follows.

1. $\Sigma \rightarrow$ Conjunction Σ^n (optional; $n \geq 2$)

2. $\Sigma \rightarrow$ Q(ualifier) P(roposition)

3. $\Sigma \rightarrow$ [±Declarative][±Interrogative][±Negative]
   [±Middle][±Necessitative][±Voluntative]
   [±Perfective][±Momentary][±Iterative][±Causative]

4. P → V (K = abstract nominal categories)
   The K-categories are as follows:

Target	Time
Receptor	Place
Agent	Source
Means (Instrument)	Manner

5. $K \rightarrow \left\{ {NP\ k^n \atop \Sigma} \right\}$

(k = inflections, or function words, selected in
accordance with the lexical entries for V)

6. NP → (Determiner) N (Σ) (optional)

These rules have various implications.

The first rule implies that all languages have compound
sentences; these may consist of two or more simple sentences.

The second implies that all languages include the
categories listed in rules 3 and 4. The K-categories are
optional in any given sentence, as indicated by their inclu-
sion in parentheses, but the verbal qualifiers are mandatorily
expressed, on a binary plus-or-minus basis. This formulation
results from the possibility of making sentences with no
nouns, such as the Latin:

(38) Pluit.   'Rains = it rains, it is raining.'

The sentence represented by this expression has no P-element
but the verb, yet is designated by either + or - for the
various Q-categories. Expressed as a factual statement it is
+declarative; -interrogative, i.e., not a question; -negative;
-middle, i.e., not formulated only with reference to the
speaker; and - for the remaining categories except momentary.
Such simple sentences have been found to be restricted to
specific situations in speech, such as observations on the
weather and on human feelings. The following utterance,
though also relatively simple, may well be more typical:

(39) Couldn't you be setting the table?

While designated as - for three of the Q-categories, necessitative, voluntative, and perfective, it is + for all the
others.

Since the qualifiers listed in rule 3, though subject to
refinement, are universals, they must be examined for their
type of expression in every language. Yet, while they are
essential elements of every grammar, their order and their
means of expression are unspecified in the universal rules.
These are determined by the specific rules for every language;
those rules lead to the wide diversity in the patterning of
expression in language. Determination of the "implicational
relations" and "correlations" among these features is a
primary concern of typological study. The principle stated in
section 1.3 was designed to represent the arrangement of the
qualifiers, which in some measure determines their means of
expression. As an example, this principle requires postverbal
expression of a marker for the interrogative in OV languages,
such as də in Sinhalese: ... däkka də? and preverbal in VSO
languages, such as an in Irish: An bhfaca ...? Expression
for the negative is placed between the interrogative and the
verb, as is also that for the other qualifiers.

Many languages remain to be explored for their expression
of even these straightforward categories. But on the basis of
those languages that are known, some conclusions can be
formulated. The qualifiers ordered first, such as declarative
and interrogative, are often expressed by intonation patterns.
This observation may be illustrated with English, where the
category for declarative is expressed by an intonation pattern
with falling final pitch, often represented: 2 3 1 #, as in:

(40) ²She came by ³plane ¹#

Moreover, the interrogative in echo questions is also
expressed by an intonation pattern, represented 2 3 3 ||, as in:

(41) ²She came by ³plane ³||

Similarly, in Japanese, questions may be expressed by
intonation alone, without the final particle ka. Yet the
subsequent qualifiers, beginning with the negative, generally
require instead of or in addition to intonation some kind of
sequence of segmental material. This observation, as well as
the relative placement of such segments, determined the order
of the qualifier categories in rule 3

Those qualifiers which stand closest to the verb, on the
other hand, notably the causative, are often merged with
lexical elements. In early Proto-Indo-European the causative
was expressed with an -n suffix; this was replaced in late
Proto-Indo-European by an -eyo suffix. This suffix is
represented with no reductions, though with vowel changes,
in Sanskrit sādáyati 'causes to sit, sets' = Proto-Indo-
European *sod-éyo-ti. By the time the Germanic dialects are
attested, *sod-éyo-ti has been reduced to the form found in
Gothic, satjiþ 'sets'. In Old English the form is seteþ, with
the causative marker lost but leaving a trace in the changed
vowel of the root. It has in this way merged with lexical
elements, and a few relics represent different forms from
the noncausative, such as set : sit, lay : lie; in general
there are no surface differences, as in drop, open, etc.
The category is either expressed lexically, as in kill,
move, or with a phrase: cause/get/have + verb, as in:

(42) a. Move the car.

b. Get that car moved.

c. Have the car moved.

Because of the causative's frequent merger with the verb, as
well as that of the iterative and the perfective, and because
of their placement with regard to it, these categories are
arranged closest to the V in rule 3.

Such observations lead to questions concerning the
relationship between surface expression and underlying
categories. Clearly there is a close relationship in some
aspects, especially in arrangement, as illustrated here.
The relationship is plainest in (S)OV languages and in VSO
languages. Yet the ordering given above may not be followed
in some languages, and further categories may well need to be
identified. In OV Quechua, for example, the following form
accords only partially with the order given here:

(43) yača-či-na-ku-ʌa-sa-nku. (Bills et al 1969: 335)
     'They are only teaching each other.'

The order of the category markers in this expression is as
follows: verb +causative +reciprocal +reflexive +delimitative
-momentary, followed by the third person plural suffix -nku.
This form and others in Quechua provide problems, for rule 3
does not include a delimitative category; moreover, the
momentary category is placed nearer the verb than is the
middle, which has separate markers for reflexive and reciproca
in Quechua. The expression of categories, especially those
other than the first three, cannot be expected to be ordered
in the same way in every language. And the delimitative,
which in Indo-European languages is expressed adverbially,
may prove more generally to be a verbal category, as it is in
Quechua. Such problems illustrate how meager our knowledge of
language is. Our linguistic generalizations are based largely
on study of the Indo-European languages, aided by consideration of those language families that have attracted some
attention, such as the Afro-Asiatic, the Finno-Ugric and
the Sino-Tibetan. Expectations of added insights from the
study of other languages provides one of the chief reasons
for intensive typological study, even if it now is carried

out with principles that seem cogent on the basis of linguistic
data in a small number of language families.

While the categories and universal rules must be regarded
as provisional, the devices of language, especially those of
syntax, seem well established; see section 1.2. These are
arrangement or order, selection, modification or sandhi, and
modulation or intonation. Of the four, as Sapir noted,
arrangement is most fundamental. For this reason it affects
the elements involved in the three other devices. Much concern
with selection has been focused on determining parts of
speech. While these have some validity, abstract underlying
features are the primary elements of concern. The study of the
other two devices, modification and intonation, has largely
been confined in the past to analysis of them in individual
languages. A well-designed typology demands attention to each
of these devices. Used as a guide in the assembling of data
as well as in their description and explanation, it will lead
to more adequate grammars than those now available.

1.9. Contributions of Typology

This book throughout aims to indicate the contributions of
typology to the understanding of language, chiefly through
examples. Yet some preliminary evaluation will be included
here, in part on the relations of a typological approach to
theoretical views which claim to deal most adequately with
languages.

Grammars set out to provide descriptions of languages.
Like handbooks in any discipline, they are produced with
varying degrees of rigor. In the past two decades much has
been made of complete explicitness, to the extent that a
computer might use a grammar to produce the grammatical
sentences of a language and only those sentences. Such

grammars have been labeled generative, resulting as Chomsky
has pointed out in the tautological term "generative grammar,"
inasmuch as any grammar aims at accurate analysis and description. Besides being explicit, generative grammars propose to
include an underlying or deep structure which reflects innate
patterns controlled by the brain. The resultant grammars have
been disappointing in two major respects: their parochiality
and their restricted scope.

The deep structures which have been proposed are based on
the analysis of SVO languages, for the most part English.
Even the rules for the underlying, and presumably universal
segment of the grammar, have been ordered to yield an SVO
output. Other arrangements, like those of OV languages, are
derived in the transformational section of the grammar. Yet
this segment of the grammar is supposedly specific to individual languages and should not regulate patterns that are
fundamental in a large proportion of the languages of the
world. The purported deep structure in these grammars then is
far removed from a universal, innate pattern.

Typological study by contrast takes into account all
languages, and accordingly it leads to a deep structure which
is indeed universal. Whether or not that proposed in section
1.8 is adequate, since barely a fifth of the world's languages
have been considered in previous linguistic research, it has
the merit of accounting for the common patterns of all known
languages.

The six rules in this deep structure component have been
surveyed above, as well as the probable inadequacies in the
categories included. All underlying constituents of sentences
can be accounted for with these rules, as a rapid review
indicates. Rule 1 permits the generation of compound sentences,
with conjunctions, sentence connectives, and the like; the

constituents of any sentence are specified in rule 2. Verbal
as well as sentence modifiers or qualifiers are generated
through rule 3; adverbial as well as nominal elements through
rule 4. Rule 5 provides for expression of simple noun phrases
and sentence complementation. Rule 6 introduces nominal
modifiers, of any pattern. Besides accounting for all basic
syntactic structures, these rules yield unordered strings
which can be arranged in accordance with any structure,
including both VO and OV and their subtypes. The findings of
typological study have led to the design of such underlying
rules.

These rules are accompanied by a well-designed lexicon.
The surface expressions in specific languages are then derived
by means of particular rules, whatever their format and
description. Transformational rules, regardless of the
shortcomings of the grammars in which they have been applied,
may well fulfill the requirements for explicating surface
expressions. Transformational grammars have contributed
especially to linguistics by sharpening the discovery procedures and formalisms used for expressing linguistic structure.
Transformational grammar's rigorous procedures must be
maintained as linguistics accounts for the patterns of
languages. In these efforts all structures of a language must
however be included. While the resulting grammar would be
huge, a theory of language cannot be limited to treatment of
favored constructions which may seem to be crucial for the
development of a given theory. In response to the view that
current theory permits only partial analyses, it may be
pointed out that language has long been recognized as a
"whole where everything is related — un ensemble où tout se
tient"; any partial treatment will very likely then be
inadequate for that segment it purports to account for, even

incorrect. Such inadequacies can be avoided if crucial patterns are noted, such as those presented in section 1.4. All of these may be amplified, but if each pattern or process is identified in any language, the result will lead to proper analysis when larger grammars are undertaken.

Identification of the patterns also provides insight into the shifting structure of a language, and into possible influences of other languages. English, as noted above, is a relatively consistent SVO language, though the arrangement of adjectives before nouns suggests that its structure was at one time OV. French and Spanish, with few adjectives still placed normally before nouns, indicate that in them the shift to SVO has virtually been completed. German presents totally different problems, inasmuch as it includes two word orders in simple clauses: VO in independent clauses and OV in dependent. If we seek to dismiss either order and characterize German as VO, or as OV, we remove the possibility of understanding remarkable developments of German in the last four centuries. During this period after the reintroduction of OV order in dependent clauses, some postpositions were introduced, and also a preposed relative construction. By providing insights into such varying patterns and the resultant phenomena, recent findings of typology have added a new dimension to historical study of languages.

Chinese, like German, includes clashing patterns. Moreover, scrutiny of Chinese has led to broader conceptions of language structure than were recognized in the past, notably the identification of topic-prominent in contrast with subject-prominent languages. The recognition of this distinction by Li and Thompson has numerous implications. Among these it points up once again the secondary position of the "subject" in language, supporting the primary classification into VO

and OV languages, and only secondary subclassification when
the subject is included in classification for language types.
Moreover, the recognition that an element with the role of
topic may be found rather than a "subject" has directed
attention to the functional approach to language, as exemplified in recent studies of Kuno and in the observations of
Li and Thompson.

Among other characteristics of topic-prominent languages
Li and Thompson have pointed out the avoidance or only marginal
use of the passive construction in them. The widespread use
of the passive in subject-prominent languages on the other
hand they account for on the grounds that if in them a noun
that is not an agent becomes a subject, the verb must "signal
this 'non-normal' choice" (1976b: 467). In Chinese, for
example, passivelike sentences are made with no special or
signaling form of the verb, e.g.:

(44) Zhèi-jian   xīnwen guǎngbò   le.
     this classifier news   broadcast completed-aspect
     'This news, (someone) has broadcast (it).' =
     'This news has been broadcast.'
     (Li and Thompson 1976b: 480)

The second English version of (44) illustrates the requirement
of a passive form in subject-prominent languages, with consequent functions that are well known and need not be discussed
here. A topic-prominent language like Chinese, on the other
hand, can simply present the verb, and an appropriate relationship will be assumed. By disclosing such traits,
typological investigation has expanded the concerns and
insights of linguistic analysis, leading to an increasingly
adequate understanding of language.

Typological study accordingly has provided guidelines
which assist linguists in their investigation of language,
and in this way has led to increased recognition that the

diverse "idioms" used in human communication are basically
one, as Saussure expressed it.

> The linguist works with facts and principles [in the
> study of Old French, for instance] similar to those that
> would be revealed in the description of an existing Bantu
> language, Attic Greek of 400 B.C. or present-day French,
> for that matter. These diverse descriptions would be based
> on similar relations; if each idiom is a closed system,
> all idioms embody certain fixed principles that the
> linguist meets again and again in passing from one to
> another ... The diversity of idioms hides a profound unity.
> (1959: 99)

The view that languages reflect an underlying unity was
propounded by another great linguist, Edward Sapir, with a
focus on language in change:

> It would almost seem that linguistic features that are
> easily thinkable apart from each other, that seem to have
> no necessary connection in theory, have nevertheless a
> tendency to cluster or to follow together in the wake of
> some deep, controlling impulse to form that dominates
> their drift ... Some day, it may be, we shall be able
> to read from them the great underlying ground-plans.
> (1921: 152 - 153)

The studies of selected languages and problems in the
following chapters have been carried out to present an account
with illustrations of those ground-plans. Space is not
adequate for complete grammatical sketches. The three
following chapters present a selection of constructions
revealing of typological structures. Chapters 5 through 7
then examine specific problems in relation to the observed
typological characteristics. While no completely consistent
language is known, the languages selected in Chapter 2 through
4 illustrate expected patterns in an OV language (Japanese),
in a VSO language (Easter Island), and in an SVO language
(English). Chapters 2 through 7, through presentation of
"linguistic features [having] a tendency to cluster,"

illustrate "principles that the linguist meets again and again" and in this way provide insights into the phenomena of language.

2. Japanese
A Characteristic OV Language

Susumu Kuno

2.0. Preface

This paper gives a typological sketch of the syntactic
structure of modern standard Japanese. Discussion of each
typological feature is necessarily brief and superficial.
There are many important features of Japanese that this paper
gives only passing mention, or excludes from discussion. An
extensive and in-depth description of the structure of the
language can be found in Martin 1975. Treatments of selected
features of Japanese in the framework of generative theory of
grammar can be found, for example, in Kuroda 1965 and 1972b,
Kuno 1973, and Shibatani, ed., 1976a. Two periodicals,
Papers in Japanese Linguistics (Department of Linguistics,
University of Southern California), and *Journal of the
Association of Teachers of Japanese* (Department of Far Eastern
Languages and Civilizations, University of Chicago), regularly
carry papers in Japanese linguistics.

2.1. Structure of Simple Clauses

2.1.1. Basic Word Order

Japanese is a verb-final language. Word order in the sentence
is relatively free, as long as the sentence ends with a main
verb (see section 2.1.2 for nonverb-final sentences involving

afterthoughts). For example, 'John introduced Tom to Mary' in Japanese can have the following word-order variations:

(1) a.   John ga Mary ni Tom o syookaisita.

    b.   John ga Tom o Mary ni syookaisita.

    c.   Mary ni John ga Tom o syookaisita.

    d.   ?Mary ni Tom o John ga syookaisita.

    e.   Tom o John ga Mary ni syookaisita.

    f.   ?Tom o Mary ni John ga syookaisita.

Ga, o, and ni are postpositional particles representing the nominative, accusative, and dative case marking. The above sentences are identical in logical content, but are different in discourse presupposition in a very subtle way. Ordinarily, constituents that represent older information precede those that represent newer information.

The subject-initial sentence pattern is the most common among the various word order patterns. In a large-scale sentence-pattern count of modern Japanese journalistic writings it was found that sentences with SOV word order occur seventeen times more frequently than sentences with OSV order. (This is a cross-language characteristic, as observed in Greenberg 1963, *Greenberg's Language Universal 1:* In declarative sentences with nominal subject and object, the dominant order is almost always one in which the subject precedes the object. Greenberg's observation is not without exception. For example, Keenan 1976a establishes Malagasy as having a basic VOS order. Derbyshire 1977 shows that Hixkaryana, a Carib language spoken in northern Brazil, has a basic order of OVS.) Despite the existence of statistical facts such as this, it is in general extremely difficult to establish an underlying word order of constituents of a free

word order language like Japanese. There is, however, at least
one syntactic argument for hypothesizing SOV, and not, say,
OSV, as representing the underlying word order for Japanese;
see Kuno 1971 for underlying word order of SOV sentences and
existential sentences. Japanese has a small class of verbals,
all stative, that mark their object, as well as their subject,
with the particle ga.

   (2) a. John ga Mary ga suki   na koto
                        fond-of is fact-that
       'the fact that John is fond of Mary'

A sentence with a stative predicate whose subject is marked
with ga instead of the thematic particle wa acquires the interpretation of exhaustive listing, i.e., 'x and only x'. Thus,

   (2) b. John ga Mary ga suki   da.
                        fond-of is

means '(Among those under discussion,) John and only John likes
Mary; it is John who likes Mary.' "Subject NP + ga" with
stative predicates in subordinate clauses does not have to
receive this exhaustive listing interpretation. Example (2a)
is given in the complement clause form to avoid this interpretation. See Kuno 1973, Chapter 2.

    The fact that (2a) can mean only that John is fond of Mary,
and not that Mary is fond of John, shows that the subject and
the object cannot switch word order when they are marked with
identical case markers. If we assume that the underlying word
order is SOV, this is a perfectly natural constraint attribut-
able to the "anti-ambiguity" factor. On the other hand, had
we assumed that the underlying word order was OSV, we would
need an obligatory "word-order-switch" requirement for
instances where the subject and the object are marked with
the same case marker. There is no natural explanation for the
existence of such a constraint.

2.1.2. Word Order in Colloquial Speech

In written Japanese, sentences are almost exclusively SOV,
but in colloquial speech nonverbal elements can appear after
the main clause verb. For example, observe the following
sentences:

(3) a. Kimi (wa)   kono hon (o)   yonda ↗ .
       you (Theme) this book (Acc.) read
       'Have you read this book?'

    b. Kimi (wa) yonda ↗ kono hon (o) ↘ .
       you   read   this book

    c. Yonda ↗ kimi (wa) kono hon (o) ↘ .
       read   you   this book

In colloquial speech, the particles wa (thematic), o (accusative) and ga (when used to mark the object of stative verbals)
are often deleted; see Kuno 1972 for conditions on particle
deletion. What is noteworthy about (3b,c) is that the rise
in intonation characteristic of an interrogative sentence is
placed on the verb, and not on the last word of the sentence.

Postverbal constituents can be elements in subordinate
clauses, as can be seen in the following examples:

(4) a. Kimj (wa) [kono-aida ano   resutoran de nani (o)
       you   other-day that restaurant at what

       tabeta ka] oboete   iru ↗ .
       ate   Q   remembering are

       'Do you remember what we ate at that restaurant
       the other day?'

    b. Kimi (wa) [nani (o) tabeta ka] oboete   iru ↗
       you   what   ate   Q   remembering are

       kono-aida ano   resutoran de ↘ .
       other-day that restaurant at

      c. [Nani (o) tabeta ka] oboete   iru ↗ kimi
         what   ate   Q   remembering are   you

        kono-aida ano   resutoran de ↘ .
        other-day that restaurant at

Postverbal <u>kono-aida</u> 'the other day' and <u>ano resutoran de</u>
'at that restaurant' in (4b,c) are constituents which appear
in the interrogative clause in (4a). If these sentences were
to be derived by a movement transformation (i.e., by Right
Dislocation), Japanese would constitute a serious counterexample to Ross's (1967) hypothesis that all rightward
movements are upward bounded.

    For example, observe the following sentences:

(i) Complex NP Shift:

    a. [That they elected *the man who was absolutely
       incompetent* the president of the company] was
       obvious.

    b. [That they elected president *the man who was
       absolutely incompetent*] was obvious.

    c. *[That they elected president] was obvious *the
       man who was absolutely incompetent.*

(ii) Extraposition of Prepositional Phrases:

    a. [That a review *of the book* appeared] was surprising.

    b. [That a review appeared *of the book*] was surprising.

    c. *[That a review appeared] was surprising *of the book.*

An exception to Ross's principle has been found in Navajo
(Kaufman 1974), but only with respect to movement of special
grammatical formatives. As far as I know, no language has
been found that can move regular lexical items rightward in
violation of Ross's principle.

    There is strong indication, however, that (3b,c) and
(4b,c) are generated not by Right Dislocation, but by a

process that adds afterthoughts to the end of a sentence.
Namely, in (3b,c), for example, the speaker first assumes
that the hearer can understand what is meant by

(5) a. Kimi yonda ↗ .
    you   read
    'Did you read (it)?'

    b. Yonda ↗ .
       read
       'Did (you) read (it)?'

The speaker adds kono hon 'this book' and kimi kono hon 'you
this book' to (5b) and (5c), respectively, to make sure that
the hearer will correctly interpret the reference of missing
subject and object. Similarly, in (4b), for example, the
speaker first utters:

(6) Kimi [nani (o) tabeta ka] oboete   iru ↗ .
    you   what   ate   Q   remembering are
    'Do you remember what we ate?'

assuming that the hearer will understand the question as
referring to 'the other day' and 'at that restaurant', later
adding the two postverbal elements to make sure that there
will be no misunderstanding.

The "afterthought" analysis of nonverb-final sentences
makes it possible to make the following two predictions:

(i) Postverbal elements are either discourse-predictable
    (or rather, the speaker assumes that they are) or
    supplementary; therefore, the sentences should have
    made sense without them.

(ii) Elements that would change the interpretation of the
     first part of the sentence cannot appear postverbally.

These predictions are borne out by the following examples:

(7) a. Kimi nani taberu ↗ .
        you what eat
        'What are you going to eat?'

    b. *Kimi taberu ↗ nani ↘ .

(8) a. Boku Nihon ni sando sika itta koto
        I   Japan to thrice only went experience

        ga nai.
        have-not
        'I have been to Japan only three times.'

    b. *Boku Nihon ni itta koto   ga nai,
        I   Japan to went experience   have-not

        sando sika.
        thrice only

(7b) shows that wh-words cannot appear postverbally. This is
because (i) wh-words are discourse-nonanaphoric; and (ii) the
postverbal addition of a wh-word would change the interpretation of the first part of the sentence completely, from
that of a yes-or-no question (i.e., 'Did you eat?') to
that of an interrogative-word question (i.e., 'What did you
eat?'). (8a) shows that sika 'only' requires that a negative
follow it; thus, the more accurate translation of sika would
be 'any more than'. (8b) is ungrammatical because the first
part of the sentence (up to the verb) states that the speaker
has never been to Japan, while the subsequent addition of
sando sika 'only three times' forces a complete switch in
interpretation.

    Postverbal elements never appear in subordinate clauses,
even in colloquial speech; (9b) is totally ungrammatical.

(9) a. Kimi [Taroo ga Hanako to   kekkonsita] koto
        you   with married   that

        sitte iru ↗ .
        knowing are

        'Do you know that Taroo married Hanako?'

b. *Kimi [Taroo ga kekkonsita Hanako to] koto
   you   married   with that

   sitte   iru ↗ .
   knowing are

c. Kimi [Taroo ga kekkonsita] koto sitte   iru ↗
   you   married   that knowing are

   Hanako to ↘ .
   with

2.1.3. Simple Sentence Types

Japanese sentences can be divided into three categories
depending upon whether their verbals are (i) verbs, (ii) adjectives, or (iii) copulas. All three of these types of verbals
conjugate with respect to tense, mode, and subordinating
types:

(10)	Verb		Adjective	Copula
	'eat'	'read'	'be young'	'be'
Nonpast	tabe-ru	yom-u	waka-i	da
Past	tabe-ta	yon-da	wakak-at-ta	dat-ta
Suppositional/ Intentional	tabe-yoo	yom-oo	wakak-ar-oo	dar-oo
Imperative	tabe-ro,-yo	yom-e	—	—
Subjunctive	tabe-reba	yom-eba	wakak-e-reba	nara
Gerundive	tabe-∅	yom-i	wakak-u	de, ni
Continuative	tabe-te	yon-de	wakak-u-te	—

Examples of the three types of sentences appear in the

following sections.

2.1.3.1. Verbs

(11) a. S V: Taroo ga kita.
                              came
                   'Taroo came.'

     b. S O V: Taroo ga tegami o kaita.
                              letter   wrote
                   'Taroo wrote a letter.'

     c. S IO DO V: Taroo ga Hanako ni tegami o kaita.
                              to   letter   wrote
                   'Taroo wrote a letter to Hanako.'

     d. S IO V: Taroo ga Hanako ni atta.
                              to   met
                   'Taroo met Hanako.'

Transitive constructions in Japanese acquire animate subjects.
For example,

(12) Taihuu   ga ie   no hei   o kowasita.
     typhoon   house 's fence   destroyed
     'The typhoon destroyed the house's fence.'

is an extremely unnatural sentence with a distinct flavor of
direct translation from English. Instead of constructions
like this, intransitive inchoative constructions are normally
used in colloquial speech:

(13) Taihuu   de   ie   no hei   ga kowareta.
     typhoon with house 's fence   broke
     'Because of the typhoon, the house's fence (Lit.)
       broke.'

There are, however, some transitive constructions with
inanimate subjects that have become part of the language,
especially in writing. Most of these constructions have
abstract nouns as their subjects:

(14) a. Sensoo ga ooku no hito   no unmei o kaeta.
        war   many   people 's fate   changed
        'The war changed many people's fates.'

    b. Koi ga Taroo o moomoku ni   sita.
       love   blind   being did
       'Love made Taroo blind.'

2.1.3.2. Adjectives

Adjectives are used as main clause verbals and are not
followed by copulas:

    (15) a. Taroo wa mada wakai.
              still is-young
          'Taroo is still young.'

        b. Kotosi   no huyu   wa samui.
          this-year 's winter   is-cold
          'It is cold this winter.'

There are a few transitive adjectives. Their objects are
marked with the particle ga, which, as we have already seen,
is ordinarily used for marking the subject of a sentence.

    (16) a. Taroo ga Hanako ga kirai   na koto
                         hateful is fact-that
          'the fact that Taroo dislikes Hanako'

        b. boku ga okane ga hosii   koto
          I   money   am-desirous fact-that
          'the fact that I want money'

2.1.3.3. Copulas

    (17) a. Taroo wa sensei da.
              teacher is
          'Taroo is a teacher.'

        b. Taroo wa sensei datta.
             teacher was
          'Taroo was a teacher.'

Japanese also has a word class called *nominal-adjective*.
Nominal-adjectives are adjectival in meaning, but do not
conjugate, and are followed by copulas:

(18) a. Kono toori wa sizuka da.
        this street   quiet is
        'This street is quiet.'

    b. Taroo wa syooziki da.
                honest   is
        'Taroo is honest.'

The present tense copula da (but not its "polite" counterpart desu) is deleted before certain sentence-final particles;
see section 2.1.4 for desu. For example, observe the
following sentences:

(19) Ka: sentence-final particle for questions

    a. Taroo wa kuru ka.
                come Q
        'Is Taroo coming?'

    b. Taroo wa syooziki datta ka.
                honest   was   Q
        'Was Taroo honest?'

    c. Taroo wa syooziki $\left\{ \begin{matrix} ^*da \\ \emptyset \end{matrix} \right\}$ ka.
                honest   Q
        'Is Taroo honest?'

(20) Sa: sentence-final particle meaning 'I assure you'

    a. Taroo wa kitto   kuru sa.
                certainly come
        'I assure you that Taroo will come without fail.'

    b. Taroo wa tensai daroo   sa.
                genius will-be
        'I assure you that Taroo will (must) be a genius.'

    c. Taroo wa tensai $\left\{ \begin{matrix} ^*da \\ \emptyset \end{matrix} \right\}$ sa.
                genius
        'I assure you that Taroo is a genius.'

Sentences such as (19c) and (20c) have the semblance of being
sentences without verbals, but the absence of verbals in
these surface sentences is simply due to a low-level copula

deletion rule, as can be seen by comparing them with the
corresponding past tense and suppositional sentences.

Another characteristic of copulative sentences is that
precopular constituents cannot be moved around:

(21) a.   Tanaka ga <u>sono hon</u> <u>o</u> katta.
                   that book bought
          'Tanaka bought that book.'

     b.   <u>Sono hon</u> <u>o</u> Tanaka ga katta.
            that book   bought

(22) a.   Tanaka wa <u>tensai</u> da.
                 genius is
          'Tanaka is a genius.'

     b.   *<u>Tensai</u> Tanaka wa da.
         genius   is

Similarly, no elements can be inserted between the copula and
the precopular constituents:

(23) a.   Tanaka wa sono hon (o) <u>mo</u>   katta.
                   that book   also bought
          'Tanaka bought that book, too.'

     b.   *Tanaka wa tensai <u>mo</u>   da.
               genius also is
          'Tanaka is a genius, too.'

2.1.4. Agreement

Verbs, adjectives, and copulas *do not* show number, person, and
gender agreements. They do show, however, agreement with
respect to levels of honorificness and politeness. Respect
for the referent of the subject is typically expressed by
prefixing the gerundive form of a verb with <u>o</u>- (honorific
prefix) and adding <u>ni</u> <u>nar</u>(-<u>u</u>) (Lit., 'become being') to the
right of the form, and by prefixing the adjectival stem
with <u>o</u>-.

(24) a. Taroo ga sono tegami o yon-da.
              that letter   read-Past
        'Taroo read the letter.'

    b. Yamada-sensei   ga sono tegami o o-yom- i ni nat-ta
          teacher   that letter   read   Past
       'Teacher Yamada read the letter.' (Respect for
       Teacher Yamada)

(25) a. Taroo wa waka-i.
                  be-young-Nonpast
        'Taroo is young.'

    b. Yamada-sensei   wa o-waka-i
          teacher   be-young-Nonpast
       'Teacher Yamada is young.' (Respect for
       Teacher Yamada)

Respect for the referent of a nonsubject noun phrase (usually
the object or dative) is expressed by prefixing the gerundive
form of a verb with o- and adding su(-ru) 'do' to the right
of it.

(26) a. Taroo ga Hanako ni sono tegami o yon-da.
                        to that letter   read-Past
        'Taroo read the letter to Hanako.'

    b. Taroo ga Yamada-sensei   ni sono tegami o o-yom-
                   teacher   to that letter   read

        i si-ta.
          Past

        'Taroo read the letter to Teacher Yamada.'
        (Respect for Teacher Yamada)

Respect for the hearer is expressed by using the polite
form of verbals, which are formed by adding mas(-u) to the
right of the gerundive form of a verb, by using the suppletive
form des(-u) for the copula, and by adding des(-u) to the
right of the nonpast or past form of an adjective:

(27) a. Taroo ga sono tegami o yom-u. (Informal level)
              that letter   read-Nonpast
        'Taroo reads the letter.'

    b. Taroo ga sono tegami o yom-<u>i</u> <u>mas</u>-u. (Polite to
       the hearer)

(28) a. Taroo wa tensai da. (Informal level)
             genius is
      'Taroo is a genius.'

    b. Taroo wa tensai <u>des</u>-u. (Polite to the hearer)

(29) a. Taroo wa mada waka-i. (Informal level)
            still be-young-Nonpast
      'Taroo is still young.'

    b. Taroo wa mada waka-i <u>des</u>-u. (Polite to the hearer)

2.1.5. Subjectless Sentences

Japanese allows deletion of subjects that are recoverable from
linguistic or nonlinguistic context. For example, observe the
following sentences:

(30) a. Soo omoimasu.
      so   think
      'I think so.'

    b. Kono hon o katte   ageyoo.
      this book   buying give-will
      'I will buy you this book.'

    c. Amerika ni ikitai.
           to go-want
      'I want to go to America.'

    d. Amerika ni ikitai ka.
           to go-want Q
      'Do you want to go to America?'

    e. Taroo no ie   ni ittara,   rusu   datta.
         's house to went-when absent was
      'When I went to Taroo's house, he was not home.'

The first and second person pronouns are rather freely deleted
because they are readily recoverable from discourse context.

(30e) allows the deletion of a third person subject, since
its antecedent is in the same sentence.

Japanese has at least two types of subjectless sentences
that cannot be attributed to deletion of recoverable subjects.
The first type includes sentences of the following kind:

    (31) a. Oya, ame da.
          oh   rain is
          'Oh, (Lit.) is rain.' 'Oh, it is raining.'

        Cf. Oya, ame ga hutte   iru.
            oh   rain   falling is
            'Oh, it is raining.'

      b. Doroboo da!
         thief   is
         (Lit.) 'Is a robber!' 'Robber!'

The x da is the template that Japanese uses in giving minimal
information while retaining the sentencehood of the statement.
The same pattern is used in answering wh-questions:

    (32) a. Kimi wa kinoo   doko e itta ka.
          you   yesterday where to went Q
          'Where did you go yesterday?'

      b. Boston   da
        (Lit.) 'Is Boston.'

    (33) a. Dare kara tegami ga kita ka.
          who from letter   came Q
          'From whom did a letter come?'

      b. Taroo   (kara) da.
        (Lit.) 'Is (from) Taroo.'

The second type of subjectless sentences can be exemplified
by the following sentence:

    (34) Boku ni wa, subete ga owatta yoo   ni
        I   to   all   ended appearance being

      omow-are-ru.
      think-Passive-Nonpast

(Lit., 'To me, is thought in the appearance of
everything having come to an end.') 'It seems to
me that everything has come to an end.'

Boku 'I' is marked with a dative particle representing the
experiencer, and therefore cannot function as a surface
subject. Subete ga owatta 'everything has come to an end' is
an adjectival clause that modifies yoo 'appearance', a formal
(grammatical) noun, which is followed by the adverbial form
ni of the copula. Therefore, ... yoo ni cannot function as
a surface subject either. Thus, the sentence is completely
devoid of a surface subject.

Some super-honorific sentences also lack surface subjects:

(35) a. Tennoo-heika wa kaze o o-hik-i
emperor   cold   Honorific-catch-ing

asobas-are-ta.
do-Honorific-Past

'The Emperor has caught a cold.'

b. Tennoo-heika ni wa kaze o o-hik-i
emperor   to   cold   Honorific-catch-ing

asobas-are-ta.
do-Honorific-Past

(Lit.) 'To the Emperor, has caught a cold.'

The super-honorific form of a verb is made by prefixing o-
to the gerundive form and adding asobas(-u) to the right of
it. (35a) has tennoo-heika 'emperor' as its subject, but
(35b) is subjectless. The sentence pattern of (35b) is due,
it seems, to a desire to avoid holding a person of high
honor responsible for an action as an agent.

2.1.6. Sentences with and without Themes

The theme of a sentence is marked with the postpositional
particle wa. Observe the following two sentences:

(36) a. John ga kita.
         'John came.'

      b. John wa kita.

(36a) is a sentence which does not have a theme. That is, it
is not a statement about John. Rather, it is a statement that
presents the whole event described as something new, or
alternatively, it presents John as the person who fulfills
the template "it is *x* that came." On the other hand, (36b)
has John as the theme of the sentence. It is a statement
about John.

There are sentences with themes that do not have corresponding themeless sentences. For example, observe the
following. (37b) is due to Mikami 1970.

(37) a. Sakana wa tai   ga ii.
         fish   redsnapper   is-good
         'Speaking of fish, the redsnapper is the best.'

      b. Basyo wa okunai-setu   ga attooteki   datta.
         place   indoor-theory   predominant was
         'Speaking of the place (of the murder), the
          indoor-theory was predominant.'

The sentence pattern of (37) is ordinarily called the "double
subject" pattern. However, there is no evidence that indicates
that Sakana wa and Basyo wa of (37a,b) function as subjects
in these sentences. The theme of a sentence which is
coreferential with the subject is marked with ga in nominal
and adjectival clauses:

(38) a. Taroo wa wakai.
              is-young
         'Taroo is young.'

      b. Taroo ga wakai.
         'It is Taroo who is young.'

      c. Taroo ga (*wa) wakai koto
         'the fact that Taroo is young'

On the other hand, it is impossible to mark sakana 'fish' and
basyo 'place' of (37) with ga in embedded clauses:

(39) a. *sakana ga tai   ga ii   koto
        fish   redsnapper is-good fact-that
        'the fact that (Lit.) speaking of fish, the
        redsnapper is the best.'

    b. *basyo ga okunai-setu   ga attooteki   datta
        place   indoor-theory   predominant was

        koto
        fact-that

        'the fact that (Lit.) speaking of the place (of
        the murder), the indoor-theory was predominant'

This shows that Sakana wa and Basyo wa cannot be regarded as
performing double functions of theme and subject. Li and
Thompson 1976b include the sentence pattern of (37) as
characteristic of topic-prominent languages.

    Since (37a,b) do not have themeless source sentences, we
have to assume that they are derived from underlying
structures that already have themes at the sentence-initial
position, as in [Theme [Sentence]].

2.1.7. Double Subject Sentences

Japanese has sentences with double subjects, both marked with
the nominative article ga; see Kuno 1973, Ch. 3, for details.
Observe the following sentences:

(40) a. Taroo no otoosan ga sinde simatta.
            's father   dying ended-up
        'Taroo's father has died.'

    b. Taroo ga otoosan ga sinde simatta.
        'Taroo — his father has died.'

(41) a. New York no koogai ni yoi zyuutakuti   ga
                    's suburbs in good residential-area

        aru.
        exist

'In the suburbs of New York, there are good
residential areas.'

b. New York no koogai ga yoi zyuutakuti ga aru.
(Lit.) 'It is New York's suburbs that there are
good residential areas.'

c. New York ga koogai ni yoi zyuutakuti ga aru.
(Lit.) 'It is New York that in the suburbs there
are good residential areas.'

Since yoi zyuutakuti ga aru 'there are good residential areas'
and koogai ni yoi zyuutakuti ga aru 'in the suburbs, there
are good residential areas' of (41b,c) are stative predicates, New York no koogai 'New York's suburbs' and New York,
with the ga marking, receive the exhaustive listing interpretation of 'It is New York's suburbs that ...; it is New York
that ...' (See the discussion of ga marking the subject of
stative predicates in 2.1.1.)

It seems that (40b) and (41b,c) have a structure that can
be represented as [S [S V]]. That the first subject is not in
the same simplex sentence as the verb can be shown by the
fact that it does not trigger Simplex Sentence Reflexivization
(see Section 2.3.3), and that it does not trigger Honorific
Agreement. Observe the following sentences, which are due
to Shibatani (1976):

(42) a. *Yamada-sensei$_i$ ga musuko ga zibun$_i$ ni
           teacher   son   self   to

   unzarisite iru.
   disgusted is

   'It is Teacher Yamada$_i$ whose son is disgusted
   with self$_i$.'

b. *Yamada-sensei ga inu ga onakunari   ni
      teacher   dog   dying-Honorific

   natte   simatta.
   becoming ended-up

   'It is Teacher Yamada whose dog has died.'

In (42a), the subscript *i* is used to show that <u>Yamada</u>-<u>sensei</u> and <u>zibun</u> are coreferential. The sentence is ungrammatical in that interpretation. (42b) is ungrammatical because <u>onakunari</u> <u>ni</u> <u>nar</u>-, an honorific form for <u>sin</u>- 'die', refers not to what it is intended for (i.e., Teacher Yamada), but to <u>inu</u> 'dog', the second subject, which does not semantically qualify as recipient of the speaker's respect. These two phenomena can be explained if we hypothesize the [S [S V]] structure for the double subject sentence pattern, and if we assume that Reflexivization and Honorific Marking apply only within the bound of simplex sentences.

Double subject sentences are very different from the "NP-<u>ga</u> + NP-<u>ga</u> + Stative Verbal" sentences that we have seen in Section 2.1.3. While (40b) and (41b,c), as shown in (40a) and (41a), have corresponding single subject sentences, (2), (16a), and (16b) do not have corresponding single subject versions:

(43) a.   Taroo ga Hanako ga suki   da.
                               fond-of is
          'It is Taroo that likes Hanako.'

     b. *Taroo no/ni Hanako ga suki da.

Similarly, when the first subject is deleted from (40b) and (41b,c), we still obtain complete sentences, as shown below:

(44) a. Otoosan ga sinde simatta.
        father   dying ended-up
        'Father has died.'

     b. Yoi zyuutakuti   ga aru.
        good residential-area   exist
        'There are good residential areas.'

     c. Koogai ni yoi zyuutakuti   ga aru.
        suburbs in good residential-areas   exist
        'There are good residential areas in the suburbs.'

In contrast, when the first NP-ga is deleted from the
"NP-ga + NP-ga + Stative Verbal" pattern, we obtain elliptical
sentences:

(45) Ø Hanako ga suki   da.
            fond-of is
     'I like Hanako; he likes Hanako; etc.'

I give below some more examples of double subject sentences:

(46) a. Taroo wa atama ga ii.
              head   is-good
        'Taroo is bright.'

     b. Zoo   wa hana ga nagai.
        elephant   nose   is-long
        'Speaking of the elephant, its trunk is long.'

     c. Taroo wa otoosan ga gakkoo no sensei da.
              father   school 's teacher is
        'Speaking of Taroo, his father is a school
        teacher.'

The interaction of this thematic pattern with the double
subject pattern produces sentences which seem peculiar to
speakers of languages that have neither of these two patterns:

(47) a. Hana wa zoo   ga nagai.
        nose   elephant   is-long
        'Speaking of noses/trunks, (Lit.) an elephant
        is long.'

     b. Me wa Merii ga aoi.
        eye   Mary   is-blue
        'Speaking of eyes, (Lit.) Mary is blue.'

At first glance, these sentences appear to have zoo ga
'elephant' and Merii ga as the surface subjects of nagai 'is
long' and aoi 'is blue', but in fact, zoo ga and Merii ga
are the higher subjects of double subject sentences, in
which the lower subjects have been deleted due to coreferentiality with the themes of the sentences:

(48) [Theme [S [S V]]]

  a. [Hana wa [zoo   ga [hana ga nagai]]]
     nose   elephant   nose   is-long

  b. [Me wa [Merii ga [me ga aoi   ]]]
     eye   eye is-blue

2.1.8. Adpositions

Japanese, as an SOV language, displays all the characteristics
that Greenberg (1963) has attributed to SOV languages. One
of the characteristics concerns adpositions. (See Kuno 1974
for perception-oriented explanation for such a universal.)

Greenberg's Language Universal 4: With overwhelmingly
greater than chance frequency, languages with normal SOV
order are postpositional.

Japanese adpositions are *all* postpositional. I give below
representative samples of adpositions classified according to
their functions, excluding those that are used in connecting
clauses, which I will discuss in section 2.5.1.

(49) Thematic and Contrastive Particles

  a. John <u>wa</u> tensai da.
    'John is a genius.'

  b. John wa tensai de   <u>wa</u> nai.
           genius being   not
    'John is not a genius.'

(50) Quantifierlike Particles

  a. Taroo <u>mo</u>   tensai da.
       also genius is
    'Taroo, too, is a genius.'

  b. Taroo <u>sika</u> konakatta.
       only came-not
    'Only Taroo came.'

(51) Noun-Coordinating Particles

   a. Taroo to Hanako ga kita.
         and   came
     'Taroo and Hanako came.'

   b. Taroo ya Hanako ga kita.
         and   came
     'Taroo and Hanako (and others) came.'

   c. Taroo ka Hanako ga kuru.
         or   come
     'Either Taroo or Hanako will come.'

(52) Case-Marking Particles

   a. Taroo ga   zidoosya de Hanako to   Tookyoo kara
         Nom. car   by   with   from

     Hirosima made   ryokoosita.
           up-to traveled

     'Taroo traveled with Hanako by car from Tokyo to
     Hiroshima.'

   b. Taroo no otoosan ga   Amerika e itta.
         's father Nom.   to went
     'Taroo's father went to America.'

(53) Sentence-Final Particles

   a. Kimi wa kono hon o yonda ka.
      you   this book   read Q
     'Did you read this book?'

   b. Boku wa kono hon o moo   yonda yo.
      I   this book already read I-tell-you
     'I tell you that I have read this book already.'

   c. Ano hito wa tensai da naa.
      that person   genius is Exclamatory
     'Boy, that man is a genius!'

   d. Kimi wa kinoo   gakkoo o yasunda ne.
      you   yesterday school   rested Tag Q
     'You didn't come to school yesterday, did you?'

Note that Japanese uses the *sentence-final* particle ka in
forming interrogative sentences as seen in (53a). The use of
sentence-final question particles is a characteristic of
postpositional languages, as observed by Greenberg:

> *Greenberg's Language Universal 9:* With more than chance
> frequency, when question particles or affixes are specified
> in position by reference to the sentence as a whole, if
> initial, such elements are found in prepositional languages,
> and, if final, in postpositional.

Some particles can occur one after another:

(54) a. Tookyoo ni wa   Taroo ga itta.
        to Theme   went
        'To Tokyo, Taroo went.'

    b. Taroo kara mo   tegami ga kita.
         from also letter   came
       'A letter came from Taroo, too.'

    c. Fuzi-san wa koko kara ga   itiban yoku mieru.
        Mt.   here from Nom. most   well can-see
       'Speaking of Mt. Fuji,(Lit.) from here is the
        best visible; one can see Mt. Fuji best from
        here.'

    d. Taroo to Hanako to ni atta.
        and   and to met
       'I met Taroo and Hanako.'

    e. Taroo to Hanako to o   syootaisita.
        and   and Acc. invited
       'I invited Taroo and Hanako.'

The above uses of Japanese particles shows that they are
postpositions rather than suffixes.

The coordinating conjunction to can optionally appear after
the last conjunct, as shown in (54d,e). Given A to B to and
given "B = C to D to," it is possible to have A to [C to D to]
to, as shown in the following:

(55) [Carter to   Mondale] to   [Kosygin to   Bresnev to] to
   and   and   and   and and
 ga kaidansita.
 conferred
 'Carter and Mondale as a team and Kosygin and Brezhnev
 as a team had a meeting.'

(55) has a three-particle sequence to to ga; see Kuno 1973,
Ch. 8, for details.

2.1.9. Comparison of Inequality

Japanese adjectives and nominal-adjectives do not inflect with
respect to comparative and superlative degrees. Instead, they
use optional degree adverbs such as motto 'more', zutto 'far',
itiban 'first', and mottomo 'most', which appear to the left
of the adjective. The postpositional particle yori 'than'
is used as a marker of comparison, with the standard with
which the comparison is made preceding yori:

(56) a. Taroo wa Hanako yori zutto wakai.
       than   is-young
    Standard Marker Adjective
  'Taroo is far younger than Hanako.'

  b. Kono kurasu de wa, Taroo ga mottomo wakai.
   this class in   most is-young
   'In this class, Taroo is the youngest.'

The order of "Standard — Marker of Comparison — Adjective"
exemplified by (56a) agrees with the following observation
by Greenberg:

Greenberg's Language Universal 22: If in comparison of
superiority, the only order, or one of the alternative
orders, is standard-marker-adjective, then the language
is postpositional. With overwhelmingly more than chance
frequency if the only order is adjective-marker-standard,
the language is prepositional.

2.2. Nominal Phrases

Greenberg makes the following observations, among others, with respect to the relative position of adjectival modifiers and head nouns in nominal phrases:

Greenberg's Language Universal 18: When the descriptive adjective precedes the noun, the demonstrative and the numeral, with overwhelmingly more than chance frequency, do likewise.

Greenberg's Language Universal 19: When the general rule is that the descriptive adjective follows, there may be a minority of adjectives which usually precede, but when the general rule is that descriptive adjectives precede, there are no exceptions.

Greenberg's Language Universal 20: When any or all of the items — the demonstrative, numeral, and descriptive adjective — precede the noun, they are always found in that order. If they follow, the order is either the same or its exact opposite.

Greenberg's Language Universal 24: If the relative expression precedes the noun either as the only construction or as an alternative construction, either the language is postpositional or the adjective precedes the noun or both.

Similarly, Lehmann (1973a) makes the following observation:

Lehmann's Structural Principle of Language: Modifiers are placed on the opposite side of a basic syntactic element from its primary concomitant.

According to this principle, nominal modifiers (relative clauses, adjectival and genitive expressions) precede nouns in (S)OV languages and follow them in V(S)O languages because

they are placed on the side of the head noun opposite its
primary concomitant, namely, V.

All the above observations apply to Japanese. Descriptive
adjectives, demonstratives, numerals, and relative clauses all
precede their head nouns, without exception. Observe the following examples: The no in these sentences is the adjectival
form of the copula, and not a particle; see example (15).

(1) a. kono ni-satu no hon
        this 2-vol. is book
        (Lit., 'these books which are 2-volumes')
        'these two books'

    b. *ni-satu no kono hon
        2-vol. is this book

(2) a. kono omosiroi   hon
        this is-interesting book
        (Lit., 'this book which is interesting')
        'this interesting book'

    b. *omosiroi   kono hon
        is-interesting this book

(3) a. kono kinoo   katta hon
        this yesterday bought book
        'this book, which I bought yesterday'

    b. kinoo   katta kono hon
        yesterday bought this book
        'this book, which I bought yesterday'

(3) shows that there is no constraint on the relative order
of a relative clause and a demonstrative. It goes without
saying that in all the above examples total ungrammaticality
results if any of the adjectival expressions appears to the
right of the head noun.

Japanese does not have indefinite or definite articles.
This does not mean, however, that nouns can be used freely
both anaphorically and nonanaphorically. Observe the following
sentences:

(4) Kinoo   Sansei-doo de hon   o katta. Yuusyoku go
    Yesterday bookstore at book   bought dinner   after

    hon   o yonda.
    book   read

    'Yesterday, I bought a book at Sanseido Bookstore.
    After dinner, I read a book/books.'

The second sentence in (4) can mean only 'I read a book; I
read books'; it cannot mean 'I read the book.' In order to
convey the latter meaning, one has to modify hon 'book' with
a demonstrative adjective:

(5) ... Yuusyoku go   sono hon   o yonda.
        dinner   after that book   read
    'After dinner, I read that book.'

The above does not mean, however, that Japanese uses a
demonstrative adjective whenever English uses the. Observe
the following sentences:

(6) Kinoo   se   no takai hito   to se   no
    yesterday height   tall   person and height Ptc.

    hikui hito   ga tazunete kita. Se   no takai hito
    low   person   visiting came height   tall   person

    wa te   ni tue   o motte   ita.
       hand in stick   having was

    'Yesterday, a tall man and a short man came to see me.
    The tall man had a walking stick in his hand.'

In the second sentence, se no takai hito 'the tall man' does
not have sono 'that'. In fact, in this context, it is not
possible to use any demonstrative adjective. Similarly,
observe the following discourse:

(7) Sono heya ni wa ookii tukue ga atta. Tukue no ue   ni
    the room in   is-big table was   table 's top in

    wa, kabin ga atta.
        vase   was

    'In the room, there was a big table. On the table,
    there was a vase.'

The second tukue 'table, desk' is not modified by a demonstrative adjective. In contrast to (6), however, it is possible to use sono 'that' in (7). The above examples show that the use of demonstrative adjectives is conditioned by various factors such as whether the noun phrase has its own modifier (adjective or relative clause), whether the noun phrase is used contrastively, or whether it is a locative. The exact conditions for the use of demonstrative adjectives are poorly understood, and await future study.

Japanese nouns do not ordinarily distinguish between singular and plural forms. For example, hon in the first sentence of (4) can mean either 'a book' or 'books'. This does not mean, however, that all nouns can be used freely for both singular and plural. Observe the following discourse:

(8) Kinoo   san-nin no gakusei ga tazunete kita.
    yesterday 3-person   student   visiting came

$\left\{ \begin{array}{ll} & \text{*Gakusei} \\ \text{*Sono} & \text{gakusei} \\ \text{Sono} & \text{gakusei-tati} \end{array} \right\}$ wa kesa   no yo-zi

    that   student   this-morning   4-o'clock

    made hanasikonde itta.
    until talking   went

'Yesterday, three students came to visit me. The students left after having talked with me until four o'clock this morning.'

The "plural" form gakusei-tati 'students' is required in the second sentence, where the noun phrase is anaphoric. The suffix -tati, which is reserved for humans, appears in the following construction also:

(9) Kinoo   Taroo-tati ga tazunete kita.
    yesterday   visiting came
    'Yesterday, Taroo and others came to visit me.'

It is not well known exactly when plural forms such as
gakusei-tati are obligatory, when they are optional, and when
they cannot be used.

Japanese has a small number of nouns that form "collective"
forms by reduplication: for example, yama-yama 'mountains',
ie-ie 'houses', ki-gi 'trees', hito-bito 'people', hana-bana
'flowers'. (A morpheme-initial voiceless consonant becomes
voiced in the second half of compounds, b being the voiced
counterpart of h.)

2.2.1 Relative Clauses

As I have already mentioned, relative clauses in Japanese
always precede their head nouns:

(10) a. Sono hito   ga kono hon   o kaita.
        that person   this book   wrote
        'That person wrote this book.'

    b. kono hon   o kaita hito
       this book   wrote person
       'the person who wrote this book'

(11) a. Taroo ga sono hon   o yonda.
                 that book   read
        'Taroo read that book.'

    b. Taroo ga yonda hon
                read book
       'the book that Taroo read'

(12) a. Taroo ga sono hito   to   issyoni benkyoosita.
                 that person with together studied
        'Taroo studied together with that person.'

    b. Taroo ga issyoni benkyoosita hito
                together studied   person
       'the person with whom Taroo studied'

The following sentence is ungrammatical:

(13) a. Taroo ga <u>sono hito</u>   <u>to</u>   benkyoosita.
         that person with studied
      'Taroo studied with that person.'

   b. *Taroo ga benkyoosita <u>hito</u>
      'the person with whom Taroo studied'

(13b) is ungrammatical in the intended interpretation (it is
grammatical if it is intended for 'the person that Taroo
studied') because the deleted particle <u>to</u> 'with' is not
recoverable. In (12b), <u>issyoni</u> 'together' makes it possible
to supply this particle. See Kuno 1973, Chs. 20 and 21, for
details.

(14) a. <u>Sono ie</u>   <u>no</u> yane wa akai.
        that house 's roof   is-red
      'The roof of that house is red.'

   b. yane ga akai   <u>ie</u>
      roof   is-red house
      'the house the roof of which is red'

(15) a. <u>Sono kodomo</u> wa otoosan ga syoogakkoo   no
        the child   father   grade-school 's

        sensei da.
        teacher is

      'Speaking of that child, (his) father is a
       grade-school teacher.'

   b. otoosan ga syoogakkoo   no sensei no <u>kodomo</u>
      father   grade-school 's teacher is child
      'a child whose father is a grade-school teacher'

In (15b), the <u>no</u> that immediately precedes the head noun
<u>kodomo</u> 'child' is not a possessive particle, but is the pre-
nominal adjectival form of the copula <u>da</u>. In more formal
speech, <u>de aru</u> (Lit., 'is being') appears in its place.

   Two facts require special mention in connection with (10)
through (15). First, the particle that marks the noun phrase
that is coreferential with the head noun of a relative clause
is not present in the surface construction. In other words,

Japanese does not allow dangling postpositions. Second, relative clauses in Japanese do not use relative pronouns. Relative clauses (and for that matter, all subordinate clauses) in Japanese are strictly verb-final, and, therefore, verbals signal the end of clauses. There is therefore no need for relative pronouns, whose main function seems to be to mark the clause boundary of embedded clauses. (See Kuno 1974 for details.)

Relativization can enter into relative clauses, adverbial clauses, interrogative clauses, and sentential subjects, namely, into those constructions which normally reject the same process in English:

(16) a. [∅ ∅ kawaigatte ita inu]_{Complex NP}
        fond-of   was dog

        ga sinde simatta kôdomo
           dying ended-up child

        (Lit.) 'the child who the dog (he) was fond
        of ∅ died'

     b. [∅ ∅ syuppansita kaisya]_{Complex NP}
           published   company

        ga toosansite simatta hon
           bankrupt   went   book

        (Lit.) 'the book which the publisher who published
        (it) went bankrupt'

     c. [∅ sinda noni   ]_{Adv. Cl.} dare   mo
           died although   anybody

        kanasimanakatta hito
        was-not-saddened person

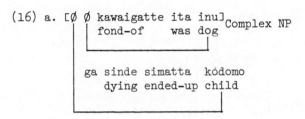

(Lit.) 'the person who, although (he) died, no
one was saddened'

d. [dare ga Ø kaita ka] Interr. Cl.
   who   wrote Q

        daremo siranai hon
        anybody not-know book

(Lit.) 'the book which no one knows who wrote (it)'

e. [Ø au koto] Sent. Sbj. ga muzukasii   hito
   see to   is-difficult person

(Lit.) 'a person who to see (him) is difficult'

The acceptability of (16a,b) is interesting from a
language-typology point of view. Both sentences involve
double relativization, namely, relativization from a relative
clause. There are many languages which prohibit double
relativization, but (16a,b) show that Japanese is not such
a language. In (16), head nouns are connected with a link to
the corresponding deletion sites in the relative clauses
(according to the conventional analysis of relativization).
(16a) is said to involve center-embedding double relativization because one link is center-embedded in another, while
(16b) is said to involve crisscrossing double relativization
because the two links crisscross each other. There are some
languages which allow relativization into relative clauses
only when the center-embedding pattern of (16a) holds, but
the acceptability of (16b) shows that Japanese is not one of
these languages. Grammatical strings of the pattern of (16b)
abound:

(17) a. [Ø Ø sidoosite kurete ita sensei] ga tenninsite
           advising giving was teacher   transferring

        simatta gakusei
        ended-up students

(Lit.) 'the students who the teacher who had been
teaching (them) moved to another school'

b. [∅ ∅ kaita hito] ga dare da ka wakaranai tegami
       wrote person   who is Q not-know letter
(Lit.) 'the letter such that who the person who
wrote (it) is, is not known'

I hypothesize that what is relativized in a Japanese
relative clause is not an ordinary noun phrase, but a noun
phrase that is the theme of the relative clause. For example,
I assume that (18a) below is derived from the intermediate
structure represented in (18b) by Theme-Deletion under
coreferentiality with the head noun:

(18) a. Taroo ga yonda hon
              read book
        'the book that Taroo read'

   b. [[sono hon wa]_Theme Taroo ga yonda]_Rel. Cl. hon
        that book   read   book

What this analysis assumes is that the head noun must
represent the theme of the relative clause; namely, the
relative clause must be a statement about the head noun.
Justification for this analysis of Japanese relativization
is given in Kuno 1973, Ch. 21. Application of the same
principle for explaining certain otherwise unexplainable
relativization phenomena in English is given in Kuno 1976b.

2.2.2. Genitives

Genitive expressions precede head nouns, as seen in the
following:

(19) a. Taroo no ie
              's house
        'Taroo's house'

b. Taroo no otoosan no ie
     's father   's house
'Taroo's father's house'

In English, genitive expressions such as the man I met yesterday's wife are rather exceptional (cf. ??the man I met's wife). By contrast, in Japanese, such expressions are very common because the relative clause precedes the head noun, and hence the genitive marker no always follows the head noun of the relative construction.

(20) a. [boku ga kinoo   atta hito] no okusan
       I   yesterday met   person 's wife
     'the man whom I met yesterday's wife'

    b. [[boku ga kinoo   atta hito] no okusan ga
       I   yesterday met   person 's wife

     tutomete iru kaisya] no syatyoo
     working is company 's president

     'the president of the company where the wife of
     the man that I met yesterday is employed'

    c. [[[boku ga kinoo   atta hito] no okusan ga
       I   yesterday met   person 's wife

     tutomete iru kaisya] no syatyoo   ga kaita hon]
     working is company 's president   wrote book

     no syuppansya
     's publisher

     'the publisher of the book that the president of
     the company where the wife of the man that I met
     yesterday is employed wrote'

Left branching constructions of the above type are extremely common in Japanese, and they do not cause any difficulty in comprehension.

2.2.3. Numerals and Quantifiers

Numerals can be used as prenominal adjectives, as nouns, and as adverbs. For example, observe the following sentences:

(21) a. San-<u>nin</u> <u>no</u> yuuzin ga tazunete kita. (Adjectival)
         3-person   friend   visiting came
         'Three friends came to visit me.'

     b. Yuuzin no <u>san-nin</u> ga tazunete kita. (Nominal)
         friend 's 3-person   visiting came
         'Three of my friends came to visit me.'

     c. Yuuzin ga <u>san-nin</u> tazunete kita. (Adverbial)
         friend   3-person visiting came
         'Friends came to visit me (Lit.) three-person-ly.'

There are restrictions on the adverbial uses of numerals and
quantifiers: they are allowable when they *semantically* modify
noun phrases that are subjects or objects; they are unacceptable when noun phrases of oblique cases are involved. However,
the exact conditions for the appearance of adverbial numerals
are not well understood:

(22) a. Yuuzin ga <u>san-nin</u> tazunete kita. (Subject)
         friend   3-person visiting came
         'Three friends came to visit me.'

     b. Yuuzin o <u>san-nin</u> syootaisita. (Object)
         friend   3-person invited
         'I invited three friends.'

     c. *Yuuzin kara <u>san-nin</u> tegami o moratta. (Oblique)
         friend from 3-person letter   received
         'I received letters from three friends.'

(23) a. San-<u>dai</u> no zidoosya de ryookoosita.
         3-car   car   by traveled
         'We traveled in three cars.'

     b. *Zidoosya de <u>san-dai</u> ryokoosita.
         car   by 3-car   traveled
         'We traveled in three cars.'

2.3. Verbal Phrases

2.3.1. Declarative, Interrogative, and Negative

Interrogative sentences are formed by using the sentence-final question particle _ka_ regardless of whether a yes-or-no question or interrogative-word question is involved:

(1) a. Taroo wa kita _ka_.
              came Q
      'Did Taroo come?'

    b. Taroo wa sono okane o dare ni yatta _ka_.
            the   money   who to gave   Q
      'Who did Taroo give the money to?'

    c. Dare ni Taroo wa sono okane o yatta _ka_.
        who to   the   money   gave   Q
      'Who did Taroo give the money to?'

The interrogative word does not have to be preposed to sentence-initial position. This is a characteristic of SOV languages, as observed by Greenberg:

> *Greenberg's Language Universal 17:* If a language has dominant order VSO in declarative sentences, it always puts interrogative words or phrases first in interrogative-word questions; if it has dominant order SOV in declarative sentences, there is never such an invariant rule.

(1c) seems to have been derived by the same word-order scrambling rule that is responsible for relatively free word order in Japanese as illustrated at the beginning of this paper.

    The interrogative word can enter rather freely into coordinate structures, complex noun phrases, adverbial clauses, and sentential subjects. Resulting interrogatives, which are quite natural in Japanese, are almost untranslatable into English.

(2) a. Taroo to   dare to   ga kekkonsita ka sitte   iru ka?
       and who and   married   Q knowing is Q
    'Do you know (Lit.) Taroo and who got married?'

   b. Dare ga dare ni kaita tegami ga itiban
      who   who to wrote letter   most

      omosirokatta   ka.
      was-interesting Q

      (Lit.) 'The letter which who wrote to whom was
      most interesting?'

   c. Taroo wa doko ni itta toki ni kore o katta   ka.
              where to went time at this   bought Q
      (Lit.) 'At the time that Taroo went where did
      he buy this?'

Negative sentences are formed by affixing the negative
adjectival morpheme (-a-)na to a verbal stem, and by adding
the negative adjective na- to the gerundive form of an
adjective or copula:

(3) a. Boku wa kyoo wa nanimo   tabe-na-i.
       I   today   anything eat-Neg.-Nonpast
    'I won't eat anything today.'

   b. Boku wa kyoo wa gakkoo ni ik-a-na-i.
      I   today   school to go-Affix-Neg.-Nonpast
    'I don't go to school today.'

(4) a. Taroo wa wakak-u   na-i.
                be-young-ing not-be-Nonpast
      'Taroo is not young.'

   b. Taroo wa tensai de   (wa) na-i.
                genius being   not-be-Nonpast
      'Taroo is not a genius.'

The negative form of ar- 'exist, have' is na-:

(5) a. Tukue no ue ni hon ga ar-u.
       desk 's top in book   exist-Nonpast
       'There is a book on the desk.'

   b. Tukue no ue ni (wa) nanimo   na-i.
      desk 's top in   anything not-exist-Nonpast
      'There is nothing on the desk.'

2.3.2. Reciprocal Verbs

Japanese has a productive process for forming reciprocal verbs.
The verb affix aw- 'match, meet' is added to the gerundive
form of action verbs (aw- + -ta > at-ta):

(6) a. Taroo to Hanako wa tasuke-at-ta.
        and   helping-Recip.-Past
    'Taroo and Hanako helped each other.'

    b. Taroo to Hanako wa hagemas-i-at-ta.
        and   encourage-ing-Recip.-Past
    'Taroo and Hanako encouraged each other.'

One of the arguments of the coordinate subject of a reciprocal
verb can be removed from the subject position and can be made
into an adverbial expression:

(7) a. Taroo wa Hanako to   tasuke-at-ta.
                    with helping-Recip.-Past
    (Lit.) 'Taroo helping-reciprocated with Hanako.'

    b. Cf. Taroo wa Hanako o   tasuke-ta.
                        Acc. help-Past
    'Taroo helped Hanako.'

    c. Taroo wa Hanako to   hagemas-i-at-ta.
                    with encourage-ing-Recip.-Past
    (Lit.) 'Taroo encouraging-reciprocated with Hanako.'

    d. Cf. Taroo wa Hanako o   hagemas-i-ta.
                        Acc. encourage-Affix-Past
    'Taroo encouraged Hanako.'

It is particularly interesting that the noun-coordinating
particle to and the comitative particle to are homophonous.
See Kuno 1973, Ch. 6 for details.

2.3.3. Reflexive

Japanese has a single reflexive form zibun 'self' for all
persons and genders. For the plural, zibun-zati 'selves'

is used if the referent is discourse-anaphoric. In simplex
sentences, reflexivization is triggered only by the subject
of the sentence:

(8) a. Taroo$_i$ ga Hanako o zibun$_i$ no ie   de korosita.
                          self   's house in killed
         'Taroo killed Hanako in his (= Taroo's) house.'

    b. *Taroo ga Hanako$_j$ o zibun$_j$ no ie   de korosita.
                           self   's house in killed
         'Taroo killed Hanako in her (= Hanako's) house.'

(9) a. Hanako$_j$ ga Taroo ni zibun$_j$ no ie   de korosareta.
                          by self   's house in was-killed
         'Hanako was killed by Taroo in her (= Hanako's)
         house.'

    b. *Hanako ga Taroo$_i$ ni zibun$_i$ no ie   de korosareta.
                          by self   's house in was-killed
         'Hanako was killed by Taroo in his (= Taroo's)
         house.'

The fact that (9a) is grammatical while (9b) is not shows
that Reflexivization applies after Passivization has applied.

    The unambiguity of reflexive inference in (8) and (9)
stands in marked contrast with the ambiguity displayed in the
following causative sentence. (This was first observed in
Akatsuka 1972.)

(10) Hanako ga Taroo ni zibun no ie   de benkyoos-ase-ta.
                         to self 's house in study-cause-Past
     'Hanako made Taroo study in his/her house.'

This phenomenon can be explained if we assume that a causative
sentence involving the causative morpheme (s)ase has a
complex underlying structure of the kind informally shown
in (11). If the lower sentence has Taroo no ie 'Taroo's
house', Reflexivization applies within this clause, with its
subject Taroo as trigger. If the lower sentence has Hanako
no ie 'Hanako's house', Reflexivization applies after the
embedded subject has been marked with ni by Agentive-Ni

(11)

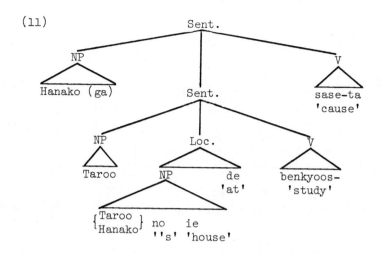

(12)

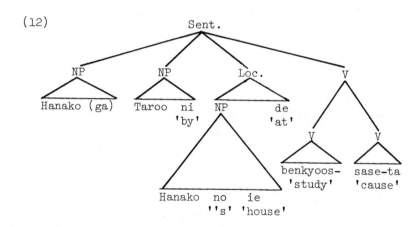

Attachment, and after the embedded verb has been raised and attached to the main verb _sase_ by Verb Raising, which yields the surface structure shown in (12). At this stage, the second occurrence of _Hanako_ is in the same simplex sentence as the first occurrence of _Hanako_, and, hence, Reflexivization applies, producing (10), which has _zibun_ as coreferential with _Hanako_.

The ambiguity of the following "adversity passive"
sentence is also in marked contrast with the unambiguity of
(9), which is a pure passive sentence:

(13) Hanako ga Taroo ni zibun no hanasi bakari s-are-ta.
                        by self 's talk   only   do-Passive-
                                                           Past
      'Hanako was adversely affected by Taroo's talking
       about nothing but himself (= Taroo)/herself
       (= Hanako).'

I assume that pure passive sentences are derived from underlying simplex sentence structures, while adversity passive
sentences are derived from complex sentence structures of the
kind shown below:

(14)

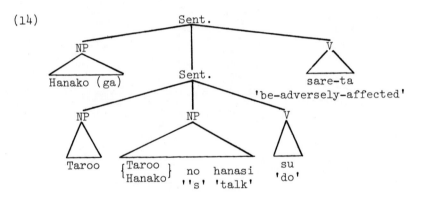

If we have Taroo no hanasi in the lower clause, Reflexivization applies within the bound of this clause. Next, Agentive-
Ni Attachment attaches ni to the lower subject Taroo, and
the lower verb is raised and attached to the left of the
main clause verb, which triggers tree-pruning processes,
yielding a surface structure similar to that of (12). If we
have Hanako no hanasi 'Hanako's talk', Reflexivization takes
place in the main clause, with the subject Hanako as trigger.
See Kuno 1973, Ch. 25, for details.

There are several characteristics of the Japanese
reflexive worth mentioning here. First, the reflexive must
refer to higher animals. Therefore, Japanese lacks reflexive
sentences like History repeats itself. Second, it is difficult
to reflexivize a nongenitive NP. Sentences (15) and (16) are
ungrammatical.

    (15) *Taroo wa zibun o korosita.
             self   killed
       'Taroo killed himself.'

Instead, the Sino-Japanese compound zi-satu si-ta 'self-
murder did' is used.

    (16) *Taroo wa zibun o tataita.
             self   hit
       'Taroo hit himself.'

Instead, one has to specify a body part, as in

    (17) Taroo wa zibun no atama o tataita.
             self   's head   hit
       'Taroo hit his own head.'

Third, reflexive sentences of the pattern of (15) and (16) are
passable if the reflexive refers not to a physical object, but
to an abstract personality (see Akatsuka 1972 and McCawley
1976 for various characterizations of Japanese reflexives):

    (18) a. Taroo wa zibun o awarenda.
               self   pitied
         'Taroo pitied himself.'

        b. Taroo wa zibun o hihansita.
               self   criticized
         'Taroo criticized himself.'

Fourth, Reflexivization in complex sentences is a "point of
view" based phenomenon. Observe the following contrast:

    (19) a. Taroo$_i$ wa Hanako ga zibun$_i$ ni kureta okane o
                          self   to gave   money

tukatte simatta.
spending ended-up

'Taroo has used up the money that Hanako gave
   him (= Taroo).'

b. *Taroo$_i$ wa Hanako ga <u>zibun</u>$_i$ ni <u>yatta</u> okane o
                          self   to gave   money

tukatte simatta.
spending ended-up

'Taroo has used up the money that Hanako gave
   him (= Taroo).'

The two sentences are differently only with respect to the
verbs of the relative clauses: <u>kureta</u> and <u>yatta</u>. They both
mean 'gave', but they are different in that the former is a
verb used when the speaker describes the action of giving
from the point of view of the recipient, while the latter
is a verb used when the speaker describes the same action
from the point of view of the giver; see Kuno and Kaburaki
1975 and Kuno 1976c. (19b) is unacceptable because there is
a conflict in the speaker's point of view: <u>yatta</u> shows that
the speaker is describing the event from Hanako's (= the
giver's) point of view, while <u>zibun</u> (= Taroo) 'self' shows
that the same speaker is describing the event from Taroo's
point of view.

2.3.4. Compound Verbs, Adjectives, and Nominal-Adjectives

Japanese is rich in compound verbal formation. I give below
representative samples:

(20) Compounding Verbals Added to the Gerundive
     Form of Verbs

   a. Verb Compounds

      yom-i-hazime-ru   'begin to read'

      yom-i das-u   'start to read'

yom-i toos-u	'read through'
yom-i a-u	'read to each other'
yom-i oe-ru	'finish reading'
yom-i tuzuke-ru	'continue to read'
yom-i sugi-ru	'read excessively'

b. Adjective Compounds

yom-i yasu-i	'be easy to read'
yom-i ta-i	'be eager to read'
yom-i zura-i	'be difficult to read'

c. Nominal Adjective Compounds

yom-i soo da	'look as if ... about to read'
yom-i sugi da	'be excessive in reading'

No elements can be inserted between the gerundive form and the compounding verbals.

(21) Compounding Verbs Added to the Continuative Form of Verbs

yon-de mi-ru	'try to read'
yon-de sima-u	'end up reading'
yon-de yar-u	'read (From the point of view of the agent)'
yon-de i-ru	'is reading'
yon-de kure-ru	'read (From the point of view of a nonagent)'

Only certain particles (wa, contrastive, mo 'also', sika 'only', dake 'only', sae 'even') can be inserted between the continuative form and the compounding verbs, as in yon-de mo mi-ru 'try also to read', yon-de sae i-ru 'is even reading'.

The position of compounding verbals relative to the gerundive and continuative forms of verbs illustrated above is consistent with Greenberg's Language Universals 13 and 16:

Greenberg's Language Universal 13: If the nominal object
always precedes the verb, then verb forms subordinate to
the main verb also precede it.

Greenberg's Language Universal 16: In languages with
dominant order VSO, an inflected auxiliary always precedes
the main verb. In languages with dominant order SOV, an
inflected auxiliary always follows the main verb.

It is also consistent with Lehmann's structural principle
given in section 2.2 because it predicts that verbal modifiers
for negation, causation, aspectual specifications, etc., are
placed after verb roots in (S)OV languages on the opposite
side of V from O.

2.3.5. Modality, Aspect, and Tense

The following examples illustrate various ways in which
Japanese expresses modality:

(22) Imperative, Necessitative

    a. Hon o yom-e. (Informal)
       book   read-Imper.
       'Read books.'

    b. Hon o yom-i   nasai. (Quasi-polite)
       book   read-ing do-Imper.
       'Read books.'

    c. Hon o yom-u   beki   da.
           read-Nonpast should is
       'You should read books.'

(Beki is the prenominal attributive form of the Classical
Japanese auxiliary verb besi 'should'. When it is used pre-
nominally, it is not accompanied by a copula: yomu beki hon
'books to read'.)

(22) d. Hon o yom-a-nak-e-reba   ikenai.
         read-Affix-Neg.-Affix-if is-not-good
    (Lit., 'If you don't read books, it is not good.')
    'You must read books.'

    e. Hon o yon-de   mo   yoi.
         read-Cont. even is-good
    (Lit., 'Even reading books, it is good.')
    'You may read books.'

    f. Hon o yom-oo.
         read-Intentional
    'Let's read books.'

(23) Epistemic Modals

    a. Ame   ga hutta ka mo   sir-e-na-i.
       rain   fell Q even know-can-Neg.-Nonpast
    (Lit., 'One cannot know whether it rained or not.')
    'It may have rained.'

    b. Ame ga huru daroo.
       rain   fall I-suppose
    'I suppose it will rain.'

(Daroo is the suppositional form of the copula da 'is'.)

    c. Ame ga huru ni tigai   nai.
       rain   fall to mistake is-absent
    (Lit., 'There is no mistake to the rain falling.')
    'It will definitely rain.'

    d. Ame ga hutta rasii.
       rain   fell seem
    'It seems to have rained.'

    e. Ame ga hutta soo   da.
       rain   fell appearance is
    'I hear that it rained.'

As shown in section 2.1.3, verbs, adjectives, and copulas
have nonpast and past forms:

(24) a. Ame   ga hur-u.
       rain   fall-Nonpast
    'It rains; It will rain.'

b. Ame   ga hut-ta.
   rain   fall-Past
   'It rained.'

(25) a. Taroo wa waka-i.
              be-young-Nonpast
         'Taroo is young.'

     b. Taroo wa wakak-at-ta.
              be-young-Affix-Past
         'Taroo was young.'

The nonpast tense of an action verb represents either a
generic, habitual action or a future action.

There is no tense agreement between the main clause verb
and the subordinate clause verb. Observe the following
sentences:

(26) a. Taroo wa siken ga <u>muzukasi-i</u>   koto o
                test   be-difficult-Nonpast that

        sit-te i-ru.
        knowing be-Nonpast

        'Taroo knows that the exam is difficult.'

     b. Taroo wa siken ga <u>muzukasi-i</u>   koto o
                          be-difficult-Nonpast

        sit-te i-ta.
               be-Past

     c. Taroo wa siken ga <u>muzukasik-at-ta</u>   koto o
                          be-difficult-Past

        sit-te i-ta.
               be-Past

(26b) means 'Taroo knew that the exam was difficult.' That is,
the time that the subordinate clause verb refers to is the
same as the time that the main clause verb refers to. On the
other hand, (26c) means that Taroo knew that the exam <u>had</u>
<u>been</u> difficult. That is, the past tense of the subordinate
clause refers to a time period prior to the time the main
clause verb refers to.

Various periphrastic expressions are used to show aspect.
For example, the following sentences show the devices
Japanese uses to express the semantics of the present perfec-
tive in English:

(27) Completion of Action: e.g., He has just left.

    a. Taroo ga ki-ta.
       'Taroo came, Taroo has come.'

    b. Taroo ga ki-ta   tokoro   da.
              come-Past place/moment is
       'Taroo has just come.'

    c. Taroo ga it-te   simat-ta.
              go-Cont. end-up-Past
       'Taroo has gone.'

(28) Continuation of Action up to Present Time:
    e.g., I have lived here for a long time.

    a. Boku wa moo   zyuunen koko ni sun-de
       I   already 10-years have in live-Cont.

       iru.
       be-Nonpast

       'I have lived here for ten years already.'

    b. Kesa   hatizi kara benkyoosi-te i-ru.
        this-morning 8   from study-Cont. be-Nonpast
       'I have been studying since eight this morning.'

(29) Past Experience: e.g., I have been to Japan once.

    a. Taroo wa itido Huransu ni it-ta   koto   ga
              once France   to go-Past experience

       ar-u.
       have-Nonpast

       'Taroo has been to France once.'

    b. Taroo wa itido mo   Huransu ni it-ta   koto
              once even France to go-Past experience

       ga na-i.
         not-have-Nonpast

       'Taroo has never been to France.'

The continuative form followed with i(-ru) 'be' that is
used in (28) to express continuation of an action up to the
present time is also used to express (i) continuation of
action at the present time, (ii) repetition of action, and
(iii) succession of the same action:

(30) a. Hanako ga asoko de nai-te   i-ru. (Continuation)
                    there at cry-Cont. be-Nonpast
         'Hanako is crying there.'

     b. Hanako wa mainiti   tenisu o si-te   i-ru.
                  every-day tennis   do-Cont. be-Nonpast
                                              (Repetition)
         'Hanako plays tennis every day.'

     c. Mainiti oozei no hito   ga kaze de   sin-de
         daily   many   people   cold with die-Cont.

         i-ru. (Succession)
         be-Nonpast

         'Many people are dying of colds every day.'

2.3.6. Compound Verbals Representing the Speaker's Attitude

Japanese is a language that often forces the speaker to
express an attitude toward the action described in a sentence.
For example, it is not possible for a speaker to simply say,
'John visited me.' One must say, 'John came visiting me.'
Similarly, it is not possible to say, 'John called me up.'
It is necessary to say, (Lit.) 'John came having phoned me,'
where came indicates that the action of telephoning was
directed toward the speaker. Likewise, it is not easy to
say simply, 'John borrowed money from me.' One ordinarily
says either 'I lent money to John,' or 'John went away,
having borrowed money from me,' where the whole event is seen
from the speaker's point of view. The following are Japanese
examples illustrating the above point:

(31) a. *Taroo ga kyoo boku o tazuneta.
              today me   visited
          'Taroo visited me today.'

      b. Taroo ga kyoo boku o tazunete <u>kita</u>.
              today me   visiting came
          'Taroo came visiting me today.'

(32) a. *Taroo ga kyoo boku ni denwa o kaketa.
              today me   to phone   called
          'Taroo called me up today.'

      b. Taroo ga kyoo boku ni denwa o kakete <u>kita</u>.
              today me   to phone   calling came
          (Lit., 'Taroo came having called me up today.')
          'Taroo called me up today.'

(33) a. ??Taroo ga kyoo boku kara okane o karita.
              today me   from money   borrowed
          'Taroo borrowed money from me today.'

      b. Taroo ga kyoo boku kara okane o karite   <u>itta</u>.
              today me   from money   borrowing went
          (Lit., 'Taroo went having borrowed money from me.')
          'Taroo borrowed money from me today.'

The requirement that expressions be speaker-centered is not
limited to the use of deictic verbs of coming and going. It is
not possible to say neutrally, 'Mary bought me a necktie.'
One must say, 'Mary gave me the favor of buying a tie.'
Similarly, one seldom says that one will buy a tie for the
hearer, but instead says that one will give the hearer the
favor of buying a tie, or 'Please give me the favor of buying
a tie.'

(34) a. ??Hanako ga boku ni nekutai o katta.
                me   to necktie   bought
          'Hanako bought me a necktie.'

      b. Hanako ga boku ni nekutai o katte <u>kureta</u>.
                me   to necktie   buying gave
          (Lit.) 'Hanako gave me the favor of buying a tie.'

(35) a. ?Kimi ni nekutai o kau.
         you to necktie   buy
         'I will buy you a tie.'

     b. Kimi ni nekutai o katte _ageru_.
         you to necktie   buying give
         (Lit.) 'I will give you the favor of buying a tie.'

(See Kuno 1973, Ch. 9, for details.)

     c. Nekutai o kaw-ase-te   _kudasai_.
                  buy-caus-ing give-Imper.
        (Lit.) 'Please give me the favor of buying a tie
        (for you).'

Likewise, if John bought chocolates for the speaker's
daughter, the speaker does not ordinarily describe this event
neutrally, but says, 'John gave me the favor of buying
chocolates for my daughter':

(36) a.??Taroo ga (boku no) musume   ni tyokoreeto o
                    I   's daughter to chocolate

        katta.
        bought

        'Taroo bought chocolates for my daughter.'

     b. Taroo ga (boku no) musume   ni tyokoreeto o
                    I   's daughter to chocolate

        katte _kureta_.
        buying gave

        (Lit.) 'Taroo gave me the favor of buying
        chocolates for my daughter.'

The above phenomena are all part of a general problem of the
speaker's point of view, for which Japanese has an extremely
rich lexical and syntactical system. See Kuno 1975, Kuno and
Kaburaki 1975, and Kuno 1976b and c.

2.3.7. Passive and Causative

We have already seen some examples of passive and causative
sentences. Japanese has two passives: the neutral passive and

the adversity passive, both of which have verbs marked with
the passive morpheme (r)are(-ru) and an underlying agentive
followed by the particle ni.

(37) a. Taroo ga sensei ni sikar-are-ta. (Pure Passive)
              teacher by scold-Passive-Past
         'Taroo was scolded by the teacher.'

     b. Taroo ga sensei ni musuko o sikar-are-ta.
              teacher by son   scold-Passive-Past
                                  (Adversity Passive)
         (Lit.) 'Taroo was adversely affected by the
         teacher's scolding his son.'

What is interesting here is the fact that the ni that is used
to mark the underlying agentive for passive sentences of both
kinds is homophonous with the dative marker ni. Observe,
further, the following sentence:

(38) a. Underlying Structure

         Taroo [saihu (ga) nakunar-] rare-ta.
                purse   disappear Passive-Past
         'Taroo was adversely affected by the purse's
         having disappeared.'

     b. Surface Sentence

         *Taroo ga saihu ni nakunar-are-ta.

Although there does not seem to be anything wrong with the
underlying structure shown in (38a), the resulting sentence
shown in (38b) is totally ungrammatical. This suggests that
the ni used both as a dative marker and as a passive agentive
marker has the characteristic that it marks a secondary agent.
(38b) is ungrammatical because saihu 'purse', which cannot
act as an agent, has ended up being followed by this secondary agent marker.

    The function of ni as a secondary agent marker can also be
seen in the following examples, which involve neither syntactic causatives nor syntactic passives.

(39) a. Boku wa Hattori-sensei ni gengo-gaku   o naratta.
         I   teacher   linguistics   learned
         'I learned linguistics from Professor Hattori.'

   b. Boku wa Hattori-sensei ni gengo-gaku
         I   teacher   linguistics

      o osowatta.
      took-lessons-from

      'I learned linguistics from Professor Hattori.'

The ni in these sentences does not represent a goal, direction,
or dative of interest; it represents a secondary agent, and as
such, alternates with kara 'from'. Similarly, observe the
following sentence:

(40) Sono koto   o Taroo ni kiita.
     that matter   asked/heard

While the primary interpretation of the sentence is 'I asked
Taroo about it,' it can also mean 'I heard about it from
Taroo,' although in this interpretation Taroo kara 'from
Taroo' is used more often than Taroo ni. The two interpreta-
tions of (40) share a common feature, that is, the fact that
Taroo is a secondary agent — as the recipient of a question
in the case of 'I asked ...', and as the source or originator
of message transmission in the case of 'I heard from ...'

   Causatives also display very interesting behavior along
similar lines. When the underlying embedded clause is transitive, there are two causatives:

(41) a. Kantoku wa sono siin de haiyuu o   nak-ase-ta.
         director   that scene at actor Acc. cry-caus-Past

   b. Kantoku wa sono siin de haiyuu ni   nak-ase-ta.
                                     Dat.
      'The director made the actor cry in that scene.'

In (41a) the underlying embedded clause subject is marked
with the accusative particle o, while in (41b) it is marked

with the dative particle ni. Shibatani (personal communication, 1976) has observed that (41a) implies that the director was harsh on the actor so that the latter cried, while (41b) implies that the director instructed the actor to cry in that scene. In other words, only the ni-marked causative involves a transmission of a message to induce the action represented by the underlying embedded clause. This observation is consistent with the fact that only the o-marked causative can be used in the following sentences. (I am indebted to S. Tonoike, personal communication, 1976, for this observation.)

(42) a. Yasai   o kusar-ase-te   simatta.
        vegetables   spoil-cause-Cont. ended-up
        (Lit., 'I have had vegetables spoil.')
        'Vegetables have been spoiled.'

    b. Yamada-san wa kazi de kodomo o sin-ase-te
            Mr.   fire by child   die-cause-Cont.

       simatta.
       ended-up

       (Lit., 'Mr. Yamada had his child die because of a
       fire.') 'Mr. Yamada lost his child in a fire.'

In (42a), there could not have been any message transmission from the speaker to the underlying embedded subject because the latter is inanimate. In (42b), the semantics of the sentence clearly relate that Yamada did not tell his son to die. The use of causatives in both sentences seems to express an underlying feeling on the part of the speaker that the subject of the main clause could have prevented the situation from happening.

    I hypothesize that the o-causative and the ni-causative are derived from the underlying structures in (43) (see Kuno 1973, Ch. 27). In (43a), Equi NP Deletion applies and deletes the embedded clause subject, which is identical to the matrix

(43) a. O-Causative ("Hands Off")

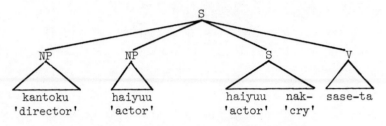

b. Ni-Causative ("Message Transmission")

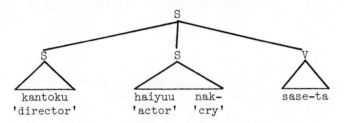

clause object. Next, Verb Raising applies, which triggers
tree-pruning rules to apply, yielding the structure shown
below:

(44)

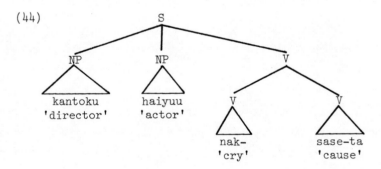

Now, the NP for haiyuu 'actor' occupies the object position
for the compound causative verb nak-(s)ase-ta 'caused to cry'.
Hence, it gets marked with the object particle o.

In the case of (43b), Agentive-Ni Attachment applies to
the embedded clause subject, followed by Verb Raising. The
resulting structure is

(45)

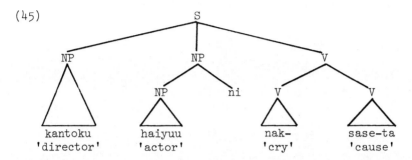

In both (44) and (45), the surface subject receives the
nominative marker ga.

When the embedded clause of a causative construction is
transitive, the underlying embedded subject receives the
ni-marking, as shown below:

(46) Taroo wa Hanako ni hon o yom-ase-ta.
                    to book   read-cause-Past
     'Taroo caused Hanako to read a book.'

This is a widespread cross-language phenomenon. For example,
observe the following French sentences:

(47) a. Underlying   J'ai fait [Jean partir]

     b. Surface Sentence J'ai fait partir Jean.
                          'I made John leave.'

(48) a. Underlying: J'ai laissé [Jean chanter l'hymne]

     b. Surface Sentence J'ai laissé chanter l'hymne a Jean.
                          'I let John sing the hymn.'

The subject of the complement clause of faire 'make'/laisser
'let' is realized as accusative object in the surface structure if the complement clause is intransitive, and as dative
object if it is transitive. See Aissen 1974 for details.

    It seems that sentence (46) is ambiguous between the
"message transmission" interpretation (i.e., 'Taroo told
Hanako to read a book') and the "hands off" interpretation.

That the latter interpretation is possible can be seen by
the following example:

(49) Taroo wa kodomo ni kaze o hik-ase-te   simatta.
          child to cold   catch-cause-Cont. ended-up
     'Taroo caused his child to catch the cold (he could
      or should have prevented it from happening).'

Thus, I hypothesize that (46) is derived from the following
two underlying structures:

(50) a. O-causative ("Hands Off")

           [Taroo Hanako [Hanako hon   yom] sase-ta].
                                 book read

     b. Ni-Causative ("Message Transmission")

           [Taroo [Hanako hon yom] sase-ta].

For (50a), Equi NP Deletion applies and deletes the underlying
embedded clause subject. Next, Verb Raising applies, trig-
gering application of the tree-pruning rules, yielding:

(51)

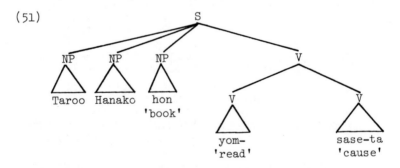

The NP corresponding to Hanako now occupies the indirect
object position with respect to the verb complex yom-(s)ase-ta
'caused to read'. Hence, it receives the dative marking ni.
For (50a), on the other hand, Agentive-Ni Attachment applies,
marking Hanako with ni. Therefore, both for (50a) and (50b),
the underlying embedded subject ends up with the ni-marking.

What is peculiar about the transitive causative is the
fact that (52b) is totally ungrammatical:

(52) a. ?Kikanzyuu   ga tekihei   o uti-korosita.
        machine-gun   enemy-troop   shoot-killed
        'The machine guns killed enemy troops.'

    b. *Taityoo   wa kikanzyuu   ni tekihei   o
        commander   machine-gun   enemy-troop

        uti-koros-ase-ta.
        shoot-kill-cause-Past

        'The commander caused the machine guns to kill
        the enemy troops.'

(52a) is artificial in that it has an inanimate subject for
a transitive sentence. However, it is at most awkward, and
it is passable as a written sentence. On the other hand, the
causative version of the sentence is totally ungrammatical.
It is clear that the sentence cannot be derived from the
underlying ni-causative structure of the pattern of (49b)
because there is no message transmission between the commander
and the machine guns. However, there does not seem to be anything semantically wrong with the o-causative underlying
structure of the pattern of (50a). It seems that the
sentence is ungrammatical for the same reason that (38b) is
ungrammatical. Namely, the inanimate noun phrase has received
the dative marking ni, which represents a secondary agent.

2.3.8. Order of Verbal Elements

We have already seen that, given a sequence of verbal forms,
the rightmost element has a higher scope than the rest of the
sequence. Thus, the sequence V + Causative + Passive is the
passive of V + Causative (i.e., 'be caused to V'), while the
sequence V + Passive + Causative is the causative form of
V + Passive (i.e., 'cause to be V-ed'). Similarly, the

sequence <u>V</u> + <u>Incipient</u> + <u>Causative</u> means 'cause to begin to
V', while the sequence <u>V</u> + <u>Causative</u> + <u>Incipient</u> means 'begin
to cause to V'. Whether a given sequence of verbal forms is
acceptable or not is determined by various syntactic and
semantic factors. For example, observe the following sentences:

(53) a. Boku wa Hanako o nagur-ase-rare-ta-i.
         I   hit-Causative-Passive-Desiderative-
                                                    Nonpast
         'I want to be made to hit Hanako.'

     b. Boku wa Hanako o nagur-are-sase-te
         I   hit-Passive-Causative-Continuative
         oita.
         kept
         'I let Hanako be hit.'

(53a) has the causative morpheme preceding the passive (i.e.,
<u>nagur-(s)ase-rare-</u> 'be caused to hit', while (53b) has the
same morphemes in reverse order (i.e., <u>nagur-(r)are-sase-</u>
'cause to be hit').

I give below some grammatical and ungrammatical sequences:

(54) a. <u>tabe-sase-rare-ru</u> 'can cause someone to eat'
        eat-Causative-Potential-Nonpast

     b. <u>nagur-are-ta-i</u> 'be eager to be hit'
        hit-Passive-Desiderative-Nonpast

     c. <u>nagur-rare-ta-gar-are-ru</u> 'be shown a sign of
           wanting to be hit'
        hit-Passive-Desiderative-'show a sign of'-
           Passive-Nonpast

     d. *<u>tabe-rare-sase-ru</u> 'cause to be able to eat'
        eat-Potential-Causative-Nonpast

     e. *<u>tabe-ta-sase-ru</u> 'cause to be eager to eat'
        eat-Desiderative-Causative-Nonpast

     f. *<u>tabe-rare-rare-ru</u> 'can be eaten'
        eat-Passive-Potential-Nonpast

(54d) is ungrammatical because the causative verb requires an action verb in subordination to it, which rare 'can' is not. (54e) is ungrammatical both for the same reason and because the desiderative ta- forms an adjectival stem, while sase 'cause' requires a verb stem preceding it. The ungrammaticality of (54f) requires explanation. Semantically, there does not seem to be anything wrong with what it is intended to mean. The ungrammaticality seems to be due to the repetition of the homophonous passive and potential morphemes. (Potential forms are produced by attaching rare to vocalic stem verbs and (r)e to consonantal stem verbs. Passive forms are produced by attaching rare to both vocalic and consonantal stem verbs. Thus, with vocalic stem verbs, rare is ambiguous between potential and passive.) In fact, tabe-rare-ru, which has only one rare, can be used for 'can be eaten' (potential of a massive action), as well as for 'be eaten' (passive) and 'can eat' (potential).

2.4. Adverbs

2.4.1. Types of Adverbs

The gerundive form -ku of adjectives and the suppletive gerundive form ni of the copula preceded by nominal adjectives (and sometimes by nouns) are used as adverbial expressions. For example, uma-i 'is good': uma-ku 'being good, well'; akaru-i 'is bright': akaru-ku 'being bright, brightly'; sizuka da 'is quiet': sizuka ni 'being quiet, quietly'; syooziki da 'is honest'; syooziki ni 'being honest, honestly'.

 Many Japanese adverbs are of nominal origin: dan-dan '(step-step) gradually'; zen-zen '(all-all) at all'; sono kekka '(that result) as a consequence from it'; sono baai '(that case) in that case'; etc.

Japanese is rich in onomatopoetic adverbs: the following
are all onomatopoetic adverbs describing manners of crying:
waa-waa 'loudly'; gyaa-gyaa 'noisily'; ogyaa-ogyaa (of a
new-born baby); siku-siku 'sobbingly'; meso-meso 'effeminately.'

Many adverbs are optionally or obligatorily followed by
the particle to: doo-doo to 'grandly'; seizen to 'in an
orderly way'; yukkuri: yukkuri to 'slowly'; honnori: honnori
to 'faintly'.

2.4.2. Sentential Adverbs

The gerundive form -ku of adjectives, followed by an
exclamatory particle mo, and the suppletive form ni of the
copula, preceded by nominal adjectives or nouns, are also
used for sentential adverbs.

(1) a. Yamada-sensei   ga onakunari ni   natta   koto
                teacher   dying   being became fact-that

   wa kanasi-i.
      is-sad

   'That Professor Yamada has died is sad.'

   b. Kanasi-ku mo, Yamada-sensei ga onakunari ni natta.
      'Sadly, Professor Yamada has died.'

(2) a. Yamada-sensei   ga onakunari ni   natta   koto
                teacher   dying   being became fact-that

   wa kanasii koto   da.
      is-sad   thing is

   'That Professor Yamada has died is a sad thing.'

   b. Kanasii koto ni, Yamada-sensei ga onakunari ni natta.
      (Lit.) '(It) being a sad thing, Professor Yamada
      has died.' 'To our sorrow, ...'

Sentential adverbs with -ku mo are used primarily in formal
and literary writing and seldom enter into colloquial speech.

   I give below representative samples of sentential adverbs:

(3) Adjectival

osorosi-i	osorosi-ku mo
'is dreadful'	'dreadfully'

yorokobasi-i	yorokobasi-ku mo
'is joyful'	'happily'

nagekawasi-i	nagekawasi-ku mo
'is regrettable'	'regrettably'

(4) Nominal-Adjectival

tasika da	tasika ni
'is certain'	'certainly'

hontoo da	hontoo ni
'is true'	'truly'

hukoo da	hukoo ni mo
'is unfortunate'	'unfortunately'

saiwai da	saiwai ni (mo)
'is fortunate'	'fortunately'

2.4.3. Some Characteristics of Adverbs

In Japanese, adverbs are placed to the left of the
constituents that they modify:

(5) a. Totemo omosiroi   hon o yonda.
        very   is-interesting book   read
        'I read a very interesting book.'

   b. Motto yukkuri aruke.
      more slowly walk-Imper.
      'Walk more slowly.'

In colloquial speech, adverbs can appear postverbally as
"afterthoughts" (see section 2.1.2).

(6) a. Kimi wa hontoo ni baka   da ne.
        you   truly   stupid   isn't-it
        'You are truly stupid.'

b.   Kimi wa baka da ne, hontoo ni.

(7) a.   Taroo ga mata kita yo.
               again came I-am-telling-you
          'Taroo has come again.'

    b.   Taroo ga kita yo, mata.

(8) a.   Motto yukkuri aruke. = (5b)
          more slowly walk-Imper.
          'Walk more slowly.'

    b.   *Aruke, motto yukkuri.

(9) a.   Hayaku koko ni koi.
          fast   here to come-Imper.
          'Come here quickly.'

    b.   Koko ni koi, hayaku.

In the above, (8b) is unacceptable because the first part of
the sentence (i.e., Aruke 'Walk!') orders the hearer to walk
as opposed to running or standing still, while the postverbal
element (i.e., motto yukkuri 'more slowly') presupposes that
the hearer has already been walking.

In many languages, adpositional phrases are ambiguous
between the adjectival and adverbial use. For example, the
following sentence is ambiguous:

(10) John called up the visitor from Iowa.

The sentence can mean either 'From Iowa, John called up the
visitor' or 'John called up the visitor who was from Iowa.'
Ambiguity of this type does not exist in Japanese, in which
adjectival postpositional phrases are always marked with no,
the prenominal attributive form of the copula.

(11) a.   Taroo wa Aiowa kara kyaku   ni denwa o kaketa.
              Iowa from visitor to phone   placed
          'From Iowa, Taroo called up the visitor.'

b. Taroo wa <u>Aiowa</u> <u>kara</u> <u>no</u> kyaku   ni denwa o kaketa.
      Iowa   from is visitor to phone   placed
   'Taroo called up the visitor who was from Iowa.'

2.5. Compound and Complex Sentences

2.5.1. Coordination and Subordination

Two clauses are combined together in coordination or subordination with the use of the gerundive, continuative, or conditional form of verbals, particles, or formal nouns. Observe the following sentences:

(1) Gerundive

Taroo ga Amerika ni <u>ik-i</u>,   Hanako ga Huransu ni itta.
          to go-Ger.   France to went
 'Taroo went to America and Hanako went to France.'

(2) Continuative

Taroo ga Amerika ni <u>it-te</u>,   Hanako ga Huransu ni itta.
          to go-Cont.   France to went
 'Taroo went to America, and Hanako went to France.'

(3) Particle

a. Taroo ga Amerika ni itta <u>si</u>,   Hanako ga Huransu
          to went and   France
  ni itta.
  to went

  'Taroo went to America, and Hanako went to France.'

b. Taroo wa hon o katta <u>si</u>, rekoodo mo katta.
        book bought and record   bought
  'Taroo bought books, and (he) also bought records.'

(The noun-coordinating particle <u>to</u> cannot be used for coordinating clauses.) The above are all examples of coordinated clauses. The three types are different in a very subtle way. (1) is neutral coordination, while (2) represents a

temporal or logical sequence (i.e., 'and then, and therefore').
(3) implies that other things also took place. Thus (3b) means
that Taroo did many things such as buying books and buying
records.

The following sentences illustrate various types of subordination:

(4) Gerundive

    a. Bukka ga agar-i,   minna ga komatte   iru.
       price   rise-Ger. all   suffering are
       'Prices rising, all are suffering.'

    b. Taroo wa tosyokan ni ik-i,   hon o yonda.
             library to go-Ger. book   read
       'Going to the library, Taroo read books.'

(5) Continuative

    a. Bukka ga agat-te,   minna ga komatte   iru.
       price   rise-Cont. all   suffering are
       'Prices having risen, all are suffering.'

    b. Taroo wa, tosyokan ni it-te,   hon o yonda.
             library to go-Cont. book   read
       'Having gone to the library, Taroo read books.'

(6) Conditional

      Kono siken wa gozyutten tor-eba, pasu dekiru.
      this test   50-points take-if pass can
      'You can pass this test if you get 50 points.'

(7) Particles

    a. Bukka ga agatta node, minna ga komatte   iru.
       price   rose since all   suffering are
       'Because prices have gone up, all are suffering.'

    b. Taroo wa, tosyokan ni itta noni, hon o yomanakatta.
             library to went though book   didn't-read
       'Taroo, although he went to the library, didn't
        read books.'

    c. Taroo ga gakkoo ni iku <u>to</u>, Hanako ga matte   ita.
              school to go when   waiting was
    'When Taroo got to school, Hanako had been waiting.'

(8) Formal Nouns

    a. Taroo ga kita toki, Hanako wa mada   nete   ita.
              came time   still sleeping was
    '(At the) time when Taroo came, Hanako was still
    asleep.'

    b. Kono-aida Tookyoo ni itta <u>sai</u>, Yamada-sensei ni
       other-day   to went case   teacher to

       omenikakatta.
       met-Honorific

    'I met Teacher Yamada when I went to Tokyo the
    other day.'

Of particular interest in the above examples is the fact
that the gerundive and continuative forms of verbals can be
used for both coordination and subordination. Which of the
two types is involved in a given sentence depends upon the
semantics of the two clauses and their relationship with each
other. (1, 2) and (4, 5) show different behaviors with respect
to various syntactic processes. For example, the subject of
the second clause in (4, 5) can be relativized, but that of
(1, 2) cannot.

    (9) a. *[Taroo ga Amerika ni <u>ik-i</u>, Huransu itta] hito
                      to go-ing France   went   person
      *'a person such that Taroo went to America and
      (he) went to France'

    b. [Bukka ga <u>agar-i</u>, komatte   iru] hito-tati
       price   rise-ing suffering are   persons
    'people who, prices going up, are suffering'

Similarly, the interrogative particle can be attached to (4, 5)
but not to

    (10) a.??Taroo ga Amerika ni ik-i, Hanako ga Huransu
                   to go-ing   France

ni itta ka.
to went Q

'Did Taroo go to America and Hanako to France?'

b. Bukka ga agar-i, minna komatte   iru ka.
   price   rise-ing all   suffering are Q
   'Prices going up, are all suffering?'

Instead, one has to nominalize the entire sentence first, and embed it in the x da '(it) is x' pattern:

(11) [Taroo ga Amerika ni ik-i,   Hanako ga Huransu ni itta]
                     to go-ing   France   to went

   no   ka.
   that Q

In the above example, da has been deleted before ka by the rule given in section 2.1.3.3.

Likewise, the subject of the second clause of (4, 5) can be a wh-interrogative word, but not that of (1, 2):

(12) a.??Taroo ga Amerika ni ik-i,   dare ga Huransu
                     to go-ing who   France

   ni itta ka.
   to went Q

   (Lit.) 'Taroo went to America, and who went to
   France?'

b. Bukka ga agar-i, dare ga komatte   iru ka.
   price   rise-ing who   suffering is Q
   'Prices going up, who is suffering?'

2.5.2. Indirect Statements and Questions, Quotatives

Subject and object complements are marked with the formal noun koto (Lit., 'thing') 'that, the fact that', the nominalizer no 'that', or the postpositional particle to 'that'. The first two are followed by case-marking particles, but to is not. Roughly speaking, koto and no are used for factive complements and to for nonfactive complements.

(13) a. Taroo ga kekkonsita <u>koto</u> wa hontoo da.
              married   that   true   is
       'It is true that Taroo got married.'

    b. Taroo ga kekkon   tyokugo   sinde simatta
              marriage right-after dying ended-up

       <u>no</u> wa higeki da.
       that   tragedy is

       'It is tragic that Taroo died right after he got
       married.'

(14) a. Boku wa Taroo ga kekkonsita <u>koto</u>   o kiita.
       I   married   fact-that   heard
       'I heard about the fact that Taroo got married.'

    b. Boku wa Taroo ga kekkonsita <u>to</u> kiita.
       I   married   that heard
       'I heard that Taroo got married.'

    c. Boku wa Taroo ga piano o hiku <u>no</u> o kiita.
       I   play that   heard
       'I heard Taroo play the piano.'

The difference between <u>koto</u> 'the fact that' and <u>no</u> 'that' lies in the degree of abstraction. <u>Koto</u> represents an abstract fact, while <u>no</u> represents an unabstracted concrete action or state. See Kuno 1973, Ch. 18, and Josephs 1972 for details.

Indirect questions are formed by embedding questions (ending with the question particle <u>ka</u>) without complementizers:

(15) a. Boku wa Taroo ga kekkonsita <u>koto</u>   o sitte   iru.
       I   married   fact-that knowing am

       'I know that Taroo got married.'

    b. Boku wa Taroo ga <u>dare</u> to   kekkonsita <u>ka</u>
       I   who with married   Q

       sitte   iru.
       knowing am

       'I know whom Taroo married.'

Indirect question formation and the use of complementizers interact with each other in a complex fashion. Compare the following sentences:

(16) a. Taroo wa Hanako ga kuru to   itta.
                          come that said
        'Taroo said that Hanako was coming.'

     b. Taroo wa Hanako ga kuru to itta ka.
        'Did Taroo say that Hanako was coming?'

     c. Taroo wa Hanako wa kuru ka to itta.
        'Taroo said, "Is Hanako coming?"'

     d. Taroo wa Hanako wa kuru ka to itta ka.
        'Did Taroo say, "Is Hanako coming?"'

     e. Taroo wa dare ga kuru ka itta.
                who   come Q said
        'Taroo said who was coming.'

     f. Taroo wa dare ga kuru ka itta ka.
        'Did Taroo say who was coming?'

     g. Taroo wa dare ga kuru to itta ka.
        'Who did Taroo say was coming?'

     h. Taroo wa dare ga kuru ka to itta.
        'Taroo said, "Who is coming?"'

     i. Taroo wa dare ga kuru ka to itta ka.
        'Did Taroo say, "Who is coming?"'

An interrogative word (e.g., dare 'who') is bound by the ka which is closest to it on its right side. A question in which ka has an interrogative word that it binds is an interrogative-word question, and one in which ka does not have an interrogative word is a yes-or-no question. If a complement clause is neither an interrogative-word question nor a yes-or-no question, it retains its own complementizer. The above three principles explain the semantics of all the sentences in (16).

2.6. Grammatical Processes

2.6.1. Pronouns and Deletion of Noun Phrases

Japanese lacks authentic pronouns for any grammatical persons. Most existing forms that correspond to pronouns in other languages are derived from nominal expressions: <u>boku</u> '(your) servant — I', <u>watakusi</u> 'personal — I', <u>kimi</u> 'lord — you', <u>anata</u> 'far away — you', <u>omae</u> 'honorable (person in) front (of me) — you', <u>kare</u> 'thing far away — he', <u>kanozyo</u> 'far away woman — she', <u>karera</u> 'far away + Plural — they'. Third person pronouns are used only in pedantic speech by educated people. Different forms of the first and second person pronouns are used depending upon the relative status of the speaker and the hearer, and upon the speech levels. The following give representative samples:

(1) First Person   Second Person

<u>watakusi</u> polite

<u>watasi</u>   quasi-polite   <u>anata</u> quasi-polite (see
                                        below); informal when
                                        used by females

<u>boku</u>   informal   <u>kimi</u>   informal (generally
              (limited to   used only by males
              male)   addressing males)

<u>ore</u>   vulgar   <u>anta</u>   slightly vulgar
              (limited to
              male)

                                <u>omae</u>   vulgar

                                <u>temae</u> extremely vulgar

Japanese lacks polite second person pronouns that can be used when addressing superiors. <u>Otaku</u> 'your honorable house — you' comes closest to such a pronoun, but it is seldom used when addressing one's superiors. The speaker uses either the

addressee's proper name plus title or title only or,
alternatively, he resorts to deletion when the second-person
reference is clear. I will illustrate this point with examples:

(2) Child to Mother

$$\left\{ {\emptyset \atop \text{?Watakusi ('I')}} \right\} \left\{ \begin{array}{ll} \emptyset & \\ \text{okaasan ('mother') ni} \\ \text{*anata ('you') to} \\ \text{*otaku ('you')} \end{array} \right\}$$

kore agemasyoo ka.
'this give-will Q'

'Shall I give this to you?'

(3) Father to Small Daughter

$$\left\{ \begin{array}{ll} \text{Papa} \\ \text{Otoosan ('father')} \\ \text{??Boku ('I')} \\ \text{*Watakusi ('I')} \end{array} \right\} \text{to kaimono ni ikoo.}$$
'with shopping for let's-go'

'How about going shopping with me?'

(4) Student to Teacher Yamada

$$\left\{ \left\{ \left\{ \begin{array}{l} \text{*Anata ('you')} \\ \text{*Otaku ('you')} \\ \text{Sensei ('teacher')} \\ \text{Yamada-sensei} \end{array} \right\} {\text{ni} \atop \text{to}} \right\} \begin{array}{l} \text{o-kik-i} \qquad \text{sitai} \\ \text{'Honorific-ask-ing do-want} \end{array} \right.$$

$$\left. \emptyset \right\}$$

koto ga arimasu.
thing   there-is'

'I have something that I would like to ask you about.'

(5) To Mr. Yamada

a. $$\left\{ \left\{ \left\{ \begin{array}{ll} \text{?Anata ('you')} \\ \text{Otaku ('you')} \\ \text{Yamada-san ('Mr. Y.')} \end{array} \right\} \text{wa} \right\} \begin{array}{l} \text{doko no} \\ \text{'where 's} \end{array} \right.$$

$$\left. \emptyset \right\}$$

go-syussin   desu ka.
Honorific-origin is   Q'

'Where do you come from?'

b. Kimi ('you') wa doko no syussin kai. (Informal)
    ∅   where 's origin Q
    'Where do you come from?'

Deletion is based on discourse recoverability. Observe
the following sentences:

(6) a. Taroo ga Koobe ni kita node, ∅ ∅ ai ni itta.
                      to came since   see to went
        'Since Taroo came to Kobe, (I) went to see (him).'

    b. *∅ Koobe ni kita node, ∅ Taroo ni ai ni itta.
           to came since   to see to went
        'Since (he) came to Kobe, (I) went to see Taroo.'

In (6a), the main clause subject 'I' is recoverable because
it refers to the speaker, which is the most discourse-
presupposed of all nouns in general. The object of _ai_ 'to
see' is also recoverable because _Taroo_ has already been
mentioned in the _node_ clause. Hence, the acceptability of the
sentence. On the other hand, (6b) is unacceptable because
the subject of the _node_ clause, barring a mention of his name
in the immediately preceding discourse, is not recoverable
from left context.

Observe, further, the following sentence:

(7) Yamada-kyoozyu no ronbun o gakusei ga eigo
        Prof.   's paper   student   English

    ni honyakusita.
    to translated

    'A student translated Prof. Yamada's paper into
    English.'

Gakusei 'student', in this sentence, is in fact ambiguous
between 'a student', 'my student', and 'Professor Yamada's
student'. To state clearly that Professor Yamada's student
translated the paper, one says the following:

(8) Yamada-kyoozyu no ronbun o kyoozyu no gakusei
       Prof. 's paper   Prof. 's student

ga honyakusita.
   translated

(Lit.) 'Professor Yamada's paper, the professor's
student translated.'

In (8), kyoozyu 'professor' is used in place of a third person
pronoun.

2.6.2. Deletion of Verbs

English has a syntactic process called Verb Phrase Deletion
that deletes a verb phrase, leaving behind an auxiliary verb
or infinitival to. For example, observe the following
sentences:

(9) Speaker A: Did you go to Boston yesterday?

    Speaker B: Yes, I did. (go to Boston yesterday
                  deleted)

(10) Speaker A: Who was killed in the accident?

     Speaker B: John was. (killed in the accident deleted)

(11) Speaker A: Do you want to go there?

     Speaker B: Yes, I want to. (go there deleted)

Japanese does not have an auxiliary verb that can be used
independently. Therefore, a rule of Verb Phrase Deletion is
nonexistent in Japanese. This situation should result in
excessive redundancy, but Japanese copes with this situation
in two ways. First, it uses the template x da to give the
minimal answer:

(12) Speaker A: Dare ga kinoo   gakkoo ni kimasen
                who   yesterday school to come-not-Polite

                desita   ka.
                was-Polite Q

                'Who didn't come to school yesterday?'

Speaker B: Taroo desu.
(Lit.) 'Is (Polite) Taroo.'

The second device that the language uses is to repeat the main verb, deleting everything else that is recoverable from context. For example, observe the following exchanges:

(13) Speaker A: Kimi wa Hanako ni moo   tegami o
                you   to already letter

kakimasita ka.
wrote   Q

'Have you already written a letter to Hanako?'

Speaker B: Hai, kakimasita.
yes   wrote
'Yes, (Lit.) (I) wrote.'

(14) Speaker A: Kimi wa Amerika ni itta koto   ga
                you   to went experience

arimasu ka.
have   Q

'Have you been to America?'

Speaker B: Hai, arimasu.
'Yes, (I) have.'

(15) Speaker A: Kimi wa Amerika ni ikitai to   omotte
                you   to go-want that thinking

imasu ka.
are   Q

(Lit.) 'Are you thinking that you want to go to America?'

Speaker B: Hai, omotte imasu.
'Yes, (Lit.) (I) am thinking.'

Copulas cannot have their precopular predicate missing. One either has to repeat the precopular predicate or say 'It is so,' as shown below:

(16) Speaker A: Tanaka-san wa syoogakkoo   no sensei
                              grade-school 's teacher

                desu ka.
                is   Q

                'Is Mr. Tanaka a grade-school teacher?'

     Speaker B: *Hai, desu.
                'Yes, (he) is.'

                Hai, syoogakkoo   no sensei   desu.
                     grade-school 's teacher is
                'Yes, (he) is a grade-school teacher.'

                Hai, soo desu.
                     so is
                'Yes, (it) is so.'

Japanese, like many other languages, has a process called
Right-Node Raising, which extracts the rightmost common
constituent from conjuncts. This process applies to the
structure underlying (17a), and yields (17b):

(17) a. Taroo ga Amerika ni ik-i, Hanako ga Huransu
                            to go-ing   France

        ni itta.
        to went

        'Taroo went to America, and Hanako went to France.'

     b. Taroo ga Amerika ni, Hanako ga Huransu ni, itta
                         to   France   to went
        'Taroo went to America, and Hanako, to France.'

On the other hand, Japanese lacks a rule of gapping,
which deletes from conjuncts (except for the leftmost one)
verbs that are repeated:

(18) a. John went to Japan, and Mary went to France.

     b. John went to Japan, and Mary ∅   to France.

The following sentence, which would derive if Gapping had
applied to the structure of (17a), is ungrammatical:

(19) *Taroo ga Amerika ni {ik-i, \\ it-ta,} Hanako ga Huransu ni Ø.

2.6.3. Scrambling

As I have illustrated with examples at the beginning of this
paper, word order in Japanese sentences is relatively free.
Sometimes, it is possible to move a constituent in a subordinate clause to sentence-initial position. Observe the following
examples:

(20) a. Boku wa [Yamada-sensei ni anata o syookaisitai]
        I   teacher to you   introduce-want

        to   omotte   imasu.
        that thinking am

        (Lit.) 'I have been thinking that I want to intro-
        duce you to Teacher Yamada.' 'I want to ...'

     b. Anata o boku wa [Yamada-sensei ni syookaisitai] to
        omotte imasu.

(21) a. Boku wa [[Yamada-sensei ni anata o syookaisitai]
        I   teacher to you   introduce-want

        to   yuu kiboo] o motte imasu.
        that say hope

        'I have been entertaining the hope that (Lit.) I
        want to introduce you to Teacher Yamada.'

     b. Anata o boku wa [[Yamada-sensei ni syookaisitai]
        to yuu kiboo] o motte imasu.

In (20b), anata o has been fronted from a reportive to clause;
while in (21b) the same expression has been fronted from a
complex NP of the type the hope that. The following example
shows that scrambling out of a subordinate clause is subject
to some kind of syntactic or semantic constraint. (See Haig
1976 for further discussion of this topic.)

(22) a.   Taroo wa [[Hanako to   Amerika ni iku] keikaku]
                              with   to go

o toriyameta.
canceled

'Taroo canceled (his) plan to go to America
with Hanako.'

b. *Amerika ni Taroo wa [[Hanako to iku] keikaku]
o toriyameta.

2.6.4. Foregrounding: Theme

As discussed briefly in section 2.1.6, Japanese has a particle
specifically used for marking the theme of a sentence. Time
and place adverbs that are used for setting up the scene for
the rest of the sentence readily serve as themes. Among
nominal constituents such as subjects, objects, and datives,
subjects qualify as themes most easily of all. However, other
constituents of the sentence can also qualify for themes:

(23) a.   Taroo wa gakusei desu.
                   student is
          'Taroo is a student.'

b.   Kyoo   wa boku wa tyuusyoku wa nuki   ni siyoo.
     today   I   lunch   skipping -ly do-will
     'Today, I will skip lunch.'

c.   Tukue no ue ni wa   hon ga sansatu atta.
     desk 's top on   book   3-volume was
     'On the desk, there were three books.'

d.   Kono hon wa dare ga kaita ka wakaranai.
     this book   who   wrote Q understand-not
     'This book — we don't know who wrote (it).'

In (23a), the wa-marked theme is coreferential with the
underlying subject of the sentence. In (23b), kyoo wa 'today'
is a scene-setting thematic time adverb; boku wa is coreferential with the underlying subject of the nominalized verb nuki
'skip', and tyuusyoku wa, with its underlying object. In

(23c), the theme is a scene-setting thematic place adverb.
What is most interesting is the grammaticality of (23d). Kono
hon wa 'this book' is coreferential with the object of the
verb of the embedded interrogative clause. Similarly, observe
the following sentence:

(24) <u>Tanaka-sensei</u> <u>wa</u>, hon o syuppansuru koto   ni
           teacher   book   publish   fact-that being

   natte   ita syuppansya ga toosansite simatta.
   becoming was published   bankrupt   went

   (Lit.) 'Professor Tanaka, the publisher that was
   scheduled to publish (his) book went bankrupt.'

In (24), the theme of the sentence is coreferential with the
underlying genitive (modifying hon 'book') in a relative
clause. On the other hand, the following sentence is
unacceptable:

(25) ??Tanaka-sensei wa hon o syuppansuru koto ni
            teacher   book   publish   to -ly

    natte   ita syuppansya ga syain   o hyakunin
    becoming was publisher   employer 100-people

    saiyoosita.
    employed

    (Lit.) 'Professor Tanaka, the publisher that was
    scheduled to publish (his) book has employed
    one hundred employees.'

As the above examples show, whether a given thematic sentence
is acceptable or not depends not so much on syntax, as on the
semantic relationship that holds between the theme and the
rest of the sentence. In (24), for example, one can establish
a semantic relationship between Professor Tanaka and the
publisher's having gone bankrupt. Perhaps the bankruptcy of
the publisher affected Professor Tanaka in that his book could
not be published. (24) is acceptable to native speakers of
Japanese to the extent that such a semantic relationship can

be established. On the other hand, it is difficult to establish
a connection between Professor Tanaka and the fact that the
publisher has hired one hundred new employees. Hence results
the unacceptability of (25). It seems that all we can say at
present is that in a thematic sentence, the rest of the
sentence must be a statement about the theme. The conclusion
that it is not possible to define any *syntactic* relationship
that must hold between the theme and the rest of the sentence
is also confirmed by the fact that, as briefly discussed in
section 2.1.6, there are thematic sentences whose themes do
not have any underlying syntactic functions, as in the
following sentences:

(26) a. Sakana wa tai   ga ii.
        fish   redsnapper is-good
        (Lit.) 'Speaking of fish, the redsnapper is the
           best.'

   b. Basyo wa okunai-setu   ga attooteki   datta.
      place   indoor-theory   predominant was
      'Speaking of the place (where the crime took
      place), the indoor-theory was predominant.'

Theme in Japanese does not interact with very many
transformational processes. It is the subject, and not the
theme, that triggers Reflexivization. (See section 2.3.3.
Kuno 1976c shows that, in rare circumstances, it is possible
to use the theme of a sentence as trigger for Reflexivization.) It is the subject, and not the theme, that triggers
the honorific marking on verbs of the type discussed in
section 2.1.4. For example, toosansite simatta 'went
bankrupt' of (24) cannot receive honorific marking with
respect to Tanaka-sensei because the latter is the theme,
and not the subject, of the sentence. It is the subject, and
not the theme, that undergoes Subject Raising. (See Kuno
1976a for Subject Raising in Japanese. The fact that the

subject, but not the theme, plays a predominant role in processes such as Reflexivization, Passivization, Equi NP Deletion, etc., has been observed in Li and Thompson 1976b.)

2.6.5. Clefting

Examples of cleft sentences are given below:

(27) a. Hanako to   kinoo   Koobe ni itta no   wa Taroo da.
        with yesterday   to went that   is
        'It was Taroo who went to Kobe with Hanako yester-
        day.'

     b. Taroo ga kinoo Koobe ni itta no wa Hanako to da.
        'It was with Hanako that Taroo went to Kobe
        yesterday.'

     c. Taroo ga Hanako to kinoo itta no wa Koobe da.
        'It was Kobe that Taroo went (to) with Hanako
        yesterday.'

     d. Taroo ga Hanako to Koobe ni itta no wa kinoo da.
        'It was yesterday that Taroo went to Kobe with
        Hanako.'

Japanese cleft sentences lack a dummy subject corresponding to the English it, and require the main clause verb (copula) to be in the nonpast tense. Lack of It-Clefting (as well as of It-Extraposition) is a characteristic of SOV languages (see Kuno 1974) and of topic-prominent languages (see Li and Thompson 1976b).

The nonpast tense da of the main clause shows that the judgment represented in the cleft sentence is made at the time of the utterance. If the past tense copula datta 'was' is used, it shows that the judgment was made in the past.

Note

Research represented in this paper has been supported in part by the National Science Foundation's grant to Harvard

University (Grant No. SOC-7412366). I am greatly indebted to Winfred Lehmann for many valuable suggestions on the organization of the paper. I am also grateful to Linda Shumaker, Ruth Stevens, and Kazue Campbell for many helpful comments on the earlier version of the paper.

3. Easter Island
A Characteristic VSO Language

Paul G. Chapin

3.0. Introduction

The Easter Island language is a Polynesian language. According
to Pawley's generally accepted subgrouping (Pawley 1966; 1967)
it is the sole member of one of two coordinate branches of the
Eastern Polynesian subgroup of Polynesian; the other branch,
Central Eastern, contains Hawaiian, Tahitian, Maori, and
other languages.

Easter Island is undoubtedly the most isolated inhabited
spot on earth, with the possible modern exclusion of the
scientific research stations on Antarctica, where habitation
depends crucially on contact with and supplies from other
places. It is separated from other human habitations by two
thousand or more kilometers of open ocean. After its initial
settlement by Polynesian people, possibly from the Marquesas,
it remained culturally and linguistically isolated for
approximately a thousand years, until the first Western
contact was made by the Dutch captain Jacob Roggeveen on
Easter Sunday in 1722. This unparalleled term of development
free from external influences gives the language of Easter
Island unique interest for linguistics. Comparison of the
modern language with its reconstructed Proto - Eastern Polynesian ancestor could offer a case study in spontaneous
language change which is not likely to be found elsewhere,

and which could give considerable insight into the internal diachronic dynamics of a verb-initial language.

Unhappily, Easter Island suffered direly in the nineteenth century from the effects of Western contact. The toll of diseases and blackbirding (the Pacific equivalent of slave-trading) was such that the precontact population of over 5,000 had diminished to 111 in the 1877 census. The population has been increasing gradually throughout the twentieth century, but the combined effects of Spanish-language administration (by Chile) and extensive interaction with Tahitians have resulted in changes in Easter Island's language and culture which have reportedly been massive.

The present study is based primarily on texts which were collected with deliberate attention to resurrection and preservation of native Easter Island diction, the state of the language prior to the Tahitian and Spanish influence. The texts were collected by Father Sebastian Englert, who wrote in preface to the most important one: "In this narrative the use of modern, Tahitian, words was avoided as much as possible, and it was attempted to use correct language, according to the old manner" (Englert 1948: 377; my translation). How well Englert succeeded in this aim can of course never be known with certainty, but the circumstances were favorable: Englert was the island's Roman Catholic priest for many years and knew the language and the people intimately; his writings give clear evidence that he was an extremely capable ethnographer and linguist; and the contemporary, nontraditional text *He Ohoga ki Tahiti* 'A Trip to Tahiti', which is the most important source, was elicited in 1936, when there may still have been some vitality to the older idiom.

After the primary research for this study was completed, I gained access to an additional body of texts collected by

Olaf Blixen (1973; 1974), which were sent to me by the kind
courtesy of Professor Blixen. The texts are traditional tales,
some told in Spanish and some told in the Easter Island
language and translated into Spanish by Blixen. I have not
discovered in these texts any major divergences from the
structural patterns adumbrated in this essay, although a
number of individual examples appear to present interesting
variations on the catalog of known possibilities. Despite the
desirability of broadening the data base, however, I have
chosen not to include any examples from Blixen's texts in
this paper. Blixen's narrator was, in Blixen's description,
of "advanced age and precarious health" (Blixen 1973: 6, n. 7),
and was prone to errors. He was also given to at least some
Tahitianisms (e.g., the use of the word nu'u 'band of
warriors'). To satisfy his anthropological purposes, Blixen
has recorded these narratives faithfully with a minimum of
editing, footnoting an explanation when one character has
suddenly been substituted for another in the midst of the
story and for other similar lapses. Hence it is difficult to
be certain of a particular, unusual sentence that appears in
these narratives that it is indeed a valid sentence of the
language and not the result of a momentary lapse on the part
of the narrator.

I believe that there are advantages for a study like this
one in deriving the data from archaic texts; the old Easter
Island language has a special interest for typological studies,
as discussed above. However, I am fully aware that there are
obvious drawbacks. The foremost drawback is that this study
can in no way be taken as descriptive of the Easter Island
language of today, which certainly deserves a study of its
own. Another difficulty of working with texts rather than
speakers of a language is that the analyst can learn what is

possible, but not what is impossible — that is, one cannot be assured that a particular pattern is ungrammatical simply because it is unattested. A third problem is that it is very difficult to explore grammatical processes systematically without the help of native speakers, particularly more complex processes such as raising and interclausal anaphora. The brevity of the section on grammatical processes is in my opinion the most serious deficiency in this essay.

A word is in order also about the relationship of this sketch to the two extant grammatical descriptions of the Easter Island language (Englert 1948 and Fuentes 1960). I believe that despite the existence of these other two works, both written with the benefit of first-hand exposure to the language which I have not enjoyed, preparation of the present study is justified, for three reasons. First is the matter of accessibility. Englert's grammar appears in a large volume on the history, ethnology, and language of Easter Island, which the scholar can expect to find only in the most complete research libraries, and which is written entirely in Spanish. Fuentes's grammar and dictionary, written out in its entirety in both Spanish and English and all bound in the same set of covers, is somewhat more widely distributed in libraries in the United States, but available to individuals only by direct order to the publisher in Santiago de Chile. It is my belief that the volume of which this report forms a chapter will reach a wider audience of linguists than the other, more specialized sources.

The second reason is that, although my direct experience with the Easter Island language cannot be compared to that of Englert or Fuentes, I write from a perspective of linguistic experience with other Polynesian languages which I believe is much broader than theirs. This perspective has allowed the coherent interpretation and analysis of a number of grammatical patterns which they have found elusive. In this respect it should be mentioned that, while this study has been informed and undoubtedly influenced by careful study of both grammars, the analyses, generalizations, grammatical terminology, and even the orthography to be found here are strictly my own, unless specifically credited to Englert or Fuentes.

Third, and I believe most important, this report has quite a different purpose from Englert's and Fuentes's descriptions of the language. This is a contribution to a comparative typological study, and not a reference grammar. Since it is not a reference grammar, I have felt free to omit such things as pronoun paradigms and tables of cardinal and ordinal numerals, indispensable in a reference grammar (and quite ably set out by Englert and by Fuentes), because I have judged them to be of limited interest for typological comparison. Conversely, I have dwelt at more length than a summary reference description would allow on discussion of phenomena which I consider of particular interest for cross-linguistic study.

3.1. Simple Clauses

Most Polynesian languages, including Easter Island (henceforth EAS), have the basic simple clause order Verb — Subject — Object — Indirect Object. Topicalization and cliticization can and frequently do bring one or another determinant to the beginning of the clause, but VSO is the discourse-neutral order. *Determinant* is my functional cover term for nominal and prepositional phrase elements of a simple clause which stand in a case and/or functional relationship to the verbal phrase of the clause, which I term the *predicate*. See Chapin 1974 for justification of this terminology. For purposes of the present discussion, *predicate* may be regarded as synonymous with V, and *determinant* as a cover term for S, O, IO, and PP.) The pattern VOS is seen infrequently, under special conditions of agent emphasis or object incorporation. Where ambiguity threatens, the order VSO is required.

The verbal phrase and nominal phrases which serve as predicate and determinants respectively are normally composed of a head preceded by one or two grammatical formatives — a tense/aspect marker in the verbal phrase, a case marker or preposition and an article in the nominal phrase. Some types of grammatical formatives may also follow the head — deictic and other markers in the verbal phrase, demonstratives in the nominal phrase. These grammatical formatives will be discussed in detail below; they are mentioned here merely to aid in interpretation of examples.

Before proceeding to the examples, some remarks are in order concerning orthography and glossing. The orthography used here is one which is standard for Samoan and for several other Polynesian languages. It is for the most part self-explanatory. The following special remarks are necessary: (a) g is the velar nasal; (b) apostrophe denotes glottal stop; (c) phonemic vowel length is indicated by a macron. The use of double vowels in possessive and interrogative pronouns and a few other words preserves a distinction made by Englert, who except in these forms marks vowel length diacritically (with circumflex or acute accent, depending on the context). I do not know whether this distinction reflects a phonetic or an underlying difference perceived by Englert.

The morphemic glosses and free translations are mine; Englert provides free translations in Spanish.

All examples are taken from Englert's texts (1948: 378 – 417) except where specifically noted otherwise.

The first five examples illustrate the configurations of
predicate and determinants which may be found in basic simplex
clauses of EAS. Sentence (1) is a VSO example; sentence (2)
VS; sentence (3) VO; sentence (4) consists of two clauses in
juxtaposition, each of which contains only a predicate; and
sentence (5) is VSOIO.

(1) He   to'o   te tenitō   i   te moni.
    $_V$[Past take] $_S$[the Chinese] $_O$[Acc. the money]
    'The Chinese man took the money.'

(2)   He   hū   te tokerau.
    $_V$[Past blow] $_S$[the wind   ]
    'The wind blew.'

(3) He   patu mai   i   te puaka.
    $_V$[Past corral here] $_O$[Acc. the cattle]
    'The cattle were corralled' or 'They corralled the
      cattle.'

(4) He   pō,   he   moe.
    $_V$[Past night,] $_V$[Past sleep]
    'It was night, and everyone slept.'

(5) Ku   hakahere ā   te Epikopō   i   toona
    $_V$[Inc. sell   Prog.] $_S$[the Bishop] $_O$[Acc. his

    kaiga o   Tahiti   ki   te rapanui.
    land Gen. T.   ] $_{IO}$[Dat. the R.   ]

    'The Bishop has sold his land in Tahiti to the Easter
      Islanders.'

Example (4), incidentally, illustrates a phenomenon which
is common in Polynesian languages: the use of a lexical item
as the head of a verbal phrase which can be translated into
English only as a noun. Polynesian languages do not rigidly
subcategorize lexical items according to privileges of co-
occurrence with particular grammatical formatives.

Prepositional Phrases

Prepositional phrases perform their usual adverbial functions,
as shown in example (6). Polynesian languages have no postpositions.

(6) He   oho   te miro   mai Magareva   ki
    _V[Past go] _S[the boat] _{PP}[from M.   ] _{PP}[to

Nuku Tava.
N.T.   ]
'The boat went from Mangareva to Nuku Tava.'

Equational Clauses

Equational clauses are formed by simple juxtaposition of two
nominal phrases.

(7) Tokorua kona   kona oone mageo.
    [Your   land] [land insalubrious]
     (kona = 'plot of land')
    'Your land is unhealthy land.'

(8) Kaiga tagata rivariva   tenei.
    [Land person good   ] [this]
    'This is a country of good people.'

The phrase oone mageo in (7) is idiomatic, and is given
the one-word gloss 'insalubrious'. Example (8) could also be
analyzed as a nominal phrase, 'this country of good people',
which could fit as a determinant into some larger clause.
However, (8) appears in the text as a complete sentence,
and has the analysis shown.

Equational clauses in EAS can also have uses which do not
correspond to those of equational clauses in English, as (9)
shows. Similar examples will appear later, in which an equational clause has been chosen as the basic sentential framework for an expression which would be structured quite
differently in English.

(9) Me'e   rahi   te   manu oruga.
    [Thing big] [the bird above]
    'There were many birds above.'

Comparatives

Adjectival comparison is expressed by a dative construction
complementary to a nominal phrase containing the adjective to
be compared, as in (10), an example from Fuentes (1960: 608).

(10) Poki nei, poki (ata) iti   ki   te   poki ena.
     Boy   this boy   more small Dat. the boy   that
     'This boy is smaller than that one.'

The use of ata 'more' is optional. Statements of equality with
respect to some attribute ('as ... as' statements') have a
similar construction, except that following the pivotal
adjective, pe he is used in place of ki te, and ata may not
be used.

3.2. Nominal Phrases

The basic form of nominal phrases has been exemplified in most
of the examples adduced so far: a head, usually but not
always preceded by an article, and sometimes followed by a
demonstrative. The full set of circumstances under which an
article may or must be omitted is not clear. Other Polynesian
languages are much more rigid than EAS in this respect. In
Samoan, for example, except before proper names, which do not
take articles, the absence of an article must be interpreted
as the zero article, which denotes definite plural. Te is the
most usual article in EAS. It may be used both in singular
nominal phrases, as in examples (1) and (6) above, and in
the plural, as in (3) and (9). It is quite unusual in Polynesian languages for an article not to distinguish number.

EAS uses <u>etahi</u> (Lit., 'one') as an article in singular specific indefinite (i.e., not previously referenced) nominal phrases, as in (11).

(11) ...i tu'u   mai   ai   etahi miro o   te   harani
      Perf. arrive here PVD one   boat Gen. the France

      mai Tahiti.
      from T.

'A French boat arrives here from Tahiti.'

(<u>PVD</u> is the abbreviation for postverbal demonstratives — see section 3.3.) A related form is <u>te</u> <u>tahi</u> 'the other', which appears in example (16) below.

The form <u>ga</u> 'Plural' appears occasionally in nominal phrases between the head and a preceding formative such as a possessive pronoun, <u>te</u>, or a numeral, as in example (23) below. (Englert asserts that <u>ga</u> is used only in nominal phrases referring to persons — 1948: 335; Fuentes disputes this, but says that the form is normally dropped in casual speech — 1960: 602. <u>Ga</u> is likely a relic form; we find the exact cognate <u>na</u> 'Plural' in Hawaiian and, in Tongan, a similar form, <u>ngaahi</u>, which is used in a similar set of syntactic contexts to EAS <u>ga</u>.)

The word <u>he</u> can appear in article position in some instances and is analyzed by both Englert and Fuentes as an article, but it is in fact probably not a true article. <u>He</u> introducing a sentence-initial nominal phrase functions as an existential, as in (12) and (13).

(12) He   manu nō   toruga.
      Exist. bird only up-there
      'There are only birds up there.'

(13) He   tokorua moni?
      Exist. your   money
      'Do you have any money?'

A nonexistential example which Englert offers to show he functioning as an article is (14).

(14) He tagata koe.
     man   you
     'You are a man.'

Englert is evidently analyzing (14) as an equational clause. An analysis which is at least as plausible, however, is that he tagata is a verbal phrase whose head happens to translate as a noun, as in example (4) above. In this instance he is exercising its normal function as a tense/aspect marker — despite the fact that (14) is not interpreted as Past; see the discussion of verbal phrases below for elucidation of this point.

He also introduces sentence-initial nominal phrases which are interpreted generically, as in (15).

(15) He poki e   hakarogo ki   te kī o   toona
     boy Nonpast listen   Dat. the say Gen. his

     matu'a.
     father

     'A boy should obey his father.'

(15) might possibly succumb to an existential analysis. (Examples 14 and 15 are from Englert's grammar, 1948: 330.)

Relative Clauses

Relative clauses are seldom used. When they appear, they follow the head of a nominal phrase, with no relative pronoun.

(16) He   kī te Kape   ki   te tahi rapanui noho
     Past say the Captain Dat. the other R.   stay

     oruga o   te miro mo   oho mai kiuta.
     upon Gen. the boat Inf. go here inland

     'The Captain told the other Easter Islanders who
     had stayed on the boat to go inland.'

"Reduced relatives," or noun complements, are found following the heads of nominal phrases rather more frequently than full relative clauses, as for example the last three words of (17).

(17) Ko   te   rua o   te   raā i   tu'u   ai   te
     Foc. the two Gen. the day Perf. arrive PVD the

     miro ki Rikitea tupuaki ki Magareva.
     boat to R.   near   to M.

     'On the second day the boat arrived at Rikitea,
     (which is) close to Mangareva.'

Genitive Phrases

Genitive phrases follow the heads of nominal phrases. Instances of genitive phrases have already been seen in examples (5), (11), (15), (16), and (17). A genitive phrase consists of a genitive marker, o or a, followed by a nominal phrase. In addition to indicating straightforward possession, genitive phrases can designate origin or source, as in (5), (11), and (15); can be used in complex prepositional constructions, as in (16) (compare English 'on top of'); and have other more idiomatic uses, as in the initial adverb phrase in (17).

All Polynesian languages including EAS distinguish two types of possession, signaled in genitive phrases by the choice between o and a as genitive marker and in possessive pronouns by alternation of these two vowels in the stressed syllable of the pronoun. The distinction has to do with the semantic relationship between the nominal head preceding the genitive phrase, or following the possessive pronoun, which I will call the *genitive object*, and the nominal head included in the genitive phrase, or the possessive pronoun itself — the *genitive subject*. A precise characterization of

the distinction has so far eluded Polynesian grammarians.
(Although there is no lack of theories. See for example
Fuentes 1960: 602 - 606.) The a/o choice generally appears
to depend on the genitive object, that is, for a given
genitive object the genitive marker will normally be the
same for the full range of possible genitive subjects, so
that some analysts have treated this as a genderlike inherent
property of substantives. Examples (18), (19), (20), and (21)
will illustrate. (Examples 18 - 21 are based on a list given
by Englert 1948: 346 - 347.)

(18) tooku matu'a, tooku hoi
    my   father my   horse

(19) taaku vĩ'e, taaku paihega
    my   wife my   dog

(20) te (matu'a, hoi) o   te tagata
    the father, horse Gen. the man

(21) te (vĩ'e, paihega) a   te tagata
    the wife, dog   Gen. the man

The inherent-property analysis, however, breaks down in the
face of the fact that a given genitive subject/genitive object
pair can sometimes have either o-genitive or a-genitive, with
a semantic distinction between the two constructions. Englert
(1948: 347) cites the example shown in (22):

(22) He   to'o toona/taana kaha   mo tata.
    Past take her   clothes to wash
    'She took her clothes to wash.'

With the possessive pronoun toona, (22) means that she took
her own clothes to wash; with taana, she took the clothes
which had been given her to wash in her capacity as laundress.

    That the distinction is rule-governed is shown by the fact
that it is still productive. New items introduced into the

culture are classified for genitive markers as soon as their names appear in the lexicon, and are classified consistently across speakers of the language.

Adjectives

Adjectival modifiers of the heads of nominal phrases may appear immediately following the head, preceding any demonstratives which may be present. Instances are seen in examples (7), (8), and (9) above.

Numerals

Numerals precede the heads of the nominal phrases in which they appear, and also precede the article if it appears, which it may not. EAS is distinct from other Polynesian languages in this respect; in other Polynesian languages numerals follow the heads of nominal phrases.

(23) "Etoru te rau te ohio, mai Rapanui ki Tahiti;
      3   the 100 the money from R.   to T.

etoru puaka katahi tagata." He   hakatakataka
3   cattle 1   person   Past gather

etoru te kauatu puaka: ehitu tagata, erua vī'e,
3   the 10   cattle 7   men   2   women

ehā ga poki.
4   Pl. boy

'"The price is three hundred (pesos), from Easter Island to Tahiti; three cattle per person." Thirty cattle were gathered together; (the fare for) seven men, two women, and four children.'

Notice in example (23) that tens and hundreds are treated as quantifiable units, and appear syntactically as the heads of nominal phrases embedded in the nominal phrases being quantified. Numerals used in quantifying nominal phrases

take the prefix e-; numerals used in enumerating or counting
take the prefix ka-.

3.3. Verbal Phrases

The verbal phrase of EAS, which functions as the predicate of
a clause, consists of a head preceded by a tense/aspect
marker, with possible one or several grammatical markers
following the head. Numerous examples of tense/aspect marker
plus head constructions have already been seen.

There are five principal tense/aspect markers in EAS. The
one which has appeared most frequently in the examples so far
is he, which has been labeled 'Past', a designation which is
accurate as far as it goes but is incomplete. He is actually
a very general, neutral sort of marker, used when none of the
more explicit, highly marked forms is called for. In narrative
texts such as the ones from which most of the examples given
here are drawn, he represents the ordinary narrative past. It
may quite consistently, however, be used in forms such as
example (14), where the present tense is more appropriate in
the English translation.

The perfective is denoted by i, as in examples (11) and
(17) above. E is nonpast, either future or present progressive. If it is present progressive, the progressive marker
ana or ā must follow the head of the verbal phrase. Examples
(24) and (25) illustrate this.

(24) E   oho au.
     Nonpast go I
     'I shall go.'

(25) E   tagi ā   te poki.
     Nonpast cry Prog. the boy
     'The boy is crying.'

Ku is the inceptive marker, used for actions or states
which began at some point in the past and are still in effect.
When ku is used, ana ∿ ā is again required after the head. The
inceptive ku ... ā combination appeared in example (5), in
which the implication is that the Bishop sold the land to the
Easter Islanders and they still possess it.

Ka is most frequently used to introduce imperatives, as in
example (27) below, and indeed that is the only use that
Englert records for it in his grammar and dictionary. In the
texts, however, a number of other uses of ka appear, including
the future as in example (26) and also uses translated in the
present and in the past. It was not possible to arrive at any
satisfactory generalization covering the various possible uses
of ka.

(26) Erua raā ka   oho nei te miro.
     Two days will? go PVD the boat
     'For two days now the boat will be moving.'

The markers following the head of the verbal phrase are
grouped into a set of classes which follow the head in a
prescribed order. At most one member of each of the classes
may be present in a given verbal phrase. The overall pattern
of the verbal phrase is as follows:

Tense/Aspect Head Adv. rō Prog. Deictic PVD

Adv. is a small class of verbs, such as hakaou 'again', which
may appear immediately following the head. Rō is an individual
marker, which according to Fuentes expresses the idea that the
action referred to is one which was imposed on the subject,
not carried out voluntarily (Fuentes 1960: 652 - 654). *Prog.*
refers to the progressive marker ana ∿ ā discussed earlier.
The deictic markers are mai 'here, hither' and atu 'away'.
PVD abbreviates postverbal demonstration, a class of four

particles: ai, nei, era, and ena. The syntax of this class,
which is rather complex, is discussed in detail in Chapin
1974: 294 - 299.

Interrogatives

Yes-or-no questions may be introduced by hoki 'whether', which
is the subordinating marker for indirect questions, as in
(27).

(27) "Ka   ui koe ki   te Kape,   hoki   ekō haga
      Imper. see you Dat. the Captain whether Neg. want

      ia mo   avai o   matou ki a   ia hai moni
      he Inf. give Subj. we   Dat. Pro. he some money

      mo te ohoga iruga i te miro."
      for the trip upon on the boat

      '"Ask the Captain whether he doesn't want us to give
      him money for the trip on the boat."'

The text immediately proceeds to (28), in which the indirect
question of (27) is expressed as a direct question.

(28) Ku   kī rō ai a   Mackinnon ki   te Kape
      Inc. say rō PVD Pro. M.   Dat. the Captain

      "Hoki e   haga rō koe mo   avai atu hai moni
       Q   Nonpast want rō you Inf. give away some money

      mo torāua ohoga iruga i te miro?"
      for their trip upon on the boat

      'Mackinnon then said to the Captain, "Will you want
      (them) to give (you) money for their trip on the
      boat?"'

Hoki is not required in direct questions; interrogation
may be indicated solely by intonation, as in example (13)
above. Compare (13) with (29):

(29) "Hoki he   moni marite   tokorua?"
      Q   Exist. money American your
      '"Do you have American money?"'

EAS has a full range of interrogative pronouns and adverbs, which normally appear with the appropriate preposition or case marker at the beginning of an interrogative clause, as in examples (30) through (33).

(30) "Aai i   toke?"
     Who Perf. steal
     '"Who stole (it)?"'

(31) "I   aai koe i   ma'a ai?"
     Ind.-Agt. who you Perf. learn PVD
     '"From whom did you learn this?"'

(32) Ki   aai koe he   ragi ena?
     Dat. who you past call PVD
     'Whom did you call?'

(33) Kihē   koe ka   oho ena apō?
     To-where you will go PVD tomorrow
     'Where will you go tomorrow?'

Notice that in examples (31), (32), and (33) the subject pronoun is moved in front of the verbal phrase. The available data are not decisive as to whether such fronting is obligatory in this context.

Copulative interrogatives are expressed simply by the juxtaposition of the preposition plus interrogative pronoun phrase with the principal other determinant. No tense/aspect marker is used.

(34) I hē   te puaka?
     In where the cattle
     'Where are the cattle?'

(35) Ko   ai   koe?
     Foc. who you
     'Who are you?'

(36) Ehia   te ohio o   taau aga?
     How-much the money Gen. your work
     'How much will you pay for the job?'

There is an apparent preference to cast questions in a copulative form, pairing with the interrogative pronoun or adverb a very general word such as me'e 'thing' or tagata 'person', with the rest of the question appearing as a relative clause on this general word. When the question concerns the addressee, the second person possessive pronoun is used before the general term. Examples (37) (from Fuentes 1960: 634) and (38) demonstrate this possibility.

(37) Heaha taau me'e haga mo   kī atu?
     What your thing want Inf. say away
     'What do you want me to say?'

(38) Koai taau tagata ma'a kai i   te korua me'e?
     Who your person can eat Acc. the your thing
     'Who can eat that thing you brought?'

Negation

Three forms are used for main clause negation in EAS: ina, kai, and ta'e. Ina appears at the beginning of the negated clause. It may be followed by kai, which in turn is followed by the head of the verbal phrase; in this configuration, ina may optionally be deleted. Example (39) illustrates the pattern with and without ina.

(39) Kai hakahoki mai te kī mai Tire ... He   noho,
     Neg. return   here the say from Chile ... Past sit,

     he   tiaki mai, ina kai hakahoki atu i   te kī.
     Past wait here, Neg. Neg. return   away Acc. the say

     'No word came back from Chile ... (He) sat and waited,
     (but they) didn't send back word.'

A subject pronoun can intervene between ina and kai, with the effect of negating the applicability of the predicate to the subject, rather than negating the predicate itself.

(40) ina matou kai ma'a i   te vānaga   magareva.
Neg. we   Neg. know Acc. the language M.
'We ourselves don't know the Mangareva language
   (though others do).'

In imperatives and in expressions with a future time
interpretation, the pattern is similar to that shown in
example (40), except that ekō is substituted for kai. Example
(41) illustrates the imperative use, and the second clause of
example (44) below the future use.

(41) ina korua ekō noho i Pamata'i.
Neg. you   Neg. stay in P.
'Don't stay in Pamata'i!'

Ina is also used to negate existential he.

(42) Ina he   moni.
Neg. Exist. money
'There isn't any money.' (I.e., we don't have any
   money.)

The negative form ta'e negates clauses in tense/aspect i
'Perfective', conditional clauses, and constituents of
clauses, exemplified in examples (43), (44), and (45), respectively. The two clauses of example (44) offer a comparison
between two types of negation.

(43) Etahi o   matou i   ta'e haga mo   hoki   mai
One   Gen. we   Perf. Neg. want Inf. return here

mai Tahiti.
from T.

'One of us didn't want to come back from Tahiti.'

(44) "Ana ta'e oho korua ki te aga, ina au ekō avai
If Neg. go you   to the work, Neg. I Neg. give

atu i   te kai mo korua."
away Acc. the food for you

'"If you don't go to work, I won't give you any food."'

(45) Hare ta'e rahi te hare tikera mai.
House Neg. large the house see   here
'Few houses can be seen.'

Ina is used for the simple response form 'no', as in example (46).

(46) He   kī   au: "Ina, ta'e mai   a   koe."
     Past say I: "No,   Neg. from Pro. you"
     'I said, "No, (it) isn't from you."'

Ta'e in example (46) negates the preposition mai 'from'. A special negative particle o is used to introduce subordinate clauses, with the interpretation 'so that not'.

(47) He   haaki atu ki   a   korua, o   kī korua, ana
     Past tell away Dat. Pro. you,   Neg. say you,   if

     mate au: i   te matu'a karega kore.
     die I: Ind.-Agt. the father property lacking

     'I told you this so that if I die you won't say: because of (our) father (we have) no property.'

Reciprocals and Reflexives

Reciprocals and reflexives have no special, distinctive form in EAS. According to Englert, in a sentence like example (48) (Englert 1948: 366) with actor-emphatic fronting of the subject, it is possible to interpret the object pronoun as coreferential with the subject, and thus express a reflexive proposition.

(48) Aana a   i   tiagi i   a   ia.
     He   Emph. Perf. kill Acc. Pro. he
     'He killed himself.'

It is likely, however, that, as in other Polynesian languages, sentences like example (48) are ambiguous, permitting also a nonreflexive reading on the order of 'He himself killed him.'

Causatives

The final point to be mentioned here concerning verbal constructions is the existence of the causative verbal prefix

haka-, from Proto-Polynesian *faka-, found in its appropriate
cognate forms in every Polynesian language. Its distribution
through the vocabulary is always extensive, but the degree of
current productivity varies from language to language. I am
uncertain of its productivity in EAS, as degree of productivity is very difficult to determine from texts, without
consultation with a native speaker. The full semantic range
of its use is highly idiosyncratic, but example (49) represents
its base use.

(49)   hoki   'return'   (intransitive)
        hakahoki 'return'   (transitive)

3.4. Coordination and Subordination

Coordination

In general, semantically coordinate phrases and clauses in
EAS are simply strung together with no overt marking to
indicate coordination. Example (23) above includes coordinated nominal phrases, and example (50) coordinated clauses.

(50) He   pū   kimu'a   erua tagata, erua kitu'a,   he
     Past pass to-front 2   man,   2   to-rear, Past

     amo i   te miro ki te gao, he   puaka
     lift Acc. the stick to the neck, Exist. cow

     to ruga, he   ma'u, he   haha'u kiroto ki te   vaka.
     thereon, Past carry, Past fasten into   the canoe

     'Two men passed to the front, two to the rear, (they)
     lifted the stick to their shoulders, the cow on it,
     (they) carried (it), (they) fastened (it) into the
     canoe.'

Note that ellipsis is accomplished wherever possible,
including gapping in the second clause, but no conjunctions
appear.

It is possible to tie sentences or clauses more closely
together with special linking words, usually in the second
clause, such as tako'a 'also', hakaou 'again', and ai 'and
then'. Example (51) is the beginning of the sentence immediately following example (23) in the text:

(51) Etoru hoi   tako'a, ...
     3   horses also
     'Three horses, also, ...'

A special comitative expression is seen in example (52).
The construction makes use of the focusing particle ko,
which precedes the head of the nominal phrase, precedes a
personal pronoun coreferential with the head in a pronominal
phrase appositive to and immediately following the head (if
the head is not itself pronominal), and precedes a possessive
pronoun plus object construction immediately following the
pronominal phrase, where the possessive pronoun is coreferential with the head and the object is the second party to the
comitative relationship.

(52) Te tagata i   oho ai ki Tahiti: Ko   Rafael
     The person Perf. go PVD to T.   Foc. R.

     Cardenale ko   ia ko   taana poki, ko   Vicente 2°
     C.   Foc. he Foc. his   boy, Foc. V.   2d

     Pont ko   ia ko   taana vi'e, ko   taana ga poki, ...
     P.   Foc. he Foc. his   wife, Foc. his   Pl. boy

     'The people who went to Tahiti (were): Rafael
     Cardenale and his son, Vicente Pont, Jr., and his
     wife and sons, ...'

Other Polynesian languages have coordinating conjunctions,
and it may be presumed that Proto-Polynesian did also, and
that EAS lost them at some point in its historical development. Englert (1948: 375) comments that Spanish o 'or' has
been adopted into EAS.

Subordination

Common types of subordinate clauses found in EAS are predicate
complements, object complements, and purposive clauses — all
three types formally similar — adverbial clauses, conditionals,
and indirect questions. Examples already given have illustrated
the indirect question (example 27), the conditional (example
44), and the predicate complement (examples 27, 28, and 37).
Predicate complement, object complement, and purposive clauses
are all introduced by the particle mo, which also functions as
the marker of the Benefactive. Example (53) shows a purposive
clause, and example (54) an object complement.

(53) He   patu   mai   i   te   puaka   mo   ma'u   kiruga
     Past corral here Acc. the cattle Inf. carry into

     ki te   miro.
     to the boat

     '(They) corralled the cattle in order to carry (them)
     onto the boat.'

(54) He   haaki mai   te   Kape   o   te   miro ki   a
     Past tell here the Captain Gen. the boat Dat. Pro.

     matou mo   hakarivariva mo   oho kiruga ki te   miro.
     we   Inf. make-ready   Inf. go upon   to the boat

     'The Captain of the boat asked us to get ready to go
     up onto the boat.'

Example (55) demonstrates that mo can also introduce a
sentential noun complement. In (55), the clause beginning
with mo is complementary to the nominal phrase immediately
preceding it, whose head is vānaga 'talk, news'.

(55) He   hakarogo au he   tu'u   atu   te   vānaga ho'ou
     Past hear   I past arrive away the talk   new

     mai Papeete, mo   oho etahi miro ki Rapanui mo
     from P.,   Inf. go one   boat to R.   Inf.

     ma'u mai i   te   mori mo   te   manu uru   tagata.
     carry here Acc. the oil for the bird carry person

'I heard that the news had come from Papeete that a
boat was going to Easter Island to take oil for
airplanes.'

Purposive clauses and predicate complement clauses may have
subjects which are the same as or different from the subjects
of the clauses to which they are subordinate. In example (53)
the purposive clause has the same subject as the main clause;
in example (56) the purposive clause has a new subject:

(56) Maana   e   aga mai mo   ma'a oou i   te tagata
     By-her Nonpast work here Inf. know you Acc. the person

     i   to'o i   toou ohio
     Perf. take Acc. your money

     'She will work so that you (will) know the person who
     stole your money.'

The predicate complements in examples (27), (28), and (37)
have subjects different from the subject of the immediately
superordinate clause; in example (57) the main clause and the
predicate complement have the same subject.

(57) Hoki e   haga rō mo   oho ki te   aga   o
     Q   Nonpast want rō Inf. go to the work Gen.

     te   tenito iuta?
     the Chinese inland

     'Do (you) want to go to work for the Chinese man
     inland?'

A truncated purpose clause may function as a noun complement, as in example (58).

(58) ina he   miro mo   oho.
     Neg. Exist. boat Inf. go
     'There isn't any boat to go (in).'

Adverbial clauses of time occur frequently. When-clauses
referring to past events appear in the perfective (tense/
aspect marker i) and are marked by a PVD — era if the

subordinate clause precedes the clause it modifies, ai if it
follows it.

(59) I   tu'u   mai   era te miro, he   tari mai i
     Perf. arrive here PVD the boat, Past bring here Acc.

     te   mori kiuta.
     the oil   inland

     'When the boat arrived, (they) brought the oil in to
     shore.'

Verbal phrases which are semantically compatible with the
notion of duration may be modified by subordinate clauses
introduced by the preposition ki, whose basic meaning is
'to, toward' and which in this instance has the sense 'until'.

(60) He   noho matou i Magareva ki tu'u   ki te hitu raa
     Past stay we   in M.   to arrive to the 7   day

     i   oho mai ai te miro mai Magareva ki Rapanui.
     Perf. go here PVD the boat from M.   to R.

     'We stayed in Mangareva until on the seventh day the
     boat left from Mangareva to Easter Island.'

The first ki in example (60) introduces the subordinate clause.
The construction immediately following it, which is translated as 'on the seventh day', literally means 'arriving at
the seventh day'.

An adversative or although-clause is introduced by the
subordinator noatu 'although', as in example (61).

(61) "Noatu   tokorua ta'e hakarogo mai ki   a   au,
     Although you   Neg. listen   here Dat. Pro. I,

     e   tikera rō e   korua, ana tu'u   korua ki
     Nonpast see   rō Agt. you   if arrive you   to

     ira."
     there

     '"Although you won't believe me, you will see if you
     go there."'

There is a general preference, reflected in the examples
given, to pull subordinate clauses to the front of the
clauses they modify. If more than one subordinate clause is
appended to a particular main clause, however, as in example
(61), only one of the subordinate clauses will precede the
main clause.

To express the reason for something, a more periphrastic
construction is used, built around the framework of an equational clause. Example (62) is a rather complex instance of
this:

(62) He me'e te   ua,   o   tooku tupuna   i
     thing the reason, Subj. my   grandfather Perf.

   tu'u   ai ki Tahiti: i   te   tariga   tagata
   arrive PVD to T.:   Ind.-Agt. the abduction person

   e   te Perū;   te ua   i   oho ai mai
   Agt. the Peruvians; the reason Perf. go PVD from

   Rapanui.
   R.

   'The reason my grandfather went to Tahiti was this:
   because of the abduction by the Peruvians; (that
   was) the reason (he) went from Easter Island.'

The first four words of (62) constitute the main clause,
an equational clause meaning literally 'The thing is the
reason.' (The function of he is unclear; see section 3.2
above for discussion.) The words following te ua 'the reason'
and going up to the colon are complementary to te ua and
complete a nominal phrase meaning 'the reason my grandfather went to Tahiti'. The words i te tariga tagata e te
Perū 'because of the abduction by the Peruvians', which
specify the reason, are grammatically in apposition to me'e
'thing'. The remainder of the sentence is a reprise and
restatement of the te ua plus complement portion of the
sentence.

The indirect agency construction in example (62), introduced
by the marker i immediately following the colon, has been seen
before in example (47). Sentence (62) is interesting also
because it contains a nominalized form in the suffix -ga
(tariga 'abduction', from tari 'to transport, to take to some
place' + -ga) which is quite common in other Polynesian
languages but is rarely seen in EAS (ohoga 'trip' in examples
27 and 28, from oho 'go' is another instance). The particular
use in example (62), te tariga tagata e te Perū 'the abduction by the Peruvians', has the flavor of a fossilized
reference to an important historical event, on the order of
"the slaughter of the innocents" in English. If this is
correct, the form tariga may well be an archaism (as
'innocents' is an archaism in English). These observations
suggest that the loss of nominalization as a productive
process in EAS may have been a comparatively recent historical
development, occurring within the last one to two centuries.

3.5. Grammatical Processes

As stated in the introductory section of this essay, adequate
treatment of grammatical processes is the most difficult part
of a linguistic description to base entirely on textual data,
without consultation with native speakers of the language. In
this chapter only a few sketchy comments are possible.

Anaphora is generally by zeroing, as in example (50), but
personal pronouns may be used anaphorically, as in example
(27). The anaphoric personal pronoun must be used in the
comitative construction illustrated in example (52).

The particle ai, seen in the last clause of example (62),
is anaphoric in other Polynesian languages, a resumptive
pronoun used to replace a deleted or moved determinant in an
oblique case. It is not used anaphorically in EAS, however,

but as a member of the class of postverbal demonstratives.
See Chapin 1974 for an extensive discussion.

It was mentioned earlier that adverbial subordinate
clauses are generally fronted. Foregrounding a determinant
or a prepositional phrase by fronting it is also quite a
common process. Examples (63) and (64) are illustrative.

(63) I   te   marama ko   Hora iti i   tu'u   mai ai
     In the month Foc. August   Perf. arrive here PVD

     te   miro.
     the boat

     'In the month of August the boat arrived.'

(64) Tooku matu'a, ko   Moises Tu'u Hereveri te   ioga,
     My   father, Foc. M.   T.   H.   the name,

     i Tahiti i   poreko ai. Tooku tupuna   ko
     in T.   Perf. born   PVD My   grandfather Foc.

     Agustin Hereveri te   igoa i   poreko ai i Rapanui.
     A.   H.   the name Perf. born   PVD in R.

     'My father, Moises Tu'u Hereveri, was born in Tahiti.
     My grandfather Agustin Hereveri was born on Easter
     Island.'

Example (64) also demonstrates the fact that more than one
determinant may be fronted in a clause. In the first sentence
of (64) the subject nominal phrase and the prepositional phrase
i Tahiti 'in Tahiti' both appear before the verbal phrase
i poreko ai 'was born'. The second sentence of (64) contains
the same set of constituents as the first, but there only the
subject nominal phrase is fronted, while the prepositional
phrase assumes its normal position following the verbal
phrase.

There is no passivization in EAS. This differentiates EAS
from many other Polynesian languages. Passivization is
extremely active in Maori, for example, and partially active
in Samoan. The existence and nature of passivization in

individual Polynesian languages interacts with the typological
division of Polynesian languages into ergative and accusative
types, which has been the topic of much discussion. See Chung
1976 for the most recent treatment and an up to date bibliography. I have been unable to determine from the textual
materials available to me the position of EAS in this typological classification, or indeed to discern any regularity
at all in the case marking system of EAS, which explains the
absence of discussion of case marking in this sketch. To
quote from my own earlier discussion of EAS syntax, Chapin
1974: 297: "I have encountered in the texts sentences with
the subject marked with the Agentive e and the object
unmarked, sentences with the subject marked with e and the
object marked with Accusative i, sentences with both subject
and object unmarked, and intransitive sentences with subject
marked with e."

One example from the texts, presented here as example (65),
suggests the possibility of raising as a rule of EAS.

(65) Hoki e   haga rō koe ki   te   puaka mo   hakahere?
     Q   Nonpast want rō you Dat. the cattle Inf. buy
     'Do you want to buy cattle?'

The raised determinant in (65) would be te puaka, raised
from an underlying function as object of hakahere 'to buy',
the head of the predicate of the predicate complement clause,
to its surface position as (Dative-marked) object of haga
'to want', the head of the main clause predicate. The evidence
for raising in example (65) rests entirely on the semantics of
the sentence, and is not entirely convincing. Other Polynesian
languages, for example Maori, have clear examples of raising
from subordinate clause subject to main clause object. See
Chapin 1974: 280, n. 27.

4. English
A Characteristic SVO Language

Winfred P. Lehmann

4.0. Introduction

In examining a language of civilization spoken throughout a
vast area, one is faced with the problem of identifying the
variant to be discussed. Different forms of pronunciation,
and different idioms, are found even within one area of use,
such as Great Britain or the United States, as well as between
these and other countries in which English is widely used.
Here a form of popular literature is chosen for examples, and
in this way assumed to be a standard: Lewis Carroll's *Alice
in Wonderland* (1865) and *Through the Looking Glass* (1872). The
references in parentheses following citations indicate page
numbers in *The Complete Works of Lewis Carroll* (New York:
Random House, n.d.).

Both pieces are read today without difficulty. The differing pronunciations in New Zealand, Australia, and other areas
where English is spoken have no effect on the grammatical
structures, or even the phonological structure, in the view
of some linguists. The language of Lewis Carroll might for
the most part be used today in speech, as well as in writing.
Accordingly his texts are taken as representative of English
today as well as a century ago. Fixing on such texts reduces
the possibility of drawing on idiosyncratic materials,
whether from one's own speech or from that of others. The
English exemplified here is then in a careful, popular

literary style designed for understanding by children but
accepted as a standard by native speakers of all ages.

English is a highly consistent SVO language. The government
constructions observe SVO patterns, as do the nominal modifying constructions — with the exception of descriptive and
limiting adjectives in an archaic order. As a consistent
language, English exemplifies characteristic features of SVO
languages, such as the many patterns that have been developed
in the verbal modifying constructions, the wide use of substitutes, and the grammatical processes used to highlight elements of sentences.

The verbal patterns make heavy use of auxiliaries, which
are also involved as substitutes and in interrogative and
negative constructions, differentiating English in this way
from (S)OV languages like Japanese and VSO languages like
Easter Island. The grammatical processes involve function
words, again in distinctive constructions like clefting. An
examination of the characteristic typological patterns
presented below in accordance with the patterns listed in
section 1.3, then discloses on the one hand the expected
constructions found in SVO languages and on the other the
basic structure of English.

4.1. The Structure of Simple Clauses

Simple, unmarked clauses agree with the SVO pattern, and
require representations for the three constituents: subject,
verb, and object.

(1.1) Alice folded her hands. (55)

Neither the subject nor the verb nor the object of a transitive verb may be omitted; the following variants of this
sentence are impermissible.

(1.2) *Folded her hands.

(1.3) *Alice her hands.

(1.4) *Alice folded.

Further, a consistent SVO language·like English does not permit any order other than the above in unmarked sentences occurring as single utterances. Thus the following are not possible:

(1.5) *Folded Alice her hands.

(1.6) *Folded her hands Alice.

(1.7) ?Her hands folded Alice.

(1.8) ?Her hands Alice folded.

(1.9) ?Alice her hands folded.

The last three are questioned rather than starred because they might be possible in the middle of a discourse.

This constraint applies also in subordination, as in the sequence:

(1.10) Margaret fidgeted while Alice folded her hands.

Such a mandatory syntactic arrangement then requires the analysis of English as an SVO language (see also section 6.1). Any attempt to propose a different underlying structure for English fails to consider the implication of such analysis for other languages. If, for example, English were to be labeled a VSO language, one would have to account for the differing characteristics in languages like Easter Island or Irish. When such attempts have been made under the rubric of a given theory, languages of VSO structure have not been considered.

Inasmuch as the basic patterns of English are so consistent, this essay will discuss at some length consequences of SVO structure. One of these has to do with the expression of verbal qualifiers. In accordance with the principle expressed in section 1.3, verbal qualifiers must precede verbs. This position, however, conflicts with the optimum position for subjects. To express negation, for example, the negative might be prefixed to the verb, as it indeed was in Old English, so that the negative of (1) might be:

(1.11) *Alice ne-folded her hands.

Such a position seems awkward, as does sentence-initial placement:

(1.12) *Ne Alice folded her hands.

The dilemma has been resolved for English by the use of auxiliaries. As will be observed at some length below, auxiliaries are characteristic of SVO languages though not confined to them.

Moreover, SVO languages typically require the S position to be filled, as well as the V and O positions, though with well-defined exceptions, in contrast with simple verb sentences in OV languages. To meet this requirement, substitutes are prominent, as in the following variants of sentence 1.

(1.13) She folded her hands.

(1.14) The griffon folded its wings. Alice did her hands.

(1.15) The griffon folded its wings and Alice her hands.

(1.16) Alice folded them.

Further examples given below illustrate at greater length the prominence of substitutes in SVO languages, substitutes not

only for nouns and verbs, but also for phrases and clauses,
e.g., so.

Further, the characteristics of SVO languages have given
rise to special constructions. Thus, if the requirement for
the S to be placed before the V were rigidly observed, an
awkward style would result, and also special emphasis on the
S. Devices then have been developed to offset these difficulties, such as the passive. This is a construction which
permits the object to be the theme. Passives are especially
characteristic of SVO and VSO languages. Other similar devices,
such as clefting, also have largely a functional role.

This chapter then illustrates the characteristics of SVO
languages, not simply the conformance of English with the
expected patterns.

In contrast with OV languages, the subject is the mandatory nominal constituent of SVO languages, as in sentences
with intransitive verbs, or in equational sentences.

(2.1) Alice turned.   (54)

(2.2) I shall be too late. (18)
                            Substantive Copula Adjective

(2.3) I'm not a serpent.   (60)
                            Substantive Copula Substantive

(2.4) The face is over.   (38)
                            Substantive Copula Adverb

Constituents in these patterns may be highlighted through
various grammatical processes, as noted further below.

(2.1) and (30) It was Alice who turned.

Marking too may be used for singling out various constituents,
by change of order or by intonation, with or without accompanying particles.

(2.3) and (VI.1)   A serpent I'm not.

(2.3) and (VI.2)   I am not a <u>serpent</u>.

The impacts of such variants are determined by the regularity of the basic SVO pattern, which assures marked effects because of the contrast introduced.

Government operates strongly in English, both in predicates and in other government constructions. Only prepositions are used in current English except for specific idioms; <u>ago</u>, as in <u>two years ago</u>, may be viewed as a postposition, but it is severely restricted in use, as may be illustrated by the attention given to Dylan Thomas's phrase: <u>a grief ago</u>.

(3)   Then Alice dodged behind a great thistle.   (50)

Moreover, constructions with a standard place this after the variable. In comparisons of inequality the adjective precedes the standard.

(4.1) It's very easy to take <u>more</u> than nothing.   (81)

In titles, the name follows, functioning like a standard for the "variable" title.

(4.2) Queen Alice.   (258)

In personal names the surname follows as standard to the given name.

(4.3) Alice Pleasance Liddell.   (272)

And in numerals in the teens, the form of ten follows, as in the other constructions of this kind furnishing a standard for the simple numerals from three to nine.

(4.4) fourteen

It is the prominence of government which leads rhetoricians to assert for English that "main elements are usually most

emphatic at the end of a sentence" (Crews 1977: 140). English
has been characterized by functional syntacticians as a
language in which the initial segment, or theme, often using
old material, sets the scene for the new material, or rheme.
Thus in sentence (1) the subject Alice is one of the important
elements of the preceding discourse, while the predicate
folded her hands introduces a new action. SVO order provides
a convenient basis for such organization of sentences. VSO
languages, on the other hand, provide greater difficulty for
initial placement of the theme, requiring special constructions for that purpose. Subjects normally furnish a link with
previous sentences, thus being less "emphatic" in Crews's
characterization and yielding the position of rhetorical
emphasis to the verb and its object or complement. This same
effect may be noted in the other government patterns, for
example, in comparative constructions, where the standard
holds the position of greatest prominence.

4.2. Nominal Phrases

As in other SVO languages, the position of relative constructions is determined by the VO constituent. They regularly
follow nouns, avoiding in this way disruption of the verb-
object constituent. The relationship of relative constructions to their antecedents is so clear that if an object is
the shared noun of the relative clause no marker is needed;
which or that is often omitted, as after rules in the
following example:

    (5.1) All because they would not remember the simple rules
          their friends had taught them. (22)

English relative constructions may be restrictive, as is the
first in the following quotation, or descriptive, like the

second. Restrictive clauses are normally spoken as part of the
intonation pattern of their head; this pattern of intonation
is generally indicated by lack of punctuation, unlike Carroll's
practice here. Descriptive clauses on the other hand have
their own intonation pattern.

> (5.2) The only two creatures in the kitchen, that did not
> sneeze, were the cook, and a large cat, which was
> lying on the hearth and grinning from ear to ear.
> (66)

The distinction between restrictive and descriptive relative
clauses is maintained for other nominal modifiers as well,
such as the participles in the following examples:

> (5.3) There stood the Queen in front of them, with her
> arms folded, frowning like a thunder-storm. (98)
> (Descriptive)

> (5.4) With tears running down his cheeks, he went on again.
> (105) (Restrictive)

The contrast also applies to adverbial clauses. The temporal
clause in (5.5) is restrictive, while that in (5.6) is
descriptive.

> (5.5) So Alice began telling them her adventures from the
> time when she first saw the White Rabbit. (110)

> (5.6) That's different from what I used to say when I
> was a child. (112)

The parallelism in this respect between relative clauses,
whether in full form or as abbreviated to descriptive adjectives and genitives, and adverbial clauses reflects the
similarity of their origins. When relative clauses were
developed in the Indo-European languages, many of the conjunctions were based on the stem of the relative pronouns.

Syntacticians have long proposed that descriptive genitives
and adjectives are reduced forms of relative clauses.

Genitives then observe the arrangement of relative clauses with regard to their head; 90 percent of the genitive constructions in contemporary English do, following their head (Fries 1940).

(6.1) with her head in the lap of her sister. (129)
(From: The lap is her sister's.)

In the course of reduction the form of the verb BE is elided together with the relative pronoun.

(6.2) She peeped over the edge of the mushroom. (52)

If genitives, however, are proper nouns, particularly single names, they often precede.

(6.3) To Tweedledum's house. (179)

Yet even single names are often postposed.

(6.4) To the house of Tweedledee. (179)

The current status of the genitive in English and its development have great historical interest, for they reflect a change from OV order in pre-Old English times to VO order today.

While the favored order for genitives has been shifted, adjectives still predominantly precede the modified noun.

(7.1) An enormous puppy was looking down at her with large round eyes. (50)

Only when they are in turn modified do descriptive adjectives regularly follow their head.

(7.2) And then they rested on a rock conveniently low. (186)

Limiting adjectives — articles and demonstratives — also stand before nouns, as do numerals; they usually precede

descriptive adjectives, with limiting adjectives standing
before descriptive adjectives.

(8.1) And at that distance too. (223)

(9.1) I haven't sent the two Messengers. (223)

(9.2) She jumped over the first of the six little books.
(169)

Parallel to the order of limiting adjectives is that of
multiplying numeral combinations with nouns representing
higher entities: millions, thousands, hundreds, tens in the
order of higher to lower (preceded by the simple numerals).
(Greenberg 1976: lecture)

(8.2) Four thousand two hundred and seven ... (223)

As with preposed descriptive adjectives, genitives, and
relative clauses, preposed limiting adjectives and the cited
numeral combinations reflect OV structure. This is the most
conservative of the English modifying patterns. In maintaining
it as a relic pattern, English provides evidence for the OV
structure which is posited for its ancestor language, Proto-
Indo-European.

Yet English nominal phrases for the most part observe the
canonical order of SVO languages, maintaining from early
stages OV order only with adjectives and numeral constructions
other than the teens.

4.3. Verbal Phrases

In SVO languages, expressions for verbal modification should
be placed before verbs, in accordance with their VO structure.
Like nominal modification, verbal modification avoids
disruption of the VO constituent. Such placement leads to
difficulties, however, through conflict between the mandatory

subject and the verbal modifying constituent. SVO languages resolve these difficulties by various means. One of the most widespread is the use of auxiliaries; these function in part like verbs, in part like empty markers which can be placed before the central verb but still not interfere with the similar preverbal placement of the subject. The English dummy verb DO admirably exemplifies such a device. It provides the qualifying marker, but because of its weakly stressed form it does not interfere with the initially placed subject. Yet, in contrast with VSO languages, auxiliaries in SVO languages do not coalesce with the central verb, providing prefixed markers. The presence of separate verblike elements called auxiliaries then constitutes one of the characteristics of SVO languages and of English.

Expressions for declarative utterances simply observe the normal word order.

(10)   This speech caused a remarkable sensation among the party. (41)

This arrangement is accompanied by an intonation pattern, with final drop in pitch from the syllable with the chief accent. The pattern, often indicated as 231#, contrasts with a pattern with final rise: 223‖, which indicates doubt or uncertainty on the part of the speaker. The 231# intonation pattern is accordingly a device for expressing certainty on the part of the speaker, that is, the declarative qualifier.

The contrasting pattern, 233‖, is one of the devices for expressing interrogation.

(11.1) You like poetry? (183)

This pattern is commonly found with an auxiliary preposed before the subject to express interrogation.

(11.2) Is this New Zealand? (19)

(11.3) Do cats eat bats? (20)

Such questions usually require an answer of either *yes* or *no*, and as a result they are often labeled *yes-or-no questions* (see Jespersen for other labels, 1924: 302 - 305).

In accordance with the general ordering principle, the interrogative marker should stand close to the sentence boundary, whether initially in VO languages or finally in OV. For SVO languages this requirement provides a difficulty, inasmuch as the subject should also occupy this position. The conflict has been resolved in two ways in English. For pronominal questions it has led to the production of a special set of words which may combine the interrogative with a substitute for the subject, the so-called <u>wh</u>-words. For yes-or-no questions it has led to the introduction of auxiliaries. Among the auxiliaries DO is the most remarkable in having today only a grammatical function, whether as interrogative marker as in (11.3), or as a device for the indication of negation or emphasis. Other auxiliaries combine uses as grammatical markers with expression of modality, aspect, and tense. The auxiliaries, which correspond to postverbal affixes in OV languages and preverbal affixes in VSO, are among the prime characteristics of SVO languages. Their gradual development in English and other SVO languages has been the topic of much fascinating research. Moreover, since understanding of the auxiliaries corresponds to an understanding of that section of the grammar of SVO languages regarding the verb phrase, the analysis of their role and functioning is required for an understanding of SVO languages.

The second large set of questions in languages is characterized by a question word. These, often referred to as <u>wh</u>-question words after the <u>wh</u>- segment in many English interrogative words, Jespersen labels <u>x</u>-questions, because they

include an "unknown quantity" (1924: 303). Initial position
of the interrogative element accords with the expectation
of this order for the theme as well as with the general
ordering principle.

(11.4) What's the French for fiddle-de-dee? (254)

(11.5) What right have you to call yourself so? (251)

(11.6) How is bread made? (254)

English, like other SVO languages, permits only one wh-word
before the finite verb, whether this is a noun as in (11.4),
an adjective as in (11.5), or an adverb as in (11.6). OV
languages, by contrast, admit more, and languages with partial
OV patterning, like the Slavic, also do. A changing language,
like Chinese, may place the wh-word in either the subject or
the predicate. The treatment of wh-words is then characteristic of language types.

Besides wh-questions and yes-or-no questions, English, like
other languages, includes devices indicating presupposition
in yes-or-no questions. One such device is the tag question,
consisting of a positive auxiliary when a negative answer is
presupposed, and a negative auxiliary for a presupposed
positive answer. The auxiliary corresponds in form to that
of the principal verb, as in the following idiosyncratic
statement.

(11.7) "I speaks English, doesn't I?" the Frog went on.
       (260)

Interrogative expressions are then closely related to
expressions for sentence negation, though negation may be
used for syntactic rather than pragmatic purposes.

Negation, in accordance with the general principle,
occupies third position from the sentence boundary, next to

interrogation. This position is reflected in English negated
yes-or-no questions.

(12.1) Isn't he a lovely sight? (188)

In patterns other than questions, however, expression for
negation is placed after the auxiliary, in this way preceding
the principal verb but also not conflicting with initial
placement of the subject.

(12.2) Manners are not taught in lessons. (252)

(12.3) I don't rejoice in insects at all. (173)

This position is observed even for emphatic negatives.

(12.4) It'll never do for you to be lolling about
       on the grass like that! (250)

Besides their attraction to auxiliaries, negatives also are
placed with indefinites, often standing initially.

(12.5) Nobody said you did. (251)

Such negated indefinites incorporate sentence negation, as
may be determined by producing a comparable sentence with a
definite pronoun, whether a statement or a question.

(12.6) She didn't say you did.

(12.7) Didn't she say you did?

Individual segments of sentences may also be negated,
with the negative indicator typically placed before the
element negated.

(12.7) Then there was an uncomfortable silence for a
       minute or two. (252)

In OV languages, by contrast, even negatives for individual
segments are postposed, as in Turkish rahat-sız 'uncomfortable, literally comfort-Neg.' Because of their placement

with indefinites and individual segments, negative indicators
are far more widely distributed in sentences of SVO languages
than are those for interrogatives. They come to approximate
the remaining Q features in lexical rather than grammatical
expression.

Of these further features, the middle is especially characteristic for its expression in SVO languages. Widely indicated
by verbal suffixes in OV languages and by verbal prefixes in
VSO languages, the middle is generally expressed with pronouns
in SVO languages. The complexities resulting from such
expression may be noted for Japanese, which in the course of
its history has introduced expressions borrowed from Chinese,
notably zibun 'self' (see section 2.3.3).

The middle is used especially for reflexive and reciprocal
relationship. An understanding of expressions for reflexive
and reciprocal reference in English is assisted by the
knowledge that its remote ancestor, Proto-Indo-European,
expressed the middle by means of a verbal suffixed inflection,
comparable to that in Turkish. By Old English times only one
reflex of the middle remained, and only in relic patterns:
hātan 'be called', whose cognate still survives in German
heissen 'be called', ich heisse x 'my name is x'. Like
other Q features the middle may come to be expressed lexically. Yet lexical expression for it fails to accord with the
general patterning of verbs with an object in SVO languages.
Even in Old English times, hātan was used transitively more
frequently than as a middle. And in Modern English only a
handful of verbs remains which are middles, e.g., agree,
cross, embrace, hug, kiss, marry, meet.

(13.1) Our letters crossed.
       (Rarely: Our letters crossed each other.)

The gradual disappearance of such verbs may be noted from their greater abundance in Shakespeare (Jespersen 1949: III.332).

(13.2) *As You Like It* 1.1.117:
  Never two ladies loved as they do.

In spite of such lexical middles, the characteristic device for expressing middle features in SVO languages is pronominalization.

The earliest expression for reflexivization through pronouns in English made use of personal pronouns, in a usage which has survived especially after some prepositions and in adjectival uses (Jespersen 1949: VII.4.8).

(13.3) If I don't take this child away with me ... (70)
       (Not: myself)

(13.4) It unfolded its arms. (55) (Not: itself's)

For the most part, however, pronouns were suffixed with forms of <u>self</u> and <u>other</u> to form the characteristic elements in reflexive and reciprocal constructions today.

(13.5) Alice was just beginning to think to herself. (70)

(13.6) Don't give yourself airs. (57)

(13.7) And here the two brothers gave each other a hug.
                                                    (182)

Compare the middle verb <u>agree</u>, which does not require an overt indicator of the middle value:

(13.8) Of course you agree to have a battle. (192)
       (Not: with each other)

The reflexive is maintained when its subject is elided.

(13.9) "Don't grunt," said Alice, "that's not at all a
       proper way of expressing yourself." (70)

While expression for the middle in English is "far from simple," whether for its history as Jespersen notes (1949: VII.162) or for its current use, as the last example and many cited elsewhere illustrate, it is basically made with pronouns, and in this way English is characteristic of SVO languages.

4.3.1. Expressions for Modality

Expressions of modality have intricate nuances of meaning, which merge with one another and shift as other Q features such as negation are aligned with them. Yet the patterning is straightforward. Specific verbs come to be used as "modal auxiliaries" in early Old English and have subsequently been enriched with others. Moreover, necessitative modality may be expressed through arrangement, in a reflection of a characteristic verb form for the imperative in earlier periods of the language. Initial verbs without a subject generally have necessitative force.

(14.1) Drink me! (22)

Auxiliaries are used, especially when tense or another Q feature is included.

(14.2) You mustn't say that.   (Nec. + Neg.)

(14.3) You should have meant! (251) (Nec. + Perf.)

The English modal auxiliaries have often been described, in treatments that are extensive. Since we aim simply to note their role in the English grammatical system, a compact analysis will be given here, based in part on Twaddell (1960: 10 - 12; see also Calbert and Vater 1975). In Twaddell's treatment the modals proper are presented in three groups, with hierarchization of contingency.

	Necessitative, Requirement, Prescription, Obligation	Voluntative, Possibility, Permission, Capability	Prediction
Absolute, Unrestricted	must, have to	can, be able to	will
Contingent, Inconclusive	need	may, might	shall
Morally Determined	ought to	dare	

As such a table suggests, the meanings of individual modals are not sharply distinct. Since modals proper do not co-occur, we may conclude, as Twaddell also notes, that "there are elements of incompatibility in their meanings." Yet co-occurrence is found for "new" expressions of modality.

(14.4) I shouldn't be able to say. (190)

Such co-occurrence, as well as other patterns, reflect the dual use of modals as full verbs and as grammatical markers expressing modality. As grammatical markers they may indicate interrogation, by initial position, or they may support negation.

(15.1) Will you walk a little faster? (107)

(15.2) I can't explain myself. (54)

Expression for modality may be accompanied by expression for aspect and tense, which is largely made through auxiliaries.

(15.3) She would have liked very much to ask them how they came there. (250)

4.3.2. Expressions for Aspect and Tense

Perfective aspect is often indicated by means of the auxiliary
HAVE accompanied by the participle; as here, adverbials may
be used with such compound verb forms.

(16.1) By the time she had caught the flamingo and brought
it back, the fight was over. (93)

Momentary aspect is indicated by contrast with an auxiliary-
based construction using BE plus the gerund.

(17.1) You're thinking about something, my dear, and that
makes you forget to talk. (96)

Simple verb forms are used to express momentary action as
opposed to continuous, which is expressed by means of be ...
ing forms.

(17.2) Alice guessed in a moment that it was looking
for the fan. (42)

Both the perfective and the momentary expression are placed
closer to the principal verb than are expressions for
modality, with +continuous or -momentary following perfective
expressions.

(16.2)   You ought to have finished. (117)

(17.3)   I must be growing small again. (30)

(16.3)   You couldn't have wanted it much. (103)

(16/17.4) You couldn't have been wanting it much.

With its adaptation of auxiliaries, English has developed
a complex verb phrase which may be compared with the large
number of affixes found in OV languages like Quechua and
Turkish. Yet the requirement that a subject be expressed
with these complexes leads, as noted above, to a less
harmonious system of verbal quantifiers in SVO languages.

For while the affixes of OV languages are parallel in their treatment, the auxiliaries of SVO languages are comparable on the one hand to principal verbs, on the other to grammatical markers.

Further, SVO languages tend to employ increasing numbers of verbs as auxiliaries, leading to expanded lexical expression of Q features. The results are especially notable in technical and scientific language, in which auxiliarylike verbs come to be highly prominent, expressing little more than Q features. In treatments of German the resulting patterns have come to be known as *Streckformen* 'extended forms'. Such verbs in English are get and make, which have come to be used to express the causative, and give and take, which in such expressions do little but express verbality and direction.

(19.1) I give you fair warning. (99) (= I warn you fairly.)

(16.5) The other guests had taken advantage of the Queen's absence. (99) (seventeenth century: advantaged themselves)

An extreme development of auxiliaries is found in Basic English, which excludes all but a dozen verbs. This ultimate development, or virtually caricature, of English devised by I. A. Richards (1943) illustrates forcibly how auxiliaries are perceived to be characteristic verbal markers in SVO structure, in contrast with prefixes in VSO and suffixes in OV.

The iterative is expressed lexically, by means of repetition or with particles.

(18.1) Still she went on growing and growing. (44)

(18.2) She generally gave herself good advice ... and sometimes she scolded herself ... (24)

The causative is also expressed with characteristic verbs, or lexically, as in the three expressions for "cause to be dry" below.

(19.2) It doesn't seem to dry me at all. (37)

(19.3) I'll soon make you dry enough. (36)

(19.4) What I was going to say ... was, that the best thing to get me dry would be a Caucus-race. (37)

The verb get puts the emphasis on the process of causing, make on the result.

(19.5) She'll get me executed, as sure as ferrets are ferrets. (42)

(19.6) The hot day made her feel very sleepy and stupid. (17)

The predominant use of auxiliarylike verbs to express causation, whatever their further connotation, reflects the history of English. In its earliest attested texts it still contained causative verbs which were distinguished from simple verbs by suffixation of -i/j-, e.g., Old English nerian 'rescue'. For the most part the suffix had been lost, with some verbs maintaining a distinction between the causative and the simplex through vowel difference, e.g., Old English settan 'set' and sittan 'sit'. Subsequently even such lexical contrasts have been lost, so that the expression of causation in verbs is distinguishable only by syntactic means: the breeze dried her hair versus her hair dried. The confusion between sit : set and between lie : lay in spoken English is proverbial. Causative expression has accordingly been lexicalized or expressed in characteristic phrasal formations as noted above. These several possibilities have given rise to much discussion among linguists concerning the relationships in meaning between such expressions as kill and cause

to die. It is not difficult to demonstrate that Q expressions
consisting of individual elements permit greater explicitness
and flexibility, especially of interrelationship among several
Q features, than does lexicalization of Q features in SVO
languages.

Of the expressions for aspect and tense, that for tense
alone still maintains the OV pattern of suffixation, e.g.,
advise : advised. Yet even here the means of expression have
been eroded, as in set : set, and in irregular forms like
dive : dove versus dive : dived. Or tense is indicated through
auxiliaries, as for other Q features. When auxiliary expression is considered as well as inflection, English distin-
guishes between the present, past, and future tenses.

(20.1) I advise you to leave off this minute. (24)
(Present tense)

(20.2) Who in the world am I? (28) (Present tense)

(20.3) Was I the same when I got up this morning? (28)
(Past tense)

(20.4) Did you ever eat a bat? (20)
(Past tense)

(20.5) Dinah'll miss me very much tonight. (20)
(Future tense)

(20.6) And then I'll tell you my history. (24)
(Future tense)

Expression of tense may be combined with expressions for
aspect. Its freedom of position permits the suggestion that
tense is closely related to nominal or adverbial indicators
of time, as in: We leave tomorrow. They dine at eight
(tonight). In a case grammar, then, tense may be introduced
through a nominal time category rather than a verbal. Its
expression may be made nominally, verbally, or adverbially,

with a freedom greater than that of the other expressions
associated with the verb.

But tense is expressed in conjunction with each of these.
Past tense is combined with perfective aspect and with
-momentary expression in the following example.

> (20.7) While she was still looking at the place where it
>   had been, it suddenly appeared again. (73)

As these examples illustrate, tense is expressed with
auxiliaries when combined with verbal expressions for
modality, aspect, and also interrogative and negative
expressions.

> (20.8) Perhaps, as this is May, it wo'n't be raving mad.
>   (73)

The expression of negation with simple verb forms now
seems archaic, and even with qualifiers it seems to be
receding, as may be illustrated with current versions of
the Bible, such as the Living New Testament of 1967 in contrast with the authorized version of 1611.

> (20.9) John 3.7:
>   Marvel not.   (1611)
>   Don't be surprised. (1967)

> (20.10) Luke 5.5:
>   We have toiled all the night and have taken
>   nothing.   (1611)
>   We worked hard all last night and didn't catch
>   a thing.   (1967)

English then has increasingly developed expression of verbal
qualifiers by means of auxiliaries, exemplifying in this way
one of the characteristics of SVO languages.

4.4. Sentence Adverbials

Another device has been developed in English which may be
characteristic of SVO languages: the so-called sentence
adverbials. These resemble modals in referring to the entire
sentence, for example, unfortunately in (IV.1) and (2) as
opposed to (3).

    (IV.1) Unfortunately, the Duchess played badly.

    (IV.2) The Duchess, unfortunately, played badly.

    (IV.3) The Duchess played unfortunately badly.

In sentences 1 and 2 the adverbial sets the tone for the
entire sentence. Linguists then equate it with a longer,
reduced sentence, such as: It was unfortunate that ...
They support this analysis by noting its independent intonation pattern.

    Some sentence adverbials, like unfortunately, are also
widely used as general adverbs, modifying adjectives, adverbs,
and verbs. Others are more widely used as sentence adverbials,
such as certainly, perhaps, possibly, probably. Comparing the
equivalents of these in OV languages like Japanese and Turkish,
one finds in them inflected verb forms, with or without
supplementary adverbs. Thus (IV.4) is expressed in Japanese
with a verb form expressing probability: daroo 'it may be',
often in conjunction with tabun 'much, in large measure'.

    (IV.4) Probably he forgot.

    (IV.5) Kare wa   tabun wasureta no   daroo.
            he   Ptc. much forgot   Ptc. it-may-be

The following pair illustrates a similar difference in Turkish.

    (IV.6) Possibly a person wouldn't know this.

(IV.7) İnsan bunu bil-mi-yebilir.
       person this know-not-it-is-possible

The flexible expandibility of OV verbal forms contrasts
sharply with the varied but limited devices of SVO languages,
which indeed use auxiliaries but also a device like sentence
adverbs. Sentence adverbs like _maybe_ (< _it_ _may_ _be_) illustrate
the relationship between the two devices.

(VI.8) Maybe it's always pepper that makes people
       hot-tempered. (95)

An OV language like Japanese, on the other hand, makes use of
postverbal elements to supplement verb forms, such as _rasii_
'(it is) likely', _soo_ _desu_ 'it is a likelihood, likely', and
_no_ _daroo_ of (IV.5). The postverbal position of such elements
in OV languages reflects their structural patterning, as the
predominantly preverbal position of sentence adverbials
agrees with the expression of verbal qualifiers in VO
languages.

4.5. Compound and Complex Sentences

Compound and complex sentences are general in all types of
languages, though the distribution of kinds of alignment and
devices for it vary. In expressing coordination, VO languages
place particles before the coordinated element, typically the
last.

(21.1) and then the different branches of Arithmetic —
       Ambition, Distraction, Uglification, and Derision.
                                                       (103)

OV languages, by contrast, place such particles after the
coordinated elements, with possible omission after the last,
as in Japanese.

(21.2) Taroo to   Ziroo (to) ga   itta.
       Taroo and Ziroo and Ptc. went
       'Taroo and Ziroo went.'

Coordination is often accompanied by ellipsis, especially
in SVO languages, both with the same subject of a verb and
with different subjects.

(21.3) So she sat still and [she] said nothing. (102)

(21.4) Some of the jury wrote it down "important," and
       some [wrote it down] "unimportant." (124)

(21.5) The Owl and the Panther were sharing a pie. (112)

The kind of ellipsis exemplified in (21.4) is particularly
characteristic of SVO languages, for the differing subjects
and objects in their fixed order permit ready reconstruction
of the elided segments of the sentence. Both in VSO and
SOV languages, on the other hand, the reduced sentence may
give rise to ambiguities, for the nouns expressed by S and O
are not separated by a verb.

Ellipsis of the verb, or gapping, is also distinct in OV
as opposed to VO structure, for in OV the early forms of the
equivalent verbs are elided, as in Japanese.

(21.6) Taroo wa   empitu o to Ziroo wa kami   o katta.
       Taroo Ptc. pencils   and Ziroo   paper   brought
       'Taroo brought pencils and Ziroo paper.'

In coordination, clauses may be adversative as well as
parallel in meaning.

(21.7) I've read that in some book, but I don't remember
       when.

When parallel, nonfinite verbs are commonly used.

(21.8) He kept shifting from one foot to the other, looking
       uneasily at the Queen. (117)

While coordination, or parataxis, is general in sentences
of SVO languages, it is far more characteristic of OV languages, which tend to have many nonfinite forms for linking
clauses paratactically, as does Turkish. SVO languages on
the other hand are more widely characterized by subordination
or hypotaxis.

Subordination is often marked with conjunctions, and is
found whether or not the two related clauses have the same
subject.

(22.1) If you can't be civil, you'd better finish the story
for yourself. (81)

(22.2) Alice watched the White Rabbit as he fumbled over
the list. (122)

In OV languages, related clauses with the same subject tend
to make use of participles, as in Turkish.

(22.3) Rakı içince   her   şeyi   unutursun.
raki drinking every thing you-forget
'When you drink raki, you forget everything.'

Such nonfinite forms in OV languages may indicate varied
relationships, which in SVO languages are introduced by means
of specific conjunctions, as illustrated in the sentences
numbered (24) below.

In keeping with the tendency toward parataxis in OV
languages, quotations are commonly expressed without modification, as so-called direct quotations concluded by a quotative
particle or other marker. SVO languages on the other hand,
with their favoring of hypotaxis, tend to have devices for
indirect statements and questions. These devices may involve
special forms of verbs, or uses of substitutes. In current
English, special inflections (subjunctives) are no longer
found, with the exception of BE, but modals or past tense
forms are introduced in the indirect quotations.

(23.1) I told you butter wouldn't suit the works. (77)
(From: I told you, "Butter won't suit the works.")

(23.2) The very first thing she did was to look whether there was a fire in the fireplace. (148)
(From: Is there a fire in the fireplace?)

Special verbal patterns may also be used in adverbial clauses, notably in contrary-to-fact conditionals.

(24.1) You'd have guessed if you'd been up in the window with me. (143)

Yet for the most part, in English, adverbial clauses have unchanged verb forms. They express various relationships, generally through conjunctions. The subordinate clause may precede or follow the main clause, though often a conditional clause precedes, in keeping with a practice that has been characterized as universal.

(24.2) Now I growl when I'm pleased and wag my tail when I'm angry. (72) (Time)

(24.3) Only as it's asleep, I suppose it doesn't mind. (75) (Cause)

(24.4) We called him Tortoise because he taught us. (102) (Cause)

(24.5) Everything's got a moral, if only you can find it. (96) (Condition)

Conjunctions may however be omitted, especially in verse and the spoken language.

(24.6) You have baked me too brown, I must sugar my hair. (111) (Result)

Subordinate clauses tend to stand in an adverbial relationship with their matrix clauses, as the labels for the examples of (24) indicate. When on the other hand the relationship of the embedded clause to the matrix clause is comparable to that

of an object, the embedded elements are often called
complements, and the process is called complementation. (The
term is also used more broadly of an element that may follow
a verb, whether an object, a predicate noun, an adverb, or a
clause.) Complementation in VO languages differs characteristically from that in OV languages, for the markers stand
in different positions with regard to the matrix and the verb
of the embedded segment.

Complementation is found characteristically with *verba
dicendi* 'verbs of saying' and *verba sentiendi* 'verbs of
perception'.

> (25.1) She said afterwards that she had never seen in all
>   her life such a face as the King made. (150)

> (25.2) The Cat seemed to think that there was enough of
>   it now in sight. (91)

As in these examples, complements in English may be full
clauses, introduced by a complementizer, typically that.
Especially when the subject of both verbs is the same,
however, a nonfinite form may be used in the embedded clause,
either the infinitive introduced by (for) to or the gerund.

> (25.3) She wants for to know your history. (102)

> (25.4) The governess would never think of excusing me
>   lessons for that. (175)

While complements in SVO languages tend to be nominal clauses
or reduced nominal clauses, in OV languages they are generally
sentences embedded before a noun, a so-called nominalizer.
Many such nouns are so used in Japanese: sidai 'situation',
mono 'thing, person', koto 'fact' and probably an abbreviation of it in the quotative particle to.

Whatever the devices used for complementation, it is
simply a process for expanding the nuclear sentence; a clause

or a reduced form of a clause serves as an object. Similarly, adverbial clauses are expanded forms of adverbs. However involved they become, compound and complex sentences in general maintain the patterns of simple sentences, whether these are SVO, VSO, VOS, or OV. Further explorations in typology will lead to increased understanding of the characteristics of the more involved constructions in each type of language.

While the involved constructions dealt with in this section exploit the possibilities of each type, they do not overcome its weaknesses. These result in part from the rigidity imposed by a given type, as we may illustrate with SVO patterns. Theoretically, all sentences in an SVO language should follow that structure, as in sentence (1) above:

(1) Alice folded her hands.

In this structure the agent of the action is also the subject — grammatical, logical, and psychological — or whatever terms may be used for these functions. Yet another constituent of the sentence may occupy one of these roles and accordingly stand in initial position. When it does, the process is referred to as foregrounding, or marking.

Various devices are used for marking, with reference both to the nuclear sentence and to grammatical processes. Sections 4.6 and 4.7 will deal with these devices. It will be observed that the term *marking* may be applied narrowly, as here, or widely, so as to include the grammatical processes discussed in sections 4.7.3, 4.7.4, and 4.7.5.

4.6. Marking

Marking, or highlighting, may be achieved by departing from the standard order, by special intonation, or through the use of particles. In written texts the special intonation patterns

may be difficult to determine; but Lewis Carroll indicated
many of these by italicizing marked constituents, as illustrated below.

A prominent aim of marking is to put the object before the
verb, with or without the use of special intonation or
particles. In English the subject is then maintained before
the verb.

(VI.1) Oh dear, what nonsense I'm talking! (27)
       (Marking through OSV order)

(VI.2) That you won't! (46)
       (Marking through OSV order and intonation)

(VI.3) This, of course, Alice could not stand. (115)
       (Marking through OSV order, intonation, and particle)

Marking is also used prominently in abbreviated sentences.

(VI.4) Who is to give the prizes? Why, she, of course. (38)

It may apply to elements other than objects of verbs, as in
(VI.4) and the following examples.

(VI.5) Adjectives you can do anything with, but not verbs.
                                                   (214)

(VI.6) Said the mouse to the cur. (40)

(VI.7) Up I goes like a sky-rocket. (48)

Yet some patterns do not admit it, whether in VO or OV
languages. Among these are adpositions and comparatives of
inequality. A sequence like 'the dog is cat from big' would
scarcely be expected in English, or in any other VO language
unless it has undergone OV influence. Such patterns were
maintained in Homeric Greek and Classical Latin from their
earlier OV stages. Marking applies particularly to the freer
patterns, such as clauses and noun modifiers. It is especially

frequent in poetry, as with the adjectives in the following
example.

(VI.8) The dream-child moving through a land
        of wonders wild and new, (13)

Moreover, it is comparable to foregrounding, though this
process is here treated separately in (29) below, in view of
its use of grammatical processes other than those indicated
above for marking.

4.7. Grammatical Processes

The various language types are characterized by grammatical
constructions which result from or are at least closely
aligned with their pattern. As noted above, languages of the
SVO pattern require overt expression of subjects. Any subject
can, of course, be elided in a suitable context, such as the
subject in the answer to: 'What did you do then?" "Went home."
And every language includes sequences like: Yes! Thanks!
Dear me! which Jespersen called amorphous sentences. But in
comparison with OV languages like Japanese, English and other
SVO languages observe some constraints in ellipsis and in the
application of grammatical rules. The subject element is normally represented in an utterance, and the object element as
well where a transitive verb is used; the Japanese examples
in Chapter 2 may serve to illustrate that OV languages do not
require these. The normal requirement of subjects and the
frequent requirement of objects lead to a mandatory use of
substitutes in SVO languages, of which the most prominent
are pronouns.

4.7.1. Pronominalization

Pronouns are in the first instance substitutes for nouns. Their
uses, while manifold, may be illustrated with a few selections,
the first somewhat extended.

> (26.1) However, the egg only got larger and larger, and
> more and more human: when she had come within a few
> yards of it, she saw that it had eyes and a nose
> and mouth; and, when she had come close to it, she
> saw clearly that it was HUMPTY DUMPTY himself.
> "It ca'n't be anybody else!" she said to herself.
> "I'm as certain of it, as if his name were written
> all over his face!" (208)

This passage, the first paragraph of a new chapter, indicates
how in a new text a noun (egg) is used, and thereupon a
pronoun (it). To be sure, a pronoun is used at once for the
heroine (she); but by this time in the story Alice has been
well established as the central figure, and accordingly a
substitute is unambiguous. Besides serving as "substitutes,"
pronouns may convey additional information, as when himself
rather than itself is used after HUMPTY DUMPTY to identify the
egg as a well-known figure in nursery rhymes. Yet essentially
they are grammatical substitutes, required by the SVO pattern.

Introduced with reference to an identified noun in anaphora,
or in a further function to external objects in deixis, pronouns lend continuity to an account. On the other hand,
without adequate context, sentences in which they occur are
murky in meaning.

> (26.2) And oh, I wish you could see her after the birds!
> (41)

This sentence is obscure unless one knows that her refers to
Dinah, Alice's cat; the references of I and you are also clear
from the context.

> (26.3) Wouldn't it be murder to leave it behind? (70)

With two uses of <u>it</u>, this sentence is obscure unless one knows
that the first <u>it</u> is an "anticipatory subject" and that the
second refers to "the child."

(26.4) "Which is just the case with <u>mine</u>," said the Hatter.
(77)

This sentence is even vaguer with its three anaphoric elements:
<u>mine</u> refers to the Hatter's watch; <u>the case</u> refers to the fact
that a watch does not indicate the year "because it stays the
same for such a long time together"; and <u>which</u> refers to the
similarity of the watch and other timepieces in not indicating
the year.

Like <u>which</u> in (26.4), pronouns often refer to situations or
actions rather than simply substitute for nouns. Similarly,
while <u>they</u> in (26.5) refers to "three sisters," <u>that</u> refers
to their "living on treacle."

(26.5) "They couldn't have done that, you know." (81)

Pronouns are accordingly substitutes for any syntactic element
with substantival use.

In their anaphoric uses pronouns are comparable to elements
in other types of languages, such as <u>kore</u> 'this', <u>sore</u> 'that',
<u>are</u> 'that there' in Japanese. But pronouns used personally
may be expressed by other devices, such as honorifics in
Japanese, or through lexical distinctions. Thus any speaker
of Japanese would interpret the verb form <u>itasimasu</u> as indicating "humility" and thus appropriate only to a first person
subject: <u>I</u> or <u>we</u>. On the other hand, the verb form <u>irassyai-</u>
<u>masu</u> is "honorific" and thus appropriate to a second or
third person subject.

(26.6) Hon o   yonde   irassyaimasu.
       book Obj. reading BE

This sentence could not be interpreted: 'I am reading a book', for the honorific _irassyaimasu_ entails a subject other than the speaker or first person. Japanese has many devices to express status, which obviate a need for pronouns (Kuno 1973: 18 - 22, 127 - 136). Whether or not other OV languages parallel it in the wealth of such devices, their structure leads to less explicit expression of the subject, and accordingly less use of pronouns than is found in SVO languages.

The availability of pronouns has led to various patterns in which their primary use is not anaphoric. They may be used to avoid the mandatory theme : rheme contrast of constituents of simple SVO sentences. By placing a demonstrative in initial position, it is possible to emphasize the situation rather than the subject.

> (26.7) Now, Kitty, let's consider who it was that dreamed it all. This is a serious question ... (271) (Not: the question is serious)

Interrogative pronouns may be used rhetorically rather than to ask a question.

> (26.8) What do you suppose is the use of a child without any meaning? (251) (Not: a child ... is useless)

Relative pronouns are used as a linking device in the construction often referred to as _cleft_.

> (26.9) I'm one that has spoken to a King, I am. (210)

Moreover, in descriptive relative constructions relative pronouns are scarcely more than grammatical markers.

> (26.10) Here he looked at Tweedledee, who immediately sat down on the ground, and tried to hide himself under the umbrella. (191)

In keeping with the heavy reliance of past grammars on morphological markers, clauses introduced by relative pronouns

have been viewed as comparable, whether they are restrictive
or descriptive. Unlike many languages, English uses relative
clauses in both restrictive and descriptive functions,
distinguishing them primarily through intonation. Even a
language as closely related to English as German has demonstrative clauses corresponding to English descriptive or
appositional relatives. The many studies devoted to explicating
differences between the two types of English relative clauses
might gain perspective from examination of comparable constructions in other languages. For in descriptive relative
clauses the pronoun is largely a grammatical marker. In
(26.10) who could be replaced with and he or but he. The
relative pronoun is a compact and convenient device in a
linguistic type requiring expression for subjects and objects.

The prominence of pronouns in SVO languages is paralleled
by that of other substitutes, both for substantives and for
other syntactic elements. Among these further substitutes
are quantity words and numerals.

(26.11) It's laid for a great many more than three. (75)

Besides the pronoun it, which refers to 'table', the quantity
word more and the numeral three refer to guests at a meal.

4.7.2. Anaphora

As for pronouns, such use of substitutes is connective, in
providing close relationships with previous matter. In this
way it is similar to use of anaphoric elements: this, that,
here, there.

(27.1) "That you won't!" thought Alice. (46)
        (That = Then I'll go round and get in at the window.)

The substitute refers to an entire sentence expressing the

rabbit's proposed action. Anaphoric particles, such as <u>so</u>, may also substitute for entire sentences.

(27.2) "There ought to be some men moving about somewhere — and so there are!" (164)
(So = Some men are moving about.)

Auxiliaries such as forms of DO commonly substitute for verbs, as <u>had</u> does below, indicating past perfect tense:

(27.3) "She's grown a good deal!" was her first remark. She had indeed. (160)

A further prominent anaphoric device is deletion, which is carried out under highly specified conditions, as has long been observed, to yield a zero substitute. Thus in coordination specific elements can be elided, such as subjects and other constituents.

(27.4) At last he said, "You're traveling the wrong way," and (0 = he) shut up the window, and (0 = he) went away. (170)

(27.5) ... and everybody jumped up in alarm, Alice (0 = jumped up) among the rest. (172)

Substitutes may also refer to adverbial phrases, as does <u>there</u> in (27.6) for a phrase like <u>along the river-bank</u>.

(27.6) There are some scented rushes! (204)

In a further use <u>there</u> has been extended as a pure grammatical marker in foregrounding, where it occupies the place of the grammatical subject but is in no way anaphoric.

(27.7) There's certainly too much pepper in that soup! (66)

The grammatical application of <u>there</u> for emphasis is so prominent in English that it will be discussed separately below. Like other anaphoric elements, <u>there</u> has come to be a grammatical marker, assisting in providing flexibility of expression in the SVO pattern.

4.7.3. Passivization

Flexibility of expression is achieved also through the process known as passivization. With the introduction of a passive the emphasis falls on the object, or the verb, rather than on the agent of the action, commonly the subject of active verbs. When misused, as often in technical language, passive constructions lead to dullness, as Carroll demonstrates with his satirization of historical writing.

> (28.1) William the Conqueror, whose cause was favored by the Pope, was soon submitted to by the English. (36)

Presumably the passive is so favored in technical and scientific writing because it permits an SV sequence when the agent is unknown, or unimportant.

> (28.2) She had read several nice little stories about children who had got burnt ... (27) (Mention of the agent of the burning is not essential.)

> (28.3) I must have been changed for Mabel. (29) (The agent of the change is not known.)

The avoidance of mention of an agent thus may lead to emphasis on the verbal phrase. In the following example the target or object is highlighted more than it would be in the active variant: "They shall not behead you."

> (28.4) "You sha'n't be beheaded!" said Alice. (88)

Such an effect results even if the agent is introduced, as in the second example followed by a participle with passive force:

> (28.5) "Not quite right, I'm afraid," said Alice, timidly: "some of the words have got altered." (58)

> (28.6) I wish they'd get the trial done. (114)

The active possible variant: 'I wish they'd finish the trial"
is less forceful.

Passivization thus leads to foregrounding of the predicate,
whether its object or its verb, or both. It achieves this
effect in part by deleting the subject.

(28.7) How is that to be done, I wonder? (62)

An active variant:

(28.7') How am I to do that?

would specify a definite actor, here I, or an unidentified
actor:

(28.7") How is anyone to do that?

Definite mention of the first person actor would go counter
to the sense, for someone besides the speaker might carry out
the action. Mention of unidentified actors also is avoided,
as unnecessary in view of the effect of the passive construction.

(28.8) There ought to be a book written about me, that
        there ought. (45)

Its function in this way may be most forcibly illustrated by
noting that indirect objects may become subjects of passive
verbs as well as direct objects.

(28.9) She was given a book.

In the same way the passive in English does not require that
an agent be included to correspond to the subject of the
active variant.

(28.10) That town can only be reached by boat.

This sentence may be derived from:

(28.10') One can only reach that town by boat.

which does not lead to:

(28.10") That town can only be reached by someone with
a boat.

The passive in English then is not simply a voice used
when "the subject is represented as the receiver or product
of an action" but rather a grammatical construction used for
highlighting constituents which by their normal order in an
SVO pattern do not receive such emphasis. It is conveniently
used for constructions in which the active subject would be an
inanimate or inert entity.

(28.11) She ... noticed that they [insides of the well]
were filled with cupboards and bookshelves. (18)
(Not: cupboards filled them)

For somewhat the same reason the passive is used with verbs
that combine an appositional element with an object.

(28.12) It was labeled "ORANGE MARMALADE." (18)
(Not: Someone had labeled it "ORANGE MARMALADE.")

In contrast with the passive in many other languages, such
as Japanese, the English passive construction then is a
grammatical device primarily for foregrounding the verbal
action or its object, but other constituents of the predicate
as well.

4.7.4. Foregrounding; Topicalization

Other devices as well may be used for highlighting or topicalization. The subject may be taken out of the clause, and its
place filled with a pronoun.

(29.1) As to the bottles, they each took a pair of plates.
(266)

Often the subject is placed last, in rhetorically emphatic

position; the construction is commonly referred to as extraposition.

(29.2) It's rather curious, you know, this sort of life!
(44)

By extraposition especially subjects are highlighted,
whether they are nouns, or nominal phrases or clauses. It
then serves as anticipatory subject.

(29.3) It'll never do for you to be lolling about in the
grass like that! (250)

(29.4) Wouldn't it be much easier to leave it behind? (70)

Other syntactic elements, such as adjectives, adverbs,
and prepositions, may also be foregrounded by placement in
initial position.

(29.5) How surprised he'll be when he finds out who I am.
(43)

(29.6) Very soon the Rabbit noticed Alice. (43)

(29.7) Up I goes like a sky-rocket. (48)

Change of order, often to initial position, then is a
frequently used device for foregrounding constituents, or
topicalization.

Distribution of emphasis is also carried out by use of the
existential there. This construction avoids foregrounding of
any one constituent of the sentence, highlighting instead
the entire situation rather than either the action or the
actor.

(29.8) There was a dispute going on between the Executioner,
the King, and the Queen. (93)

Neither the dispute nor its progress nor the set of dispu-
tants is of central concern but rather the dispute in its
progress among them. This pattern then is a device to avoid

the inherent highlighting given to subjects in SVO languages
or to elements in final position, as the following examples
also illustrate.

(29.9) There was a large mushroom growing near her. (52)

(29.10) And certainly there was a most extraordinary noise
         going on within. (64)

Grammatical devices have then been developed in English which
highlight individual constituents or the substance of the
entire sentence.

4.7.5. Clefting

A special construction which has come to be highly prominent
for highlighting individual constituents is known as clefting.
By "cleaving" the clause through use of it with a form of BE,
this construction gives special emphasis to the element after
BE, whether it is the subject, object, or other constituent.

(30.1) It was this last remark that had made the whole
        party look so grave and anxious. (94)
        (Not: This past remark had made the whole party
        look grave and anxious.)

The sentence in parentheses would single out the appearance of
the whole party as grave and anxious; the cleft sentence
highlights the remark.

    The emphasized elements may or may not be followed by a
relative pronoun.

(30.2) It's the most curious thing I ever saw in my life!
                                                    (74)

Conjunctions may also be used when appropriate.

(30.3) It was so long since she had been anything near
        the right size that it felt quite strange at first.
                                                    (62)

Cleft sentences may be interrogative, or subordinate.

(30.4) Is that the reason so many things are put out here?
(80)

(30.5) Alice knew it was the Rabbit coming to look for her.
(46)

As in this last example, the clefted sequence may be reduced to a participial clause.

Clefting has led to patterns which use other devices than the anticipatory subject it, notably there.

(30.6) There could be no doubt that it had a very turn-up nose. (70)

The nonclefted sentence would be impossible without further change (*That it had a turn-up nose could be no doubt.). Such extensions of clefting illustrate its special force in the language.

A similar construction, known as pseudo-clefting, distributes foregrounding so that it does not fall on the object or other constituent put in first place.

(30.7) A loaf of bread ... is what we chiefly need. (186)

The simple version of this sentence would highlight the object as last element.

(30.7') We chiefly need a loaf of bread.

Typically, a pseudo-cleft places what initially, rather than in the modification applied by Carroll:

(30.7") What we chiefly need is a loaf of bread.

The construction is then similar to the use of interrogatives in exclamations or indirect questions.

(30.8) What a fight we might have for the crown, now! (231)

(30.9) Where the noise came from, she couldn't make out.
(237)

Like these it achieves emphasis for an element by arranging it
nearer the first position in the sentence.

Grammatical processes have in this way been developed in
SVO languages which compensate for some of their rigidities
or even inadequacies. English is not unique in developing such
processes. Nor are the processes developed in English the only
possible ones for variety of expression in the SVO type.
Those in other languages, such as German es (ist) 'it (is)'
in clefting, or the French c'est 'it is', might be similarly
explored and illustrated here. Yet English provides adequate
illustration of the devices used to introduce flexibility in
a language, whatever the strengths and disadvantages of its
simple structures. Further typological study will identify
the array of such constructions in SVO languages, as well as
in languages of the other types, and in this way increase our
understanding of language.

4.8. Morphological Characteristics

A number of morphological characteristics have been identified
for specific language types. Prominent among these is the
placement of affixes, notably those expressing the verbal
qualifiers. In VSO languages these precede the central verb;
in OV languages, on the other hand, they follow, as is
illustrated by the Japanese verbal inflections in Chapter 2.
The placement of qualifier affixes is in accordance with
the principle of arrangement stated in section 1.3. VSO
languages have prefixes; OV languages have suffixes.

The principle applies also in some degree to expressions
for case in the noun and to derivational processes. VSO

languages thus often modify the initial word in genitive constructions, e.g., Classical Hebrew dāvār 'word', dəvar elohim 'word of God'; inflection for congruence may not however observe the principle. Like inflection for qualifiers, in VO languages derivational affixes are commonly prefixed while in OV languages they are suffixed. Yet it must be observed that morphological characteristics are highly conservative, and accordingly the patterning of affixes in any language at a given time must be carefully interpreted. It may represent an archaic situation, or a characteristic which is being eliminated but is still relatively widespread. English illustrates such situations. In the older period, especially in its most archaic materials, it maintains a relatively rich system of suffixed inflections. These have steadily been reduced in the course of the history of English, until today the remaining inflections are secondary in importance to the device of arrangement and to the use of function words.

4.8.1. Inflection

As noted above, English has very few inflections, many fewer than did Old English. Hypotheses have been proposed in attempts to account for their loss. Some scholars have ascribed it to phonological reasons, pointing to the introduction of a strong initial stress accent in Proto-Germanic which in their view led to a consequent loss of inflectional suffixes. Others have advanced as counterargument to this hypothesis the observation that new elements might have been introduced as the older inflectional suffixes were lost.

It may also be observed that SVO languages by their basic structure do not require elements to identify the most

frequent cases, those for the subject and object. Such
identification is achieved by position of the verb. Accordingly inflection for case may well be unnecessary in SVO
languages when the order of elements is fixed. Before it is
fixed, however, affixes are significant in indicating case
forms and concord classes. Languages moving toward an SVO
structure, like Classical Greek and Latin, and to a lesser
extent Old English, then tend to have a full set of affixes
to indicate concord of descriptive and limiting adjectives
with nouns, and of nominal elements with verbs, as well as
some cases.

In SOV and similarly in VSO languages, on the other hand,
devices are necessary to distinguish subjects and objects, or
to distinguish sequences of two nouns, as is often done for
genitive : noun sequences with a device like that illustrated
above for Classical Hebrew. Such distinction may be made with
affixes, but also as in Japanese with particles. In OV
languages these particles are postposed; in VO languages they
are preposed. Greenberg has advanced a universal that an SOV
language "almost always has a case system" (1966: 113 #41).
As may be noted in the Japanese examples of Chapter 2, this
universal is valid if nouns plus postpositions are assumed to
make up case systems; these then are semantic systems, not
necessarily morphologically marked. Under such assumption,
then, case systems are important for both VSO and SOV languages; in VSO languages preposed particles or prepositions
may distinguish different case relationships as postposed
elements do in SOV languages.

In English on the other hand case relationships may be
unspecified, as with the frequently cited verbs which permit
a variety of semantic cases to be used without special
marking, such as open.

(VIII.1) The custodian opened the door. (Subject = agent)

(VIII.2) The key opened the door. (Subject = instrument)

(VIII.3) The door opened. (Subject = target or object)

Moreover, clauses having verbs with an indirect object as
well as a direct may distinguish these simply by means of
arrangement.

(VIII.4) The attendant showed the visitors their room.

Inflection then, or even the expression of case relationships
by means of particles, is not prominent in English.

In nouns all inflection for case has been lost with the
exception of the genitive. Yet as noted above the inflected
genitive has also been replaced largely by phrases with the
preposition of. Pronominal inflection is more conservative
in maintaining distinct object forms in six elements: I : me,
he : him, she : her, we : us, they : them, who : whom. Here too,
however, the usage is observed less than in the past;
especially after prepositions the old nominative form is often
used. Case inflection then has been receding in English, and
is still.

Of the various verb qualifiers, apart from the participles
only the past tense has retained a morphological marker,
generally by means of the D suffix: heed : heeded, hiss :
hissed, heel : heeled, with internal inflection yielding to it.
The other qualifiers, as discussed above, are expressed
through function words.

English then, as a characteristic SVO language, makes
little use of inflection. The most prominent inflected
elements maintained are those for concord categories: plural
number in the noun and third person singular in the verb.
Having preserved these inflections, English has not succeeded

to the state of Chinese, which has had SVO structure far
longer. While loss of final elements as a result of strong
initial stress must be taken into account, English lends
support to the hypothesis that SVO languages with fixed word
order will tend to give up inflection for case in the noun and
for qualifiers in the verb.

4.8.2. Derivation

The derivational processes of English are in great part conservative, for compounds are made in accordance with OV patterning. Nouns and adjectives prepose the modifying element to
the modified element, as in Cheshire Cat, queer-looking, and
so on. Moreover, suffixation is the primary derivational
process in complex words, as in curiosity, remarkable,
cheerfully.

   Yet in the past two millennia prefixes have come to be
prominent, whether in nouns, verbs, or other elements, as in
insolence, adjourn, aloud. These formations, as noted above,
go counter to the OV constraint against prefixes. Other OV
patterns of the early period have been abandoned, such as
the use of object-verb compounds, as in Old English yrfe-numa
'inheritance + taker = heir'. Nor have they been modified to
the VO pattern of such compounds, which is prominent in
Chinese and also in Japanese borrowings based on Chinese, as
in the well-known pair: (OV) hara-kiri 'stomach-cut', (VO)
seppuku 'cut-stomach' for a traditional Japanese form of
suicide. The English verbs of this OV compounding pattern,
like baby-sit, are generally assumed to be back formations
from adjectival compounds, such as baby-sitting. Accordingly
they are not productive formations of the OV pattern. The
predominant patterns of derivation are then archaic residues
from the Proto-Indo-European and early dialect periods.

4.8.3. Morphophonemic Processes

Sandhi changes have for the most part been treated as processes
of individual languages rather than as processes to be associated with specific types of language. The lack of concern for
general principles may be understood, for phonological processes seem remote from patterns of arrangement related to
expressions of meaning. Yet a general tendency has been
proposed: OV languages tend to have progressive assimilation
if the appropriate phonological conditions are present, and VO
languages to have regressive. If appropriate conditions exist
for vowels to be modified, OV languages then would have vowel
harmony — defined as modification of later vowels in a word
by earlier vowels — and VO languages would have umlaut, that
is, modification of earlier vowels by later. Similar directions of modification would prevail in consonant assimilation.

Modern English shows no consistent direction of modification. In the major inflectional suffixes, such as the suffixes
in the past and past participle [əd t d], the assimilation is
progressive. In most derivational suffixes, however, the
assimilation is regressive; t > š before a former palatal j
with -ious, e.g., vivacious, or t > š/č with -ion, e.g.,
action, and -ure, e.g., posture, and so on. The progressive
assimilation of the inflectional affixes involves the oldest
morphological markers, yet it would be hazardous to suggest
that in contrast with that in derivation this assimilation
should be related to the older OV structure of pre - Old
English. Phonological processes have not been extensively
investigated with attention to the structure of their
language. When they are, the many variables involved in
specific developments must be noted with regard to both
specific languages and specific phonological changes. On
the basis of such investigations, more precise generalizations

may be proposed in the future. If English were to be characterized for phonological processes at present, these like
its derivational patterns would be said to reflect in great
part its earlier OV structure, accompanied by phonological
changes expected in VO languages.

4.9. Phonological Characteristics

4.9.1. Syllabification

English syllables show a wide range of structures, from
simple vowels as in a to sequences opened and closed by
several consonants, as in sprints. While English shows such
diverse syllabic structures, these can only tenuously be
related to language types. The most readily observable correlation is that between OV languages and sequences of open
syllables. The Japanese examples in Chapter 2 provide good
illustrations, though similar observations could be cited
from other OV languages, such as the Dravidian or the Turkic.
The early Germanic material also manifests such a structure,
as in the frequently cited Gallehus inscription.

> (31.1) Ek Hle-wa-ga-stiʀ Hol-ti-jaʀ hor-na ta-wi-do.
> I Hlewagastir   of-Holt   horn   made
> 'I Hlewagastir of Holt made the horn.'

When one notes that the first person pronoun ek had lost a
final a vowel, and that syllables like Hol- and hor- reflect
vocalic resonants, the syllabic structure of Proto-Germanic
from which English developed was virtually as open as that of
Japanese. On this basis we can account for the regularity of
the first Germanic consonant shift, for virtually all the
shifted consonants stood in the same position in their
syllables, either before syllabics or before resonants.

The change in Modern English to closed syllables with
final consonant clusters, as in guest versus ga-stiʀ and

horn versus hor-na, is ascribed to losses of finals resulting
from a heavy initial stress accent. Yet, as with the change
to little inflection in English, the relationship between
change of language type and change of syllabic structure is
intriguing. OV languages are often agglutinative in morphology,
and the suffixed syllables seem readily added if of a C(C)V
structure, as in Japanese, or in other OV languages, as the
following Quechua verb form illustrates:

(31.2) maga-yku-na-ku-sqanku
'they finally fought each other'

(Bills et al provide many further examples — 1969: 335.)
In nonagglutinative languages, by contrast, there are no
grounds for such syllabic structure. The English syllabic
patterning may then be characteristic of SVO languages, and
accordingly may contrast with a favored pattern for OV
languages with their predominantly open syllables.

4.9.2. Suprasegmentals

The current English suprasegmental system was established some
time before the beginning of our era, but not so much earlier
that the final syllables were reduced by the time the Gallehus
inscription was produced — about 350 A.D. When it was
established, a stress accent system was introduced for words
or wordlike groups, and a pitch system maintained for clause
intonation patterns. Earlier both word groups and clauses were
characterized by pitch patterns, somewhat as in Japanese today.
Sentence (1) may be used to illustrate the two systems of
the current language.

(1) Alice folded her hands.
    Word-grouping, based on stress groups:
    æləs fówlded ərǽndz

Clause grouping, based on pitch alignments:

^{2}æləs   fowlded   ər^{3}ændz^1

As the indications above for strong stress ($^{\prime}$) and high pitch
(^{3}) indicate, the highest pitch of an English clause or simple
sentence coincides with a strong stress. Some uses of the
resulting intonation patterns have been discussed above, in
section 4.3, examples (10) and (11).

Suprasegmental patterns have not been adequately studied
in relation to language types, so that also with reference to
them any generalizations will have to wait for considerably
further study. Yet stress systems, accompanied by reduction
of vowels, seem to be associated with VO languages, whether
VSO or SVO, and pitch systems with OV languages. But the
patterning and relationship of possible systems with specific
language types is imprecise. To judge from their distribution
in specific areas of the world, suprasegmental systems seem
to be diffused among neighboring languages. Information on the
basis and history of a suprasegmental system in any given
language must be known, as well as the system of neighboring
languages, before any useful statements can be made about its
relationship with the structure of that language. For English
and its earlier stages in any event, the suprasegmental
systems are quite clear, that for the stage preceding ca. 500
B.C. as well as that today.

4.9.3. Segmentals

English has a moderate number of consonant and vowel phonemes,
however its segmental system is analyzed. The figure of
twenty-four consonants can be well supported; the vowels
range in the neighborhood of fifteen, depending on the
analyst's views. The structure of the segmental portion of

phonological systems seems to have little relationship with
the typological structure of a language. Yet OV languages
commonly have relatively small sets of vowels, as in Japanese
and Proto-Indo-European. VSO languages, however, may also
contain few vowels, as does Arabic. While the sets of consonants and vowels seem to be the last formal elements which
might be governed by principles regulating other characteristics of a language, they too must be carefully studied,
for possible relationship with language types.

There seem to be no grounds for relating semantic structures with the syntactic, morphological, or phonological
structures of a language. To propose associating a numeral
system, for example, a decimal or a quaternary, with any
formal linguistic structure is totally unwarranted in view of
our information about languages. As another example the
distribution of kinship systems, like the Omaha, shows no
relation with formal linguistic characteristics. Semantic
systems must accordingly be treated apart from typological
patterns based, as here, on form.

In recent treatments of typological patterning, even many
syntactic constructions have been excluded. One example is
the order of descriptive adjectives preceding nouns, as in
the little old tumble-down houses. Their order seems determined more by semantic than by formal criteria which are
language specific.

Further study may disclose such relationships, and also
significant patterns beyond the thirty dealt with above.
Investigation of additional languages will also clarify the
relationships between functional, pragmatic, and syntactic
forces. The three following chapters exemplify procedures
that may be pursued in such investigations. Yet English too,
as the examples in this chapter illustrate, shows the forces

at work in living language which modify the basic patterns to produce richness of communication without interfering with the underlying principles that determine its basic structure.

5. An Exploration of Mandarin Chinese

Charles N. Li & Sandra A. Thompson

5.1. Introduction

The language whose typology we are going to describe is
Mandarin Chinese; genetically, Mandarin is a member of the
Chinese branch of the Sino-Tibetan family. It is the major
Chinese language in that (1) it is the native language of
more than half of the people of China, (2) these native
speakers inhabit about 75 percent of the land area of China,
(3) it is the official language of both mainland China and
Taiwan, and (4) the written language is structurally and
lexically closer to Mandarin than to any of the other Chinese
languages.

A number of Chinese languages are mutually unintelligible.
This mutual intelligibility is largely due to phonological
and lexical factors; from the grammatical point of view, these
languages are rather similar. Thus, most of the typological
features of Mandarin discussed in this paper are shared by
the other Chinese languages with some differences of detail.
However, from here on, we will speak of Mandarin without the
qualifying phrase "and in the Chinese languages in general."
We will point out those few characteristics which distinguish
Mandarin from its sister languages.

When Mandarin is compared to other languages of the world,
it displays a number of typologically salient features. On

the phonological level, Mandarin is a tone language, and its syllable structure is relatively highly constrained. On the grammatical side, we will try to show that the most note-worthy feature is the fact that Mandarin is an isolating language with practically no grammatical morphology. From this fact follow the other typological features that we will be discussing: its word order characteristics, the prominence assigned to the notion of "topic," the lack of a case system, the system of "serial verb constructions," and the fact that there is very little evidence for claiming syntactic (as opposed to semantic) knowledge on the part of its speakers.

5.2. Tone and Syllable Structure

All the Chinese languages are lexical tone languages: part of the lexical representation of each syllable in every word includes the information as to what tone it carries. However, of all the Chinese languages, Mandarin's tone system is the simplest: first, it has only four lexical tones, the smallest number of tones of any Chinese language (e.g., Standard Cantonese has nine tones). Second, Mandarin has relatively few tone sandhi rules, as compared with most of the dialects of the Amoy language, such as Taiwanese and Fukienese. Since excellent descriptions of the tone system of Mandarin are readily available in the literature, we will be very brief here (see, for example, Chao 1961; 1968; Cheng 1971; Kratochvil 1968).

For stressed syllables, there are four possible tones:

High	bā
Rising	bá
Dipping	bǎ
Falling	bà

Pinyin, the official spelling system for Mandarin proposed by
the People's Republic of China, which we will be using
throughout, represents these tones by four iconic diacritic
tone marks, as illustrated above for the ba syllable.

Unstressed syllables have what is known as the "neutral
tone": its pitch is determined entirely by the tone of the
preceding syllable. Unstressed syllables have no tone diacritic in the Pinyin spelling system.

The syllable structure of all the Chinese languages is
relatively simple compared with that of, say, English: for
example, all of the languages forbid consonant clusters and
allow only a restricted number of consonants in a syllable-
final position. But, as with tone, Mandarin is the simplest
in syllable structure:

$$(C) \ (V) \ V \ (\ \{^V_N\} \ )$$

Every syllable has a nuclear vowel; diphthongs and triphthongs
may occur; an initial consonant is optional, and the only
final consonants which are permitted are the nasal segments
n and ŋ.

The essential lack of morphology, which we will show to
have significant ramifications throughout the grammar of
Mandarin, can easily be seen to affect the phonology of
Mandarin as well: there are few morphophonological processes.
The phonologically interesting phenomena all center around
the effects of rate of speech on tones and segments, and the
vowel height constraints on diphthongs and triphthongs (see
Cheng 1971 for details).

5.3. Word Order

Since the appearance of Greenberg's milestone paper on word
order typologies (1963), linguists have been attempting to

characterize languages in terms of his basic three-way
distinction according to the position of the verb: VSO, SVO,
or SOV. Mandarin is not at all a straightforward example of
distinctions of this type, for three reasons.

First, the notion of "subject" is not a well-defined one
in the grammar of Mandarin.

A second and closely related fact is that the order in
which basic constituents occur is governed to a large extent
by pragmatic and semantic considerations rather than grammatical ones. What this means is that both verb-medial and verb-
final sentence types exist, neither being clearly more "basic"
or "neutral" than the other. Languages which are relatively
easy to characterize in Greenberg's terms are always those in
which the word order is principally determined on strictly
grammatical grounds (i.e., independent of pragmatic or semantic principles), such as French and Turkish.

Third, whether Mandarin is taken to be verb-medial or
verb-final, it is inconsistent with respect to the features
that correlate with VO or OV order according to Greenberg's
typological scheme. For example, sample texts reveal a greater
number of VO than OV sentences, yet modifiers must precede
their heads, which is an OV concomitant.

Let us examine in more detail each of these three problems
in determining word order for Mandarin.

The first problem has to do with the fact that Mandarin is
a language in which "subject" is not a clearly definable
notion. In Li and Thompson 1976b we suggested that Mandarin
is in fact a topic-prominent rather than a subject-prominent
language. That is, in Mandarin, the basic structure of
sentences can be more insightfully treated in a description
in which the topic-comment relation rather than the subject-

predicate relation plays a major role, although many sentences, of course, do have identifiable subjects. An example of a topic-comment sentence is:

(1) Nèikuài tián wǒmen zhòng daòzi.
    that   field we   grow rice
    'That field (Topic), we grow rice (on it).'

In such a sentence, the initial noun phrase <u>nèikuài</u> <u>tián</u> 'that field' is playing the role of the topic with respect to the comment <u>wǒmen</u> <u>zhòng</u> <u>daòzi</u> 'we grow rice.' Evidence that it does not bear the grammatical relation *subject* to the rest of the sentence includes the fact that there is no selectional relationship between this topic and the comment. Now, in a language in which such sentences are part of the repertory of basic sentence types, it is clearly no simple matter to determine what the basic word order is according to Greenberg's criteria: the verb is preceded by two nouns, but neither the SOV nor the OSV label characterizes sentences like (1).

A second problem in determining the basic word order for Mandarin is the related fact that it is primarily pragmatic and semantic factors rather than grammatical ones which determine the order of major constituents with respect to the verb. Thus, on the pragmatic side, preverbal position is a signal for definiteness for topics, subjects, and objects (see Li and Thompson 1975; 1976a; 1976b). On the semantic side, pre- or postverbal position signals a meaning difference for adverbial expressions (see Tai 1973a and Light 1976).

Let us briefly illustrate these two points. First, we have said that definiteness is signaled by preverbal position for topics, subjects, and objects. Since topics, as in (1), are definite by definition, they are always preverbal, but subjects and objects may appear on either side of the verb:

(2) a. <u>Zéi</u>   pǎo le.
    thief run Asp.
    '<u>The thief</u> has run away.'

   b. Pǎo le   <u>zéi</u>.
    run Asp. thief
    '<u>A thief</u> has run away.'

(2a) shows that the preverbal subject is interpreted as
definite, while the postverbal subject of (2b) is interpreted
as indefinite. In (3a) it can be seen that the unmarked postverbal object is taken as indefinite, while any of the three
possible preverbal positions render it definite (3b - d):

(3) a. Wǒ mǎi <u>shū</u> le.
    I buy book Asp.
    'I bought a <u>book</u>.'

   b. Wǒ bǎ   <u>shū</u> mǎi le.
    I def. obj. book buy Asp.
    'I bought <u>the book</u>.'

   c. <u>Shū</u> wǒ mǎi le.
    book I buy Asp.
    '<u>The book</u>, I bought it.' (Topic/Contrastive)

   d. Wǒ <u>shū</u> mǎi le.
    I book buy Asp.
    'I bought <u>the book</u>.' (Contrastive)

(The pragmatic difference signaled by pre- versus postverbal
position holds for nouns which are not morphologically marked
for definiteness with a demonstrative; under certain conditions it is possible for a noun marked for definiteness to
appear postverbally, particularly when contrastively stressed:

  (i) Wǒ mǎi le <u>nèiben</u> shū.
    I buy Asp. that   book
    'I bought that book.')

Second, to illustrate the semantic difference between pre-
and postverbal position for adverbial expressions, we can
examine time phrases and place phrases.

Time phrases. Preverbal time phrases tend to signal punctual time, while postverbal time phrases tend to signal durative time:

(4) a. Wǒ <u>sān-diǎn-zhōng</u> kāi-huì.
    I   3:00   hold-meeting
    'I have a meeting <u>at 3:00</u>.'

   b. *Wǒ kāi-huì   <u>sān-diǎn-zhōng</u>.
     I hold-meeting 3:00

(5) a. Wǒ shuì le   <u>sānge</u> <u>zhōngtou</u>.
    I sleep Asp. 3   hours
    'I slept <u>for</u> <u>three</u> <u>hours</u>.'

   b. *Wǒ <u>sānge</u> <u>zhōngtou</u> shuì   le.
     I 3   hours   sleep Asp.

Place phrases. Preverbal position signals location of actions, while postverbal position signals location of participants or object:

(6) a. Tā <u>zài</u> <u>zhuōzi-shang</u> tiào.
    he at table-on   jump
    'He jumped (up and down) on the table.'

   b. Tā tiào <u>zài</u> <u>zhuōzi-shang</u>.
    he jump at table-on
    'He jumped onto the table.'

   c. Tā <u>zài</u> <u>zhuōzi-shang</u> huà.
    he at table-on   draw
    'He is drawing at the table.'

   d. Tā huà <u>zài</u> <u>zhuōzi-shang</u>.
    he draw at table-on
    'He is drawing (something) on the table.'

With both pragmatic and semantic factors influencing the order of noun phrases with respect to the verb, then, it is eminently clear that "basic word order" will be difficult to establish.

Before leaving this point, however, let us see what happens
if we select some criterion according to which we might try to
pick either VO or OV order as "basic" for Mandarin. One such
criterion, which most linguists would consider reasonable,
might be the *unmarked* pragmatic value for subjects and objects,
the unmarked value for subjects being definite, for objects,
indefinite. According to this criterion, the least marked word
order for Mandarin will be SVO for sentences which have
subjects and objects. Corroborating this observation is the
fact that a sample text count yields more SVO than SOV
sentences.

Unfortunately, we cannot be entirely happy with the results
of applying this criterion, because we must still face the
third problem in determining a word order for Mandarin:
according to Greenberg's discussion, certain features should
correlate with the order in which the object and verb occur.
Mandarin can be seen to have some of the features of an OV
language and some of those of a VO language, with more of the
former than of the latter (see Li and Thompson 1974a and
1974b for more discussion). The presence of both OV and VO
features has been observed by other linguists, e.g., Tai
(1973b), Light (1976), and Teng (1975):

OV Language Features	*VO Language Features*
1. OV sentences occur.	1. VO sentences occur.
2. Prepositional phrases precede the V (except for time and place phrases) (see above).	2. Prepositions exist.
3. Postpositions exist.	3. Auxiliaries precede the V.
4. Relative clauses precede the N.	4. Complex sentences are almost always VO.

OV Language Features	*VO Language Features*

5. Genitive phrases precede
   the N.

6. Aspect markers follow
   the V.

7. Certain adverbials
   precede the V.

Example sentences illustrating each of the OV features are:

1. OV sentences occur.

(7) Zhāng-sān bǎ   tā mà   le.
    Zhang-san Obj. Marker (OM) he scold Asp.
    'Zhang-san scolded him.'

The ba-construction is one of the most-discussed and least-
understood constructions in Mandarin grammar. It is a feature
not found in most of the other Chinese languages. In essence,
ba functions to mark a definite direct object:

(7) b. Tā mǎi le   shū le.
       he buy Asp. book Asp.
       'He has bought a book.'

    c. Tā bǎ shū mǎi le.
       he OM book buy Asp.
       'He bought the book.'

For further discussion, see Thompson 1973a; Li 1971; and
Cheung 1973 and references cited there.

2. Prepositional phrases precede the V, and

3. Postpositions exist.

(8) Tā zài chūfáng-lǐ chǎo-fàn.
    he at kitchen-in cook-rice
    'He's cooking in the kitchen.'

4. Relative clauses precede the N, and

5. Genitive phrases precede the N.

(9) Huì jiǎng guóyǔ   de   nèige xiǎohái shì wǒ-de érzi.
    know speak Chinese Rel. that child   be I-gen. son
    'The child who knows how to speak Chinese is my son.'

6. Aspect markers follow the V.

(10) Wǒ qù-<u>guo</u>   Táiběi.
     I go-experienced Taipei
     'I have been to Taipei.'

7. Certain adverbials precede the V:

(11) Tā <u>mǎn</u>   bù zàihu.
     he completely not care
     'He is completely indifferent.'

(12) Nǐ kuài yidiǎn   chī.
     you fast a-little eat
     'Eat a little faster.'

Here are examples illustrating the VO features:

1. VO sentences occur.

(13) Wǒ xǐhuān tā.
     I like   he
     'I like him.'

2. Prepositions exist.

(14) Tā <u>cóng</u> Zhōngguo lái le.
     he from   China   come Asp.
     'He has come from China.'

3. Auxiliaries precede the V.

(15) Tā <u>néng</u> shuō zhōngguo-huà.
     he can   speak Chinese
     'He can speak Chinese.'

4. Complex sentences are almost always VO.

(16) Wǒ tīnshuō nǐ mǎi le   tāde   shū-diàn.
     I hear   you buy Asp. he-Gen. bookstore
     'I heard that you bought his bookstore.'

Until more is understood about the basis for these word order correlates, it is difficult to see any clear pattern in this distribution of OV and VO features.

To summarize this section, then: discussions in the literature on word order do not enable us to decide what the basic word order of Mandarin is; the notion of "subject" is not a prominent one in Mandarin; pragmatic and semantic factors influence word order more than grammatical factors do; and Mandarin has properties which have been suggested as concomitants of both OV and VO languages.

5.4. Morphology

5.4.1. Compounding Mechanisms

As we suggested above, Mandarin has very little grammatical morphology relative to other languages. The language, however, is rich in compounds, both nominal and verbal. The most common type of verbal compound is the "resultative" compound, composed of an action verb followed by a stative verb, e.g., dǎsǎo 'dust and sweep' + gānjing 'clean' = 'tidy up'. It is also known as the causative compound since the first verb specifies the cause and the second verb denotes the result. An example of a sentence with such a compound would be:

(17) Wǒmen bǎ fángjian dǎsǎo-gānjing.
    we   OM room   sweep-clean
    'We swept the room clean.'

(For further discussion, see Thompson 1973b.) In the formation of nominal compounds, Mandarin is essentially like English: nominal compounds can be created at will, and the language is also full of lexicalized compounds. For example,

Newly Created Compounds

English: ketchup blot

Mandarin: jiàng-yóu wū-diǎn
            soy   stain

Lexicalized Compounds

English: pocket book

Mandarin: xiǎo-yǒu
            school-friend
            'alumnus'

(For more discussion, see Zimmer 1971; 1972; Li 1971.)

Mandarin has two other interesting compounding devices, which are somewhat less commonly found in languages of the world. One is exemplified by the so-called verb-object compound. This term is used to refer to compounds consisting of two morphemes which could function in a verb-object relationship syntactically but which are frozen lexical items functioning as nouns or verbs in the language. Examples include:

Nouns

guǎn-jiā
take-care-of-home
'housekeeper'

dǐng-zhēn
push-needle
'thimble'

zhěn-tóu
rest-head
'pillow'

Verbs

dān-xīn
bear-heart
'worry'

jué-shé
chew-tongue
'gossip'

diū-liǎn
'lose-face
'be ashamed'

(This type of compound is discussed at some length in Chi
1974.)

The other compounding device, which is more productive than
the verb-object type, involves the shortening of a multi-
morphemic phrase into a bimorphemic lexical item called a
"stump compound." For example, the official name of the Soviet
Union is:

> sūwéiāi shèhui-zhǔyì lián-bāng gòng-hé-kuó
> soviet socialism   union   republic
> "Union of Soviet Socialist Republics"

which is typically shortened to sū lián 'Soviet Union' where
sū is the first syllable of the first morpheme sūwéiāi
'soviet' and lián is the first morpheme of the third word
lián-bāng 'union'. Another example is:

> xiē-nán   lián-hé dà-xué
> west-south united university
> "South-Western United University"

which is shortened to xiē-nán lián dà. Such "stump compounds"
are commonly used in naming agencies and branches of the
military or government. (Excellent discussion of the various
types of compounds in Mandarin can be found in Chao 1968 and
Kratochvil 1968.)

5.4.2. Lack of Grammatical Morphology

We have suggested that the fact that the language has essentially no grammatical morphology may be a significant

typological feature. Here we will discuss the implications of
this typological fact for Mandarin grammar.

First, there is no case morphology signaling "primary"
case relations, that is, the grammatical relations of subject,
direct object, and indirect object.[1] While in certain sentence
types, the word order SVO indicates that the preverbal noun
is the subject and the postverbal noun is the object, we have
shown that word order is semantically and pragmatically
conditioned in Mandarin, and that there are simple, basic
sentence types whose word order does not signal grammatical
relations (although in complex sentence constructions, such
as serial verb construction to be discussed later in this
section, the word order SVO is fairly rigid). Needless to say,
Chinese also does not have agreement to signal the notion of
subject. Hence, one may conclude that grammatical relations
are not systematically manifested in surface coding. In Li
and Thompson 1976b, we also argued that there are relatively
few grammatical processes that refer to grammatical relations.
(There do, however, appear to be certain processes, such as
Equi and reflexive, which are sensitive to "subject"; see Li
and Thompson 1976b for discussion.) A corollary to this
de-emphasis of grammatical relations is the fact that the
"topic" notion, as we suggested above, plays a much more
prominent role in Mandarin than in languages which predomi-
nently code grammatical relations. That is, topic-comment
sentences such as the following are basic sentences in
Mandarin:

(18) Nèi-zuo   fángzi xìngkui   qù-nián   méi xià-yǔ.
     that-Classif. house   fortunate last-year not rain
     'That house (Topic), fortunately it didn't rain
      last year.'

(19) Yú   wǒ zuì   xǐhuān chī xīnxian-de.
    fish I   most like   eat fresh-Nominalizer
    'Fish (Topic), I like fresh ones best.'

(20) Tāmen shéi zhīdào?
    they   who   know
    'As far as they are concerned, who knows?'

(21) Zhè-men   kè   wǒmen děi   dāngxīn.
    this-Classif. course we   must careful
    'This course (Topic), we must be careful.'

(22) Dà-xúexiào zhè-jian   zuì   hǎo.
    university this-Classif. most good
    'Universities (Topic), this one is the best.'

A second implication of the lack of grammatical morphology is
that Mandarin is missing a morphological system for signaling
the definiteness of a noun phrase; correlated with this is the
fact that word order is used for that function, as discussed
in section 5.3.

The third implication of the dearth of grammatical morphology which we would like to discuss is the serial verb construction. A serial verb construction contains two or more
predicates juxtaposed without any morphological marker
indicating either (1) the relationship between the nouns and
the predicates or (2) the relationship between the predicates.
Thus, it takes the form

NP   V   (NP)   V   (NP)

Sentences of this form in Mandarin are understood in radi-
cally different ways. For ease of presentation, we group the
interpretations into the following types and give examples
of each:

A. "Canonical" Serial Verbs

(23) a. Tā mǎi piào   jìnqu.
    he buy ticket go-in
    'He bought a ticket to go in/and went in.'

b. Tā tiāntian huì   kè   xiě   xìn.
   he every-day receive guest write letter
   'Every day he receives guests and writes letters.'

c. Wǒmen kāi huì   tǎolùn nèige wènti.
   we   hold meeting discuss that problem
   'We're holding a meeting to discuss that problem/
   and discussing that problem.'

d. Tā shàng lóu   shuìjiào.
   he go-up stairs sleep
   'He's going upstairs to sleep.'

B. Complementation

1. Object Complementation

(24) a. Wǒ yào tā qù.
     I want he go
     'I want him to go.'

b. Wǒ zhīdao Z. S. lái le.
   I know   Z. S. come Asp.
   'I know Z. S. has come.'

c. Tā kànjian wǒ xiě xìn.
   he see   I write letter
   'He saw me writing a letter.'

2. Subject Complementation

(25) a. Tā shàng dàxué   shì dà shì.
     he go-to university be big matter
     'His going to the university is a big deal.'

b. Tā shēng-bìng hěn kěxí.
   he get-sick   very sad
   'It's very sad that he has gotten sick.'

c. Xiě   Yīngwen hěn nán.
   write English very hard
   'It's very hard to write English.'

3. "Pivot" Sentences

(i.e., NP$_2$ = Subj. of V$_2$ and Obj. of V$_1$)

(26) a. Wǒ jiào tā qù.
    I tell he go
    'I told him to go.'

   b. Wǒ pīping   tā bù yònggōng.
     I criticize he not diligent
     'I criticized him for not being hardworking.'

   c. Wǒ pài tā qù mǎi jiǔ.
     I send he go buy wine
     'I sent him to go buy wine.'

   d. Háizi dōu xiào   tā shì yíge pàngzi.
     child all laugh-at he be a   fatso
     'The children all laughed at him for being a fatso.'

C. "Intention" Clauses

(27) a. Wǒmen zhòng cài   chī.
    we   raise vegetable eat
    'We raise vegetables to eat.'

   b. Wǒ yǎng zhū mài.
     I raise pig sell
     'I raise pigs to sell.'

   c. Wǒ zhǎo xuésheng jiāo.
     I seek student teach
     'I'm looking for students to teach.'
     (Ambiguous as in English)

D. "Descriptive" Clauses

(28) a. Wǒ yǒu yíge mèimei hěn piàoling.
    I have a   sister very pretty
    'I have a sister who is very pretty.'

   b. Wǒ mǎi le yíjiàn yīfu   tài dà.
     I buy Asp. a   outfit too big
     'I bought an outfit that was too big.'

    c. Tā chǎo le   yíge cài   hěn   xiāng.
    he cook Asp. a   dish very delicious
    'He cooked a dish that was very delicious.'

                E. Circumstantial Adjuncts

(29) a. Wǒ zài chúfang-li shāo-fàn.
        I at kitchen-in cook-rice
        'I'm cooking in the kitchen.'

     b. Tā zuò zài yǐzi-shang kàn bào.
        he sit at chair-on   read paper
        'He sat in the chair reading a newspaper.'

     c. Wǒ yòng kuàizi   chī-fàn.
        I use chopsticks eat-rice
        'I eat with chopsticks.'

     d. Wǒ bǐ   tā gāo.
        I compare he tall
        'I'm taller than he is.'

                F. Ambiguities

(30) a. Tā tiāntiān kàn diànying chī pǐngguo.
        he every-day see movie   eat apple
        'Everyday he sees movies and eats apples/to eat
         apples.'

     b. Tā tiāntiān kàn péngyou chī pǐngguo.
        he every-day see friend   eat apple
        'Everyday he sees a friend and eats apples/eat an
         apple/to eat apples.'

     c. Wǒmen yǒu yíge wènti   hěn   máfan.
        we   have a   problem very troublesome
        'We have a problem that's very troublesome/
         That we have a problem is very troublesome.'

     d. Wǒ yǒu yíge jiějie yǒu yíge háizi.
        I have a   sister have a   child
        'I have a sister who has a child/
         I have a sister and a child.'

What is evident from the above examples is that the serial
verb construction is used to encode a number of different
relationships between predicates in Mandarin. These predicate
relationships are structurally distinct in most other languages because of the presence of grammatical markers. The
interesting question that such constructions pose is: given
such a minimally specified string, how do speakers assign
appropriate interpretations to it?

Our answer to this question is that speakers *infer* the
appropriate interpretations for such strings on the basis of
four types of knowledge: language-dependent knowledge, pragmatic factors, certain language-independent principles, and
universal linguistic principles. Let us elaborate on each of
these.

A. Language-Dependent Knowledge

Speakers of a language know the meanings of predicates in
their language and the nature of the arguments each predicate
takes. It is easy to see that this knowledge accounts for a
fair amount of a speaker's ability to interpret serial verb
sentences. For example, in a sentence such as the object
complement type (31),

    (31) Wǒ xǐhuan chī bīng-ji-líng.
       I like   eat ice-cream
       'I like to eat ice-cream.'

the interpretation follows directly from the fact that xǐhuan
'like' is a two-argument verb requiring an animate subject;
since wǒ 'I' is an animate noun and is in a preverbal position, the sequence chī bīng-ji-líng 'eat ice cream' can only
be interpreted as its object. (That such knowledge is, in
fact, language-*dependent* rather than universal semantic knowledge, is evident from the fact that, although verbs such as

Mandarin xǐhuan and its English counterpart like are both
two-argument verbs, the Mandarin xiào 'laugh' can be either
a one-argument or a two-argument verb, corresponding to the
English laugh as well as laugh at. These properties of verbs,
then, must be viewed as facts which speakers know about their
own language.)

Another significant kind of language-dependent knowledge is
the knowledge of the range of grammatical devices available
in the language. Thus, given a serial verb sentence like:

(32) Tā kàn diànyǐng chī píngguo.
     he see movie   eat apple
     'He saw a movie and ate an apple.'

an interpretation in which the two events are understood to
have occurred simultaneously is ruled out because there is an
explicit construction in Mandarin for signaling simultaneity
of two events, the -zhe-construction (see section 5.5).

(33) Tā kàn-zhe diànyǐng chī píngguo.
     he see   movie   eat apple
     'He ate an apple while watching a movie.'

Similarly, unlike the serial verb construction in Thai
which may take on a causative reading, a serial verb construction in Chinese will not be given a causative interpretation.
The reason is that there is another grammatical device, namely
the resultative verb compound mentioned earlier, available to
the speaker of Chinese who wishes to signal a causative relationship between two verbs.

The basic principle suggested here regarding the native
speaker's knowledge of the range of grammatical devices
available in the language is that a language tends not to
employ several distinct multipredicate structures to signal
one specific semantic relationship between two predicates.
This principle may be viewed as a tendency toward economy in

linguistic codification. It does not call for an isomorphism
between multipredicate structures on the one hand and semantic
relationships between predicates on the other. In fact, a
language may employ two distinct structures to signal a
specific semantic relationship between two predicates. Such a
situation frequently òccurs when the language is undergoing
syntactic changes involving the structure in question. For
instance, the resultative compound historically displaced the
causative serial verb construction in Chinese (see Li and
Thompson 1976c). But the process of actualization concerning
the displacement took several centuries, during which both
serial verb construction and resultative compounds were
used to signal the causative relation between predicates.

A third type of language-dependent knowledge which must be
attributed to speakers is an understanding of certain basic
syntactic principles of their language, such as word order
in certain constructions. For Mandarin, the fact that in
complex sentences word order is consistently SVO plays a role
in determining the interpretation of serial verb sentences.
Because of this relatively rigid word order in complex sentences, the native speaker is able to identify the first NP
in a serial verb sentence as the subject of the first verb and
also the potential subject of the second verb. Consider for
example:

(34) Tā tiāntiān kàn diànying chī pingguo
     he every-day see movie   eat apple

By the word order principle, we understand that the subject of
see is the first NP of the sentence, tā 'he'. Now the second
NP of the sentence, diànying 'movie', which should be the
subject of the second verb by virtue of its position immediately preceding the second verb, is an *inanimate* noun; but the

second verb, chī 'eat', requires an *animate* subject. Hence, the second NP cannot serve as the subject of the second verb, and we are forced to take the first NP as the subject of both the first and second verb. Thus the SVO word order for complex sentences and the meaning of the verbs (i.e., their selectional and categorial co-occurrence restrictions) are sufficient for us to determine the grammatical relationships between the NP's and the predicates in sentence (34).

B. Pragmatic Factors

Situation-dependent, or pragmatic, factors are responsible for narrowing down interpretations in cases such as the following:

(35) Tā yǒu yíge wènti   hěn máfan.
he have a   problem very troublesome

    a. 'That he has a problem is very troublesome.'
    b. 'He has a problem that is very troublesome.'

The difference between interpretations (a) and (b) is whether the clause tā yǒu yíge wènti 'he has a problem' is understood as being presupposed, as in (a), or asserted, as in (b). The pragmatic fact of whether this proposition is known to both speaker and hearer clearly determines whether interpretation (a) or (b) is appropriate in a given situation.

C. Language-Independent Principles

A good part of the knowledge of possible relationships between clauses in a sentence is acquired by normal people as a result of their experiences in the world. This knowledge is language-independent and results from our perception of and experience with the world. Given any two events, there can be only a small, finite number of relationships between them. Language merely reflects and codifies these relationships in

various multipredicate constructions, although different
languages employ different strategies in their codification.
This language-independent knowledge of various relationships between clauses plays a significant role in the interpretation of serial verb sentences in Mandarin. Before
discussing how this works, however, let us describe the
central relationship between events and/or states commonly
occurring in the world. Below we list the relationships
together with a description of the construction used in
Mandarin for signaling each relationship:

1. Parallel Events

Most languages employ a coordinate structure with a coordinate
marker linking the clauses to codify parallel events. In
Mandarin, however, they are signaled by the serial verb
construction, e.g.,

(36) Tā xiě   xiǎoshuo mài   gǔdong.
     he write novel   sell antique
     'He writes novels and sells antiques.'

2. Consecutive Events

When two events occur sequentially, languages may either use
a temporal adverbial clause such as an after-clause, a before-
clause, or a coordinate structure with or without a consecutive marker such as the English then. Temporal adverbial
clauses with after or before seem to be nearly universal.
However, in Mandarin, consecutive events may also be codified
by the serial verb construction.

(37) Tā tuō-le   yīfu   shàng   chuáng.
     he take-off-Asp. clothes get-into bed
     'He took off his clothes and then got into bed.'

3. Simultaneous Events

Two events may occur simultaneously. Mandarin signals the
simultaneous relationship between two clauses with the -zhe-
construction, e.g.,

(38) Tā chī-zhe fàn kàn bào.
     he eat   food read newspaper
     'He reads newspapers while eating food.'

4. Result

One event may be the result of another. The construction used
in Mandarin to signal this relationship takes on the particle
de, marking the predicate denoting the event which leads to
the result, e.g.,

(39) Tā pǎo-de hěn lèi.
     He run   very tired
     'He is very tired from running.'

5. Purpose

An action may be carried out for a specific purpose. When both
the action and the purpose are expressed by clauses, the
relationship between the two clauses may be described as
"purposive." In Mandarin, the serial verb construction
signals this relationship:

(40) Tā huí   jiā kàn qīnqi.
     he return home see relative
     'He went back home to see his relatives.'

6. Cause

One event may be the cause of another. The causative relationship in Mandarin, as mentioned above, is signaled by the
"resultative compound," e.g., dǎsǎo-gānjing 'sweep-clean'.
The causative relationship between these two verbs is inferred

from the juxtaposition of the two verbs just as the meaning
'is made of' is inferred from an English compound such as
steel blade.

7. Conditional, Concessive

A conditional or concessive relationship between two events
is typically expressed by explicit morphology. All languages
appear to have some morphological marker signaling conditional
or concessive relationships between two clauses. In Mandarin,
a marker such as rúguo 'if' on the clause indicating condition
is optional, but the marker jiù 'then' on the consequent
clause is obligatory. (See section 5.6 for more discussion of
conditional clauses.)

(41) (Rúguo) tā lái wǒ jiù qù.
     if   he come I then go
     'If he comes, I will go.'

Concessional clauses are marked with such pairs as suīrán
'although' ... kěshi 'but'.

(42) Suīrán tā lái-le, kěshi wǒ hái juéde bú
     although he come-Asp. but I still feel not
     shūfu.
     comfortable
     'Although he has arrived, I still don't feel good.'

It is clear that the knowledge of such relationships
between events and/or states in the world plays a role in
the interpretation of serial verb sentences by the speaker
of Mandarin. For example, given a sentence such as (40),
which juxtaposes two verbs semantically requiring agents
acting willfully, the Mandarin speaker knows that given the
small set of relationships described above a most likely
inference is that the first action was undertaken *in order to*
accomplish the second.

D. Universal Linguistic Principles

As we have seen in the preceding discussion, a small set of language-independent principles representing our perception and knowledge of the world accounts for most of the relationships between clauses in multipredicate constructions. However, the relationships between clauses in certain multipredicate constructions which appear in all languages cannot be understood as manifestations of the language-independent relationships between events in the world, but seem to be purely linguistic. Two of the most important and fundamental of these relations are predication and description.

1. Predication

A proposition may be predicated on another proposition. In other words, a proposition may serve as an argument of a predicate. Multipredicate constructions of this type are currently referred to by the term "complementation." Let us examine two examples given earlier:

(24) b. Wǒ zhīdào Z. S. lái le.
      I know   Z. S. come Asp.
      'I know Z. S. has come.'

(25) b. Tā shēng-bìng hěn kěxí.
      he get-sick   very sad
      'It's very sad that he has gotten sick.'

In these examples, the underlined propositions are serving as arguments in the propositions whose predicates are respectively zhīdao 'know' and kěxí 'sad'; these predicates can be said to be making a predication, then, on the underlined propositions. The relationship between the two propositions does not reflect the relationship between events/states in the world. It is a purely linguistic relationship.

2. Description

The most commonly found type of sentence in which one
proposition serves a descriptive function with respect to a
noun phrase is, of course, a relative clause construction.
Mandarin has a relative clause construction (see below), but
there is also a serial verb construction in which the second
proposition (or verb phrase) is understood as a description
of the last noun phrase in the first proposition. Consider
again an earlier example:

(28) a. Wǒ yǒu yíge mèimei <u>hěn piàoling</u>.
         I have a   sister very pretty
        'I have a sister who is very pretty.'

The descriptive clause in Mandarin must be in sentence-final
position as shown by the underlined clause in (28a), and the
noun phrase it describes must be specific and indefinite.
What is being coded in (28a), we are suggesting, is not a
relationship between two events or states in the world, but a
linguistic relationship between two propositions. The particular construction, which we have labeled "descriptive clause"
is language-specific, but the knowledge of the descriptive
function of propositions, like the knowledge of complementation, is surely universal linguistic knowledge.

The interpretation of serial verb sentences, then, is best
viewed as the result of an interplay of universal linguistic
principles and language-dependent, language-independent, and
pragmatic factors. The interpretive strategy is an inferential
process on the part of the speakers of the language. To
illustrate the interplay among these factors, let us examine
two examples in more detail.

First consider a serial verb sentence such as (43).

(43) Tā tiāntian huì   kè   xiĕ   xìn.
he every-day receive guest write letter
'Every day he receives guests and writes letters.'

Given the small set of possible relationships between predicates, the Mandarin speaker considers those for which the
serial verb construction is a possible codification. These
relationships are represented as: parallel events, consecutive
events, purpose (intention), complementation, descriptive
clause, circumstantial adjunct. Sentence (43) is not a case
of complementation because neither of the two predicates takes
a proposition as one of its arguments. It does not involve a
descriptive clause because it fails to meet a requirement of
the descriptive clause; i.e., the last NP of the first clause
which the descriptive clause modifies must be specific and
indefinite. Thus, the sentence-final clause xiĕ xìn 'write
letter' cannot serve as a descriptive clause because the
preceding noun phrase kè 'guest' is not specific. Finally,
(43) does not involve a circumstantial adjunct because
circumstantial adjuncts employ specific predicates — the so-
called co-verb in Mandarin. We are now left with only three
possible interpretations: parallel events, consecutive events,
purpose. In fact, in isolation, sentence (43) is indeterminate
with respect to these three interpretations; only contextual
information could determine which of them would be appropriate
in a given setting.

Next, consider a serial verb sentence such as (44),·

(44) Tā yǎng zhū mài.
he raise pig sell
'He raises pigs to sell.'

The complementation, the descriptive clause, and the circumstantial adjunct interpretations are ruled out in (44) for
the same type of reasons that they are ruled out in (43).

We will not repeat the discussion here. The question posed by serial verb sentences such as (44) is: why doesn't it convey a reading of parallel or consecutive events in addition to the purposive reading, as sentence (43) does? The answer lies in the structural characteristics of (44). We observe that the second predicate in (44), mài 'sell' requires the presence of at least two arguments: the source of the transaction and the object of the transaction. The goal of the transaction may be absent in both English and Mandarin. However, in (44), the NP, zhū 'pig', immediately preceding the verb, mài 'sell', cannot serve as its subject, which is semantically the source of the transaction on the basis of selectional restrictions. Thus, mài 'sell' in (44) has neither a subject NP preceding it nor an object NP following it. Another structural characteristic of (44) is that the verb mài 'sell' does not and cannot have any aspect marker. A verb lacking the arguments required by its meaning in their normal positions and having no aspect marker is a nonfinite verb, which signals irrealis. An irrealis verb such as mài 'sell' in (44) simply carries the message "unspecified future" with respect to the other verb, which is nonstative and whose arguments are fully specified. Thus sentence (44) conveys two events, one coded in full and one understood to occur in an unspecified future: both require the presence of an agent. The semantics of such a situation naturally results in a purposive reading, just as in English, where the irrealis verb form, the infinitive, is understood in a purposive sense in the translation of (44): 'He raises pigs to sell'. The important point here is that, on the one hand, there is no morphology for signaling irrealis in Mandarin, and, on the other hand, the irrealis interpretation results from the absence of nominal and aspectual concomitants.

It is this absence that rules out parallel and consecutive event interpretations for sentences such as (44).

In conclusion, we have seen that the lack of grammatical signals does not impair communication. Furthermore, as the Mandarin serial verb construction shows, the lack of grammatical signals does not necessarily result in other complications. The strategies used by a Mandarin speaker are essentially the same ones available to speakers of any language. One could conclude that many of the familiar grammatical signals for relationships between predicates are not essential for communicative purposes; Mandarin appears to be, however, quite rare among languages of the world in making use of so few of these signals.

5.5. Marked Subordination

In this section, we will discuss those subordinate structures that are characterized by subordination markers.

5.5.1. Simultaneous Action (-zhe-construction)

The -zhe-construction has the following structure:

$$\text{NP} \left[\text{[V-zhe} \ (\text{NP)} \text{]} \ \text{V} \ (\text{NP)} \right]_{\text{VP}}$$

where the first NP is always interpreted as the subject of the two following verbs. E.g.,

(45) Tā dī-zhe tóu zǒu-lù.
he lower head walk
'He walks with his head bowed.'

(46) Tā kū-zhe pǎo huí jiā qù.
he cry   run back home go
'He ran home crying.'

(47) Tā kàn-zhe shū shàng kè.
he read   book attend class
'He goes to class reading.'

The following evidence suggests that the -zhe-clause is subordinate: (a) it is marked with -zhe, which makes the clause nonfinite; its verb may not take any aspect markers. (b) There are a number of semantic constraints on the verb in the -zhe-clause; it must be nonstative and durative. A momentary verb occurs in the -zhe-clause only if the action it denotes can be iterative. Such constraints are typical of subordinate clause verbs, but are not usually found with coordinate clause verbs.

The evidence supporting our claim that the -zhe-clause is part of a VP constituent, shown in the structure

$$\text{NP} \left[\text{[V -zhe (NP)] V (NP)} \right]_{\text{VP}}$$

is as follows:

(1) Auxiliaries, negatives, and certain adverbs which normally occur in the second position preceding the VP in Mandarin occur only before the -zhe-clause. (2) The entire -zhe-clause together with the following constituents may be fronted for the purpose of focusing:

(48) Guāng-zhe jiǎo shàng kè,   tā yuànyi.
     bare   foot attend class, he willing
     'He is willing to attend classes barefooted.'

Hence, syntactically, the -zhe-construction involves a nonfinite clause embedded in the verb phrase. Semantically, the construction expresses two simultaneous actions with the action denoted by the verb in the -zhe-clause providing the "background" for the main clause predication. The particle -zhe functions as a subordinate marker.

5.5.2. Relative Clause versus Descriptive Clause

The relative clause in Mandarin, like the genitive, the article, and the adjective, precedes the head noun it modifies. E.g.,

(49) Wǒ xǐhuan de   rén
I like   Rel. people
'The people I like'

(50) Xǐhuan wǒ de   rén
like   I Rel. people
'The people who like me'

As (49) and (50) show, the relative clause is marked by the
particle de, and the NP within the clause that is coreferential
with the head noun is deleted. As far as accessibility to
relativization is concerned, subject and direct object are
most readily accessible in all Chinese languages. In the case
of indirect objects, prepositional objects, and genitives,
their accessibility to relativization is not as straightforward. For most speakers of Mandarin, indirect object
relativization is permissible, but rare:

(51) Wǒ gěi-le   tā yǐ-běn shū de   nèige rén.
I give-Asp. he one   book Rel. that person
'The person I gave a book to.'

Notice that in (51) where the head noun is coreferential with
the indirect object of the relative clause, the indirect
object is replaced with a pronoun (underlined) rather than
deleted.

Relativization of prepositional object and genitive noun
is unacceptable to most native speakers of Mandarin:

(52) ??wǒ cóng nèr   lái   de   dìfang
I from there come Rel. place
'the place I come from'

(53) ??wǒ rènshi tā   mèimei de   nèige rén
I know   his sister Rel. that person
'the person whose sister I know'

The relative clause sentence is similar to another Mandarin
construction, the descriptive clause, mentioned above in the
discussion of serial verb sentences, in some respect, but the

two constructions also differ from each other both semantically
and syntactically. Let us consider a pair of examples:

(54) *Relative Clause:*

    Wǒ mǎi-le   yī-tiáo <u>hěn</u> <u>xiōng</u>   de   gǒu.
    I buy-Asp. a   very ferocious Rel. dog
    'I bought a dog that was very ferocious.'

(55) *Descriptive Clause:*

    Wǒ mǎi-le   yī-tiáo gǒu <u>hěn</u> <u>xiōng</u>.
    I buy-Asp. a   dog very ferocious
    'I bought a dog that was very ferocious.'

(54) and (55) are similar in that both sentences contain a
clause which says something about a dog being ferocious. But
the similarity stops there. (54) and (55) have different
meanings. The meaning of (54) containing the relative clause
may best be paraphrased as: "I bought one of those ferocious
dogs," whereas the meaning of (55) may be described as: "I
bought a dog and it happened to be ferocious." Thus, the
relative clause construction assumes the existence of a class
of dogs, namely, "ferocious dogs," whereas the descriptive
clause construction does not. In other words, the descriptive
clause describes an incidental property about the object
denoted by the preceding noun, whereas the relative clause
provides a property for the establishment of a subclass of
objects denoted by the following head noun. There are several
other salient characteristics of the descriptive clause
construction that set it apart from the relative clause
construction. One is that the descriptive clause can occur
only in sentence-final position. Another is that the clause
does not form a constituent with the preceding NP. The last
is that the preceding NP must be indefinite. (For a detailed
discussion of the descriptive clause, see Li and Thompson,
forthcoming a). One important consequence of the distinctions

mentioned above is that whereas the relative clause is a
prototype of subordination, it is not at all clear that the
descriptive clause involves subordination at all.

5.5.3. Time Adverbial Clause

There are three noteworthy characteristics of time adverbial
clauses in Mandarin: (1) they must precede the main clause;
(2) they are marked with time adverbial particles; (3) these
particles appear at the end of the time clause, unlike the
markers for such clause types as conditional and concessive
(see section 5.6). For example,

(56) a. <u>When</u>:

        Tā lái <u>de</u> <u>shíhou</u>, wǒ hěn gāoxing.
        he come Rel. time, I very happy
        'When he came, I was very happy.'

    b. <u>Before</u>:

        Tā rènshi nǐ <u>yǐqián</u>, wǒ chángchang jiàn tā.
        he know you before, I often   see him
        'Before he knew you, I often saw him.'

    c. <u>After</u>:

        Tā zǒu-le <u>yǐhou</u>, wǒmen chīfàn.
        he go-Asp. after, we   eat
        'We'll eat after he goes.'

In the <u>when</u>-clause and the <u>before</u>-clause, the verbs may not
take an aspect marker:

(57) a. *Tā lái-le   de   shíhou, ...
        he come-Asp. Rel. time,   ...
    b. *Tā pīping -le nǐ yǐqián, ...
        he criticize-Asp. you before, ...

In an <u>after</u>-clause, the verb must take the completive aspect
marker <u>-le</u>, as in (56c), or a completive expression, as in:

(58) Wǒmen niàn dào dì-   wǔ kè   yǐhou, jiù
     we   read to Ordinalizer-five lesson after, then
     róngyi le.
     easy   Asp.

'After we've read to the fifth lesson, it will be easy.'

The meaning of the Mandarin subordinator yǐhou 'after'
requires that the proposition to which it is suffixed be
explicitly marked as completed.

5.5.4. Extent Clause Construction

The extent clause construction signals roughly the same
meaning as so ... that in English, as in:

  (59) He is so fat that he can't dance.

However, in Mandarin, the clause that indicates the extent
appears to be the main clause, while the predicate whose
"extent" is being discussed appears to be in the subordinate
clause:

  (60) Tā pǎo de tóu dōu hūn-le.
       he run   head even dizzy-Asp.
       'He ran to such an extent that he got dizzy.'

  (61) Tā pàng de bù néng tiàowu.
       he fat   not can dance
       'He is so fat that he can't dance.'

  (62) Tā xiào de wǒmen dōu bù-hǎoyìsi.
       he laugh   we   all embarrassed
       'He laughed to such an extent that we were all
        embarrassed.'

The first verbs, pǎo 'run', pàng 'fat', xiào 'laugh' in
(60) - (62) are marked by the particle de. They cannot be
followed by aspect markers or preceded by the negative
particle bù or by auxiliaries such as néng 'can'. However,
(60) - (62) show clearly that aspect markers, bù, and

auxiliaries can occur in the extent clause. These facts
provide some of the evidence indicating that the first clause
in the extent construction is the subordinate clause, whereas
the second clause, the extent clause, is the main clause.

It can now be seen that the result clause, exemplified
above in (39), repeated here, is simply a special case of the
extent construction:

> (39) Tā pǎo-de hěn lèi.
>   he run   very tired
>   'He is tired from running.'

The only difference between (60) - (62) and (39) is that in
(39) the extent clause consists of simply a stative verb plus
a modifier, while the predicates in (60) - (62) are more
elaborate. Note that in both (61) and (39) the nonexpressed
subject of the second predicate is understood as coreferential
with the subject of the first verb. (For more discussion of
these constructions, see Hashimoto 1971.)

The four types of subordination characterized by the
presence of subordinate markers which we have discussed in
this section are: the -zhe-construction (simultaneous action),
the relative clause construction, the time adverbial clause
construction, and the extent clause construction. The relative
clause obligatorily precedes the head noun. As for the other
three constructions, the subordinate clause generally precedes
the main clause. If the subordinate-main relationship may be
viewed as analogous to the modifier-modified relationship,
then the constraint that the modifier must precede the
modified is a very strong one in Mandarin. This constraint
also extends to simple adverbs such as hěn 'very', tài 'too',
bù 'not', chángchang 'often', tiāntiān 'every day', which
must precede the word they modify. For example:

(63) a. Tā <u>hěn</u> gāo.
         he very tall
         'He is very tall.'

     b. *Tā gāo <u>hěn</u>.
         he tall very

(64) a. Tā <u>tài</u> lèi.
         he too tired
         'He is too tired.'

     b. *Tā lèi <u>tài</u>.
         he tired too

(65) a. Tā <u>chángchang</u> shēng-bìng.
         he often   sick
         'He often gets sick.'

     b. *Tā shēng-bìng <u>chángchang</u>.
         he sick   often

(66) a. Tā <u>tiāntiān</u> kàn shū.
         he every-day read book
         'He reads books every day.'

     b. *Tā kàn shū <u>tiāntiān</u>.
         he read book every-day

5.6. Paired Correlative Markers

As suggested above, certain relationships between events and
states are signaled by structures involving two clauses each
of which begins with a marker, although one of the pair may
be optionally deleted:

         CONJ S CONJ S

Examples include the following:

                    A. Reason

(67) <u>Yīnwei</u> wǎn le, (<u>suǒyi</u>) wǒ méi qù.
     because late Asp. so   I   not go
     'I didn't go because it was late.'

(68) <u>Jìrán</u> tā bù kěn,   (<u>jiù</u>) suàn   le.
since he not willing, then forget Sentence Ptc.
'Since he is not willing, forget it.'

B. Concessive

(69) <u>Suīrán</u>   wǒ xǐhuan nèige fángzi, <u>kěshi</u> wǒ méi
although I like   that house   but I not-have

qián.
money

'Although I like that house, I have no money.'

(70) <u>Suīrán</u>   nǐ néng jiègei wǒ qián, <u>háishi</u> bú gòu.
although you can lend me money, still not enough
'Even if you can lend me money, it still won't be
enough.'

C. Conditional

1. Future

(71) (<u>Yàoshi</u>) nǐ qù, wǒ <u>jiù</u> qù.
if   you go, I then go
'I'll go if you go.'

(72) <u>Chúfei</u> nǐ máng, <u>bùran</u> wǒmen yídìng   lái kàn nǐ.
unless you busy,   we   certainly come see you
'We'll come to see you unless you are busy.'

2. Unreal Hypothetical

(73) (<u>Yàoshi</u>) jīntian fàngjià, wǒ <u>jiù</u> shuìjiào.
If   today   holiday, I then sleep
'If today were a holiday, I would sleep.'

(74) <u>Jiùshi</u> wǒmen qù de zǎo, <u>yě</u>   děi zǒu yíge zhōngtou.
even-if we   go   early still must walk one hour
'Even if we left early, we would still have to walk
an hour.'

3. Unreal Counterfactual

(75) <u>Jiǎru</u> wǒ shì nǐ fùqin, wǒ <u>jiù</u> bù xǔ nǐ qù.
If   I   be you father, I   not let you go
'If I were your father, I wouldn't let you go.'

(76) (<u>Yàoshi</u>) tā zǎo yìdian huílai, <u>jiù</u> hǎo le.
if   he early a-little return, then fine Asp.
'If he had returned a little earlier, it would be fine.'

It is to be noted that the three subcategories of the
conditional clause constructions are not determined by the
paired markers in each sentence. The markers in (71), which
is a future conditional, for instance, are exactly the same
as the markers in (76), which is an unreal counterfactual,
and in (73) which is an unreal hypothetical. Thus, whether a
structure marked with such paired coordinators as <u>yàoshi</u> ...
<u>jiù</u>, <u>jiǎru</u> ... <u>jiù</u>, <u>jiùshi</u> ... <u>yě</u>, or <u>chúfei</u> ... <u>bùran</u> is
interpreted as a simple future conditional construction or an
unreal hypothetical construction or an unreal counterfactual
construction depends entirely on pragmatic factors. For
example, (76) would be interpreted as counterfactual in a
context in which it is known to all participants that "he" in
fact returned too late.

D. Miscellaneous Paired Conjunctions

(77) <u>Búshi</u> wǒ lái, <u>jiùshi</u> tā qù.
not   I   come, be   he go
'Either I come or he goes.'

(78) Nǐ <u>yuè</u> dàshēng shuōhuà, wǒ <u>yuè</u> tóu-teng.
you more loud   talk,   I more headache
'The more you talk so loudly, the worse my headache
gets.'

(79) Tā <u>búdàn</u>   mǎi chēzi, <u>yě</u> mǎi fángzi.
he not-only buy car,   also buy house
'He is not only buying a car, but is also buying a
house.'

It is clear that in constructions such as these, the relationships between the clauses are made explicit by the correlative
markers, which have very specific meanings.

One of the most interesting questions raised by these
constructions is whether the clauses are in a coordinate or a
subordinate-main relationship. Our position is that these
constructions are syntactically parallel to each other,
though semantically they may express relationships which
other languages express with subordinate clauses, such as
conditionality and reason.

Before leaving the correlative clauses, we note that,
again, it is quite possible for two clauses to simply be
juxtaposed, with no markers, leaving the relationship to the
inferential abilities of the participants. For example,

(80) Bú gòu   zài jiào.
     not enough again order
     'If it's not enough, we'll order more.'

5.7. Pronominalization

Mandarin has a six-person pronoun system, representing one of
the most common pronoun systems in languages of the world.

wǒ	'I, me'	wǒmen	'we, us'
nǐ	'you'	nǐmen	'you' (Pl.)
tā	'he/she, him/her'	tāmen	'they, them'
	zìji	'self'	

As the glosses clearly indicate, pronouns in Mandarin are
not distinguished on the basis of gender or case, and their
plural suffix is the invariant -men. It should be mentioned
that pronouns in Mandarin refer only to humans. In the
twentieth century, due to the influence of European languages,
the third person pronoun in Mandarin has been extended from

human reference to animate reference in the written language.
In speech, however, it is still not common to use the third
person pronoun to refer to a nonhuman animate being. Pronominalization follows strictly the "precede" constraint, i.e.,
if NP_1 and NP_2 are coreferential and NP_1 precedes NP_2, then
only NP_2 may be pronominalized. For example,

> (81) a. Zhāngsān zhǐshi xiǎngdao (tā)-zìji.
>   Zhangsan only   thinks-of (he)-self
>   'Zhangsan only thinks of himself.'
>
>   b. *(Tā)-zìji, Zhāngsān zhǐshi xiǎngdao.
>   (he)-self, Zhangsan only   think-of
>
> (82) a. Yàoshi Zhāng-sān dào nèr   qù, tā jiù bù gāoxing.
>   if   Zhang-san to there go, he then not happy
>   'If Zhang-san goes there, he'll be unhappy.'
>
>   b. *Yàoshi tā dào nèr   qù, Zhāng-sān jiù bù gāoxing.
>   if   he to there go, Zhang-san then not happy

If (82b) is to be grammatical, tā and Zhāng-sān cannot be
coreferential. The "command" relationship, which may supercede
the "precede" constraint in English to allow the first of two
coreferential NPs to be pronominalized, is not operable in
Mandarin. The typologically distinct characteristic of Mandarin
pronominalization is that often an NP preceded by another
coreferential NP is simply deleted. This deletion process may
occur within a complex sentence or across sentence boundaries
in discourse. Languages that allow such a deletion process are
called zero-pronominalization languages. Let us consider some
examples in Mandarin.

A. Zero-Pronominalization for Subject
Obligatory in Adverbial Clause Construction

> (83) a. Zhāng-sān qù-le   měiguó yǐhòu, jiù bù gāoxing.
>   Zhang-san go-Asp. America after, then not happy
>   'After Zhang-san went to America, he was unhappy.'

b. #<u>Zhāng-sān</u> qù-le   měiguó yǐhòu, <u>tā</u> jiù bù
   Zhang-san go-Asp. America after, he then not

   gāoxing.
   happy

B. Zero-Pronominalization for Subject
Optional in Correlative Structures

(84) Yīnwei <u>Zhāng-sān</u> xǐhuan nǐ, suǒyi   (<u>tā</u>) lái   zhèr.
     because Zhang-san like you, therefore (he) come here
     'Because Zhang-san liked you, he came here.'

The pronoun, <u>tā</u>, in the second clause is optional in (84) as
well as in (82a).

C. Zero-Pronominalization in Discourse

The most common type of zero pronominalization in discourse
is topic-controlled, i.e., a topic followed by a sequence of
comments each of which is an independent clause. For example,

(85) Nèichang huǒ xìngkui   xiāofang-dùi lái de kuài.
     that   fire fortunately fire-brigade come   quick

     Zhǐ shāo-le   sān-ge fángzi, fàng-le   yǐ-xie yān.
     only burn-Asp. three house, release-Asp. some smoke

     Wǔ-fēn-zhōng yǐhòu, jiù miè-le.
     five-minutes later, then extinguish-Asp.

     'That fire (Topic), fortunately the fire-brigade came
     quickly. It only burned up three houses, and
     released some smoke. Five minutes later, it was
     extinguished.'

Zero-pronominalization is a complex and widespread phenomenon in Mandarin, which we have not yet begun to elucidate
here (but see Li and Thompson, forthcoming b, for some discussion). We mention it here as an important typological
characteristic of Mandarin.

5.8. Conclusion

We have considered here a number of typological parameters and
outlined the position of Mandarin with respect to these
parameters. We have concluded that the lack of grammatical
morphology has a number of far-reaching consequences for the
grammar of this language, and that such a language may provide
important clues to the understanding of language use which we
might miss if we restricted our attention to languages with
complex morphological systems.

Note

1. An apparent counterexample to the claim that grammatical
   relations are unmarked is the indirect object. The indirect
   object is marked with the preposition gěi 'to' in sentences
   with certain three-place predicates such as sòng 'present',
   jì 'mail', huì 'to send by money order'. For example,

    (i) a. Wǒ sòng-le   yǐ-ben   shū gěi tā.
          I give-Asp. a-classifier book to he
          'I gave a book to him.'

        b. Wǒ jì-le   yǐ-feng   xìn   gěi tā.
          I mail-Asp. a-classifier letter to he
          'I mailed a letter to him.'

However, with other three-place predicates, the indirect
object is indeed unmarked:

    (ii) a. Wǒ wèn tā yíge wènti.
          I ask he a   question
          'I'll ask him a question.'

        b. Wǒ gěi tā yǐ-ben   shū.
          I give he a-classifier book
          'I'll give him a book.'

For a typology of indirect object constructions, see Chao
1968: 317 - 319.

Another putative exception to the claim that Chinese does not have case morphology is the ba-construction described earlier:

(iii) Wǒ bǎ Zhāng-sān pīping   le.
      I OM Zhang-san criticize Asp.
      'I criticized Zhang-san.'

In the ba-construction illustrated by (iii), the patient noun is marked with the particle ba. However, as pointed out above, this marker appears only when the patient is in preverbal position.

6. The Syntax of Subject-Final Languages

Edward L. Keenan III

6.0. Introduction

In section 6.1 I present a defininition of *subject-final language* and exhibit eight languages which appear to meet the definition. In section 6.2 I present some of the general syntactic properties of subject-final languages. And in section 6.3 I propose a partial answer to the question "Why are so few languages subject-final?"

6.1.0. Definition of Subject-Final Languages

By *subject-final language* I understand any language in which full noun phrase subjects must follow full noun phrase direct objects in the pragmatically less marked sentence types (which contain both subjects and direct objects) of the language. By *pragmatically less marked* (henceforth *least marked* or *unmarked*) I refer to those sentences which place the fewest restrictions on their contexts of appropriate use. Thus English would not be considered a subject-final language, since in general those sentences which present objects before subjects, like (1a) below, place more restrictions on their context of appropriate use than do sentences like (1b) in which the object follows the subject.

(1) a. Ice cream the children will eat.

b. The children will eat ice cream.

(1a) is most appropriate in a context in which ice cream is
being contrasted with, or mentioned to the exclusion of,
something else, say spinach. And since (1b) does not put such
restrictions on its context of use, it is (pragmatically) less
marked than (1a).

Further, the use of *must* in the definition of subject-final
language rules out of consideration languages like Walbiri
(Australia; see Hale 1967), Tagalog (Philippines, Malayo-
Polynesian; see Schachter and Otanes 1972), and Ignaciano
(Bolivia, Arawakan, Andean-Equatorial Phylum; see Ott and
Ott 1967). In these languages changing the relative order of
subject and object in unmarked sentences appears to effect no
change in the pragmatic markedness of the sentence. Thus
attention here is restricted to languages in which the relative order of subject and object is an important property of
the language. Any change in relative order of subject and
object in the languages considered then will either yield
ungrammatical structures or else ones which are more marked
(pragmatically) than the original.

Determining which sentences in a language are less marked,
however, can be a far from simple task. In the languages
discussed below, assessment of the least-marked word order is
based, depending on the language, on the following:

1. In one instance, extensive field work with the language.
2. In a few instances, intensive elicitation with native
   speakers.
3. In several other instances, only published material,
   sometimes scanty, on the language.

In the third case, most of the sources were not specifically
concerned with the question of least-marked word order, so I
have made the following assumptions: first, that the least-
marked sentences will be among the most frequently occurring;

second, that the citation order in simple sentences in the
grammar is among the least-marked word orders; and, third,
that the least-marked sentences have the greatest syntactic
distribution. Thus they will in general present the greatest
range of marking for tense/aspect, mood, voice, etc.; they
will nominalize and embed more easily than more marked
sentences; they will be the easiest to question and relativize
into, etc. For example, in (1a,b) above from English, one can
relativize on the children in the unmarked sentence (1b) but
not in the more marked sentence (1a).

(2) a. *the children who ice cream will eat

   b. the children who will eat ice cream

6.1.1. Distribution of Subject-Final Languages

Using the definition given in the previous section, it is clear
that very few languages appear to be subject-final. Indeed,
Greenberg's first universal (Greenberg 1966: 110) states: "In
declarative sentences with nominal subject and object, the
dominant order is almost always one in which the subject
precedes the object." Greenberg does, however, cite Coeur
d'Alene, Siuslaw, and Coos, all Amerindian languages, as
presenting the order V(erb) O(bject) S(subject) as dominant.
While lacking substantiating data on these languages, I have
found eight other languages which appear to present VOS, in
one variant or another, as the least-marked word order. These
I refer to as the "sample" throughout my essay. There are,
however, no convincing examples of languages whose unmarked
word order is either OVS (but see postscript) or OSV, the
other two logical possibilities for being subject-final
(considering only the relative order of subject, verb, and

object). See Pullum 1977 for discussion and rejection of the
few tenuous examples of languages suggested as being OSV.

6.1.2. Some Subject-Final Languages

Malagasy (Madagascar; Malayo-Polynesian)

My data on Malagasy is based on a year of field work *in situ*,
continued informant work, and several good grammars, (e.g.,
Malzac 1926). For sentences which present both subject and
direct object, the least-marked word order is clearly VOXS,
where X is any other full noun phrase required by the verb,
such as indirect object, benefactive, locative, instrumental,
etc. If several such noun phrases occur, it is possible for
some locatives and temporals to occur to the right of the
subject. The direct object, however, is rigidly bound to the
immediate postverbal position; putting any other noun phrase
between the verb and direct object results in resoundingly
ungrammatical sentences.

(3) Manasa lamba   (ho'an ny ankizy)   ny zazavavy.
    wash   clothes (for   the children) the girl
    'The girl is washing clothes (for the children).'

(4) Nametraka ny harona teo   ambon'ny latabatra Rabe.
    placed   the basket there on-the table   Rabe
    'Rabe put the basket on top of the table.'

The only alternate word order in which the subject would
precede the object is SVO. This order, however, is clearly
more marked. It occurs rarely in discourse and has a contrastive emphatic effect. (5) would be a natural context of use.

(5) — Inona no   ataon'ny   mpianatra?
      what Ptc. done-by-the students
      'What are the students doing?'

    — Ny zazavavy mihira, ny zazalahy mianatra.
      the girl   sing   the boy   study
      'The girls are singing; the boys are studying.'

Of more common occurrence in Malagasy is an SVO order in
which the subject is separated from the predicate phrase by
the particle dia.

(6) Rasoa dia   manasa lamba   (izy).
    Rasoa Ptc. wash   clothes 3Sg.
    'Rasoa (she) is washing clothes.'

This construction, however, represents a clear, if weak,
topicalization of the subject (or any noun phrase). Its
distribution is largely limited to main clauses. Sentences with
such fronted noun phrases cannot be nominalized, relativized
into, etc. The sentence type is thus clearly not among the
least marked in Malagasy. See Keenan 1976a for further
discussion.

Furthermore, one could question whether (4) above is really
among the least-marked sentences (pragmatically speaking; see
Keenan 1976a for justification that it is among the least-
marked syntactically). Sentence (7) below, the passive variant
of (4), would probably be a more usual way to express the idea
in (4).

(7) Nopetrahan-dRabe teo   ambon'ny latabatra ny   harona.
    placed-by   Rabe there on-the   table   the basket
    'The basket was put on the table by Rabe.'

(7) however, does not present (in surface) a direct object
phrase and so is not one of the sentences on which the
definition of subject-final is based. Apparently then the set
of least-marked sentences in Malagasy contains fewer ones with
direct objects than does the set of least-marked sentences in,
say, English. If this set contained no sentences with direct
objects in Malagasy, we would not be justified in calling
Malagasy a subject-final language. But this is not true.
Sentence (3) cannot be construed in a passive form, since the
semantic direct object lamba 'clothes' is indefinite and

surface subjects in Malagasy must be definite; that is, they
are presupposed referential. See Keenan 1976a for more discussion. Thus (8) is clearly ungrammatical.

(8) *Sasan'ny   zazavavy (ho'an'ny ankizy) lamba.
    washed-by-the girl   (for-the child) clothes
    'Clothes are being washed (for the children) by
      the girl.'

Thus the simple sentence in (3), without the oblique noun
phrase, is the only unmarked way to express this idea. Malagasy, then, does present unmarked sentences with both subjects
and direct objects; in such instances the subject always
follows the object.

Batak (Toba Dialect, Northern Sumatra, Malayo-Polynesian)

Data here are based on informant work with two native speaker
linguists, Dr. Maruli Butar-Butar and Mr. Liberty P. Sihombing,
as well as on Silitonga 1973. (Page numbers by examples below
all refer to Silitonga 1973.) I consider here only the Toba
spoken in Northern Sumatra. There is a large Toba community
in Djakarta (Java) which, on the basis of elicitation from
one native speaker, appears to use SVO as the least-marked
word order. It is likely that this is due to the influence of
Bahasa Indonesia.

The unmarked order in active sentences in Toba Batak is
VOSX. No noun phrase can intervene between the verb and its
direct object. Oblique noun phrases, including indirect
objects, follow the subject.

(9) Mangisap sandu nasida di djabu. (p. 21)
    smoke   opium they in house
    'They are smoking opium in the house.'

(10) Mangalean poda   guru   i   tu dakdanak i.
     give   advice teacher the to child   the
     'The teacher gives advice to the child.'

Here again, however, SVO is a grammatically possible order, as in (11a).

(11) a. Ibana mangisap sandu.
      he   smoke   opium
      'He is smoking opium.'

    b. Ndang ibana mangisap sandu. (p. 69)
      not he   smoke   opium
      'He isn't smoking opium.'

But the SVO order again seems contrastive. Thus (11b), the negation of (11a), only denies that _he_, in distinction to someone else, is smoking opium. It is still implied that someone else is smoking opium. Thus (11a) makes presuppositions on its context of use concerning whether other people than those mentioned in the sentence are smoking opium or not. Hence (11a) is more marked than the corresponding sentence in VOS order. As further support that VOS is the least marked order, SVO sentences occur only rarely in Silitonga (1973) and in my elicited data, while VOS occurs commonly. In addition, Silitonga argues that VOS is the syntactically most basic order, and he derives SVO sentences from VOS ones via a transformation. I conclude then that VOS sentences like (9) and (10) are among the least-marked sentences in Toba Batak. The direct objects in these sentences are, however, indefinite. While it is possible for direct objects to be definite, as in (12) below,

(12) Manghindat poti i   baoa i. (p. 40)
     lift   case   the man the
     'The man lifted the case.'

it is more usual for sentences in which there is a definite patient to present themselves in either of two ways. First, as in Malagasy, the sentence can be passivized, as in (13).

(13) Dihindat baoa i   poti i.
     lift-by man   the case the
     'The case was lifted by the man.'

The use of passives, which exist in a considerable variety of
forms, is extremely common in Toba Batak (see Silitonga 1973,
Ch. 11, for discussion). And some verbs can appear only as
passive in simple sentences (although the active form shows
up in more complex constructions).

(14) a. *Mananda   baoa i   ibana.
        Act.-know man   the he
        'He knows the man.'

     b. Ditanda   ibana baoa i. (p. 27)
        Pass.-known he   man   the
        'The man is known to him.'

     c. Ise mananda   baoa i?
        who Act.-know man   the
        'Who knows the man?'

These data suggest then that, as in Malagasy, the set of
unmarked sentences in Toba Batak contains fewer sentences
presenting direct object phrases than does the corresponding
set in English. Nonetheless, those sentences like (9) and
(10) with indefinite direct objects appear to be in this set.
Furthermore, there is a second type of active construction
in which definite direct objects precede subjects and which
may be among the unmarked constructions in the language; a
particle do is inserted between the direct object and the
subject, as in:

(15) Manghindat poti na   borat i   do   baoa i. (p. 30)
     lift   case that heavy the Ptc. man   the
     'The man lifted the heavy case.'

Most usually do serves to single out the constituent which
precedes it with the force of a cleft construction, as in (16).

(16) Si   Bissar do   mangisap sandu.
Art. Bissar Ptc. smoke   opium
'It is Bissar who smokes opium.'

Sentences like (16) presuppose it is known that someone smokes opium and assert merely that the person is Bissar. Hence they are more marked than the simple VOS statement. We expect then that in sentences like (15) it is the whole predicate phrase lift the heavy case which is being contrasted with some other relevant action, such as locking up the room. However, such sentences occur quite frequently, either in active or passive forms, as translations of unmarked declarative sentences of English, so that it appears that this contrastive force of do is hardly felt as a predicate focus. Rather do seems to function as a mere particle separating the predicate phrase from the subject.

I conclude then that active sentences with indefinite objects are clearly among the unmarked sentences in Toba Batak, and that ones with definite objects probably are for certain verbs but not for others.

Fijian (Fiji, Malayo-Polynesian)

My data here come principally from a two-term field methods course given by me with the collaboration of a native speaker of Fijian. I wish to thank the participants in that field methods course for their help in procuring the Fijian data. Specifically I have used examples here from papers by Eser Ergavanli, Ammon Gordon, and Lynn Gordon.

The unmarked word order in Fijian appears to be VOXS, as in Malagasy, but with a considerably greater degree of word order freedom as discussed below.

(17) A   tauva nai lavo mai   na   kato na   tagane.
past take Art. money from Art. box   Art. man
'The man took money from the box.'

(The "articles" nai/na above merely indicate that the nouns
that follow them are common nouns and not that they are
definite. In particular, direct objects occur easily as
definite; lavo 'money' above could as well have been glossed
as the money.)

Simple sentences in Fijian may sometimes, however, appear
in either a VOS or a VSO order:

(18) a. Sa   kila na   taro   o   Wati.
        Past-3Sg. know Art. question Subj. Wati
        'Wati knows the question.'

     b. Sa   kila o   Wati na   taro.
        Past-3Sg. know Subj. Wati Art. question
        'Wati knows the question.'

The particle o precedes proper noun or independent pronoun
subjects, so it is clear that (18b) has order VSO. The VSO
order, however, is much more restricted in its distribution
than the VOS order. Thus if both subject and object are proper
nouns, or both are independent pronouns, the VSO order is not
acceptable.

(19) a. Sa   kila-i   Bale o   Wati.
        Past-3Sg. know-Obj. Bale Subj. Wati
        'Wati knows Bale.'

     b. *Sa   kila-(i) o   Wati Bale.
        Past-3Sg. know-Obj. Subj. Wati Bale
        'Wati knows Bale.'

When the direct object is a proper noun or a pronoun, the
verb takes a characteristic suffix, -i for the example chosen.
Further, preceding the verb is a pronominal clitic whose form
varies as a function of the person and number of the subject.

It would appear then that VOS order is usable in a greater
variety of instances than VSO order and so should be considered
the less marked of the two. Further, there are two other
reasons for considering VOS as the more basic of the two orders.

First, "heavy" noun phrases (with lexical heads) occur
easily in the object slot in VOS order, but heavy subjects
cannot occur in the VSO order (Gordon 1976). Once again then
the distribution of VOS is wider than that of VSO.

(20) a. A   raica na   tagane ka vakamatea na   toa
         Past see   Art. man   who kill   Art. chicken

         o   koya.
         Subj. he

         'He saw the man who killed the chicken.'

     b. *A   raica na   tagane ka vakamatea na   toa
         Past see   Art. man   who kill   Art. chicken

         koya.
         him

         'The man who killed the chicken saw him.'

(Koya in (20b) must be interpreted as the object since it
lacks the subject particle o.)

Second, in sentences in which subject and object are both
common nouns, and so not distinguished by case marking or
verbal "agreements," the informant generally preferred the
VOS interpretation of the sentence rather than saying it was
ambiguous (although judgments here were not always consistent,
so this evidence is less convincing than it might be).

(21) A   raica na   tagane na   yalewa.
     Past see   Art. man   Art. woman
     'The woman saw the man.'
    ?'The man saw the woman.'

In addition to VSO, Fijian presents another alternate word
order in which the subject precedes the object: SVO. Thus,
(22) is an acceptable variant of (21), according to our
informant.

(22) Na   yalewa a   raica na   tagane.
     Art. woman Past see   Art. man
     'The woman saw the man.'

(22) has only the reading on which the woman is the subject.

It appears likely, however, that the possibility of SVO order here was an artifact of the elicitation situation (in English) and the informant's having lived in America for some years. For example, in a survey of three recent newspaper articles in Fijian (where one might expect English language influence) no SVO sentences were observed, while verb-initial structures were very common. SVO is not the ordinary citation order in the literature. See, for example, Arms 1974 and references cited there. Furthermore, even for the informant SVO has a more limited distribution. Thus from (21) the phrase na tagane 'the man' can be relativized as in (23) below.

(23) na   tagane ka   raica na   yalewa
     Art. man   Rel. see   Art. woman
     'the man who saw the woman' or
     'the man whom the woman saw'

In (23) there is no way to tell whether yalewa 'woman' functions as the subject or the object of the verb, and the relative clause is fully ambiguous as between the two readings. If, however, we could relativize on tagane 'man' from (22), the meaning would be unequivocal since yalewa 'woman' would be left in the preverbal position and hence necessarily be the subject. However, despite this good motivation, our informant in general rejected such structures.

(24) *na   tagane ka   na   yalewa a   raica
      Art. man   Rel. Art. woman Past see
      'the man whom the woman saw'

So, again, VOS seems the more unmarked of the two structures and I conclude that Fijian is basically a VOS language, but less rigidly so than Malagasy, for instance.

Gilbertese (The Gilbert Islands, Micronesia;
Malayo-Polynesian)

The data here are based on informant work and Cowell 1971.

In very many respects, both syntactically and morphologically, Gilbertese patterns like Fijian. For example, it has
preverbal subject clitics and object "agreement" suffixal to
the verb. The least-marked word order is VOSX, where X
covers all prepositional noun phrases including indirect
objects. As my data on Fijian are considerably more extensive
than those for Gilbertese, I merely give an example of
subject-final order here and do not discuss Gilbertese otherwise. My claim that Gilbertese

(25) E   kamatea te   naeta te   moa.
     it$_i$ kill-it$_j$ Art. snake$_j$ Art. chicken$_i$
     'The chicken killed the snake.'

is subject-final is based on two considerations: first, that
was the order of elicited material, and, second, it is the
cited basic order in Cowell 1951. I lack information, however,
as to whether SVO and VSO are grammatical orders, whether they
represent topicalized or more marked orders, and so on.

Tzeltal (Southern Mexico; Mayan Family, Penutian Phylum)

The data here are based on field notes, elicitation, and
texts provided by Penny Brown (see also Brown, forthcoming).

The least-marked word order in Tzeltal appears to be VOXS,
with the possibility of locatives occurring after the subject
attested in texts for intransitive sentences:

(26) La   y- il te'tikil mut   ta hamal te   Ziak-e.
     Past he-see wild   chicken in forest Art. Ziak-Art.
     'Ziak saw a wild bird in the forest.'

SVO however is also an attested order; while VSO is not:

(27) 'In   te   winik-e,   la   s- mil s-   bankil.
     that-one Art. man- Art., Past he-kill his-brother
     'That man killed his brother.'

The VOS order appears clearly to be the less marked of the
two orders, VOS and SVO, for the following reasons:

1. It is easily the most commonly occurring citation form.

2. It is easily the most common order in the three texts
available. In these texts, collected by two different field
workers, there are eighteen clear instances of sentences containing full noun phrase subjects and direct objects (from a
corpus of 288 sentences, many of which contain more than one
clause). Sixteen of these sentences present VOS order and only
two present SVO order (there is one additional, incompletely
translated, sentence which may also have SVO order).

3. The SVO sentences occurring in texts are instances in
which the sentence is definite. There are examples of indefinite subjects occurring postverbally, however, which suggests
that the preverbal position is a topic position, since normally only definite noun phrases can be topics. There are
also examples, though not many, in which locatives and direct
objects occur in preverbal position.

Further, in intransitive sentences by far the most common
order is V-Obl.-S rather than S-V-Obl. (where Obl. indicates
Oblique). Clearly, then, it is quite common for a full noun
phrase to intervene between a verb and a final subject:

(28) ... ya   š-b'aht ta na   te   anc- e.
     ... Pres. 3-go   to house Art. woman-Art.
     '... the woman goes to the house.'

4. In instances where an SVO order would disambiguate between which noun phrases were subject and object of the verb,

we do not find in elicitation that SVO order is used, which suggests that SVO has a more restricted distribution, as was true in Fijian above. Thus (29) below is ambiguous according to whether <u>Ziak</u> is understood to be the subject or object of <u>hit</u>.

(29) te   winik-e   te   mač'a la   s-mah te   Ziak-e
     Art. man- Art. Art. who   Past 3-hit Art. Ziak-Art.
     'the man who hit Ziak'
     'the man whom Ziak hit'

Often, however, there is a pause between the verb phrase and the subject in VOS sentences, which may suggest that VOS is a kind of "afterthought" order. The relative frequency of VOS over SVO, however, argues against this. Further, the SVO sentences in the text also present the subject followed by a pause. What may be more generally true is that any full noun phrase marked on the verb is separated by a pause, usually, from the rest of the sentence. Verbs mark both subjects and indirect objects, with the corresponding full noun phrase present; indirect objects may also be marked by a pause.

(30) La   y-ak'- be   s-na,   te   anc,   te
     Past 3-give- to-her 3-house, Art. woman, Art.

     winik-e
     man -Art.

     'The man gave his house to the woman.'

          Otomi (Mezquital Dialect, Hidalgo, Mexico;
                   Oto-Manguean Phylum)

All data here come from Hess 1968.

The least-marked word order for transitive sentences is given by Hess as:

Temp.-Foc.-V-O-S/IO-Obl.

(31) Bihĕ   yá   dútu   nú?ą ra   dąmé.
     he-donned-it his-Pl. clothing that the man
     'That man put on his clothing.'

(32) Pĕ?ca   ?na ra   ngŭ   nú?ą ra   ríko.
     he-has-it one the house that the rich-man
     'That rich man has a house.'

Thus the subject and the indirect object occur in complementary distribution, but either follows the direct object.
The immediate preverbal position is what Hess calls a focus
position; it can be filled by any major noun phrase, such as
the subject, direct object, or locatives. "Focus indicates
to the listener by a shift of the item from post-nuclear to
pre-nuclear that the speaker is shifting attention to
something not already calling for special attention in the
preceding clauses" (Hess 1968: 80-81).

It appears clear then that Otomi is subject-final, and
that instances of SVO order are focused or pragmatically more
marked. Further, VOS is the citation order of examples in Hess.
In the two texts given in Hess there are four sentences with
full noun phrase subject and direct object; three have VOS
order and the other has SOV order, presumably indicating some
sort of double focus.

Ineseño Chumash (Southern California,
Chumash Family, Hokan Phylum)

The data here come entirely from Applegate (1972), whose work
is based on the field work of John P. Harrington, done in 1911
and 1919. Ineseño Chumash is now presumed extinct. I am
indebted to Pamela Munro for drawing my attention to Applegate's work and for providing a typological sketch of Ineseño

Chumash, which summarizes the lengthy description in Applegate.
(Page references cited below are to Applegate.)

Applegate (p. 475) states that the "favored, neutral (word)
order" in I-Chumash is V-IO-DO-S-Obl., noting (p. 473) that
there is some variation in the relative order of IO and DO.
He notes further (p. 466) that full noun phrases carry no case
marking (excluding obliques) and that relative position after
the verb is the primary indicator of grammatical relations
(subject, direct object, etc.).

> (33) S-ul'iš-it ha-   k- tu?   ha- ?ɨhɨy-?. (p. 471)
>   3-grab- me Art.- my- ear   Art.-man
>   'The man grabs my ear.'

> (34) S-uluaqpey-us-wun   ha- weselu ha- mɨy.
>   3-chase-   3- 3Pl. Art.-calf   Art.-wolf
>   'The wolf chases the calves.'

There are, however, two ways, in simple sentences, in which an
SVO order may arise (VSO does not seem to be attested at all).
First, most major noun phrases may be moved to a preverbal
position by a process of topicalization. Subjects, direct
objects, and locatives are among those which can be so
topicalized:

> (35) Šow   ha   s-?uw hi   Ponoya.
>   pespibata Ptc. 3-eat Ptc. Ponoya
>   'Ponoya eats pespibata.'

We may assume that the topicalized order is less basic than
the VOS order, since it has the effect of emphasizing the
topicalized noun phrase. For example, if the topicalized noun
phrases are independent pronouns, they often occur in a special
emphatic form when preverbal (p. 484).

Second, apparently it is not possible for more than two full
noun phrases to follow the verb. Thus if the sentence has more

than two, the subject may occur preverbally, as in (36); but
nonsubjects can also be fronted, as in (37).

(36) Ma-   ʔeneq hi   s-sin'ay ha-   malak hi   mam'
     Art.- woman Ptc. 3-put   Art.-tar   Ptc. inside

     ha- s-ʔawaq.
     Art.-3-jug

     'The woman puts tar inside her jug.'

(37) Ma-   takak ha-   s-am-   axšɨs ha-   maxal'amɨs
     Art.-Quail Art.-3-Indef.-invite Art.-fiesta

     hi   ʔas'aka.
     Ptc. ʔas'aka

     'They invite Quail (to) the fiesta (at) ʔas'aka.'

It appears clear then that for simple sentences the least-
marked order is VOS; orders in which the subject precedes the
object are either emphatic or grammatically conditioned if the
sentence is complex.

Baure (Bolivia, Arawakan Family, Andean-Equatorial Phylum)

All data here come from a single article, Baptista and Wallin
1967. (Page numbers in this section all refer to that article.)
The least-marked word order appears to be VOS, as illustrated
in (38) and (39). However, very few sentences presenting full
noun phrase subjects and direct objects occur in Baptista and
Wallin texts, so Baure is the least well supported candidate
for being subject-final in our sample.

(38) Ro-   pónoek-iyo- wo-   ni   to čor teč ni-šír?
     3Sg.M.-plant- where-Punct.-Incom. the corn that my-son
     'Where did my son plant the corn?'

(39) Wečon   to neč te hir ačó-w   to ro-píri.
     fighter the those this man and-Punct. the his-brother
     'This man and his brother are fighting those.'

SVO however is a grammatically possible word order:

(40) To šiyé ro-   hínokopaw kon to rámpikow
     the fox 3-Sg.M.-see   what the he-carry-come

     teč toéroker.
     that field-man

     'The fox was seeing what the farmer was bringing.'

In my view VOS represents the least-marked order in Baure for
the following reasons: first, of the twenty-four clause types
formulaically described in Baptista and Wallin, twelve present
subjects and direct objects. Of these, eleven present the
subject slot after the object slot and one presents SVO order.
These orders are described as the most frequent (p. 36),
although it is also stated there that the order varies freely.
Second, for all the intransitive sentence formulae presented,
the subject follows the verb. To my knowledge, basic intransitive order VS associated with transitive order SVO is nowhere
attested among the languages of the world. Third, and perhaps
most important, clause-initial position is claimed to be
emphatic (p. 33), although no exemplified discussion is given
regarding the meaning differences between SVO and VOS orders.

I conclude then that the Baure evidence suggests that it is
subject-final, but clearly more extensive investigation would
be needed to establish this convincingly.

6.2. Some General Properties of Subject-Final Languages

In this section I present several generalizations (Gs)
concerning the syntax of subject-final languages.

G-1: Subject-final languages are always verb-initial
(but see Postscript).

That is, in the least-marked sentence types in a subject-
final language, the verb normally precedes the major noun

phrases required by the verb. Thus in intransitive sentences
the unmarked word order is VSX (e.g., Batak) or VXS (e.g.,
Malagasy, Chumash). For the languages in our sample, G-1
needs only sporadic qualifications. Perhaps the most significant is that in Chumash, intransitive sentences with nominal
predicates usually have an SV order, although VS order is
also possible:

   (41) Kay ka   wot'. (Applegate 1972: 452)
        he Ptc. chief
        'He is a chief.'

   (42) Šiša-k- pepe?   hi   kay. (Applegate 1972: 452)
        half-my-brother Ptc. he
        'He is my half-brother.'

   *G-2: Subject-final languages normally occur in linguistic
   phyla in which verb-initial languages are common.*[1]

The most serious qualification of G-2 concerns Chumash,
presumably a member of the Hokan phylum. The more common order
in Hokan would appear to be verb-final, as for Yuman languages
generally, such as Digueño and Mojave (see Munro 1974 for
discussion). (My knowledge about the distribution of word
order types in other Hokan languages is limited. Specifically,
I know nothing of the Hokan languages in northern California
to which Applegate asserts Ineseño Chumash is related. It is
quite generally true however that Amerindian languages of the
northwest coast are verb-initial. Thus Salish, e.g., Bella
Coola, is dominantly verb-initial. So are Wakashan languages
like Nootka, at least some Penutian languages like Chinook,
and various isolates like Quileute.) On the other hand, one
may infer from Applegate that the affiliation of Chumash with
Hokan is not entirely well established: "The Chumashan languages are thought to be related to the Hokan stock, repre-

sented primarily in northern California, but this relationship
is not an easy one to establish" (1972: 1).

The phyla to which the other languages in my sample belong
evidence significant verb-initiality. The best established
evidence is for the Malayo-Polynesian (Austronesian) phyla.
The four languages cited here from those phyla, Malagasy,
Fijian, Gilbertese, and Toba Batak, are all verb-initial. In
addition, Philippine languages (Tagalog, Kapampangan, etc.)
are all verb-initial, as are the Polynesian languages, Maori,
Tahitian, etc.

As regards Tzeltal (Mayan family, Penutian phylum) verb-
initial is a common order in Mayan (e.g., Jacaltec; see Craig
1977 for discussion). Elsewhere in Penutian, e.g., Chinookan
on the northwest (American) coast, verb-initial occurs.
As regards Otomi (Oto-Manguean phylum) the Zapotecan language dialects are verb-initial (see Picket 1960 for
discussion).

Finally, as regards Baure (Arawakan family, Andean-Equatorial phylum) the picture is slightly more complex. Several
other Arawakan languages (we know little about the distribution of word order types more generally in Andean-Equatorial)
are known to be verb-initial, e.g., Ignaciano (Ott and Ott
1967) and Machiguenga (Snell and Wise 1963). But at least one
other Arawakan language, Piro (Matteson 1965), is cited as
verb-final. And furthermore, Baure, as well as Ignaciano and
Machiguenga, presents several morphosyntactic properties
characteristic of verb-final languages as opposed to verb-
initial ones. Most of these properties (see below) concern
the position of small morphemes which are either completely
bound or else have their position rigidly fixed relative to
a major constituent (verb or noun phrase) of a sentence. On
the assumption that the position of bound or nearly bound

morphemes changes more slowly historically speaking than the
relative position of unbound constituents, the hypothesis that
the verb-initial order in Arawakan is a relatively recent
innovation, the bound morphology not yet having "caught up"
so to speak, is tempting and worthy of further investigation.

G-3: *SVO is a grammatical (although marked) word order
in all VOS languages.*

This point has been substantiated in section 6.1 above.
Here I note only that, as Greenberg has pointed out, SVO is
quite generally an "alternate" order available in verb-initial
languages.

My next generalization concerns verb agreement. A verb
agrees with a full noun phrase in a sentence if it has bound
morphemes or clitics whose form varies with the noun class of
the full noun phrase.

G-4: *If a language is subject-final then either transitive
verbs of unmarked sentences agree with no full noun
phrase in the sentence or they agree with two noun
phrases.*

G-5: *If transitive verbs in subject-final languages present
agreement at all, then they have a prefixal (pre - verb
stem) agreement with the subject noun phrase and a
suffixal agreement with a nonsubject.*

For the languages in our sample, Malagasy and Batak present no
verb agreement at all. All the others have a prefixal subject
agreement and some form of suffixal object agreement. In
Tzeltal and Otomi the suffixal agreement is with the indirect
object rather than the direct object. It is unclear from Hess
1968 whether verbs also inflect for direct object, or whether
there is simply a distinction in stem forms for transitive and

intransitive verbs. In Baure, object agreement is, according
to Baptista and Wallin 1967, optional when the full noun
phrase direct object is present, but shows up with pronominal
force when the full noun phrase is not present, as in (43):

(43) Pi- kótokoše- ro.
     you grab-will-it
     'You will grab it.'

And for some sentence types, the suffixal proform on the verb
must be interpreted as referring to the indirect object if a
full noun phrase direct object is present.

*G-6: Subject-final languages have relatively little nominal
case marking.*

By *nominal case marking* I mean that full noun phrases carry
affixes or pre- or postpositions which indicate the semantic
and/or the grammatical relation they bear to the verb. Thus
for no language in my sample is there a general way of
distinguishing full noun phrase subjects and objects by
nominal case marking. Malagasy and Fijian do however present
limited means for making a subject-object distinction by
case marking.

   In Fijian, proper nouns and the independent personal
pronouns (but not common nouns) are preceded by a particle o
when they occur as subjects:

(44) E   mokut-i   Wati o   Bale.
     3Sg. hit- Obj. Wati Topic Bale
     'Bale hit Wati.'

This particle is more properly considered a topic marker rather
than principally a subject marker, since pronouns and proper
nouns, when they are fronted as topics, also carry this
particle:

(45) O   Wati e   mokuta o Bale.
     Topic Wati 3Sg. hit   Bale
     'Wati Bale hit.'

Nonetheless in unmarked sentences o̲ does distinguish pronoun
and proper noun subjects from objects. If the subject is a
common noun phrase, however, it is not morphologically distinct
from the object.

In Malagasy, proper noun human direct objects as well as
direct objects beginning with the phoneme /i/ may take a
locative-genitive particle an̲-. For some speakers the use of
this particle is optional. Compare (3) and̲ (4), in which the
object is unmarked, with (46) below:

(46) Nahita an-   dRabe Rasoa.
     saw   Acc.- Rabe Rasoa
     'Rasoa saw Rabe.'

Further, it might appear from examples like (30) that in
Tzeltal subjects carry a special discontinuous form of the
article t̲e̲ ... -e̲, while nonsubjects have only t̲e̲. It appears
from my data however that the discontinuous form of the
article is generally used for the last noun phrase in a
sentence, regardless of grammatical role. Thus in (29) Ziak
has the discontinuous form of the article even though it may
be interpreted as the object, not the subject. The distribution of the discontinuous form of the article would however
bear further investigation.

Despite these qualifications, it seems clear from the
data that in general in subject-final languages common noun
phrase subjects and objects are not distinguished by adpositions or case affixes, and proper noun subjects and objects
are only sporadically distinguished by these means.

Furthermore, it is not uncommon in these languages for
indirect objects to carry no nominal case marking. Thus full

noun phrase indirect objects are most usually unmarked by
affixes or adpositions in Malagasy, Chumash, Tzeltal, Otomi,
and to judge from very limited data, Baure. On the other hand,
such indirect objects are constructed with prepositions in
Fijian, Gilbertese, and Batak.

> G-7: *Subject-final languages are generally prepositional
> rather than postpositional.*

Baure is a partial counterexample to G-7. The adpositions which
occur as bound morphemes are clearly postpositions, not
prepositions:

(47) Biyónopoekopaša pon   soratí-ye.
     we-walk-down   other town- to
     'We are going by land to another town.'

Oh the other hand, the postpositional system in Baure does
seem to be of limited productivity. Thus postpositions occur
only on nouns but do not follow entire noun phrases: (48) and
(49) are from Baptista and Wallin 1967: 45:

(48) a. to pon   bipér típoreko-ye čiča
        the other Class. chicken- in big
        'in the other big chicken'

     b. to no-   sóri-ye to ni-ronáneb
        the their-town-in the my-parents
        'in my parents' town'

Furthermore, adpositions which are morphemically independent occur as prepositions:

(49) a. iyowón soratí-ye
        from   town- in
        'from within the town'

     b. iškón embére
        until tomorrow
        'until tomorrow'

Since postpositions are highly characteristic of verb-final
languages, this patterning is quite consistent with my earlier
suggestion that Baure (as well as Ignaciano and Machiguenga,
which also present bound adpositions as postpositions) has
recently changed from a verb-final to a verb-initial language.

Otherwise, all the other languages in the sample here are
exclusively prepositional. Yet most of the American Indian
languages in the sample seem to have very few unanalyzable
prepositions. Thus in Tzeltal, ta is just about the only
unanalyzable preposition in the corpus; it translates instrumental and locative prepositions in English. Chumash (see
Applegate 1972: 431) may have no unanalyzable prepositions
at all. Even locatives are normally presented without prepositions, as in example (37), although the verb may take an
affix indicating that a locative element is present. The few
candidates for prepositions appear to be derived from independently existing nouns or verbs. Finally, in Otomi there
again appear to be only a few indigenous prepositions. Many
locatives, for example, are presented without overt locative
prepositions. And many of the prepositions which do exist are
clearly borrowings from Spanish, as Hess (1968: 145) points
out.

Finally, verb-initial languages generally are prepositional
(Baure and related Arawakan languages plus a few others such
as Quileute on the northwest coast notwithstanding), so it is
not likely that prepositionality is directly dependent on the
property of being subject-final.

*G-8: In subject-final languages noun phrase questions can
always be formed by putting the question word, e.g.,
Who? What? etc., in a preverbal position, provided
the question word is not a bound morpheme.*

This generalization holds for all the languages in our sample. The Malagasy example below is typical, although it is not true that the question word is separated from the rest of the sentence in all the languages.

(50) Iza no   manasa lamba?
     who Ptc. wash   clothes
     'Who is washing clothes?'

The proviso to G-8 regarding morphemically independent question words is necessitated by Baure. Some question words, as in (38), occur as bound morphemes on the verb, and these are not fronted in questions. Others, such as Who? and Why? do occur as independent morphemes, however, and so are fronted, taking, curiously, subject and object clitics (at least in the case of Why?).

(51) Ko-   ro- pi poékon?
     who-why him-you allower
     'Why do you let him?'

Furthermore, in the languages in my sample, it is not always necessary to front independent question words. For example, both Malagasy and Batak allow certain types of non-subjects to be questioned merely by inserting the appropriate question word in the noun phrase position, as (52) from Malagasy illustrates.

(52) Manasa lamba   amin'inona Rasoa?
     wash   clothes with-what Rasoa
     'With what is Rasoa washing clothes?'

(52) need not be an echo question.

It is possible that G-8 can be stated in a more general fashion, something along the lines of "focused, or relatively new, information is fronted." I cannot give a general definition of *focused constituent*, but the intent here is to characterize the information role of John in sentences like (53).

(53) It was John whom Mary saw.

Intuitively, (53) presupposes that Mary saw someone and asserts that that person was John. Similarly in questions like <u>Whom did Mary see?</u> it is presupposed that Mary saw someone, and the identity of that person is requested. Several of the languages in the sample here, notably Malagasy, Batak, and Fijian, present constructions which focus on noun phrases in the way (53) focuses on <u>John</u>. And all three languages focus the noun phrase by presenting it in a preverbal position. The Malagasy (54) is illustrative:

(54) Rasoa no   manasa lamba.
     Rasoa Ptc. wash   clothes
     'It is Rasoa who is washing clothes.'

Data on focusing in the other languages of the sample are lacking, but if they have such focus constructions and they follow the pattern of question formation, as is plausible on semantic grounds, then the generalization of G-8 would be established.

G-9: All subject-final languages present morphemically independent subordinate conjunctions which precede a finite subordinate clause.

(55) from Malagasy is illustrative:

(55) Tsy faly   Rabe satria   marary Rasoa.
     not happy Rabe because sick   Rasoa
     'Rabe is not happy because Rasoa is sick.'

The significance of G-9 however is considerably weakened by the fact that subordinate conjunction plus finite subordinate clause is not a dominant way of expressing subordination in the Amerindian languages of my sample. Subordinate conjunctions exist in Tzeltal, but the corpus contains very few examples, so it does not look like a well-developed category.

In Otomi several of the subordinate conjunctions are clearly
borrowings from Spanish, so again the category does not look
well entrenched in the language. In Baure, those subordinating
particles which are morphemically independent clearly do
precede finite clauses, but a more usual way to indicate
subordination in this limited corpus is by bound suffixes on
the verb. Such clauses, however, usually translate headless
relatives and embedded questions in English, rather than true
adverbial clauses of the "if, when, because" sort. And finally,
in Chumash again, while there are a few examples of words
analyzable as subordinate conjunctions (see Applegate 1972:
421 for examples), the more common way to express subordinate
clauses is by nominalization of sentences. These nominalizations, however, generally translate headless relatives or
embedded questions.

The next several generalizations concern the internal
structure of the noun phrase:

*G-10: In possessive constructions subject-final languages
always present full noun phrase possessors after the
head (the possessed) noun phrase.*

In the Amerindian languages of this sample, the possessor noun
phrase is not marked as genitive or introduced by a preposition, and the head noun carries a pronominal prefix or clitic
which agrees in person and number with the possessor (something which is otherwise common in Amerindian languages).
Otomi (56) is illustrative:

(56) rá   noyá ʔaxwã
     his word God
     'God's word'

In the Malayo-Polynesian languages of this sample, heads do
not normally agree with possessors; but there is usually some

sort of particle between the head and the possessor, as in
Malagasy (57):

(57) ny trano-nd-   Rabe
     the house-Poss.-Rabe
     'Rabe's house'

(The /d/ in /nd/ above is not part of the possessor morpheme;
it is inserted whenever an /n/ and an /r/ would otherwise occur
together, in that order.)

In Chumash the full noun phrase possessor may be placed
before the head for emphasis, and in all the Amerindian languages in this sample pronominal possessors are represented
(in the least-marked way) solely by the pronominal prefix or
clitic. Thus <u>his</u> <u>word</u> in Otomi would be expressed merely by
deleting <u>ʔaxwǎ</u> 'God' from (56).

> G-11: *In subject-final languages relative clauses always*
>   *present the head noun to the left of the restricting*
>   *clause.*

(58) from Malagasy is illustrative:

(58) ny   zazavavy (izay) manasa lamba
     the girl   (that) wash   clothes
     'the girl who is washing clothes'

> G-12: *Subject-final languages do not have relative pronouns.*

By *relative pronoun* I understand some kind of pronominal
element which marks the grammatical role (subject, object,
etc.) of the position relativized. G-12 clearly holds for
the Malayo-Polynesian languages of the sample. All these
languages present a morphologically invariable particle which
occurs (optionally or obligatorily depending on the language)
between the head and the restricting clause, as Malagasy <u>izay</u>
in (58). In Fijian and Gilbertese, personal pronouns may be
retained directly in the position relativized if the position

is constructed with a preposition or is a possessor noun
phrase. In Batak only possessor noun phrases allow pronoun
retention. Malagasy allows no pronoun retention.

The application of G-12 to the Amerindian languages in
this sample is less clear however, in large part due to lack
of data. In Baure and Chumash the head noun phrase of relative
clauses is followed by the restricting clause, which is in
nominalized form and could stand alone as a headless relative
(the one that...). The nominalized verb carries an article and
various subordination particles, but these particles do not
appear to differ according to whether the head functions as
a subject or object of the verb. Nor do they otherwise appear
to have any pronominal function — that is, they are subordi-
nators used in many contexts besides relative clauses and do
not appear to have a referential function. -al- in Chumash is
illustrative:

(59) ha- k- ʔuw-muʔ ha   ka   ha- k-al- aqšiyɨk
     Art.-my-food   Art. Ptc. Art.-I-Sub.-like
     'my food that I like'

In Tzeltal and Otomi, on the other hand, interrogative
pronouns sometimes appear as (part of) the relativizer
word(s). Since locative interrogative words, for example, are
distinct from those which question subjects and objects, one
might (to extrapolate from the limited data) be able to
distinguish, e.g., the house that I saw from the house where
I live. The interrogative pronouns however are not distinct
for subject and object, so to that extent at least the
languages lack relative pronouns.

G-13a: *All subject-final languages possess articles.*

G-13b: *With more than chance frequency subject-final
        languages have definite articles (distinct from the
        ordinary demonstrative adjectives).*

As regards G-13b, Malagasy, Batak, Otomi, Tzeltal, and Baure have definite articles, while Gilbertese, Fijian, and Chumash do not. In Gilbertese, however, there is a singular article (definite or indefinite) and a plural indefinite article. In Fijian, common nouns carry an article, but it appears to give no semantic information, e.g., definiteness, number, or noun class, concerning the noun. And in Chumash almost all common nouns are constructed with an article, although again no semantic information seems to be indicated by it. Its presence does, however, distinguish nominalized verbs from non-nominalized ones.

Concerning other common elements within noun phrases I find no fully universal generalizations. The closest is:

G-14: With much greater than chance frequency numerical expressions precede the nouns they modify.

Only Malagasy is exceptional here. Numerical expressions behave by and large like descriptive adjectives and as such follow the noun (although there are one or two frozen expressions with numerals preceding nouns). In some of the other languages, notably Tzeltal and Gilbertese, the constructions of numerical expressions are complicated by the existence of numeral classifiers.

G-15: With much greater than chance frequency articles precede nouns.

Only Batak is exceptional here in having the article (which also functions as the third person inanimate personal pronoun) follow the noun.

As regards the positioning of descriptive adjectives only the weak generalization is possible that it is slightly more usual for such adjectives to follow nouns than to precede. However the normal order is adjective plus noun in Tzeltal and Otomi, and both orders, adjective before or after noun, are about equally common in Chumash.

And as regards demonstrative adjectives, I have no generalization at all. They precede nouns in Chumash, Otomi, and Baure. They follow nouns in Gilbertese, Fijian, and Batak. And they "frame" noun phrases in Malagasy and Tzeltal, as illustrated in (60) from Malagasy and (61) from Tzeltal:

(60) ity   trano fotsy ity
     this house white this
     'this white house'

(61) men   k'shk'al winik-i
     that fiery   man- that
     'that fiery man'

The next generalizations concern the internal structure of verbs and verb phrases.

G-16: Negative elements precede the verb in subject-final languages.

G-16 holds for all the languages in the sample. (55) above from Malagasy is illustrative.

G-17: A causative element precedes the root of the causativized verb in subject-final language.

In all the languages in the sample except Tzeltal and Otomi, causative constructions are formed by prefixing the verb root with a causative morpheme. (62) below from Malagasy is illustrative.

(62) Mamp- ianatra ny   ankizy Rabe.
     cause-study   the child Rabe
     'Rabe teaches the children.'

In Tzeltal the only examples I have of causative constructions are constructed with the verb 'give' followed by a nominalization of the causativized verb:

(63) Ya   yák'   ta   mánei.
     Pres. he-give Prep. buying
     'He causes (him) to buy (it).'

Similarly in Otomi an overt verb of causation precedes the causativized verb.

G-18: *All subject-final languages have passive forms of verbs (ones in which the object of the active verb functions as the subject).*

Sentences (4) and (7) above from Malagasy illustrate active-passive pairs.

G-19: *'Passive' is generally marked in the verbal morphology in subject-final languages.*

The only clear exception here is Tzeltal, where passives are constructed from the active verb <u>receive</u> followed by a nominalized form of the "passivized" verb (these nominalized forms occur in a great variety of complex verbal constructions, e.g., the causatives mentioned above).

(64) La   y- ich'   'utel   yu'un   s- tat   te
     Past he-receive bawling-out because his-father Art.

     Ziak-e.
     Ziak-Art.

     'Ziak was bawled out by his father.'

In Baure 'Passive' appears to be marked on the verb, but more examples illustrating the full verbal morphology are needed to make this conclusion certain.

G-20: *Subject-final languages generally do not have overt copulas.*

By *copula* I mean a morphophonemically independent element which has the characteristic properties of stative verbs in its language and which functions as the main verb in sentences with nominal predicates, like John is a thief. Malagasy is a typical here:

(65) Mpampianatra Rajaona.
teacher   John
'John is a teacher.'

Otomi may be a counterexample to G-20. In sentences like (66) below there is a morphophonemically independent element which codes categories of person and, apparently (no full paradigms are given), of tense.

(66) Nugí ma nǎna   mrá   měngu ʔbɛtʔí.
     I   my mother 3Past native Beti
     'As for me, my mother was a native of Beti.'

It is not clear from Hess (1968) however that mrá in (66) has otherwise the morphology of verbs. Rather it looks as though the apparent copula shows more affinity with nominal construc-tions than verbal ones, although more complete data would be needed to justify this suggestion. Furthermore, mrá is not present when the main predicate would be adjectival, as in Mary is pretty.

Otherwise both Malagasy and Chumash allow the subject to be separated from a nominal predicate by a particle, but this particle is invariable in form and otherwise has none of the properties of verbs. (41) above from Chumash is illustrative, and the Malagasy construction, (67) below, is clearly a form of topicalization (see section 6.1 for more discussion).

(67) Rabe dia mpampianatra.
     Rabe Ptc. teacher
     'Rabe is a teacher.'

Finally, other possible word order correlates in verb phrases based on Greenberg, such as the relative position of modals, adverbs, and the verb, have proven difficult to verify, since for many of the languages in the sample it appears doubtful that there are distinct grammatical categories of modal and adverb.

Nonetheless elements which translate modal concepts like obligation, necessity, desire, intention, etc., usually precede the verb; they follow the verb however in Chumash and, where they occur as bound affixes, in Baure (where they are independent morphemes in Baure they occur preverbally).

Manner adverbs, however, are even harder to establish as a basic grammatical category in the languages of the sample. They appear as a distinct category in Malagasy and Fijian, where they follow the verb. They seem to follow the verb in Otomi, but more examples are needed. Certain adverbial-like particles appear suffixal to verbs in Baure. In Tzeltal and Chumash, adverbs appear to be merely verbs and occur pre-verbally, as in (68) from Chumash.

(68) S- towič   ha   s- wala-tepet
     it-go-fast Ptc. it-turn
     'It turns fast.'

The few available examples of manner adverbials in Gilbertese appear to occur preverbally, in the same position as negation and other sentential adverbs like _truly_.

6.3. Explaining the Scarcity of Subject-Final Languages

Subject-final languages, as indicated here, comprise a small and erratically distributed percentage of verb-initial languages. Verb-initial languages are themselves a clear minority among the world languages, probably not constituting more than 10 percent of the total. Verb-final languages, with various degrees of word order freedom, are the most widely distributed of word order types; SVO languages are a reasonably close second. Together these two types include about 90 percent of the world's languages. Given this distribution, it is

natural to wonder why so few languages avail themselves of
the syntactic possibility of presenting the subject in final
position.

Here I suggest that at least part of the explanation is
cognitive, that is, it concerns how humans understand the
meanings of sentences, and part of the meaning is pragmatic,
that is, it concerns the purposes for which humans use
language. (I do not claim however that this constitutes the
whole explanation.) Specifically I argue that syntactically
"simple" or *basic* sentences present certain cognitive and
pragmatic difficulties for users of subject-final languages.
And second I argue that several major syntactic processes for
forming complex (less basic) sentences aggravate the basic
difficulties and in addition introduce further cognitive
difficulties.

6.3.1. Basic Difficulties

Many might consider that the principle that "old information
comes first" is sufficient to explain the preponderance of
subject-initial languages, given that most commonly the
subject is old information in the sense that it usually refers
to some person or object already known to the speaker and
addressee(s.) at the time of speaking. However, I find this
principle, as it stands, insufficient. Specifically, why
should old information come first? After all, usually when we
communicate we want to say something not specifically known
to the addressee. Why not begin then with the novel information and trail off with what is already known? Furthermore, I
find no clear sense in which the information in the predicate
is new and that in the subject old. What is new in a simple
sentence like Ché lives! is not the information in either Ché
or lives but rather that the referent of the subject has the

property, or performed the action, expressed by the predicate.
To understand what is new then we need both the subject and
the predicate, so why not put randomly either one first? Or at
least why don't languages vary randomly with regard to the
choice they make? Below I propose a *Relevance Principle* which
in my view covers perhaps some of the same ground as was
intended for the old-information principle but which I think
has somewhat greater explanatory force.

The Relevance Principle: The reference of the subject
(phrase) determines in part, the relevance of what is said,
regardless of what it is, to the addressee.

In other words, if all we know is what the subject phrase of
a sentence is, we have some expectation whether what will be
said is of any importance to us, depending on whether the
subject phrase refers to an individual (or object) which is
of concern to us or not.

Suppose, for example, we are discussing the success of a
political meeting and someone claims:

(69) John left the meeting early.

Immediately upon hearing the subject phrase John we have some
idea of the relevance, and importance, of whatever is said to
our interest. If John is the candidate we are supporting, we
are concerned to understand what is said about him; whereas
if John is, say, merely the man who was supposed to set up
the tables, we might be less concerned to understand what was
said about him. In a subject-final language on the other hand
we must attend to most of the sentence before we have much
idea as to whether the new information is of much concern to
us.

Subjects then are old information in the sense mentioned
above, but more important they are the topics (of the least-

marked sentences in a language) and thus specify what it is
that the speaker is talking about. And a major advantage of
mentioning the topic first is that the hearer immediately has
at least a serious idea of how what is said (whatever it is)
will concern him or her. We note further that:

1. Probably in all languages (Dyirbal may be an exception;
see Keenan 1976b for discussion) there are many more verbs
which take human subjects than any other sort of noun. Thus
relatively few verbs in any language require that their
subjects refer to times, locations, or even instruments of
actions. Now if subjects are, in part, those noun phrases
which serve to identify the interest of the address in the
discussion it is natural (given that we are in general more
interested in humans than in other things) that subjects should
be dominantly human. (See Givón 1976a for discussion of the
relation between topichood and humanness.)

2. Overt (marked) topicalization operations in most languages move noun phrases to the front of the sentence. Thus
there may well be instances in which we are primarily interested in a participant in an action who would not normally
have been identified by the subject phrase. In such instances
languages generally have the means of marking that constituent
in some way, very commonly by fronting it (perhaps introducing
other changes in the sentence). And the same reason for saying
that subjects in unmarked sentences come first usually also
explains why topics in general ought to come first — they
identify (at least in part) the interest that the addressee
may have in understanding what is said. To put it differently,
subjects usually come first because they are the topics of
the least-marked sentences in a language. And topics in
general come first because they determine the relevance of
what is said for the addressee.

It should be noted perhaps that relevance for the addressee
need not be restricted to mean relevance for the addressee's
interests considered independently of the linguistic discourse
in which the sentence is uttered. It may well be that identifying the reference of the subject or topic (phrase) functions
to allow the addressee to determine the relevance of what is
going to be said to what has already been said. Thus as Givón
(1976a) has argued, topics have a discourse linking function.

*A Principle of Semantic Interpretation: The meaning of the
predicate phrase often depends on the reference of the
subject.*

If this principle is correct, it is cognitively advantageous
to present the subject before the predicate (= verb + its
closely associated objects), since otherwise the addressee
will have to "store" the predicate phrase without fully
understanding it until the subject appears.

One might suppose that the meaning of a predicate phrase
could be described, say as an event or activity, or a state,
independently of who or what was asserted to be in the state
or to engage in the activity. But this, it seems to me, is
not true. Consider for example a predicate like be strong.
As a first approximation at least it can be said that if the
subject is animate, as in John is strong or Weightlifters are
strong, we indicate that the referent of the subject can exert
a lot of force. But if the subject is inanimate, as in This
chain is strong or The table is strong, we indicate that
the referent of the subject can withstand a lot of force.
Similarly the activity denoted by drop on the bed is rather
different according as the subject is John, as in John dropped
on the bed, or pieces of the ceiling, in Pieces of the ceiling
dropped on the bed. And consider the different activities all

referred to by <u>run</u> in sentences like <u>The</u> <u>children</u> <u>are</u> <u>running</u>,
<u>The</u> <u>fish</u> <u>are</u> <u>running</u>, <u>The</u> <u>buses</u> <u>are</u> <u>running</u> <u>today</u>, <u>This</u> <u>watch</u>
<u>is</u> <u>running</u>, <u>The</u> <u>colors</u> <u>are</u> <u>running</u>, <u>The</u> <u>water</u> <u>is</u> <u>running</u>, <u>The</u>
<u>stockings</u> <u>are</u> <u>running</u>, <u>My</u> <u>nose</u> <u>is</u> <u>running</u>, etc. In each the
exact activity which we interpret <u>running</u> as referring to
depends on the nature of the referent of the subject. This
fact about language probably reflects a more general fact
about our ontology: discrete objects may exist in some sense
independently of the properties or activities we ascribe to
them on particular occasions, but the existence of properties
or activities in the absence of objects which have these
properties or engage in the activities is dubious.

It seems to me that, although the point would have to be
further researched, in general, considering the entire lexicon
of a language, simple nouns are relatively fixed in meaning or
reference (though there are certainly genuine cases of ambiguity) and the meaning of verbs and adjectives depends, somewhat subtly perhaps, on what object they are predicated of.
Accepting this claim then it seems that the cognitive advantage
of a subject-predicate language over a predicate-subject
language follows.

Furthermore, it may well be that subject-final languages
present, even in simple sentences, a more acute version of the
dependency problem. We have already seen that, with the
exception of Malagasy and Batak, the subject-final languages
present two pronominal affixes whose form varies with the
noun class of the subject and either the direct or indirect
object; see (34) above from Chumash, for example. Further, the
affixes on the verb are clearly pronominal in function, that
is, they are referential. Thus if, for example, the agent and
patient of an action have already been mentioned in the
discourse and we want to assert that <u>He</u> <u>hit</u> <u>her</u>, we would not

normally (unless some emphasis or contrast were implied) use
the independent pronouns in the full noun phrase positions.
Rather we would just use what appears to be the simple verb as
it occurs in the sentence with full noun phrases. The pronominal affixes on the verb are sufficient to reference the
participants of the action.

But this means, from the point of view of the speaker, that
it is necessary to anticipate to a significant extent the
subject and object phrases in a sentence when enunciating the
verb, in order to know which pronominal affixes to use. And
the hearer on the other hand will interpret these affixes as
referential, but in many instances their reference won't be
determinable until the full noun phrase subjects and objects
have been enunciated.

The anticipation and interpretation problems would not
appear to arise in Malagasy and Batak, because they lack the
pronominal affixes on the verb. But an analogous problem, at
least from the point of view of the speaker, does arise.

We have seen that in these two languages the use of various
forms of passive verbs is quite common, and in selected
instances is clearly the pragmatically least marked option.
But this means that at the time of enunciating the verb of
the sentence the speaker must have anticipated the agent and
patient phrases to know which participant will be placed in
the subject slot. In a subject-initial language on the other
hand we can mention the subject/topic without yet having
decided exactly what we want to say about it. It may be then
that a cognitive dependency between verb and subject exists
in subject-final languages but not in subject-initial ones.
My general suggestion here then is that subject-final languages
may be cognitively somewhat more difficult than subject-initial
languages, since they require a longer "look-ahead" on the

part of the speaker and a longer "unprocessed storage" on the part of the hearer. (A partial counterexample here is afforded by SOV languages which are ergative. Here the case-marking on the subject must anticipate the transitivity of the verb, though nothing more specific about its meaning. I note that nominative-accusative case-marking systems are more widely distributed than ergative-absolutive ones.) What remains open in this analysis, however, is whether it is merely an accident of our small sample of languages that verbs in all of them generally code properties of the subject to a greater extent than verbs in subject-initial languages.

6.3.2. Derived Difficulties

Many of the major processes which form complex structures from simpler ones, and which most if not all languages have to varying degrees, are ones which aggravate the basic difficulties discussed above. Thus they either force the subject farther from the beginning of the sentence ("farther" here relative to the subject's distance from the beginning of a simple or basic sentence) or they increase the amount of material) whose meaning or reference cannot be completely evaluated until the subject phrase is processed. Below I discuss several such processes.

First, however, I note that the processes which aggravate the basic difficulties appear to trigger an additional difficulty, which I shall refer to as *cognitive dissonance*. (To the best of my recollection the term *cognitive dissonance* was first used in psychology, by Festinger.)

The Principle of Cognitive Dissonance: A language is cognitively dissonant to the extent that principles of semantic interpretation which apply to basic sentences of the language must be modified to yield the correct interpretation for complex sentences.

Thus it will appear in many of the examples to follow that the syntax of complex sentences in subject-final languages differs in certain ways from that of simpler ones, ways which avoid the aggravation of the basic difficulties, but which mean that the assignment of meaning to complex sentences by listeners is not done in analogy with the way simple sentences are interpreted. Thus, somewhat indirectly perhaps, subject-finality is responsible for a more complex set of inter-pretation "rules" than is needed for subject-initial languages.

6.3.3. Some Nonbasic Sentence Types
        in Subject-Final Languages

Reciprocals

Consider the interpretation of sentences like (70) from English:

(70) The children were hitting each other.

We know from the special form of the object pronoun <u>each</u> <u>other</u> that the recipients of the action are the same as the actors, and immediately upon hearing the object pronoun we know just what set of people this is, since it is necessarily the same as the set referenced by the subject, and the subject has already been mentioned.

In a subject-final language, however, we might expect (70) to be rendered roughly as (71):

(71) Were hitting each other the children.

And indeed this is basically the way reciprocals are expressed in Tzeltal:

(72) La   s-mah s-ba- ik   te   winike-tik.
     Past 3-hit 3-self-Pl. the man-   Pl.
     'The men were hitting each other.'

In this type of reciprocal construction, however, we cannot
fully interpret (assign a meaning or reference to) the
reciprocal pronoun at the moment of hearing. Rather, we must
wait until the subject phrase has been enunciated, and only
then do we know which individuals were being hit. Reciprocal
Formation then (however it is formulated) extends the amount
of material whose interpretation must await the subject phrase.

　　Interestingly however, of the subject-final languages in my
sample, only Tzeltal forms reciprocals in just this way. All
the other languages in the sample, except possibly Otomi, for
which relevant data are lacking, form reciprocals by affixing
the verb. Malagasy below is typical:

(73) Mif-   anoratra taratasy Rasoa sy Ravelo.
     Recip.-write   letter   Rasoa and Ravelo
     'Rasoa and Ravelo write each other letters.'

　　Forming reciprocals by verbal affixing seems to have the
effect of reducing somewhat the distance between the subject
and the beginning of the sentence. Moreover, it does not
introduce a noun phrase whose interpretation must await that
of another noun phrase, but it still does aggravate the
dependency of meaning of the predicate upon the subject in
the sense that, for example, in Malagasy the verb _mifanoratra_
'to write each other' contains more information than does the
nonreciprocal form _manoratra_ 'to write', but that information
is not fully determinate in the sense that we still don't know
who is receiving letters until the subject phrase appears.

Reflexives

Reflexives, as illustrated in (74a) for SVO languages and (74b) for VOS languages, pose basically the same interpretation problem as do reciprocals.

(74) a. John hit himself.

b. Hit himself John.

Here, however, four of the eight languages in my sample present an independent pronoun in the object position whose interpretation cannot be made until the subject is enunciated. Malagasy and Tzeltal have specifically reflexive forms of pronouns. (75) from Malagasy is illustrative. The reflexive pronoun in Tzeltal is just the nonplural form of the reciprocal pronoun in (72).

(75) Namono tena Rakoto.
     killed self Rakoto
     'Rakoto killed himself.'

Fijian and Gilbertese lack specifically reflexive pronouns altogether, but use ordinary personal pronouns in the object position, illustrated by (76) from Fijian:

(76) A   mokut-i   koya o   Bale.
     Past hit- Obj. him Topic Bale
     'Bale hit him/himself.'

The interpretation of koya 'him' in (76) is not so dependent on the subject as is the reflexive pronoun in Malagasy or Tzeltal. It might corefer to the subject, or it might refer to some other third party already prominent in the context of speech. It is understood like the pronoun him in John thinks that Mary adores him, where him may refer to someone other than John.

Thus, to some extent, Fijian and Gilbertese avoid the dependency of reference problem by sacrificing logical

explicitness (in the sense that they cannot unequivocally
distinguish in surface between John hit him and John hit
himself; see Keenan, forthcoming, for more discussion).
Further, the dependency problem is not altogether avoided,
since the object pronoun in (76) could be uttered in a context
in which no particular individual had been mentioned, as in
"What happened at school yesterday?"

In addition, the Malagasy and Fijian types of reflexive
construction may create a small amount of cognitive dissonance,
as follows: If the subject phrase is an independent pronoun,
as in (77a,b) from Malagasy and Fijian respectively, the
subject pronoun must be interpreted as difficult in reference
from the object pronoun.

(77) a. Namono an- dRabe izy.
        killed Acc.-Rabe he
        'He killed Rabe.'
        'Rabe killed himself.'

     b. a   mokut-i   Bale o   koya.
        Past kill- Obj. Bale Topic he
        'He killed Bale.'
        'Bale killed himself.'

Thus we have here a simple instance of a pronoun following a
referential noun phrase of the right sort but with which it
cannot be interpreted as coreferential. But elsewhere in the
language, in fact almost everywhere, a pronoun occurring
after a full noun phrase of the right category can be interpreted as coreferential with it. Thus it appears as though
one small principle of semantic interpretation which applies
to fairly simple sentences does not apply to more complex ones.

As regards reflexives in the other subject-final languages,
Baure and Chumash reflexivize by affixing verbs, much as was
done in the instance of reciprocals. Otomi may also reflexivize
in this way, but I lack sufficient data to be certain. Batak,

however (together with Tagalog and other Philippine languages),
provides one of the very rare exceptions to the generalization
that, in simple sentences, subjects control reflexivization
and nonsubjects are presented as reflexive pronouns or omitted.
The most usual way to overtly reflexivize in Batak is to
present the sentence as passive in form with the derived
subject being the reflexive pronoun.

> (78) di-   pukkul si   Bissar diri-na.
>   Pass.-hit   Art. Bissar self-his
>   'Bissar struck himself.'
>   (Lit., 'Was struck by Bissar he-self.')

We note that _dirina_ 'himself' is fully pronominal, in that the
form of the reflexive varies in person and number with its
antecedent. (_Dirina_ is a slightly collapsed form of _diri-ni-ia_
'self-of-he'.)

Batak then appears to avoid the problem of having to
suspend the interpretation of object phrases until the subject
phrase is reached, but at the expense of violating an extremely
general property of subjecthood — namely, being an expression
whose reference is determinable independently of other expressions within the same simple sentence (see Keenan 1976b for
more discussion).

Batak does, however, present at least two other ways of
expressing reflexives. In some instances at least, it can have
recourse to an SVO order, as in (79):

> (79) Si   Bissar makkaholongi diri-na.
>   Art. Bissar love   self-his
>   'Bissar loves himself.'

To the extent that the subject is not being specifically
topicalized the option is cognitively dissonant, since usually
fronted noun phrases are understood to be more topical than
those in the least-marked sentences.

A further option for presenting reflexive sentences in
Batak, as well as in Malagasy, is to use an intransitive
though not specifically reflexive form of the verb. Thus both
Batak and Malagasy form verbs by affixing (prefixing is
dominant) roots which most commonly do not otherwise occur as
words in the language. If a given root accepts both transitive
and intransitive affixes, as is fairly common, then, when
semantically appropriate, the intransitive form may be interpreted reflexively. Thus in Batak the transitive verb 'to
wash' is formed from a root plus the prefix maN to yield
mandidi; the intransitive form is maridi, and it is the intransitive form which my informant used to translate the
English reflexive:

(80) Maridi si   Rotua.
     wash   Art. Rotua
     'Rotua washes herself.'

Analogous claims hold here for Malagasy. In fact, the total
number of verbs in Malagasy which would construct a reflexive
with the reflexive pronoun is rather limited. To judge from
claims made in early, nineteenth-century, grammars of Malagasy, the use of tena 'body, self' is an innovation as a
reflexive pronoun. And certainly in many instances where we
expect a reflexive pronoun in English, an intransitive verb
form such as misasa 'to wash (intransitive)' would be used
rather than the transitive form (manasa 'to wash') plus the
reflexive pronoun.

We are left then with the general impression that frequently
in subject-final languages specifically reflexive constructions
are not well-developed.

Heavy Objects

Quite generally the most common position for full sentences to
be embedded as noun phrases is the direct object position.
Thus, for verbs of saying and thinking, the sentence expressing
what is thought or said occurs as an object in languages like
English:

(81) John said that Fred left the party early.

In subject-final languages we might expect that (81) would be
rendered as (82):

(82) Said that left the party early Fred John.

Such a construction would obviously aggravate the basic
problems of subject-finality, however, since the subject is
now far removed from sentence-initial position; and, since
now many verbs and nouns precede the subject, there is a
greater possibility than in simple sentences for elements to
depend for their meaning or reference on the subject.

In fact no subject-final language seems to express sentential complements of saying with the word order in (82). Most
commonly a subject-final language simply uses a VSO order,
illustrated in (83) from Malagasy.

(83) Nihevitra Rabe fa   namaky boky ny   mpianatra.
     thought   Rabe that cut   book the student
     'Rabe thought that the students were reading books.'

The use of the VSO option is common in Malagasy, Fijian,
Chumash, and, to judge from a limited corpus, Otomi. It occurs
in elicitation in Tzeltal and occurs in texts in Baure (where
however the sentential object is always a direct quotation).
The relevant data on Gilbertese are lacking.

The VSO order is, however, cognitively dissonant, since in
simple sentences the noun phrase immediately following the

verb is normally interpreted as the object, not the subject, of the verb. The use of an SVO order here would also be dissonant to the extent that the subject was not being specifically topicalized. Chumash does, infrequently, present an SVO order here, but in general this is not a common option in the sample.

Another option, which is not cognitively dissonant, though utilized significantly only in Malagasy and Batak, is to present the verb of saying as passive. (84) from Batak is illustrative.

(84) Ndang di-   boto ibana na   mangisap sandu hamu.
     not   Pass. know he   that smoke   opium we
     'That we smoke opium isn't known by him.'

It appears in fact that verbs of saying and thinking in Batak always appear in a passive form when construed with a sentence complement.

Sentential Objects with Like Subjects

In English, and in many other languages, it is often possible to omit, in one way or another, the subject of a sentential object if it is understood to be the same as the subject of the main verb. Thus we might posit that the underlying syntactic structure of (85a) below is (85b).

(85) a. John wants to close the shop.

     b. John wants [John close the shop]

Since the understood subject of 'close' is the same as that of 'want' we may omit it and obtain a derived sentence of the usual subject-predicate form, where the predicate contains in effect two verbs, one of which (in English) is nonfinite, that is, it does not have the same form it would have if it were the main verb of a simple sentence.

We might expect then that, to the extent that subject-final languages are not dissonant, sentences like (85a) would be presented as:

(86) Wants to close the shop John.

And (86) in fact is a commonly occurring order in a majority of the languages in the sample: Malagasy, Batak, Otomi, Tzeltal, and Chumash. I lack the data on Baure and Gilbertese; Fijian does not in general delete coreferential noun phrases in such contexts but merely pronominalizes them. In all the languages in the sample the embedded verb remains finite. (87) from Batak is illustrative:

(87) Nunga   mulai manussi abit   si   Rotua.
     already begin wash   clothes Art. Rotua
     'Rotua has already begun to wash clothes.'

This order obviously aggravates the basic problem, however, especially since, at least in principle, arbitrarily many "higher" verbs may be added to the beginning of the sentence. (88) below from Malagasy illustrates the case of three such higher verbs.

(88) Te-   hanaiky   hanasa   ny zaza Rasoa.
     want- agree-Fut. wash-Fut. the child Rasoa
     'Rasoa wants to agree to wash the child.'

An option which avoids increasing the distance of the subject from the beginning of the sentence is to place the subject immediately after the first, or main, verb. Thus (87) above from Batak could also be rendered as:

(87') Nunga   mulai si   Rotua manussi abit.
      already begin Art. Rotua wash   clothes
      'Rotua has already begun to wash clothes.'

This word order option is also used in Malagasy and Tzeltal. But, as with the previous examples concerning sentence

complements, this option is clearly anomalous, since for
transitive verbs the noun phrase immediately following the
verb is interpreted as the direct object for the least-marked
sentences in the language.

Conjunction Reduction

Given a sentence formed by the coordinate conjunction of two
sentences with the same subject it is possible in most if not
all languages to eliminate one of the subject noun phrases.
In subject-initial languages the predicate phrase remaining
after the deletion of the subject can be naturally conjoined
with the predicate phrase of the other sentence to yield a
derived sentence with a single subject and a compound predicate phrase, illustrated in (89a,b) below from English:

(89) a. John came early and John left late.

b. John [came early and left late].

In subject-final languages however, if the result of the
deletion is to yield a compound predicate phrase with a single
subject, it would have to be the subject of the first sentence
which is deleted:

(90) a. Came early John and left late John.

b. [Came early and left late] John.

Clearly such a pattern of conjunction pushes the derived
subject far indeed from sentence-initial position. Surprisingly,
however, this pattern is an option in many of our languages:
Malagasy, Fijian, Batak, Chumash, and Tzeltal, as in (91a,b)
from Malagasy:

(91) a. Misotro taoka   Rabe ary mihinam-bary Rabe.
       drink   alcohol Rabe and eat-   rice Rabe
       'Rabe is drinking alcohol and Rabe is eating rice.'

   b. [Misotro taoka   sy mihinam-bary] Rabe.
      drink   alcohol and eat-   rice Rabe
      'Rabe is drinking alcohol and eating rice.'

(Sy above conjoins only phrases, never sentences, whereas ary
conjoins sentences but not, in general, phrases; see Keenan
1976b for more discussion.)

   In discourse, however, it is possible in all these languages, and to my knowledge in all languages, to omit the
subject of a sentence when it is the same as the subject of
the preceding sentence (though it may not always be possible
to conjoin such sentences with an overt coordinate conjunction). Thus in Malagasy:

   (92) Misotro taoka   Rabe ary mihinam-bary.
        drink   alcohol Rabe and eat-   rice
        'Rabe is drinking alcohol and (he) is eating rice.'

Such structures, however, with an overt coordinate conjunction,
are arguably dissonant to some extent. For normally if X and
Y are joined by a coordinate conjunction we expect that X and
Y are of the same grammatical category. But (92) exemplifies
a sentence conjoined with a mere predicate phrase. Further,
the only noun phrase which could be understood as the subject
of the entire construction is not in the normal position,
sentence-final, for subjects. And in fact in Malagasy (I do
not have the pertinent data for other languages) that noun
phrase does not behave like a subject. Thus many syntactic
operations in Malagasy are restricted in the operation to
subjects (see Keenan 1976a for further discussion). For
example, in Malagasy, clefting, which moves a noun phrase to
the front and inserts the particle no, operates on subjects
but not on objects. And (93) can be formed from (91b), indicating that Rabe is the derived subject of (91b):

(93)   Rabe no   misotro taoka   sy mihinam-bary.
       Rabe Cleft. drink   alcohol and eat-   rice
       'It is Rabe who is drinking alcohol and eating rice.'

But from (92) above we cannot cleft on <u>Rabe</u>, indicating that
in fact <u>Rabe</u> does not function as the subject of (92).

(94) *Rabe no   misotro taoka   ary mihinam-bary
      Rabe Cleft. drink   alcohol and eat-   rice
      'It is Rabe who is drinking alcohol and eating rice.'

6.3.4. Ambiguity

Finally, I consider a general problem which, in principle,
all verb-terminal (verb-initial or verb-final) languages face.
If all major noun phrases are on the same side of the verb in
unmarked sentences, then any operation which moves or deletes
a noun phrase may leave the resulting structure ambiguous
according to whether the subject or the object was moved or
deleted. Consider, for example (95a,b) below from Fijian.

(95) a. A   raica na   tagane na   gone yalewa.
        Past see   Art. man   Art. child woman
        'The girl saw the man.'

     b. Na   gone   yalewa ka   a   raica na   tagane
        Art. child woman that Past see   Art. man
        'the girl who saw the man' or 'the girl whom the
        man saw'

Given that the relative clause construction (95b) has been
formed by moving the subject (or object) to the front, the
relative order of noun phrases after the verb can no longer
be used to distinguish subject and object. Thus had we
relativized on <u>girl</u> from (96) below we would have equally
obtained (95b) above:

(96) A   raica na   gone yalewa na   tagane.
     Past see   Art. child woman Art. man
     'The man saw the girl.'

We expect then that relative clause constructions like (95b) in Fijian are ambiguous, and in fact they are, as our translation indicates. So also are the corresponding noun phrase questions, which are formed by fronting the question word.

There are, however, several ways a language may be constructed so that such ambiguities do not arise. If, for example, subject and object have distinct case-marking, then moving one of them will not create an ambiguity, since the grammatical role (subject, object) of the one that is left will be signaled by its case-marker and hence the noun phrase that was moved (or deleted) will be the one that is missing (from the argument position of the verb from which the movement took place). And because case-marking is prevalent in verb-final languages, such languages do not in general create ambiguities by moving or deleting noun phrases. Verb-initial languages however are generally not endowed with rich case-marking systems; and as we have seen, subject-final languages in particular do not in general distinguish subject and object by case-marking.

A second way out of the problem is to leave a pronominal "trace" in the position from which a full noun phrase was "moved" or "deleted." Thus if (95b) above were rendered literally as the girl that saw her the man, we would know by the relative position of the pronoun and full noun phrase that girl was the object of the verb, not the subject. And in general, verb-initial languages use pronoun-retaining strategies much more than do verb-final languages in relative clause formation (though rarely in question formation; see Keenan and Comrie 1977 for discussion of the former point). And Gilbertese does in fact retain object pronouns under relativization as illustrated in (97a,b,c), thus avoiding the ambiguity in (95b).

(97) a. E   ore-a   te   mane te   aine.
        3Sg. hit-3Sg. Art. man Art. woman
        'The woman hit the man.'

     b. Te   aine   are ora-a   te   mane
        Art. woman   that hit-3Sg. Art. man
        'the woman who hit the man'

     c. Te   mane are oro-ia   te   aine
        Art. man who hit-him Art. woman
        'the man that the woman hit'

However it is not common in this sample for subject or object
pronouns to be retained, although noun phrases that would be
governed by prepositions more commonly are represented by
pronouns when relativized, as particularly in Fijian.

    A final way of avoiding the ambiguity is simply to restrict
the positions which can be moved or deleted. This is particularly common in many languages as regards deletion. Thus in
many contexts, many languages allow only subjects to be
deleted when coreferential with some other noun phrase. Many
fewer languages restrict the movement of noun phrases in a
similar way. Both Malagasy and Batak however do. Thus in both
of those languages direct objects cannot be directly relativized; only subjects can, as (98a,b) from Malagasy illustrate:

(98) a. ny   zazavavy izay manasa ny lamba
         the girl   that wash   the clothes
         'the girl who is washing the clothes'

     b. *ny lamba   izay manasa ny zazavavy
         the clothes that wash   the girl
         'the clothes that the girl is washing'

(98b) could only mean the clothes that are washing the girl
in Malagasy. If it is desired to relativize on a patient of
an action, the sentence from which relativization takes place
must be passivized so that the patient is a derived subject,
and then we can say the clothes that were washed by the girl.

On the basis of the data available to me, then, subject-final languages are only partly successful in avoiding the ambiguity problem. Fijian and Tzeltal tolerate the massive ambiguity. Gilbertese (at least in certain contexts — I lack extensive data) avoids the ambiguity by pronoun retention. Malagasy and Batak avoid the problem by restricting the positions which can be moved. I lack sufficient data on Chumash, Otomi, and Baure to know whether they tolerate the ambiguity or not, although nothing in the data suggests that the positions from which relativization can take place are restricted. And since there is no case-marking and, in the few available examples, pronouns are not retained in positions relativized, it would appear that the ambiguity is tolerated.

In conclusion then, it seems that subject-finality poses both cognitive and pragmatic problems for understanding basic sentences, and many quite general means of forming complex structures from simpler ones both aggravate these basic problems and introduce new cognitive problems.

Postscript

The following pieces of data were brought to my attention too late to be included in the chapter:

1. Derbyshire (1977) discusses a Carib language, Hixkaryana (Brazil), whose basic word order is argued to be OVS. The examples given there suggest that Hixkaryana follows more closely a verb-final typology than a verb-initial one, and thus does not pattern in general like the verb-initial languages presented here. We should then restrict our claims here to languages which not only are subject-final in the sense discussed in this paper but also present the other major NPs after the verb.

2. There are at least three other languages not discussed
here which are subject-final in our original sense: Tzotzil
and K'ekchi, both Mayan, and thus related to Tzeltal (data
from Ava Berenstein, personal communication), and Tsou, a
Malayo-Polynesian language indigenous to Taiwan (see Tung
1964). Tzotzil and K'ekchi conform well to our generalizations
for subject-final languages, patterning generally like Tzeltal
but with better-developed passives and subject and object
agreement. We know less of Tsou, but superficial inspection of
Tung 1964 suggests that Tsou also conforms to our generalizations. It does at least have well-developed passives and both
subject and object agreement, and it occurs in a phylum in
which verb-initiality is common.

Notes

The work on subject-final languages was supported by a grant
(No. 2944) from the Wenner-Gren Foundation for Anthropological
Research; the work on Malagasy was supported by an NSF Post-
doctoral Fellowship and a grant from Wenner-Gren (No. 2384).

1. A possible counterexample to the claim made in 6.2 is
   Zenéyze, that variety of Romance spoken in and around Genoa,
   Italy. It appears that simple sentences without a "theme"
   or topic have VOS order as in (i) below, cited from Pullum
   1977.

   (i) U- vend-e i   peši   a Zêna   a   Kataynin.
       it-sell-s the fishes in Genoa the Catherine
       'Catherine sells the fish in Genoa.'

On the other hand, when the agent is the topic, the order
is SVO and the verb agrees with the topic/subject.

   (ii) A   Kataynin a- vend-e i   peši   a Zêna.
        the Catherine she-sell-s the fishes in Genoa
        'Catherine sells the fish in Genoa.'

Vattuone (1975) argues that the VOS order is syntactically the more basic and that the SVO order is derived by a rule of thematization. Pullum (1977) however argues, convincingly to my mind, that the SVO order is basic and that the VOS order is derived.

A critical point for me in the argument is that the verb-initial structure uses an impersonal verb: it is always third singular masculine regardless of the number and gender of the "subject." Such impersonal constructions are common in European languages. Note (iii) below from Dutch (Kirsner 1976) and (iv) from French.

(iii) Er   wordt   (door de jongens) gefloten.
      there becomes by   the boys   whistled
      'There is whistling (by the boys).'

(iv) Il est   arrivé   un homme et deux femmes.
     it is-3Sg. arrived-Sg.M. a man   and two women
     'There arrived a man and two women.'

I consider then that the existence of impersonal constructions of that sort in Zenéyze is not sufficient to class Zenéyze as a subject-final language in the sense established here for two reasons:

First, even if such impersonal constructions are among the pragmatically least marked sentence types in Zenéyze they are clearly (as with other European languages presenting such constructions) a small minority among the unmarked sentence types.

Second, it is part of understanding what we mean by "subject" that the subject is the topic (of unmarked sentences — see section 6.3 for further discussion of that point). Arguably then sentences like (i) in Zenéyze are subjectless, and hence not among the sentences on which my definition of subject-final is based.

I further note that the use of a predicate-first order
in presentational or topicless contexts, e.g., as discourse-
initial in stories, is not uncommon in Romance. See Givón
1976b for discussion of predicate-first order in Spanish.
Similarly in French, newspaper reports not uncommonly begin
with a predicate-first order, as in (v) below:

(v) Ont   assisté à   la réunion hier   à l'Elyseé
    have attended to the meeting yesterday at the-Elyseé

    Mssrs. X, Y, et Z.
    Mssrs. X, Y, and Z

    'Attending the meeting yesterday at the Elyseé
    were Mssrs. X, Y, and Z.'

(Sentences like (v) are primarily about the existence of
a meeting, not about who attended.) Thus to the very
limited extent that Zenéyze might be considered subject-
final it seems likely that other varieties of Romance
could also be considered verb-initial, so G-2 would not be
violated.

7. Ergativity

Bernard Comrie

7.0. Introduction

7.0.1. Scope

Ergativity is a term used in traditional descriptive and
typological linguistics to refer to a system of nominal case-
marking where the subject of an intransitive verb has the same
morphological marker as a direct object, and a different
morphological marker from the subject of a transitive verb.
The following Tongan sentences provide examples (Churchward
1953: 67, 68): intransitive subject and direct object (referred
to collectively as *absolute* have the preposition '<u>a</u>, and
transitive subject (*ergative*) has the preposition -<u>e</u>:

(1) Naʻe tāmateʻi ʻe   Tēvita ʻa   Kōlaiate.
    Past kill   Erg. David Abs. Goliath
    'David killed Goliath.'

(2) Naʻe lea   ʻa   Tolu.
    Past speak Abs. Tolu
    'Tolu spoke.'

This chapter aims to examine constructions of this and related
types in a variety of languages, in order both to give some
idea of the kinds of manifestations of ergativity that are
found in different languages and to try to establish generalizations concerning ergativity, both as a synchronic phenomenon
and in its diachronic relations with nonergative systems.

The chapter does not seek to put forward any one single theory
of ergativity, but rather to illustrate the range of data that
any such theory must be able to encompass, in the hope that
future theoretical accounts of ergativity will take account
of the full range of data provided by different subtypes of
ergativity. The last few years have seen a significant increase in the amount of data available on ergative languages,
in particular on the syntax of ergative languages, and I have
taken account of this below.

7.0.2. S, A, P, and Case-Marking

Discussion of Tongan examples (1) and (2) above is in one
sense premature: it presupposes that, despite the formal
identity of morphological marking of 'a Kōlaiate and 'a Tolu
and the different morphological marking of 'e Tēvita, it is
possible to group 'e Tēvita and 'a Tolu together as subjects
(transitive and intransitive) versus 'a Kōlaiate as direct
object. Indeed, many linguists looking at ergative constructions like (1) have concluded that the term *subject* of the
transitive verb in this construction should refer to 'a
Kōlaiate, rather than to 'e Tēvita, or even that the term
subject is completely inapplicable in the ergative construction. We return to the definition of *subject* in section 7.1.2;
in the meantime, to avoid begging this question, I shall use
the three symbols S, A, and P, rather than subject and direct
object. S refers to the single argument of an intransitive
verb, e.g., 'a Tolu in (2), or Tolu in its English translation;
the symbol is clearly reminiscent of the word *subject*, and
generally in such single-argument sentences it is clear that
the one argument is the subject. A refers to that argument
of a transitive verb which would be its subject in a nonergative language like English (e.g., 'e Tēvita in (1), David

its English translation); and P refers to the argument that
would be the direct object (e.g., 'a Kōlaiate in (1), Goliath
in its English translation). A and P are reminiscent of the
semantic terms *agent* and *patient*, but though there is a high
correlation between the semantic opposition agent/patient and
the syntactic opposition A/P, the two are not identical (see
further section 7.2); for instance, in the English sentence
John underwent an operation, John is A and an operation P,
although John is not semantically an agent.

   Given this tripartite distinction (S, A, P) there are five
logically possible systems for assigning case to S, A, and P,
as in Figure 1. V here refers to verb; the order of the
constituents is not relevant to the argument, and verb-final
has been chosen purely for expository convenience.

   In type (a), the same morphological marker (here, as
elsewhere, morphological markers may be null) is used for all
three syntactic positions; this type is illustrated by English,
with nonpronominal noun phrases:

(3) John came.

(4) John kissed Mary.

   In type (b), S and A have the same morphological marker
(nominative), while a different marker is used for P (accusative). This case-marking system may be referred to as
nominative-accusative, and is illustrated by Latin, for
instance:

(5) Puer   vēnit.
    boy-Nom. came
    'The boy came.'

(6) Puer   puellam   amat.
    boy-Nom. girl-Acc. loves
    'The boy loves the girl.'

Figure 1. Case-Marking Systems for S, A, and P

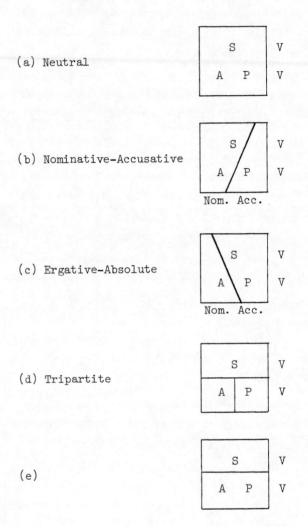

(a) Neutral

(b) Nominative-Accusative

(c) Ergative-Absolute

(d) Tripartite

(e)

In type (c), S and P have the same morphological marker
(absolute), while a different marker is used for A (ergative);
this is the ergative-absolute system, often referred to simply
as the ergative system. It is illustrated by Tongan examples
(1) and (2) above, as well as by the following Basque examples
(adapted from Lafitte 1962). In Basque, the ergative ending
is -(e̲)k̲; the absolute case has no ending:

(7) Martin   ethorri da.
    Martin-Abs. came   Aux.-3Sg.S
    'Martin came.'

(8) Martin-ek   haurra   igorri du.
    Martin-Erg. child-Abs. sent   Aux.-3Sg.A-3Sg.P
    'Martin sent the child.'

(In Basque, the auxiliary codes the person and number of S,
A, and P. Thus da̲ is the appropriate form if there is a
third person singular S (3Sg.S) and no P, and du̲ the appropriate form if there is a third person singular A and a third
person singular P.)

Type (d), with three different morphological markers, is
relatively rare across the languages of the world. Some
languages have this system of case-marking for a limited
number of noun phrases: in the Australian language Dyirbal,
for instance, the interrogative pronoun 'who?' has distinct
forms for S (wanᵞa̲), A (wanᵞdᵞu̲), and P (wanᵞuna̲) (Dixon
1972: 53), but this is not true of noun phrases in general
(see further section 7.4.2). Motu, an Austronesian language
of New Guinea, might appear to be a type (d) language from
the data cited by Capell (1969: 36, 43, 54), with the postposition na̲ for S, ese̲ for A, and no overt marker for P:

(9) Mero na e ginimu.
    boy S he stands
    'The boy is standing.'

(10) Mero ese aniani e   heni-gu.
     boy A   food   he gave-me
     'The boy gave me food.'

Motu, however, is not a pure type (d) language, since the A
postposition <u>ese</u> is in fact optional, and the conditions on
the occurrence of the S postposition <u>na</u> are more complex
(and vary from dialect to dialect), so that some instances of
S also lack any overt marker. (I am grateful to A. J. Taylor
for providing me with Motu material additional to that cited
by Capell.)

Type (e), with the same marker for both A and P and a
different marker for S, seems not to occur as an attested
case-marking system; we return to this in section 7.4.1, where
I try to give an explanation for the apparent absence of this
logical possibility. For the purposes of the present chapter,
I shall be concerned primarily with type (c), contrasting it
in particular with type (b). Type (a) makes no distinctions
at all between S, A, and P, so provides no interesting material for the present chapter; type (d) can be viewed typologically (perhaps also diachronically, though I leave this
question open) as the intersection of types (b) and (c).

7.0.3. General Problems

So far I have spoken about ergativity solely in terms of
case-marking of noun phrases. One might therefore ask whether
ergativity is a purely superficial morphological phenomenon,
bearing no relation to any other syntactic or semantic
properties of the language in question; or whether it is
rather a more deep-seated typological trait of languages with
this case-marking system, permeating much more of the syntactic and semantic structure, and perhaps calling into question
the whole theoretical apparatus of the subject/direct object

distinction with respect to such languages. I discuss this
problem in detail in section 7.1, showing that there is
empirical evidence that can be brought to bear in answering
this question, although the answer is by no means straightforward: rather, languages with morphological ergativity
differ in the extent to which they have further repercussions
of ergativity in their syntactic structure. In section 7.2
I discuss the attempt to define ergativity in semantic rather
than syntactic terms, that is in terms of semantic agentivity;
again, it turns out that languages vary in the extent to which
this approach is applicable to them.

A second set of questions one can ask concerning ergativity
relates to the motivation for this system; that is, why do
languages exist with the ergative-absolute system, rather
than all languages being nominative-accusative to the extent
that they have case-differentiation of S, A, and P? One
possible answer would be diachronic, that is, investigating
how an ergative-absolute system can arise from a nonergative
system: this possibility is examined in section 7.3, which
also looks at relationships between ergativity and passive
constructions. Another possible approach would be synchronic,
asking whether the ergative-absolute system makes sense as a
purely synchronic phenomenon, a question to which I turn in
section 7.4. The questions in this paragraph have been posed
from the viewpoint of a nominative-accusative system, as if
such a system were the norm, and the ergative system to be
regarded as some kind of aberration requiring special explanation. But, in sections 7.3 and 7.4 I adopt a more neutral
stance, since one can equally ask, from the viewpoint of an
ergative-absolute system, why the nominative-accusative type
should exist. Although the ergative-absolute system is often
regarded as an exotic linguistic type, this seems to stem

largely from the fact that the most widely spoken European
languages are not ergative, which in turn results from the
historical accident of the spread of Indo-European languages
to the exclusion of most other European languages (though
Basque, surrounded by Indo-European, does have an ergative-
absolute case-marking system). Indeed, apart from Europe,
where ergativity is absent except for Basque and the Caucasus,
and Africa, where there seem to be no ergative languages,
ergative languages are to be found in nearly all parts of the
world.

7.1. Morphological and Syntactic Ergativity

The five systems illustrated in Figure 1 have been discussed
so far solely in terms of case-marking of noun phrases.
However, there is no a priori reason for the differences
among these five systems to be restricted solely to case-
marking, or indeed solely to morphology, rather than being
applied to a variety of syntactic phenomena. In other words,
concentrating in particular on the nominative-accusative
and ergative-absolute systems, we can ask whether there are
syntactic phenomena in a given language which treat S and P
alike in contrast to A, i.e., on the basis of the ergative-
absolute system, where in other languages the same syntactic
phenomenon might operate on the basis of S and A in contrast
to P, i.e., on the basis of the nominative-accusative system.
In this section, I examine both morphological and syntactic
aspects of ergativity.

The general problem can be illustrated with examples from
English. In English, as far as the vast majority of syntactic
phenomena are concerned, the system is nominative-accusative.
For instance, sentences (11) - (15) below show that in forming
constructions of the type X wants Y to Z, irrespective of

whether Z is transitive or intransitive, Y is always interpreted as the subject (S or A) of Z, and never as its object
(P):

(11)   The birds chirp.

(12)   The wolf hunts the fox.

(13)   I want the birds to chirp.

(14)   I want the wolf to hunt the fox.

(15)   *I want the fox the wolf to hunt.

However, even in English there are some fairly marginal
constructions that operate rather on an ergative-absolute
basis. For instance, in English it is possible to form compound nouns of the type N-V-ing, such as bird-chirping, fox-
hunting. However, the interpretation of such compounds
depends on whether the verb is transitive or intransitive:
with an intransitive verb like chirp, the noun is interpreted
as its S, i.e., bird-chirping is related to birds chirp;
whereas with a transitive verb like hunt the noun is interpreted as its P, i.e., fox-hunting is related to (someone)
hunts foxes, not to foxes hunt (something). (It seems,
incidentally, to be generally true across languages that
where nouns can be incorporated into verbs, as in these
compounds in English, P is easiest to incorporate, followed
by S, with A being most resistant to incorporation.)

7.1.1. Morphological Ergativity: Case-Marking
         and Verb-Agreement

In section 7.0.2 I explained and illustrated the ergative-
absolute case-marking system; there is then no need to
repeat what was said there with regard to morphological
ergativity of nominal case-marking. There is, however,

another kind of morphological ergativity, namely ergativity
in the verb-agreement system. Just as case-marking can
operate in accordance with the five logically possible systems
of Figure 1 (though, as already noted, e seems not to occur
in practice), so too can verb-agreement. It is possible for
verb-agreement to follow the nominative-accusative system,
as for instance in the Bantu language Swahili, where the same
agreement markers are used for S and A (preceding the tense
morpheme), and a different set for P (following the tense
morpheme):

(16) Hamisi a- li- fika.
     Hamisi he-Past-arrive
     'Hamisi arrived.'

.(17) Hamisi a- li- mw- ona Juma.
      Hamisi he-Past-him-see Juma
      'Hamisi saw Juma.'

In some languages with an ergative-absolute case-marking
system, the verb-agreement is determined equally on an ergative-absolute basis. This is so in Avar, a northeast Caucasian
language, where verbs agree in noun class (this includes a
male/female division for human nouns) with S and P, but have
no overt agreement with A (Anderson 1976: 4):

(18) Vas   v-   ekerula.
     boy-Abs. Sg.Masc.Abs.- run
     'The boy runs.'

(19) Jas   j-   ekerula.
     girl-Abs. Sg.Fem.Abs.- run
     'The girl runs.'

(20) Vas-as: jas   j-   ec:ula.
     boy-Erg. girl-Abs. Sg.Fem.Abs.- praise
     'The boy praises the girl.'

As the glosses indicate, verbs agree with the absolute noun
phrase.

There are even some languages that have verb-agreement on
an ergative-absolute basis but have no overt case-marking of
noun phrases; in fact, this type is not particularly rare,
being found for instance in some of the Northwest Caucasian
languages (Abkhaz, Abaza; see, for instance, Allen 1956), and
quite generally in the Mayan languages of Mexico and Central
America. The examples below are from Quiché, a Mayan language
of Guatemala (Quiché examples here and below are from the
Mayan Linguistics course given by Lyle Campbell at the 1976
Linguistic Institute).

(21) K-   ox   kam- ik.
     Asp.- 1Pl.Abs.- die- Ptc.
     'We die.'

(22) K-   at-   kam- ik.
     Asp.- 2Sg.Abs. die- Ptc.
     'You die.'

(23) K-   at-   ka-   cuku- x.
     Asp.- 2Sg.Abs.- 1Pl.Erg.- seek- Act.
     'We seek you.'

(24) K-   ox-   a-   cuku- x.
     Asp.- 1Pl.Abs.- 2Sg.Erg.- seek- Act.
     'You seek us.'

The independent pronouns are normally omitted, unless stressed.
Like other noun phrases, they have no case-marking in Quiché;
the usual word order is V-S or V-P-A. Verb-agreement is on an
ergative-absolute basis: for the first person plural, ox- is
the absolute prefix: S in (21), P in (24); and ka- the
ergative prefix: A in (23). For the second person singular,
at- is the absolute prefix: S in (22), P in (23); and a- the
ergative prefix: A in (24). In Mayan linguistics, it is
customary to refer to the two sets of verbal affixes as Set
A (ergative, e.g., first person plural ka-) and Set B
(absolute, e.g., first person plural ox-). Although arbitrary,

this terminology has certain advantages — the affixes of Set
A, for instance, are also used as noun prefixes indicating
possession, e.g., Quiché ka-c'i:' 'our dog' — especially in
dealing with the more complex distribution of the two sets in
languages like Chol and Jacaltec, discussed in sections 7.1.3
and 7.3.2.

Assuming that neutral nominal case-marking is compatible
with either a nominative-accusative or an ergative-absolute
system, in that it does not make any distinction cutting
across either of these two distinctions, we can say that the
languages examined so far with regard to nominal case-marking
and verb-agreement are either consistently nominative-
accusative or consistently ergative-absolute. We might go on
to ask whether there are any languages that combine the
nominative-accusative morphological system with the ergative-
absolute morphological system, having one for nominal case-
marking and the other for verb-agreement. In fact, there are
many languages which have an ergative-absolute system for
nominal case-marking and a nominative-accusative system for
verb-agreement (the inverse is rare or nonexistent). One
such language is Walbiri, a Pama-Nyungan language of Central
Australia (Hale 1973: 309, 328):

(25) ŋatʸu ka   - na   puḷami.
      1-Abs. Tense -1Sg.Nom. shout
      'I shout.'

(26) ŋatʸuluḷu ka   -na   -ŋku   nʸuntu   nʸanʸi.
      1-Erg.   Tense -1Sg.Nom. 2Sg.Acc. you-Abs. see
      'I see you.'

(27) Nʸuntuluḷu ka   -npa   -tʸu   ŋatʸu   nʸanʸi.
      you-Erg.   Tense -2Sg.Nom. -1Sg.Acc. 1-Abs. see
      'You see me.'

Inspection of these examples shows that the independent
pronouns (which behave in this respect like other noun

phrases) have case-marking on an ergative-absolute basis: for the first person singular, ŋat ᵛu is absolute: S in (25), P in (27); while ŋat ᵛululu is ergative: A in (26). The forms for the second person singular are absolute n ᵛuntu, ergative n ᵛuntululu. The verb-agreement affixes, however, which appear in sentence-second position together with the tense-marker ka, are assigned on a nominative-accusative basis, so that the first person "nominative" affix -ga occurs as S agreement affix in (25) and as A agreement affix in (26), while a separate form, -t ᵛu, is used as P agreement affix in (27); for the second person, the forms are nominative -npa, accusative -ŋku. In Walbiri, then, we see for the first time a discrepancy within the (core) grammatical structure; part of the morphology is based on the ergative-absolute distinction, and another part on the nominative-accusative distinction.

We may note in passing that one occasionally comes across a subvariety of type (d) of Figure 1 with verb-agreement, namely where portmanteau morphs are used to indicate certain combinations of A and P. Thus in Rembarnga, an Australian language of Arnhem Land, the agreement markers for Ss of the first and second persons singular are, respectively, ŋa and ŋin ᵛ, but the agreement marker for a second person singular A with a first person singular P is tan (although for most other combinations of A and P, verb-agreement is on a nominative-accusative basis, with relatively transparent morphophonemic variation in some of these instances) (McKay 1977: 501).

Even type (3) is occasionally found with verb-agreement, as in the Iranian dialect Dānesfāni (Yar-Shater 1969: 204), where the past participle agrees with S, but with no constituent of a transitive sentence:

(28) Hasan   buma.
     Hasan-(Masc.) came-Masc.
     'Hasan came.'

(29) Zeynaba   bumia.
     Zeynaba-(Fem.) came-Fem.
     'Zeynaba came.'

(30) Hasan   /Zeynaba   šet   -eš
     Hasan-(Masc.)/Zeynaba-(Fem.) milk-(Masc.) -Aux.-3Sg.A

     uxa.
     drink

     'Hasan/Zeynaba drank the milk.'

(31) Hasan   /Zeynaba   āwa   -š̌
     Hasan-(Masc.)/Zeynaba-(Fem.) water-(Fem.) -Aux.-3Sg.A

     uxa.
     drank

     'Hasan/Zeynaba drank the water.'

In all such instances known to me, however, the verb agrees
with S, and shows no agreement whatsoever with either A or P;
moreover, the examples with which I am familiar are all in
languages where the ergative system is breaking down, being
replaced by a nominative-accusative or neutral system. It
seems likely that at an intermediate stage in the development
from ergative-absolute to nominative-accusative, a situation
can be reached where the conflict between moribund ergative-
absolute morphology and nascent nominative-accusative morphology is resolved by simply omitting all morphological markers,
giving rise to the type illustrated above from Dānesfāni: in
the intransitive sentence there is no conflict, and the
participle agrees with S; in the transitive construction,
there is conflict as to whether the participle should agree
with A or with P. The compromise reached is for it to agree
with neither. Thus we expect type (e) to arise only as a
result of conflict of this kind.

7.1.2. Syntactic Ergativity

In treating ergativity from a syntactic viewpoint, we are
looking for syntactic phenomena in languages which treat S and
P alike, and differently from A. Syntactic nominativity likewise means syntactic phenomena where S and A are treated alike,
and differently from P. This distinction is connected with the
general problem of subject identification: if in a language S
and A are regularly identified, that is, if the language is
consistently or overwhelmingly nominative-accusative, then
we are justified in using the term *subject* to group together
S and A; if in a language S and P are regularly identified
(consistent or overwhelming ergative-absolute system), then we
would be justified in using the term *subject* rather to refer
to S and P, that is, in particular, to refer to P, rather
than A, of the transitive construction. The fullest attempt
to date to isolate syntactic subject properties is Keenan
1976b, which examines a large number of properties, including
syntactic properties characteristic of subjects across a wide
range of languages (in particular, nonergative languages).
For present purposes, I shall examine a much more restricted
range of properties, using these as illustrations of general
trends.

In English and a number of other languages, certain verbal
forms dependent on another verb may lack an overt subject if
and only if the subject of the dependent verb is the same as
the subject of the main verb. In English, the verbs want and
can, for instance, behave in this way, with identity of
subject of main and dependent verb:

(32) John wants to come.

(33) John wants to kiss Mary.

(34) John can come.

(35) John can kiss Mary.

Where the subject of the dependent verb is not the same as that of the main verb, as is possible with want, the subject of the dependent verb must be expressed overtly (in English, as surface direct object of want):

(36) John wants Bill to come.

(37) John wants Bill to kiss Mary.

I have stated this condition in terms of subjects (of the dependent verb), and the examples cited show that surface S and A are treated alike, in contrast to surface P. I now examine the same construction types in Khinalug, a Northeast Caucasian language with morphological ergativity in both case-marking and verb-agreement.

The morphologically ergative nature of Khinalug can be seen from the following (Kibrik et al 1972: 192-193):

(38) Lɨgɨld   sacaχ-∅ -q'iqomä.
     man-Abs. silent -Masc.
     'The man is silent.'

(39) Xiñimk'ir   sacaχ-z -q'iqomä.
     woman-Abs. silent -Fem.
     'The woman is silent.'

(40) Bɨj   -i   ši   tɨ   -∅   -kˊ'i.
     father -Erg. son-Abs. awaken -Masc.
     'The father awakened the son.'

(41) Bɨj   -i   riši   tɨ   -z   -kˊ'i.
     father -Erg. daughter-Abs. awaken -Fem.
     'The father awakened the daughter.'

The verb-agreement marker, which separates the two parts of a compound verb, agrees in noun class (including a male/female distinction for humans) with the absolute noun phrase. The verbs meaning 'want' and 'can' take a nonfinite dependent verbal form, the so-called dependent participle; where the

subject of the dependent participle is not the same as that of
the main verb, it appears in the same form (ergative or
absolute) as it would with a finite form of that verb (Kibrik
et al 1972: 194 - 195):

(42) Asɨr   gada   točkwi   jukwatʰmä.
     I-Dat. boy-Abs. to-get-up want
     'I want the boy to get up.'

(43) As   jukwatʰmä hini   pʰšä q'izi.
     I-Dat. want   she-Erg. bread to-bake
     'I want her to bake bread.'

(The verbs 'want' and 'can' take their subject in the dative
case; as and asɨr are alternative dative forms of the first
person singular pronoun.) Where, however the subject (S or A)
of the dependent participle would be the same as the subject
of the main verb, it must be omitted:

(44) As   jukwešämä endžik   -ondä.
     I-Dat. wanted   to-descend-not
     'I wanted not to descend.'

(45) As   uχur   kʰičʰeb   läk'iri jet´:imä.
     I-Dat. to-you book-Abs. to-give non-want
     'I do not want to give the book to you.'

(46) Hinu   lik´'uvri muxwižmä.
     she-Dat. to-sing   can
     'She can sing.'

(47) Hinu   pʰšä   q'izi   muxwižmä.
     she-Dat. bread-Abs. to-bake can
     'She can bake bread.'

From these examples, it is clear that this construction in
Khinalug is controlled by the nominative-accusative opposition,
since the dependent participles in (44) - (47) are both intransitive and transitive, and not by the ergative-absolute
opposition. Thus despite morphological ergativity, Khinalug
is syntactically a nominative-accusative language.

In the study of most languages that have morphological
ergativity (nominal, verbal, or both), it seems to turn out
that, apart from a few syntactic processes like incorporation
that tend always to operate on an ergative-absolute basis
rather than a nominative-accusative basis, the vast majority
of syntactic phenomena operate on a nominative-accusative
basis rather than on an ergative-absolute basis. That is, the
majority of languages that are morphologically ergative are
not syntactically ergative; in the majority of ergative
languages ergativity seems to be a relatively superficial
phenomenon, at least as far as morphology and syntax are
concerned (I turn to semantics, especially agentivity, in
section 7.2); for further exemplification of this point see
Comrie 1973, Anderson 1976, Keenan 1976b. In such languages
then we are justified in using the term *subject* to refer to
S and A, and *direct object* for P, just as we are in English.

A different picture is provided, however, by Dyirbal, an
Australian language of Northern Queensland. The illustrative
construction chosen here is the formation of coordinate
sentences where one of the components is a transitive sentence, the other an intransitive sentence, of the type The
man came here and hit the woman, or The man hit the woman and
came here. I present the material, for English and then for
Dyirbal, by indicating first of all the relevant noncoordinate
sentences (e.g., the man came here, the man hit the woman),
then the possibilities for combining them, with omission of
the common noun phrase from the second clause; the coordinate
sentences will be written out with an indication of which
simple sentences enter into their formation. The English
examples are as follows:

(48) The man came here.

(49) The man hit the woman.

(50) The woman came here.

(51) The woman hit the man.

(52) The man came here and hit the woman.   (48) + (49)

(53) The man hit the woman and came here.   (49) + (48)

(54) The woman came here and hit the man.   (50) + (51)

(55) The woman hit the man and came here.   (51) + (50)

From the coordination possibilities — note, for instance, that (48) can be coordinated with (49), but not with (51) — , it is clear that the relevant criterion for this kind of coordination is that the two simple sentences should have the same subject (S or A); the subject of the second clause in the coordinate construction may then be omitted. Since (48) and (49) have the same subject, they can be coordinated to give (52) or, with reverse order of the clauses, (53). It is not possible to coordinate (48) with (51), since although both have the noun phrase the man, this noun phrase is subject in (48) but direct object in (51). In other words, this kind of coordination in English works on a nominative-accusative basis.

Dyirbal has an ergative case-marking system (there is no verb-agreement): the ergative suffix has several allomorphs, including -ŋgu and -ṟu; the absolute case has no marker. In addition to these markers on nouns, a noun may be preceded by a nominal classifier indicating its noun class (for human nouns, this means a male/female distinction) and its case (including ergative versus absolute). Although word order is free, the usual order is P-A-V or (S)-V (Dixon 1972: 59, 130):

(56) Bayi   yaṛa   bani-nᵞu.
Masc.-Abs. man-Abs. come-Tense
'The man came here.'

(57) Balan   dᵞugumbil baŋgul   yaṛa-ŋgu   balga-n.
Fem.-Abs. woman-Abs. Masc.-Erg. man- Erg. hit- Tense
'The man hit the woman.'

(58) Balan   dᵞugumbil bani-nᵞu.
Fem.-Abs. woman-Abs. come-Tense
'The woman came here.'

(59) Bayi   yaṛa   baŋgun   dᵞugumbi-ṛu   balga-n.
Masc.-Abs. man-Abs. Fem.-Erg. woman- Erg. hit- Tense
'The woman hit the man.'

(60) Bayi yaṛa baninᵞu, baŋgun dᵞugumbiṛu balgan.
                                    (56) + (59)
'The man came here and the woman hit him.'

(61) Bayi yaṛa baŋgun dᵞugumbiṛu balgan, baninᵞu.
                                    (59) + (56)
'The woman hit the man and he came here.'

(62) Balan dᵞugumbil baninᵞu, baŋgul yaṛaŋgu balgan.
                                    (58) + (57)
'The woman came here and the man hit her.'

(63) Balan dᵞugumbil baŋgul yaṛaŋgu balgan, baninᵞu.
                                    (57) + (58)
'The man hit the woman and she came here.'

Coordination in Dyirbal is indicated without any overt conjunction, simply by juxtaposing the two sentences, with optional
omission of the appropriate noun phrase from the second clause.
Inspection of the coordination possibilities shows that they
are different from those for English, in fact strikingly so:
the combinations that are possible in Dyirbal are impossible
in English, while the combinations that are possible in English
are impossible in Dyirbal. In Dyirbal, coordination operates
on an ergative-absolute basis, that is, it is possible to
treat as identical for purposes of coordination two absolute
noun phrases even if one is an S and the other a P. But it

is not possible to treat as identical for purposes of coordination an S and an A:

(64) *Bayi yaṛa baninʸu, balan dʸugumbil balgan.

(56) + (57)

'The man came here and hit the woman.'

In Dyirbal one finds, quite generally, that syntactic processes which in English operate on a nominative-accusative basis operate on an ergative-absolute basis. Given this situation, one is led to consider that perhaps, with regard to languages of this type, it is incorrect to identify A as the subject in transitive sentences: in a sentence like (57), nearly all the subject properties characterize the absolute noun phrase (P) balan dʸugumbil, rather than the ergative noun phrase (A) baŋgul yaṛaŋgu. If one were to consider P as the subject, and A as an agentive complement, then one is effectively claiming that such Dyirbal sentences have the syntactic structure of English passive sentences. We can illustrate this by considering again coordination possibilities, as in (48) - (55), but taking passive rather than active sentences with transitive verbs:

(65) The man came here.

(66) The woman was hit by the man.

(67) The woman came here.

(68) The man was hit by the woman.

(69) The man came here and was hit by the woman.

(65) + (68)

(70) The man was hit by the woman and came here.

(68) + (65)

(71) The woman came here and was hit by the man.

(67) + (66)

(72) The woman was hit by the man and came here.

$$(66) + (67)$$

(We return to the relation between ergative and passive for further discussion in section 7.3.) One factor that has to be taken into account is that languages do not divide neatly into those that are purely morphologically ergative (like Khinalug) and those that are consistently syntactically ergative (as well as morphologically ergative) (like Dyirbal); many languages occupy an intermediate position, with certain syntactic phenomena operating on a nominative-accusative basis, others on an ergative-absolute basis, so that the ergative languages of the world as a whole show a continuum from purely morphological ergativity to syntactic ergativity, though with a preponderance of languages at the purely morphologically ergative end of the spectrum. In languages where subject properties are roughly evenly distributed between A and P, the value of the term *subject* is seriously called into question. For a detailed discussion of a language with some syntactic phenomena on a nominative-accusative basis and others on an ergative-absolute basis, reference should be made to Dixon's (1977a) account of Yidinʸ, another Australian language of Northern Queensland, and for more general discussion, based on Australian material, to Blake 1976, and the articles on ergativity in Dixon, ed. 1976: 485 - 611.

7.1.3. Split Ergativity

One general conclusion that can be drawn from the discussion of section 7.1 so far is that it is rather misleading to speak of ergative languages, as opposed to nominative-accusative languages, since we have seen that it is possible for one phenomenon in a language to be controlled on an ergative-absolute basis while another phenomenon in the same language

is controlled on a nominative-accusative basis. Thus one
should ask rather to what extent a language is ergative-
absolute or nominative-accusative, or, more specifically,
which constructions in a particular language operate on the
one basis and which on the other. In fact, the situation is
even more complex than this, because we sometimes find the
same phenomenon in the same language operating in some
instances on a nominative-accusative basis, in others on an
ergative-absolute basis. In the present section I shall
examine some examples of this kind of "split ergativity";
most of them will be discussed further in sections 7.3 and
7.4, where explanations will be suggested for the various
kinds of split ergativity.

One of the commonest ways in which languages manifest split
ergativity is according to tense/aspect: in some tenses or
aspects the language is nominative-accusative, in others it
is ergative-absolute. I illustrate this by means of Georgian
examples; languages with similar systems include Hindi and
many other Indo-Iranian languages. In Georgian, a South
Caucasian (Kartvelian) language, the aorist tense system has
an ergative-absolute system, with the ending -i for the
absolute and -ma for the ergative; the present tense system
has a nominative-accusative system, with the ending -i for
the nominative and -s for the accusative:

(73) Student-i   midis.
     student-Nom. goes
     'The student goes.'

(74) Student-i   çeril -s   çers.
     student-Nom. letter-Acc. writes
     'The student writes the letter.'

(75) Student-i   mivida.
     student-Abs. went
     'The student went.'

(76) Student-ma   çeril -i   daçera.
     student-Erg. letter-Abs. wrote
     'The student wrote the letter.'

In these examples I continue to gloss the case-markers
according to their role in the ergative-absolute or nominative-accusative system, although this means that Georgian -i,
for instance, is glossed as nominative in (73) and (74), but
as absolute in (75) and (76) — this to avoid the confusion
that is inevitably engendered when traditional case labels
(nominative, ergative, etc.) are used to refer to forms that
occur in both ergative-absolute and nominative-accusative
systems.

In Georgian (and likewise in the relevant Indo-Iranian
languages), there is morphological identity between nominative
of the nominative-accusative system and absolute of the
ergative-absolute system, but this is by no means a necessary
pattern in languages with split ergativity. In Chol, a Mayan
language of Mexico, the tense/aspect basis of split ergativity
is similar to that of Georgian (present tense nominative-
accusative versus past tense ergative-absolute), but the
distribution of the forms is different. (It will be recalled
from section 7.1.1 that ergativity in Mayan languages is
revealed primarily in the verb agreement. I am grateful to
R. Freund for bringing the Chol data to my attention.)

    (77) Ca   čəmiy-on.
         Past die- 1Sg.Abs.
         'I died.'

    (78) Ca   čəmiy-et.
         Past die- 2Sg.Abs.
         'You died.'

    (79) Ca   h-   k'eley-et.
         Past 1Sg.Erg.-see- 2Sg.Abs.
         'I saw you.'

(80) Mi   k-   čəmel.
    Pres. 1Sg.Nom.-die
    'I am dying.'

(81) Mi   a-   čəmel.
    Pres. 2Sg.Nom.-die
    'You are dying.'

(82) Mi   h-   k'el-et.
    Pres. 1Sg.-Nom.-see- 2Sg.Acc.
    'I see you.'

In Chol, the Set A affixes — first person singular k̲- (h̲-
before a velar), second person singular a̲ — function as
ergative in the ergative-absolute system, but as nominative
in the nominative-accusative system; the Set B affixes — first
person singular -o̲n, second person singular -e̲t — function
as absolute in the ergative-absolute system, but as accusative
in the nominative-accusative system. In some Mayan languages,
for example Jacaltec, a similar split occurs between main
clauses (ergative-absolute) and subordinate clauses (nominative-accusative), with morphological identity of ergative
and nominative; see section 7.3.2.

Another major type of split ergativity is where the
conditioning factor is the status of the A and P noun phrases,
that is, where certain noun phrases have a nominative-accusative case-marking system, but others an ergative-absolute
case-marking system. I return to this kind of split ergativity,
and further variations thereon, in section 7.4; for the
present I simply give some examples from Dyirbal. As already
noted, (56) - (59), most noun phrases in Dyirbal have an
ergative-absolute case-marking system. Independent personal
pronouns of the first and second persons, however, have rather
a nominative-accusative case-marking system (Dixon 1972: 60):

(83) ŋadʸa bani-nʸu.
     I-Nom. come-Tense
     'I come.'

(84) ŋinda   bani-nʸu.
     you-Nom. come-Tense
     'You come.'

(85) ŋadʸa ŋinuna   balga-n.
     I-Nom. you-Acc. hit- Tense
     'I hit you.'

(86) ŋinda   ŋayguna balga-n.
     you-Nom. I-Acc. hit- Tense
     'You hit me.'

As can be seen from these examples, ŋadʸa 'I' and ŋinda 'you'
function as both S and A, whereas ŋayguna 'me' and ŋinuna
'you' function only as P. Pronominal and nonpronominal noun
phrases may of course co-occur in the same sentence, and then
the case-marking system for each operates independently:

(87) ŋadʸa bayi   yaṛa   balga-n.
     I-Nom. Masc.-Abs. man-Abs. hit- Tense
     'I hit the man.'

(88) ŋayguna baŋgul   yaṛa-ŋgu balga-n.
     I-Acc. Masc.-Erg. man- Erg. hit- Tense
     'The man hit me.'

With this kind of split ergativity, not only can we not
characterize a whole language as discretely ergative versus
nonergative, we cannot even characterize the nominal case-
marking of a whole sentence in these terms, since sentences
like (87) and (88) contain elements of both the ergative-
absolute and the nominative-accusative case-marking systems.

As a final observation on this split ergativity in Dyirbal,
we should note that the nominative-accusative system found
with certain pronouns is purely morphological; as far as
syntax is concerned, for example coordination possibilities,

such sentences still behave according to the ergative system
(Dixon 1972: 131):

(89) ŋadʸa baninʸu, baŋgul yaṟaŋgu balgan.   (83)   (88)
     'I came here and the man hit me.'

(90) ŋayguna baŋgul yaṟaŋgu balgan, baninʸu.   (88)   (83)
     'The man hit me and I came here.'

(91) ŋadʸa bayi yaṟa balgan, baninʸu.   (87)   (56)
     'I hit the man and the man came here.'

In this respect, Dyirbal shows how different it is from most
languages with ergativity, where the ergativity is essentially
only morphological, not syntactic; in Dyirbal ergativity is
syntactic and also characterizes most of the morphology, and
the only exceptional nominative-accusative morphology does
not affect the basic syntactic ergativity of the language.

Finally, with regard to split ergativity, we may note that
some languages present idiosyncratic exceptions to the general
system (ergative-absolute or nominative-accusative) that is
used for a particular phenomenon. Thus Khinalug is basically
ergative-absolute with regard to verb-agreement — cf. (38) -
(41) — but the transitive verb č'aχi 'bring' takes nominative-
accusative verb-agreement, although case-marking is still
on an ergative-absolute basis (Kibrik et al. 1972: 193):

(92) Bɨj   -i   xu   čʰkʰa-∅   -Ršämä.
     father Erg. water-Abs. bring-Masc.
     'Father brought water.'

(93) Däd   -i   xu   čʰkʰa-zɨ   -Ršämä.
     mother-Erg. water-Abs. bring-Fem.
     'Mother brought water.'

7.2. Ergativity and Agentivity

In many discussions of ergativity, a key role is played by
the notion of agentivity, and readers may be surprised that

this notion has not been discussed so far in the present
chapter. By *agentivity* I mean, roughly speaking, the degree
of control which the referent of a noun phrase has over the
situation described by the verb with which it is associated.
Thus, in the following examples, the degree of agentivity of
the subject noun phrase diminishes progressively through the
list:

(94) John deliberately fell down.

(95) John, through his own negligence, fell down.

(96) John, through no fault of his own, fell down.

(94) assigns absolute control to the subject, that is,
highest agentivity: his falling was due to a conscious
effort on his part directed toward this goal. (95) assigns
intermediate control: John could have avoided falling down,
but he did not, that is, he had potential control over the
situation, which he did not in fact exercise. (96) assigns
no control at all; the fall was entirely outside John's
control. Thus the claim that there is a close connection,
perhaps even of identity, between ergativity and agentivity
amounts to the claim that the function of the ergative case
is not so much syntactic as semantic, to mark a noun phrase
which has high agentivity — e.g., (94) versus (95) and (96),
or (94) and (95) versus (96). The use of the ergative to mark
A would then be an automatic consequence of the fact that in
most transitive sentences A has high agentivity, at least
relative to P. In this discussion I explicitly reject the
identification of ergativity and agentivity, for reasons
discussed in the present section; the line of argument will
be to show that, despite some similarities between ergativity
and agentivity, evidence from a wide range of ergative
languages points against this identification.

The first piece of evidence against this identification is
that in many languages ergative noun phrases do not have to
be agentive, as in the following Basque examples (Lafitte
1962: 322):

(97) Herra -k   z- erabiltza.
hatred-Erg. you-move
'Hatred inspires you.'

(98) Ur-handia-k   d- erabilka eihara.
river   -Erg. it-move   mill-Abs.
'The river works the mill.'

Second, languages with split ergativity on a tense/aspect
basis provide examples where the same noun phrase appears now
in the ergative, now in the nominative, without any difference
of agentivity, as in Georgian examples (74) and (76), repro-
duced below as (99) and (100):

(99) Stuḍenṭi (Nom.) çerils çers.
'The student writes the letter.'

(100) Stuḍenṭma (Erg.) çerili daçera.
'The student wrote the letter.'

The main kind of evidence to be cited in this section is an
extension of the second kind noted above, and consists in
finding pairs of sentences where, for syntactic reasons or for
semantic reasons unconnected with the agentivity of the given
noun phrase, in one of the sentences it appears in the ergative, in the other in a nonergative case (in the examples
cited here, usually the absolute case). The first set of
examples concerns verbs that are basically transitive, but
which can be used also without a P, although the same interpretation of agentivity is present in both, as in English:

(101) John is eating a fish.

(102) John is eating.

In some ergative languages, the subject of such an objectless
transitive verb remains in the ergative case, thus providing
perhaps some evidence of a link between ergativity and agentivity, as in Basque:

(103) Martin-ek   jan du.
      Martin-Erg. ate Aux.-3Sg.A (-3Sg.P)
      'Martin ate.'

Martinek has the ergative ending -ek, and the auxiliary is
the form used with a transitive verb having a third person
singular A and a third person singular P; in fact, (103) can
also mean 'Martin ate it.' As in many other languages, third
person singular acts as an unmarked category, since Basque has
no specific auxiliary forms to indicate the absence of a
direct object with a transitive verb. In many other ergative
languages, however, the subject of such a verb stands in the
absolute case, for example, in Tongan:

(104) Na'e inu   'a   e   kava 'e   Sione.
      Past drink Abs. the kava Erg. John
      'John drank the kava.'

(105) Na'e inu   'a   Sione.
      Past drink Abs. John
      'John drank.'

In many languages with a case-marking system like Tongan in
this respect, a marker is also required on the verb in such
constructions to indicate that it is being used intransitively.
In Dyirbal this is the reflexive suffix (Dixon 1972: 90):

(106) Balam wudʸu   baŋgul   yaṛa-ŋgu dʸaŋga-nʸu.
      Abs. fruit-Abs. Masc.-Erg. man- Erg. eat- Tense
      'The man eats fruit.'

(107) Bayi   yaṛa   dʸaŋgay-mari- nʸu.
      Masc.-Abs. man-Abs. eat-   Refl.-Tense
      'The man eats.'

In Quiché, the corresponding suffix is -n:

(108) K-   at-   ka-   kamisa-x.
      Asp. 2Sg.Abs.- 1Pl.Erg.- kill- Act.
      'We kill you.'

(109) K-   ox-   kamisa-n-ik.
      Asp. 1Pl.Abs.- kill-   Ptc.
      'We kill.'

Similar pairs can be found where the same verb can be constructed either with a direct object or with some other kind of object (often with a difference in meaning between the two versions — I return to this below). Occasionally, the ergative is found in both members of such a pair, as in Walbiri, where the nondirect object appears in the dative (Hale 1973: 336):

(110) ŋatʸululu ka   -na   wawiri   luwani.
      I-Erg.   Tense-1Sg.Nom. kangaroo-Abs. shoot
      'I am shooting at the kangaroo.'

(111) ŋatʸululu ka   -na   -la   -tʸinta   wawiri
      I-Erg.   Tense-1Sg.Nom.-3Sg.Dat.-Intrans. kangaroo-
      -ki luwani.
      Dat. shoot
      'I am shooting at the kangaroo (but may not hit it).'

More commonly, however, the difference in syntactic structure of the object brings about a difference in syntactic structure of the sentence, with the absolute case being used for the subject where the object is nondirect, as in the Bzhedukh dialect of West Circassian (Northwest Caucasian) (Anderson 1976: 21; the examples are attributed to John Colarusso):

(112) Č̣'aaλa-m   č'əg°-ər   yaẑ°a.
      boy-   Erg. field-Abs. he-plows-it
      'The boy is plowing the field.'

(113) Č̣'aaλa-r   č'əg°-əm   yaẑ°a.
      boy-   Abs. field-Nondir. he-plows-it
      'The boy is plowing away at the field (but may
         not complete it).'

Here the use of a nondirect object indicates noncompletion of
the action. With some verbs, there is also a change in the
form of the verb to indicate the change away from transitivity:

(114) P:śaśa-m   cʰəy   -ər   yadə.
      girl- Erg. cherkesska-Abs. she-sews-it-Trans.
      'The girl is sewing the cherkesska.'

(115) P:śaśa-r   cʰəy   -əm   yada.
      girl- Abs. cherkesska-Nondir. she-sews-it-Intrans.
      'The girl is sewing away at the cherkesska.'

In some other languages, the use of a special affix on the
verb to indicate intransitivity is more widespread. In Dyirbal,
for instance, either the reflexive suffix or the suffix -ŋay
is used, and the object appears in the dative (or instrumental) (Dixon 1972: 90, 151-152):

(116) Balam wudʸu   baŋgul   yaṛa-ŋgu dʸaŋga-nʸu.
      Abs. fruit-Abs. Masc.-Erg. man- Erg. eat-   Tense
      'The man eats fruit.'

(117) Bayi   yaṛa   bagum wudʸu-gu   dʸaŋga-mari-
      Masc.-Abs. man-Abs. Dat. fruit-Dat. eat-   Refl.-
      nʸu.
      Tense

      'The man eats fruit.'

(118) Balan   dʸugumbil baŋgul   yaṛa-ŋgu balga-n.
      Fem.-Abs. woman-Abs. Masc.-Erg. man- Erg. hit- Tense
      'The man is hitting the woman.'

(119) Bayi   yaṛa   bagun   dʸugumbil-gu balgal-
      Masc.-Abs. man-Abs. Fem.-Dat. woman-   Dat. hit-
      ŋa-nʸu.
        Tense.

      'The man is hitting the woman.'

Similarly in Quiché, the form of the verb in -n is used in
such instances. In Quiché the verbal affixes for first person
singular and the polite second person happen not to have any

overt distinction between Set A and Set B, so that the first
person singular in- can be either ergative or absolute, as can
polite second person singular la, so that a form like the
following is potentially ambiguous:

(120) K-   in-   loq'o-x   la.
      Asp. 1Sg.-love- Ptc. 2Sg.Polite
      'I love you' or 'You love me.'

The ambiguity can be resolved by constructing the object as a
nondirect object and giving the verb the intransitivizing
suffix -n:

(121) K-   in-   loq'o-n čeh la.
      Asp.-1Sg.-love   to you
      'I love you.'

Since the verbal form in (121) has no direct object, the
first person singular prefix in- can only refer to its
subject.

   In recent work on ergativity, constructions where an
otherwise transitive verb occurs with an oblique object —
particularly where the verb has a special marker like Dyirbal
-ŋay or Quiché -n, and where there is an absolute rather than
an ergative noun phrase — are often referred to as the "antipassive." Although this term can be rather misleading, for
instance in that (unlike the situation with the passive) in
the majority of languages with this construction there does
not seem to be any difference in the subject status of the
ergative and absolute noun phrases of the nonantipassive and
antipassive respectively (with the possible exception of more
consistent syntactically ergative languages like Dyirbal), it
does provide a convenient nomenclature and one that has
recently become widespread. The difference between nonantipassive and antipassive can be diagrammed as in Figure 2.

Figure 2. The Antipassive

(a) Nonantipassive   (b) Antipassive

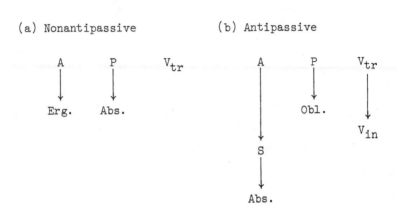

It should also be noted that although the antipassive is, from a formal viewpoint (oblique object rather than P) a relatively uniform phenomenon across languages, its function can vary quite considerably from language to language. In Walbiri and Circassian, for instance, its main function is to express a difference in sentence-internal semantics, namely incompleteness of the situation described in so far as it affects the object: in (111) there is no suggestion that I actually hit the kangaroo; in (113) there is no suggestion that the boy will complete the plowing of the field. Many nonergative languages have similar pairs of sentences with direct and oblique objects expressing a similar difference in meaning: compare the English glosses with shoot versus shoot at, plow versus plow away at (Anderson 1971).

In Kala Lagau Langgus (Mabuiag, Western Torres Strait Language), an Australian language, another difference in sentence-internal semantics is carried by the antipassive. The antipassive is in complementary distribution with incorporation (used for body parts) and indicates complete

affecting of P, which is a predetermined set (Bani and Klokeid
1976: 278):

(122) Ngath ngaungu ithab koei puil   pathamadhin.
      I-Erg. myself these big tree-Abs.-Pl. cut-Pl.P-Past
      'I cut down these big trees.'

(123) Ngai   ngaungu ithab koei puin   pathaidhin.
      I-Abs. myself these big tree-Obl.   cut-Past
      'I cut down all these big trees.'

(I am grateful to S. C. Dik for bringing these data to my
attention.) We may note that incorporation, discussed below,
also has different functions in different languages, although
detailed discussion is beyond the scope of the present
chapter.

In Dyirbal, on the other hand, the function of the antipassive is primarily related to discourse structure: anti-
passives are not usually found as the first clause of a
discourse. But thereafter they can be found where the nonantipassive form is excluded because of the restrictions on
coordination, and the like, of an absolute noun phrase with
an ergative noun phrase. The following, for example, coordinate the intransitive sentences (56) and (58) with the
antipassive versions of (57) and (59), and thus translate
the English coordinate structures (52) and (54), which, as
already noted, are impossible in Dyirbal using the nonantipassive form (Dixon 1972: 130):

(124) Bayi   yaṟa   bani-nʸu,   bagun   dʸugumbil-
      Masc.-Abs. man-Abs. come-Tense Fem.-Dat. woman-
      gu   balgal-ŋa-nʸu.
      Dat. hit-   Tense
      'The man came here and (he) hit the woman.'

(125) Balan   dʸugumbil bani-nʸu,   bagul   yaṟa-gu
      Fem.-Abs. woman-Abs. came-Tense Masc.-Dat. man- Dat.

balgal-ŋa-nʸu.
hit-   Tense

'The woman came here and (she) hit the man.'

Given that the prime function of the Dyirbal antipassive is
in constructing discourses with all clauses having the same
absolute noun phrase expressing the topic, it is not surpris-
ing that the antipassive should be paralleled by another
derived verbal form allowing coordination of two sentences
where A of the first is coreferential with S or P of the
second, namely the -ŋura form, which allows the following
coordination possibility (Dixon 1972: 77 - 78):

(126) Bala yugu   baŋgul   yaṟa-ŋgu mada- n,
      Abs. stick-Abs. Masc.-Erg. man- Erg. throw-Tense

      waynʸdʸi-ŋura.
      ascend

      'The man threw the stick and went uphill.'

A final set of pairs where absolute and ergative alternate
without any necessary difference in degree of agentivity is
where one member of each pair involves incorporation of P
into the verb, that is, the formation of a complex intransitive verb from a construction with a verb and P. A particularly clear example is provided by Chukchee, a language of
Eastern Siberia (Chukotka Peninsula):

(127) Tumg -e   nantəwatən kupre-n.
      friend-Erg. they-set-it net- Abs.
      'The friends set the net.'

(128) Tumg -ət   kopra-ntəwatg'at.
      friend-Abs. net- they-set
      'The friends set the net/engaged in net-setting.'

(127) is an ergative construction: P is a separate word in the
absolute case, A is in the ergative case, and the verb agrees
with both A and P. In (128), the object has been incorporated

into the verb; it is part of the same word as the verb. In
Chukchee this can be seen quite clearly because instead of the
vocalism of the separate word kupre-, vowel harmony assimi-
lates the vocalism to that of the verb, giving kopra- (in
Chukchee, vowel harmony is coextensive with word boundaries).
In the incorporated version (128), the construction is
intransitive, since P no longer exists as a separate word, so
the subject is in the absolute case; moreover, the verb is in
the appropriate form for an intransitive verb with a third
person plural subject (and, of course, no direct object). Not
all languages have such clear phonological and morphological
evidence of incorporation, but it is probably in this way that
we should analyze the "direct objects" that occur in the
following examples, (130) from Tongan (Churchward 1953: 77)
and (131) from Quiché:

(129) Na'e inu   'a   e   kava 'e   Sione.
      Past drink Abs. the kava Erg. John
      'John drank the kava.'

(130) Na'e inu   kava 'a   Sione.
      Past drink kava Abs. John
      'John drank kava/engaged in kava-drinking.'

(131) K-   e-   q'oxoma-n   le čirimiy le
      Asp.- 3Pl.Abs.- play-   Antipass. the chirimí the
      ax q'oxom-ab'.
      player-   Pl.
      'The players played the chirimí/engaged in chirimí-
      playing.'

In some languages, however, even incorporated Ps still require
an ergative subject, as in Dargi (Abdullaev 1971: 82), a
Northeast Caucasian language:

(132) Nu-ni q'as-   barra.
      I-Erg. decision- made
      'I decided.'

More literally, (130) would be 'I made a decision', except
that P is incorporated into the verb; nonetheless, the subject
is in the ergative.

The ergative subjects in sentences like Basque (103),
Walbiri (111), and Dargi (132) might provide some slight
evidence for a link between ergativity and agentivity; yet
these examples can equally, or even better, be accounted for
in terms of intransitive derivatives of transitive verbs which
retain some properties of the transitive from which they
derive, in particular the ergative subject. But the weight
of the examples discussed so far is strongly against identification of ergativity and agentivity.

We must now turn to some examples that suggest there is
some connection, in some languages, between ergativity and
agentivity, although this connection is by no means identity.
It should be noted initially that there is bound to be a high
correlation between ergative noun phrases and agentive noun
phrases simply because As are typically high on the scale of
agentivity; this is a factor quite independent of ergativity,
however: as pointed out to me by Susumu Kuno, Japanese has a
rather strong agentivity requirement on As, but no morphological or syntactic ergativity correlating with this. In
some languages, however, one finds that A goes into the
ergative case, and that S stands sometimes in the absolute
case, sometimes in the ergative case, the ergative being used
where S is more agentive, as in the following pair of Batsbi
sentences (Batsbi is a Northeast Caucasian language) (Dešeriev
1953: 226):

(133) Tχo   naizdraχ   qitra.
      we-Abs. to-the-ground fell
      'We fell to the ground (unintentionally, not our
      fault).'

(134) Atχo   naizdraχ   qitra.
      we-Erg. to-the-ground fell
      'We fell to the ground (intentionally, through our
      own carelessness).'

Such examples suggest that languages may evince a connection
between ergativity and agentivity, although there is no
necessary connection. Diachronically, this could arise from
the high correlation between As and agentive noun phrases,
so that a marker of A status could easily be reinterpreted as
a marker of agentivity, and vice versa. (Klimov 1973 argues
that morphological ergativity almost invariably arises diachronically from agentivity; for a critical assessment of his
arguments, see Comrie 1976b.) This process could be facili-
tated by the presence of objectless transitive verbs with
ergative subjects (cf. Basque sentence 103), or by verbs with
incorporated objects and ergative subjects (cf. Dargi example
132); note moreover that in Dargi, many such examples are
probably to be analyzed synchronically as morphologically
complex intransitive verbs, rather than as involving synchronically a derivation via incorporation). Lest it should
be felt that this chapter is unjustly negative with regard to
the connection between ergativity and agentivity, I should
point out that the close relation between ergativity and
agentivity in some languages is counterbalanced by a close
relation between ergativity and nonagentivity in some others
(see further section 7.4.2), e.g., Dalabon, an Australian
language spoken in Arnhem Land, where the ergative suffix -yi
occurs with all inanimate As, but not with all animate As,
although the latter are more agentive than the former.

7.3. Ergative-Absolute and Nominative-Accusative Systems: Diachronic Relationships

When linguists, for the most part speakers of nonergative languages, first started investigating ergativity, one of the main questions that concerned them was: how can a language come to be ergative? There was thus a presupposition that ergativity is somehow aberrant and its deviation from the norm has to be explained as the result of some historical development from a more normal language-type. Had linguists developed first among speakers of ergative languages, the question might well have been posed in the opposite way: How could the aberrant nominative-accusative system arise from the normal ergative-absolute system? In this section, I shall try to show that both directions of development are possible and provide examples of both, although for the majority of ergative languages, our knowledge of their history is so limited that we can do little more than speculate on earlier stages.

7.3.1. Passive and Ergative

From the viewpoint of a nominative-accusative language, the ergative-absolute system is most reminiscent of passive constructions in a nominative-accusative language. In this part of the discussion, I shall continue to use A and P to refer to the two arguments of a transitive verb irrespective of which is subject (or which is treated like S for specific morphological or syntactic phenomena). Thus, in both active and passive sentences of English like Mary kissed John and John was kissed by Mary, the same noun phrase (here, Mary) will be A in both, and the same noun phrase (here, John) will be P in both. In nominative-accusative morphology, it is

typical (though not quite universal) for the nominative to be
less complex morphologically, abbreviated below as (-), than
the accusative and oblique (+), whereas in ergative-absolute
morphology it is typical for the absolute to be less complex
morphologically (-) and the ergative and oblique more complex
(+). The similarity between the passive construction in a
nominative-accusative language and the ergative construction
may be illustrated by the following structures:

(135) Nominative-accusative: active transitive
A   P   V
Nom. (-)   Acc. (+)

(136) Nominative-accusative: intransitive
S   V
Nom. (-)

(137) Nominative-accusative: passive
P   A   V
Nom. (-)   Obl. (+)

(138) Ergative-absolute: transitive
A   P   V
Erg. (+)   Abs. (-)

(139) Ergative-absolute: intransitive
S   V
Abs. (-)

(The word order is not relevant to this argument, although
the typical, but by no means universal, difference in the word
order of passive and ergative constructions as illustrated by
the actual order used in 137 and 138 is one argument against
their identification.) In both the passive and ergative
constructions, the A noun phrase is more complex morphologically than the P noun phrase, whereas the inverse is usually
true in the active construction of the nominative-accusative
system. In both the passive and the ergative, P is morphologically identical to S, whereas in the second nominative-

accusative construction A is morphologically identical to S.
The only difference would be that the passive contrasts with
an active nominative-accusative construction, whereas the
ergative does not enter into such a contrast; in other words,
the ergative would be like an "obligatory" passive construction. From what has been said so far, it should be clear that,
for the majority of languages with ergativity, this is not
acceptable as a synchronic analysis: in most languages with
ergativity, the majority of subject properties identify the
A of the transitive verb as its subject, whereas in the
passive construction the majority of subject properties
identify the P as the subject of the sentence. Only for
languages with consistent syntactic ergativity, such as
Dyirbal, is the obligatory passive analysis a candidate for
analysis of the ergative construction.

Another piece of evidence often cited against the obligatory
passive analysis is that many languages have passive constructions contrasting with the active ergative, as in Basque:

(140) Haurra   igorria   da.
      child-Abs. sent-Pass. Aux.-3Sg.S
      'The child was sent.'

However, this is not an absolutely telling argument, since
there are languages with more than one passive construction,
so it could be the case that Basque, for instance, had two
passives and no active. However, in the Basque ergative
construction subject tests identify A as subject, whereas in
the Basque passive they identify P as subject, i.e., the
subject tests do not require the dubious reinforcement from
the presence of a distinct passive form.

Diachronically, however, there is good evidence that some
instances of morphological ergativity do arise from passive
constructions, through loss of the corresponding actives. The

best evidence comes from the development of ergativity in the
Indo-Iranian languages (Pirejko 1968), especially in the Indic
languages; these languages typically are ergative only in the
past tense forms or, more restrictedly still, in the perfective past forms. In earlier stages of these languages, for
instance Sanskrit, such tense/aspects had both active and
passive forms. However, the passive forms increased in
frequency relative to the active forms, until eventually the
active forms became obsolete. Parallel with this development,
the subject properties were transferred (no doubt gradually,
although it may not be possible to reconstruct all the details)
from the P noun phrase (of the passive construction) to the
A noun phrase (of the ergative construction). In many modern
Indo-Iranian languages, the only subject properties still
characterizing P are its less complex morphology and verb-
agreement with P rather than with the A, as in Hindi:

(141) Is   laṛke ne   pustak   paṛhī.
      this boy   Erg. book-(Fem.)-Abs. read-Fem.
      'This boy read a book.'

In many Indo-Iranian languages, even these last vestiges of
ergativity (purely morphological) are being lost, often in
stages which, synchronically, seem to make little sense, but
can be explained in terms of the gradual loss of ergativity,
such as constructions where the auxiliary clitic agrees in
person and number with A, whereas the participial form of
the verb agrees in gender (sometimes also in number) with P,
as in the Iranian language Munjani (Grjunberg 1972: 431):

(142) Mən   vow   ž   -əgh- əm.
      I-Erg. she-Pl. hit Fem. 1Sg.S
      'I hit her.'

In Modern Persian, ergativity has been lost completely, so
that in the development from the oldest Persian to the modern

Figure 3. Development of Ergative from Passive

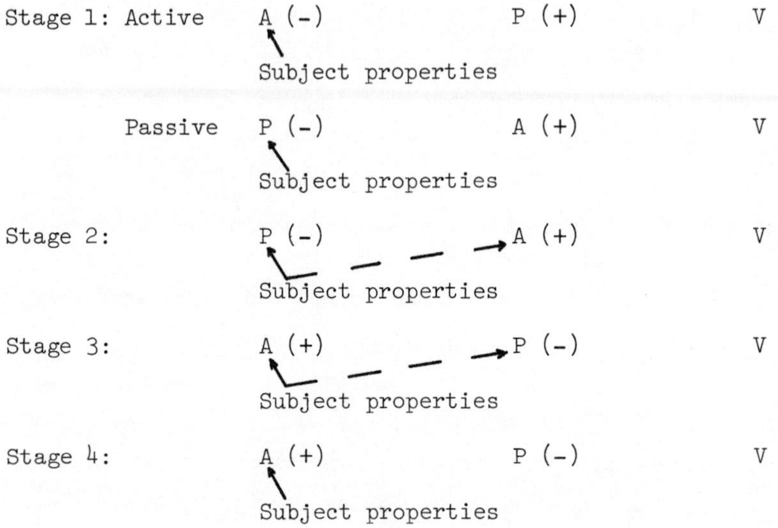

Stage 1: Active   A (-)   P (+)   V
                   ↖
                   Subject properties

         Passive   P (-)   A (+)   V
                   ↖
                   Subject properties

Stage 2:   P (-)   _ _ _ →A (+)   V
                   ↖___ _ _
                   Subject properties

Stage 3:   A (+)   _ _ _ →P (-)   V
                   ↖___ _ _
                   Subject properties

Stage 4:   A (+)   P (-)   V
                   ↖
                   Subject properties

language one can see the rise and fall of ergativity. The
development from passive to ergative can be represented
schematically as in Figure 3. The further stage found in
Modern Persian involves loss even of the morphological
ergative system.

A similar development has been posited for the Polynesian
languages (Hohepa 1969), though there it is a much more
recent development than in Indo-Iranian. Some Polynesian
languages are still almost completely nominative-accusative;
some are well on the way to becoming ergative (the passive
is very frequent relative to the active; subject properties
are being transferred away from P in this construction to A);
while others are completely ergative; in some, there has even
been realignment of the morphology, in the loss of the passive
suffix on verbs in the ergative construction, although the
noun phrase morphology does not yet show any signs of loss,

as it does in many Indo-Iranian languages (Polynesian
languages do not typically have verb-agreement, so there is
no possibility of ergativity being manifested there).

Further evidence for the passive origin of ergativity in
some languages can be seen in the fact that certain correlations that hold between passive and other features hold equally
between ergativity in these languages and these same features.
For instance, passive tends to be more frequent with the perfect
aspect (in particular the perfect of result) than with other
verbal forms (Comrie 1976a: 84 - 86); in the development of the
ergative in Indo-Iranian, the ergative is first found only in
the perfect, and the later wider range of ergativity follows
from the extension of these forms to oust all other past perfective forms (as in most Indic languages with ergativity), or even
all other past forms (as in most Iranian languages with ergativity). Thus the current split ergativity along a tense/aspect
basis in most Indo-Iranian languages with ergativity is a reflex of this correlation. Second, in many languages passives
can only be formed, or can only be formed readily, or are formed
much more readily, from dynamic, as opposed to stative, verbs.
In Samoan, a Polynesian language, the ergative construction
is used with more dynamic verbs, the nominative-accusative
construction with more stative verbs (I am grateful to Dixie C.
Samasoni for discussion of the Samoan examples):

(143) Ua   sogi e   le tama ∅   le ufi.
      Tense cut Erg. the boy Abs. the yam
      'The boy cut the yam.'

(144) Ua   alofa ∅   le tama 'i   le teine.
      Tense love Nom. the boy Acc. the girl
      'The boy loves the girl.'

The absolute and nominative are morphologically identical (in
Samoan, with no preposition, contrasting with ergative e), as
is expected from the diachronic development; both develop from

subjects at an earlier stage of the language, the absolute from
the subject of a passive construction, the nominative from the
subject of an active construction. Synchronically, in Samoan,
both (143) and (144) have passives with the same syntactic and
morphological structure as each other, suggesting that the actives have the same syntactic structure as each other too:

(145) Ua   sogi-ina   Ø   le ufi e le tama.
      Tense cut- Pass. Abs. the yam by the boy
      'The yam was cut by the boy.'

(146) Ua   alofa-gia   Ø   le teine e le tama.
      Tense love- Pass. Abs. the girl by the boy
      'The girl is loved by the boy.'

Having observed the possible development from passive to
ergative, we may note the opposite possibility whereby a nominative-accusative system could develop from the antipassive. Just
as ergativity can develop through replacement of an active construction by a passive construction (and transference of subject
properties to the passive agent), so a nominative-accusative
system could develop through replacement of an ergative construction by an antipassive construction (though without the
need for transference of subject properties). This has been suggested as a possible origin for split ergativity in Georgian,
where the aorist tense forms seem to be earlier than the present
tense forms; accordingly the ergative system for noun case-
marking in the former might well be earlier than the nominative-
accusative system in the latter. The nominative-accusative system in the present tense system would then represent widening
of the aspectual value of the antipassive to replace all
nonperfective (nonaorist) aspectual forms.

7.3.2. Nominalizations and Ergative

In many discussions of the origin of ergative constructions,
nominalization is advanced as one possible source for ergativity.

Often, the details of the development are not worked out; in particular, no explanation is offered for the crucial difference between the ergative-absolute and other systems, namely the differential treatment of A and S, the latter being treated in the same way as P. In many languages nominalization results in the replacement of all subjects (S and A) by the genitive, with direct objects being unaffected (cf. Comrie 1976c), and clearly this would not lead to an ergative system.

The same proviso actually applies also to the passive as a possible source of ergativity. The possibility of this development is fostered by the fact that in a large number of languages passives exist only of transitive sentences, so that reinterpretation of a passive as an (ergative) active can only apply to sentences with transitive verbs. In some languages, passives can be formed equally from intransitive sentences, and reinterpretation of the passive agent as subject in such a language would not lead to ergativity. This development seems to have taken place in some North Russian dialects (Timberlake 1976).

In examining nominalization, one must therefore be careful to ask what feature of the nominalization construction is responsible for the ergative-absolute system. In English, which has both prenominal and postnominal genitives, both active and passive nominalizations of transitive verbs are possible:

(147) the enemy's arrival
(148) the enemy's destruction of the city
(149) the city's destruction by the enemy

In Russian, on the other hand, which has very much the same nominalization construction as English, but which does not have two different kinds of genitive, in effect only the passive nominalization is possible for transitive verbs.

(150) priezd vraga
      arrival enemy-of
      'the enemy's arrival'

(151) razrušenie   goroda   vragom
      destruction city-of enemy-by
      'the city's destruction by the enemy'

Russian has no direct equivalent of the English active nominal
the enemy's destruction of the city; that is, as far as nominalizations are concerned, Russian has in effect an ergative
system: S and P stand in the genitive (functioning as an
absolute), while A stands in the instrumental (functioning as
an ergative). The verbal system of Russian, however, does not
share this kind of ergativity, although ergativity would be a
logically possible development if finite verbal forms were to
be replaced by nominalizations. I am not aware of any actual
instances where ergativity in the verbal system arises from
such an ergative nominalization construction.

     In many ergative languages, the transitive sentence
construction can be derived etymologically, either with
certainty or with a high degree of plausibility, from a
nominalization, whereas the intransitive sentence construction
does not derive etymologically from a nominalization (Allen
1964). In one sense, this is ergativity via nominalization,
but it should be noted that nominalization does not explain
the differential treatment of transitives and intransitives
in such instances — the explanation is required at an even
earlier stage; namely, why are only transitive constructions
replaced by nominalizations, and not intransitive constructions? The kind of situation discussed in this paragraph
holds, for instance, in the development of ergativity in
Iranian, from constructions like Old Persian manā kr̥tam 'I did
this, this was done by me', where manā is the genitive of the
first person singular pronoun, and kr̥tam is a past participle
used as a noun phrase, i.e., more literally something like
'this is the my-having-been-done-thing'. Indeed, Cardona
(1970) suggests that this nominalization was reinterpreted as

a passive in the development of Iranian (interpretation of manā
as passive agent), so that the ergative construction would
derive most directly from a passive, and only indirectly from a
nominalization. (A further factor in the development of ergativity in Indo-Iranian is that the past participle is already
incipiently ergative in Proto-Indo-European, having active
meaning when formed from an intransitive verb, 'having come',
but passive meaning when formed from a transitive verb, 'having
been killed'. Compare the discussion of ergativity in derivational morphology in section 7.4.3.) In all instances known to
me where ergativity is alleged to derive via nominalization, it
seems at least a priori plausible that a development similar
to that in Iranian occurred, with nominalization originally a
device for forming passive constructions, and subsequent reinterpretation of these passives as ergatives.

Moreover, there are attested examples where nominalization
is the prime factor in the destruction of ergativity, its replacement by the nominative-accusative system. This development
can occur in languages where nominalization involves putting
both S and A into the genitive, whereas P remains in the absolute case. The development is attested, for instance, in the
verbal affixes of Chol. The Set A affixes are used in most Mayan
languages as ergative affixes on verbs and as possessive affixes
on nouns (including nominalizations, where the affixes refer to
S and A alike — in this respect, the languages are syntactically
nominative-accusative), the set B affixes as absolute affixes on
verbs. In Chol (see examples 77 - 82), the past tense retains the
earlier system; the present tense, however, has been replaced by
a nominalization, so that all subjects have the Set A affixes
(functionally, nominative), while direct objects, as usual
unaffected by nominalization in Mayan languages, have the
Set B affixes. Similarly in Jacaltec, many subordinate clauses

derive from nominalizations, so that, whereas main clauses are ergative-absolute, these subordinate clauses have the nominative-accusative system deriving etymologically via nominalization (examples from Craig 1976: 102):

(152) Sikinax hač.
      tired   2Sg.Abs.
      'You are tired.'

(153) Šk- ač   w-   ila.
      Asp.- 2Sg.Abs. 1Sg.Erg.- see
      'I saw you.'

(154) Šk- oŋ   to ku-   saxčox.
      Asp.- 1Pl.Abs. go 1Pl.Nom.- play
      'We went to play.'

(155) Šk- oŋ   to hač   ku-   kolo'.
      Asp.- 1Pl.Abs. go 2Sg.Acc. 1Pl.Nom.- help
      'We went to help you.'

In these Jacaltec examples, the Set A affixes are w- (first person singular) and ku- (first person plural); the set B affixes are (h)ač (second person singular) and oŋ (first person plural).

Since genitive noun phrases are typically more complex morphologically than absolute noun phrases, nominative-accusative systems that arise in the way just discussed would be expected to have a nominative (etymologically, genitive) more complex morphologically than the accusative (etymologically, absolute), unlike the general pattern in nominative-accusative languages where the nominative is less complex. There are, however, some nominative-accusative languages with the nominative more complex morphologically and the accusative less complex, such as some of the Yuman languages with nominative in -č (S and A) and accusative with no overt marker; nominalization is a possible diachronic explanation for such systems. (I am grateful to Pamela Munro for drawing the Yuman data to my attention.)

In conclusion to section 7.3: I have tried to show that the diachronic relations between ergative-absolute and nominative-accusative systems are rather more complex than is often assumed: there are indeed possibilities for a natural development from nominative-accusative to ergative-absolute, but equally there are possibilities for a natural development in the opposite direction.

7.4. Synchronic Function of Ergative Case-Marking

Having looked at some possible diachronic explanations for the ergative-absolute system, in this section I wish to examine some possible synchronic explanations for this kind of system, in particular with regard to noun-phrase case-marking. The question posed here is thus: is there any sense to the ergative-absolute case-marking system internal to this kind of case-marking system? We take as our starting point the notion that one of the functions of a case-marking system, in so far as it applies to S, A, and P, is to enable recovery from the form of the sentence of the syntactic relations contained in it, that is, to enable identification of the S, A, and P of the sentence. (There are, of course, other ways of coding the difference between S, A, and P, for example by verb-agreement or word order; I return to verb-agreement briefly at the end of this section, concentrating in the meantime on case-marking.) Various factors can operate to make identification of S, A, and P more difficult — for instance, in the absence of overt cues for S, A, or P status, a sentence containing both A and P will give more difficulty than one allowing only S, or only P. Therefore one might expect that utilization of overt markers of syntactic relations would be most likely to occur, across the languages of the world, in those instances where confusion of syntactic relations would be most likely in the absence of such overt markers. I shall try to illustrate this general principle, in its relation to ergativity, in the following sections.

7.4.1. Ergative and Antiergative

As already indicated, one factor complicating the identification of S, A, and P, in the absence of overt markers, is a syntactic construction allowing the presence of both A and P (in the same clause). Thus the transitive construction A-P-V presents more problems from this viewpoint than does the intransitive construction S-V, since in the former there is greater need to hit at least one of A and P to avoid misinterpretation (e.g., of John hit Mary as Mary hit John). If we refer back to Figure 1, we note that of the five systems presented there for marking of S, A, and P in transitive and intransitive sentences, two of these types are very highly motivated from the viewpoint of the discriminatory function of case-marking (discrimination of S, A, and P): type (b) (nominative-accusative) and type (c) (ergative-absolute) both distinguish A from P in the A-P-V (transitive) construction, in the one type (nominative-accusative) using a special form for P of the transitive construction and the same form for both A and S, in the other type (ergative-absolute) using a special form for A of the transitive construction and the same form for both S and P; both types have only two morphological categories, with which they make the relevant distinction among S, A, and P where it is most needed (clauses with both A and P), and from this viewpoint it is irrelevant whether S is identified morphologically with A or with P. In the majority

of nominative-accusative languages the accusative is morphologically more complex than the nominative, and in nearly all
ergative-absolute languages the ergative is morphologically
more complex than the absolute, so that we can make the
general claim: nominative-accusative languages distinguish A
from P in the A-P-V construction by marking P; ergative
languages distinguish A from P in the A-P-V construction by
marking A. Of the other types given in Figure 1: type (a)
does not use noun-phrase case-marking to distinguish S, A,
and P (and typically languages with this system use some other
means, e.g., verb-agreement or word order, to indicate this
distinction); type (d) is, from the viewpoint of the discriminatory function of case-marking, unnecessarily explicit, but
at least it does make the distinction between A and P of a
transitive construction (type d appears also to be extremely
rare among the languages of the world); type (3) seems to be
nonexistent, and certainly the discussion of the present
section would suggest that it should be at least extremely
rare, if not totally excluded: A and P are not distinguished
in the transitive construction, while a functionally unnecessary distinction between S on the one hand and A and P of
the transitive construction on the other is maintained; that
is, the distinction that it is most important to maintain is
not in fact maintained, while an unnecessary distinction is
made elsewhere. The absence or near-absence of type (e) is
one piece of evidence in favor of this approach to the
ergative case-marking system.

Another piece of evidence comes from the morphology of
subjectless sentences. In some languages, subjectless sentences form a distinct sentence-type, with syntactic
properties distinguishing them from sentences with subjects.
Thus in addition to the constructions S-V and A-P-V, for

such languages one should also consider the type P-V. (There
is also the type V in such languages, lacking both subject
and direct object, but since this leaves no possibility for
case-marking, it is not relevant to the present discussion.)
This last type, P-V, is another type where, parallel to S-V,
there is no need to have an overt marker for the direct object,
since there is no subject with which it can be confused in
the clause. (In languages of this type, S-V and P-V are
typically distinguished from one another by the fact that
only certain verbs, or certain verbal forms, appear in P-V.)
Therefore one might expect to find languages where a special
marker is used for the direct object if and only if there is
also a subject in the same clause, subjects and direct objects
being otherwise unmarked. This would be the mirror-image of
the ergative-absolute system, and might therefore be termed
the 'antiergative-absolute' system, the antiergative being
used for the P of A-P-V (compare the ergative for the A of
A-P-V), and the absolute for the S of S-V, the A of A-P-V,
and for the P of P-V (compare the absolute in the ergative-
absolute system for the P of P-V, if this exists as a separate
sentence-type, and of A-P-V and for the S of S-V), as in
Figure 4.

Languages of this antiergative type do indeed exist, for
instance, Finnish, where, with singular pronominal noun
phrases, the so-called accusative in -n is used for P where
there is an A, but not where there is no A (e.g., in
imperatives):

(156) Maija   tuli.
      Maija-Abs. came
      'Maija came.'

(157) Maija   söi kala-n.
      Maija-Abs. ate fish-Antierg.
      'Maija ate the fish.'

Figure 4. Ergative and Antiergative

(a) Ergative-absolute

		V
	S	V
A	P	V
	P	V

Erg.   Abs.

(b) Antiergative-absolute

		V
S		V
A	P	V
P		V

Abs.   Antierg.

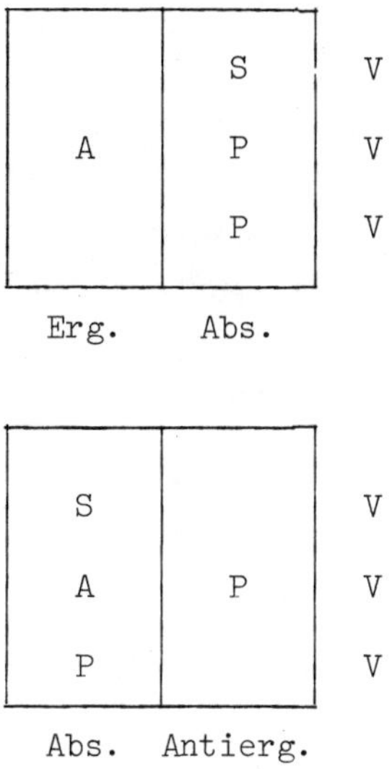

(158) Syö   kala!
      eat-Imperat. fish-Abs.
      'Eat the fish!'

Further discussion of the antiergative-absolute system with
more exemplification, will be found in Comrie 1975; see also
Bechert 1977, which became available to me only after completion of the body of this chapter. For present purposes,
the important point to note is that the existence of the
antiergative-absolute system provides further evidence in
favor of the approach toward the synchronic explanation of
ergativity advocated in this section.

7.4.2. Case-Marking and Interpretation Probability

So far, we have been assuming that case-marking will tend to
be used to distinguish A from P, wherever both are present in
the same clause, since otherwise confusion would be more
likely. Clearly, however, the possibility of confusion also
depends on the kinds of noun phrases used as A and P. Thus,
given a transitive verb like eat and two noun phrases, one
animate like man and the other inanimate like bread, even in
the absence of any overt markers there would be a much greater
likelihood of someone speaking about the man eating the bread
than about the bread eating the man; similarly, the hearer
would normally assign the former interpretation to an otherwise ambiguous sentence of this type. We might therefore
expect to find languages where case-marking of A or P of the
A-P-V construction is made only where the likelihood of
confusion, allowing for the fact that certain situations are
so unlikely in absolute or relative terms as to be able to be
excluded from consideration, is still very high. Thus there
would be no marking if we were to talk of the man eating the
bread, but there would be marking if we were to talk of the
man eating a lion (given that lions can readily eat men), and
even more so if we wanted to talk about (metaphorical or
science-fiction) bread eating the man. There are indeed
languages which exhibit case-marking systems of this type.
Since this chapter is on ergativity, I shall concentrate on
such case-marking of A. (For a discussion of case-marking of
direct objects from this viewpoint, see Comrie, forthcoming.)
     Haiman (forthcoming) notes that in Hua, a language of the
New Guinea Eastern Highlands, there is an ergative suffix
-bamu', whereas the absolute case has no overt marker:

(159) Busa' rmie.
      Busa' he-went-down
      'Busa' went down.'

(160) Busa'-bamu' egbie.
      Busa'-Erg. he-hit-him
      'Busa' hit him.'

(161) Busa' egbie.
      Busa' he-hit-him
      'He hit Busa'.'

However, Haiman notes that although the ergative suffix can
only be used with A (and never with S or P), it is not
necessary to use this suffix with A, since it can be omitted
where confusion would not otherwise result. Thus, of the
following two sentences, (162) with -bamu', can only mean
'Who gave it to him?', whereas (163), with no marking on
kzo' 'who', can mean either 'Whom did he give it to?' (Hua
does not distinguish morphologically between direct and
indirect object) or, in the appropriate context, 'Who gave it
to him?':

(162) Kzo'-bamu' mie?
      who   Erg. he-gave-it-to-him

(163) Kzo' mie?
      who he-gave-it-to-him

Ergativity and the Animacy Hierarchy

In many languages where case-marking of A and P is restricted
to situations in which confusion is most likely, there is a
more rigid specification of what class of situations is
considered to be most likely to engender confusion, rather
than the more general specification (where the speaker feels
clarification is required) that seems to hold for Hua.

There seems to be a general supposition in human discourse
that certain entities are inherently more agentive than others,

and as such inherently more likely to appear as A of a
transitive verb and less likely to appear as P of a transitive verb. The mainstay of this supposition is the animacy
(agentivity) hierarchy, which claims basically that more
animate entities will tend to act upon less animate entities
rather than vice versa. The animacy hierarchy has first and
second person pronouns at the top (i.e., active participants
in the speech act are most agentive), followed by third
person personal pronouns, followed by other human noun phrases,
then other animate noun phrases, with inanimate noun phrases
at the bottom. (Languages may make finer or less fine distinctions, and different languages vary with regard to some
of the finer distinctions, but the general schema remains the
same.) Given a transitive verb with A and P, there are three
possibilities with regard to the animacy hierarchy: (a) A is
higher on the hierarchy than P; (b) both A and P are of equal
animacy; (c) P is higher on the hierarchy than A. In terms of
the animacy hierarchy, (a) is expected, whereas (c) is
unexpected, while no prediction is made with respect to (b).
In some languages, one finds that no case-marking is used in
(a), whereas case-marking is used in (c), and usually also
in (b). This system obtains in Dalabon, an Australian language
of the Northern Territory (Silverstein 1976: 129):

    (164) Buluŋan   ga'manbuniŋ.
          my-father he-made-it
          'My father made it.'

In (164), there is an animate noun phrase and an inanimate
pronoun coded in the verb form; the expectation is that the
animate noun phrase will be A and the inanimate noun phrase P,
and as this expectation is borne out, there is no case-marking
of A.

(165) bulunan   -yi   wuduwud ga'nan.
      my-father -Erg. baby   he-looks-at-him
      'My father is looking at the baby.'

In (165), both noun phrases are human, and, at least in
Dalabon, are treated as being at the same level in the animacy
hierarchy: the hierarchy thus makes no prediction as to which
is more likely to be A and which P, so case-marking is
required, and since Dalabon marks A in such instances, we
have an ergative case, in -yi. As noted by Silverstein (1976:
129), inanimate As are invariably lower than or on the same
level as their Ps, since inanimate is the lowest position on
the hierarchy, and this accounts for the invariable marking
of inanaimate As of transitive verbs with the ergative suffix
-yi in Dalabon, contrary to the positive correlation noted
in some other languages between ergativity and agentivity.

In some languages, this kind of case-marking is determined
by the absolute position of a noun phrase on the hierarchy,
rather than by the relative position of A and P on the
hierarchy: noun phrases high on the hierarchy will not be
marked when they are A, but will be marked (accusative) when
they are P; noun phrases low in the hierarchy will not be
marked when they are P, but will be marked (ergative) when
they are A. We have already observed a language of this
kind, namely Dyirbal (section 7.1.3), where first and second
person pronouns and nonpronominal noun phrases have an
ergative-absolute morphology, the latter being lower on the
animacy hierarchy than the former. Further examples of this
pattern, drawn mainly from Australian languages, are given
by Silverstein (1976), in terms of a more detailed explanatory hypothesis similar to that advanced here. Silverstein
also notes that in some languages there may be an area of
overlap between the two systems, that is, some noun phrases

that have both marked ergative and marked accusative cases,
with an unmarked case used only as S, thus giving rise to a
tripartite system as in Figure 1 (d); Dyirbal has this system
for the human interrogative pronoun 'who?': wanᵞa (S),
wanᵞdᵞu (A), wanᵞuna (P) (Dixon 1972: 53).

Note that this differs in terms of morphological marking
from the Motu system given in (9) and (10) as an illustration
of type (d) in Figure 1: in Motu, P, rather than S, is less
complex morphologically. In Motu, moreover, this tripartite
system is much more widespread than in languages with split
ergativity involving limited overlap, so that all in all the
tripartite case-marking system may well be a rather different
kind of phenomenon in the two kinds of language (though
involving some kind of intersection of ergative-absolute and
nominative-accusative in both).

7.4.3. Synchronic Explanation of Other Manifestations
        of Ergativity

The discriminatory function of the ergative-absolute system
as discussed in the present section relates primarily to
morphological ergativity, in particular to ergativity in the
case-marking system. It can also be extended to ergativity
in verb-agreement, particularly in those languages (such as
the Mayan languages) where there is no case-marking of S, A,
and P, and verb-agreement is the prime indicator of S, A, and
P (with word order playing a secondary role, more especially
relevant when both A and P are third person). Indeed, in
languages where verb-agreement does not play this role of
distinguishing A from P, it might be more helpful to regard
ergative-absolute verb-agreement as an instance of syntactic,
rather than morphological, ergativity; the boundary is, in
any event, rather fluid, and different grammatical traditions

differ as to whether the use of morphological categories is
properly part of morphology or rather part of syntax. Thus
the major phenomenon still requiring an explanation — and one
for which no explanation will be put forward here with any
confidence — is syntactic ergativity, especially bearing in
mind that syntactic ergativity is much less common, across the
languages of the world, than is morphological ergativity. As
noted in section 7.0.3, there is really no statistical basis
for saying that morphological ergativity is abnormal, whereas
there may be a statistical basis for arguing that syntactic
ergativity is abnormal.

In section 7.1, we noted that one kind of syntactic ergativity is, however, quite widespread in languages, even in
languages which are otherwise not ergative, namely ergativity
in derivational morphology. I cited the example of formation
of compound nouns by incorporation, where English allows
incorporation of P of transitive verbs (e.g., fox-hunting)
and of S of intransitive verbs (e.g., bird-chirping), that
is, allows incorporation of absolute noun phrases. In looking
at incorporation across languages, including languages where
this is much more productive and much more a central syntactic
process of the language than in English, one finds that P is
easiest to incorporate, followed by S, with A most resistant
to incorporation. This suggests that incorporation may
originate with P, with subsequent spread to S, followed only
very occasionally by spread to A. If we imagine an early stage
where incorporation is restricted to P, then it follows that
incorporation is restricted to transitive verbs; intransitive
verbs will not be amenable to incorporation, which thus
imposes a syntactic restriction on a morphological process,
although there is no morphological reason for this restriction
to exist, that is, incorporation applied to an intransitive

verb is syntactically ill formed, but morphologically well
formed. A logical development from this stage would be for
incorporation to be extended to intransitive verbs; here,
however, the only candidate for incorporation is S. As far as
transitive verbs are concerned, the original situation is
maintained, so that overall an ergative system is built up,
although the motivation for the change would not be ergativity
itself, but rather pressure against accidental morphological
gaps. There is evidence for a development of this kind within
Modern English derivational morphology. Although it is possible
to incorporate both P and S to form compound nouns in English,
the forms with incorporated S (e.g., bird-chirping) are much
less natural than those with incorporated P (e.g., fox-
hunting). English can form adjectives referring to a quality
of the P of a verb with the suffix -able, e.g., washable
'able to be washed', not 'able to wash'; in addition, there
are a few forms from intransitive verbs, and here the quality
is attributed to S, e.g., perishable 'likely to perish'. The
suffix -ee functions similarly, e.g., employee 'one who is
employed', not 'one who employs', escapee 'one who has
escaped', and, at least in some idiolects, standee 'one who
stands', used of a standing passenger (though the validity of
this last example is somewhat weakened by the use of the term
dilutee in Britain during the Second World War to refer to an
unskilled worker who diluted the existing work-force, rather
than to those who were thus diluted). Thus this extension from
P only to P and S seems to be an ongoing process in current
English, and the explanation suggested here may be able to
account for instances of syntactic ergativity involving
derivational morphology, though extensions beyond this into
more clearly syntactic phenomena are questionable, given the
requirement of an initial stage where subjects (in most

languages, S and A) are not amenable to the syntactic process
in question. (Compare the claim in Keenan and Comrie 1977 that
relative clause formation, and possibly many other syntactic
processes, apply most readily to subjects, transitive or
intransitive.)

In treating derivational morphology, we are approaching,
if not entering, the field of the lexicon. In much recent work
on ergativity, or at least in much recent work using the term
ergativity, the term has been extended to cover sets of sentences like the following English pair:

(166) John broke the window.

(167) The window broke.

The claim would be that <u>John</u> in (166) is ergative, while
the <u>window</u> in both (166) and (167) would be absolute. This
use of the term can be very misleading, in that *ergativity*
does have a reasonably well defined traditional meaning in
its application to case-marking and verb-agreement, and also
in that this extended use of the term conceals the real
differences between the morphology of languages like English
and Basque, the real differences between the syntax of languages like English and Dyirbal; probably all languages have
pairs of sentences like (164) and (165) in English, though
usually with a morphological indicator of the difference
between the transitive and intransitive verb, unlike English.
Incidentally, ergative languages (morphological only or both
morphological and syntactic) tend equally to have distinct
transitive and intransitive forms in such pairs. But if we
compare the above English pair with the following pair, there
may be some sense in which we can use the term *ergativity*
here:

(168) John ate a pie.

(169) John ate.

In (168) and (169), the S of the intransitive is identified,
in terms of semantic roles, with the A of the transitive verb,
whereas in (166) and (167) the S of the intransitive is
identified with the P of the transitive. We might refer to
the pattern of (166) and (167) as "lexical ergativity," and
that of (168) and (169) as a "lexical nominative-accusative
system." If we were to use this terminology, however, it would
be essential to bear in mind that this is an extension of the
traditional terminology, an extension that moreover seems to
have little value in terms of typological classification —
presumably all languages have a large amount of "lexical
ergativity" — unlike morphological and syntactic ergativity,
which provide useful means of grouping together a number of
parameters along which languages may vary. Compare Dixon
(1977b) on ergative-absolute and nominative-accusative patterns
in the Dyirbal lexicon.

7.5. Conclusions

The discussion of section 7.4, moving from presentation of
data to attempting explanations for the kind of data found,
necessarily became much more speculative than that of the
preceding sections. There is much in the area of the internal
cohesion of ergative systems that still requires explanation;
the formation and testing of such explanatory hypotheses is
an important task for future research on ergativity.

However, much still remains to be done also in terms of
gathering and processing data on ergative languages. By a
combination of geographical, social, and political accidents,
ergative languages have until recently been largely neglected

(the major European languages have ergativity only in small
parts of the derivational morphology), with information on
the syntax of these languages being particularly scarce. One
example will suffice to show how this scarcity of syntactic
information can bias our general view on ergativity: the
availability of a description of Dyirbal syntax, in the shape
of Dixon's (1972) monograph, has revolutionized our view of
ergativity, since for the first time it has become apparent
that there is a language with near-consistent syntactic ergativity (though it has to be realized that not all ergative
languages are like Dyirbal; the discovery of a continuum from
purely morphological to near-consistent syntactic ergativity
has also proved an important stage in the development of our
ideas on ergativity). In this chapter I have tried to present
in a systematic way the range of phenomena which, in my
opinion, characterize and correlate with ergativity. It may
be that further data from other languages will force us to
widen this framework even further, but in the meantime it is
essential that more theoretical, explanatory discussions of
ergativity should take into account the range of phenomena
which we at present know to be encompassed within ergativity.
If this chapter does something to help bring this about, it
will have served its purpose.

Note

This chapter is a revised and expanded version of a lecture
on "Ergativity" given originally as one of the American Council
of Learned Societies Distinguished Scholar lectures at the
1976 Linguistic Institute of the Linguistic Society of
America, Oswego, New York. This talk was also given at the
Department of Modern Languages and Linguistics of Cornell
University, the Institute of Linguistics of the Soviet Academy

of Sciences, and the Leningrad Section of the Soviet Academy
of Sciences. I am grateful to all those who participated in
the ensuing formal and informal discussions.

For my initiation into ergativity in Mayan languages I am
grateful to Lyle Campbell, and also to the other members of
his Mayan Linguistics course at the 1976 Linguistic Institute.
I must also acknowledge the debt I owe to the many people who
have discussed ergativity with me, orally or by letter, or by
exchange of unpublished material. In addition to those cited
specifically in the text and in the bibliography, mention
should be made of J. C. Catford, Talmy Givón, David E. Johnson,
András Komlósy, Igor A. Melchuk, and G. K. Pullum.

My work on non-Slavic languages of the Soviet Union is
supported by a grant from the Social Science Research Council,
London.

8. Conclusion
Toward an Understanding of the
Profound Unity Underlying Languages

Winfred P. Lehmann

8.1. Principles Governing Language

Preceding chapters, especially Chapters 2, 3, 4, and 6,
illustrated how specific principles govern language structure.
Because these chapters deal primarily with consistent languages and with consistently regulated constructions the
conclusions may suggest that any individual language is
rigidly confined within a limited set of patterns. It is true
that many characteristics of languages are so determined;
yet change leads to inconsistencies in structure, as examples
below illustrate. It will also become clear from these
examples that change is limited to the patterns available
for languages of specific structures, whether OV, or VO in
the variants VSO, SVO, and VOS. A knowledge of principles
governing language and their effects is then essential for
analysis, description, and understanding of languages. Typological study is fundamental to linguistics, whether synchronic or diachronic, practical or theoretical.

As the treatment above has demonstrated, patterns in a
specific language are controlled by linear structure in that
language, and by the two forces molding its production:
government and agreement.

Government regulates basic patterns of the nuclear clause,
those numbered 1 - 4 (see section 1.4). Nominal and verbal

modifiers, patterns 5 - 20, are introduced in keeping with
these, so that they as well as compound sentences, 21 - 25,
are determined by general principles. Through agreement,
elements in these patterns may be interrelated, as well as
elements involved in grammatical processes, especially 26 - 28.
Basic patterns of any language are accordingly governed by
simple but powerful principles, which affect morphological and
phonological as well as syntactic characteristics.

But the regularity possible for a consistent language of
any type encounters interference through a characteristic
aim of communication, an aim often labeled pragmatic. In
studies of pragmatic effects in SVO languages, the initial
sentence constituent — the theme — has been shown generally
to present old material, in this way providing textual
continuity; the latter part of the sentence — the rheme — then
is preferred for new material. The theme is often the logical
and psychological as well as the grammatical subjects, as in:

(1) Alice folded her hands.

But pragmatic aims may lead to arrangements in which elements
other than such subjects are selected as theme, for example,
adverbial elements. Specific grammatical processes, as well
as marking, are involved in such selection, as in the following passage.

(2) a. The moment Alice appeared, she was appealed to by
all three to settle the question, and they repeated
their arguments to her, though, as they all spoke
at once, she found it very hard to make out exactly
what they said. (Carroll n.d.: 93)

This passage could be presented in straightforward SVO
sentences.

(2) b. Alice appeared. All three appealed to her at that
moment. "You settle the question." ... Making out
exactly what they said was very hard.

Apart from the dullness of such a presentation, its strict adherence to regular syntactic sequences obscures the emphases of the shifting situation. Immediacy of the "appeal" on the other hand is highlighted by the marking device of preposing the adverbial The moment, promoting it to the function of theme. The passive in the second clause, putting Alice in subject position, identifies her as the theme of that clause. Similarly the last clause makes she (= Alice) the theme, at the same time highlighting the difficulty caused by the simultaneous speaking of the executioner, the King, and the Queen.

SVO languages in this way include possibilities for expressions which contrast with straightforward sequences in their structure. So also do other language types. Special devices introduced in continuous texts are studied especially in discourse analysis. These devices, or pragmatic concerns, may lead to diverse patterning.

Diverse patterns are also found in languages as a result of linguistic change. When change occurs in language, it is handled so as to interfere minimally with communication. Accordingly, small segments of a language are affected, and the process of change is carried out over a long period of time. For example, voicing of t in some areas of American English is confined to those members of the t-phoneme which occur medially, as in Minnesóta, and which stand before an unstressed vowel — contrast detér — but not if the unstressed syllable ends in n — contrast bútton with bútter. The phonological change has been going on for at least a century and is continuing. Syntactic, morphological, and semantic changes may require even longer periods to be carried out. For example, regularization of English verbs, e.g., dive :

dived vs. dive : dove, has been going on more than a millennium,
as has the shift from OV to VO structures.

Facts of change are occasionally misunderstood when one's
own speech is taken as norm. For any individual a specific
change may well be immediate; change is adopted at a certain
point, and the old pattern is abandoned. For a speech community, however, old patterns persist among many speakers, so
that the change is adopted only slowly by the entire community,
as illustrated with the examples cited here. The most comprehensive study of change in a community for an extended period
of time has been carried out at Charmey, Switzerland. The
study provides excellent examples of the position presented
here concerning change (see Lehmann 1973b: 163 - 164).

Given this situation regarding change, no language is
completely regular or symmetrical, whether in phonological
structure or in the structure of any other component. Yet
the lack of symmetry does not nullify the general principles
discussed above. These instead are supported by observation
of languages over long periods of time, when, as Sapir
recognized, the changes may be viewed in accordance with underlying ground-plans, as a drift.

It is useful, however, to distinguish between languages
which are in process of change and those which are relatively
stable, like Japanese. Since typological conclusions are based
on empirical data, generalizations presented above have been
ascertained through observation of consistent languages.

When a language is at a stage in change that has affected
only some patterns, so that some constructions are VO, others
OV, it is said to be inconsistent. The characteristics of
inconsistent languages can be best determined for languages
with long documentation, such as Indo-European, Afro-Asiatic,
and Sino-Tibetan. On the basis of such demonstration we can

then analyze languages with only brief periods of documentation, such as the Amerindian languages and the languages of
Australia and New Guinea. Positing of general principles for
inconsistent languages is now an important goal of typological
study, and indeed of general linguistic study.

It is also instructive to examine means of expression that
are attested as opposed to theoretically possible means of
expression. For expressions widely found in human language as
opposed to potential though undocumented patterns lead to
important observations for the understanding of language.
Widely recorded and undoubtedly universal patterns, like the
interrogative and negative, might well be expressed by means
of a variety of devices, phonological, syntactic, or semantic.
The phonological device of nasalization (indicated by ~)
could, for example, be employed in questions as opposed to
statements.

(3) *Jõhn sẽẽs Mãrỹ? vs. John sees Mary.

Many other such phonological devices — palatalization,
pharyngealization, and so on — could be applied to distinguish
questions from statements or to express other verbal
quantifiers.

Semantic devices also could be utilized, as by use of
labels to characterize sentence types, for example:

(4) a. *John sees Mary — this is a question.

   b. *This is a question — John sees Mary.

While this suggestion too may seem odd, Old Irish actually
includes such a mechanism, though it may be orthographic; the
prefatory word ceist [ke^iʃt] 'question' is found before some
interrogative clauses.

More such instances of semantic or phonological devices
may be uncovered in time; but typically the expressions for
questions, and for other verbal qualifiers, are syntactic,
whether of arrangement, selection, or intonation. Expression
of such modifications of meaning through syntactic devices is
a further indication of the central position of syntax in
language, and consequently also its central position in typological study. Moreover, even when modifications are brought
about by pragmatic and functional aims, or as a result of
language change, the principles regulating syntactic structure
are remarkably simple and general among languages of different
structures. Such properties of language account for the rapid
acquisition of language by children, for pidginization, and
for the readiness with which languages are translated.

8.2. Inconsistency in Languages

While syntactic structures of languages are governed by
pervasive principles, few languages are even approximately
consistent. Japanese itself, selected here because of its
relative consistency, underwent strong VO influence from
Chinese, which is evident in many of its learned compounds
and in its reflexive. Its history illustrates how inconsistent
patterns can be introduced through diffusion or borrowing.
Inconsistencies are also found because some patterns change
more readily than others. For fuller understanding of
linguistic structures specific inconsistencies must be
studied, as well as their reasons and their effects in a
given language.

Detailed illustrations will not be provided here, in part
because any such study involves examination of the interrela-
tions between many constructions in language over a long
period of time. A brief illustration may however be given in

the Turkish ki construction. Borrowed from Persian within the
last millennium, it affords in Turkish a VO relative clause
pattern. The tie between ki clauses and their matrix is loose,
permitting a large number of interrelationships, as any
grammar of Turkish will illustrate. Since ki clauses are used
especially in technical and literary texts, most sentences
including them are lengthy; two simple examples are given
here, the first a standard relative clause, the second causal
in its effect (from Jansky 1954: 233 - 234):

(5) Muvaffak olunca   beni unutma   ki   sana
    success if-you-have me   don't-forget Rel. you

    yardım ettim.
    help   I-did

    'If you are successful, don't forget me who helped you.'

(6) Senden   yarım bekliyorum ki   ben de   sana yardım
    you-from help I-expect   Rel. I   also you help

    ettim.
    I-did

    'I expect help from you since I also helped you.'

As these examples illustrate, use of postposed (VO) clauses
with ki provides a flexible alternative in Turkish to the
preposed relative clauses required in an OV language.

    Yet ki clauses have fallen into disuse, especially since
attention was turned to "purifying" the language following
the Atatürk revolution. Both their current rejection, and
their introduction from Persian would repay careful study.
One may speculate, for example, that they were readily adopted
because of the earlier presence in Turkish of a native
particle ki indicating attributive relationship. This ki is
found already in Old Turkish, as in temporal and locative
expressions: söki 'former', yirdäki 'who is found on earth'
(von Gabain 1974: 64 - 65). It is also maintained in Modern
Turkish:

(7) Bu   sandıklardaki   portakallar çok iyidir.
    this case-Pl.-which-are-in oranges   very good-BE
    'The oranges found in these cases are very good.'

Just as we assume that the Persian ki was favorably regarded
by Turkish speakers because of their somewhat similar native
pattern, we might also propose that foreign patterns are more
readily adopted when comparable constructions are already
found in the language. These may well be chance similarities,
like ki in Turkish; or they could be found in residues due to
incomplete change, or in patterns due to marking. Investigation of further inconsistencies in specific languages, their
possible reasons, and their effects on the language will
contribute greatly to our understanding of change in language.
The course of their possible rejection is also illuminating,
not only the cause, such as the aim to purify a language and
its effects, but also the consequences for alternate patterns
that fill the former role of the rejected pattern.

Inconsistency may also lead to special processes in language.
An example is that vowel modification known as umlaut in the
early Germanic dialects. Umlaut was noted in Chapter 1 as a
potential process in VO languages, for it is a kind of progressive assimilation. Vowels in earlier syllables of words,
characteristically in the accented syllable, are modified in
accordance with final syllables. Thus -gastiʀ, attested in
the Gallehus inscription ca. 350 A.D., illustrates an earlier
stage of the form found in Old English giest, NE guest, where
e is an umlauted form of a. In Germanic, back vowels of stem
syllables were modified by high front elements [i j], and
front vowels by high back elements [u w]. Umlaut was carried
through with great regularity, especially in northern
Germanic dialects, such as Old Norse and Old English.

When a sound change is carried out so consistently,
similarity of phonological environment is generally a factor.
The consistency of umlaut can be ascribed to the preponderance
of open syllables in initial portions of Germanic words, as
in the complete Gallehus name: Hle-wa-ga-stiʀ. Such syllabic
structure is expected in OV languages, as exemplified in the
Japanese examples of Chapter 2.

These observations lead to the conclusion that umlaut
might be expected to occur in an inconsistent language which
is moving from OV to VO structure. Germanic umlaut illustrates
some of the subtleties involved in changes from one structure
to another. Other such phenomena will be noted below, though
many further investigations of specific languages must be
undertaken, to better explicate processes like umlaut as well
as to understand specific languages at any stage in their
development. It should be observed these proposals do not
imply that shift in type causes phenomena like umlaut; on the
other hand, these shifts are instrumental in setting the stage
for such phenomena. Investigations of well-attested changes
like Germanic umlaut provide further evidence on processes of
change in language, on conditions under which they occur and
their possible causes. Such information can be used to account
for patterns of languages known only from the present.

Nez Perce provides an intriguing example. In it the vowels
in words are regulated morphologically, neither progressively
as in umlaut nor regressively, as in vowel harmony; because
the vowels "harmonize," however, the term *vowel harmony* is
used of Nez Perce. The mechanism is morphological rather than
phonological, as in Germanic umlaut or in Turkish vowel
harmony; for example, a specific morphological marker accounts
for the specific vowels of /caqá·t'ayn/ 'for a raspberry'
opposed to /cé·qet/ 'raspberry' (Aoki 1966: 760 - 761).

A similar situation is found in Chukchee (Comrie, personal
communication). These languages reflect results of inconsistencies, whether through internal changes or through borrowing.
This assumption, or any other regarding the Nez Perce and
Chukchee phenomena, is highly tentative because of our igno-
rance about their earlier history. Investigation of languages
with known histories may in time furnish information through
which we can account for phenomena in languages like Nez Perce
having texts only from the recent past and present. Besides
characterizing consistent languages, as was done in Chapters
2, 3 and 4, further studies should set out to provide characterizations of languages with various kinds of inconsistencies.

8.3. Change in Typological Patterning

Some languages attested for considerable time permit observation of effects of change in typological structure on
individual patterns. Sinhalese, for example, is relatively
well documented, at least in that its basic patterning is
disclosed around the beginning of our era as well as today.
Two millennia ago Sinhalese included many VO characteristics.
In this respect it is comparable to Classical Sanskrit and
Middle Indic dialects like Pali. Subsequently Sinhalese has
become a highly consistent OV language, without doubt through
Dravidian influence.

In the course of this change to OV structure all patterns
noted above have been modified. Even such relatively conservative patterns as the teen numerals have for the most part
adopted Dravidian order (Ratanajoti 1975: 51, 80). The
numerals 11, 12, 15, which have not, are of further interest,
as noted below; 13, 14, 18 are given to illustrate the regular
Sinhalese pattern — others may be noted in Ratanajoti's lists.

	Classical Sanskrit	Pali	Old Sinhalese	New Sinhalese	Tamil
11	ékādaśa	ekādasa	ekalos	ekaloha	padin-onru
	1 10	1 10			10 1
12	dvādaśa	dvādasa	dolos	dolaha	pan-n-iraṇḍu
13	tráyodaśa	terasa	teles	dahatunə	padin-munru
14	cáturdaśa	catuddasa	tudus	dahahatərə	padi-nali
15	páñcadaśa	pañcadasa	pasalos	pahaloha	padin-aindu
18	aṣṭādaśa	aṭṭhadasa	aṭadaśa	dahaaṭə	padin-eṭṭu

The New Sinhalese patterns in 11 and 12, reminiscent of the
forms not changed to VO order in English and German — eleven,
Gothic ainlif 'one left'; twelve, Gothic twalif 'two left' —
may have escaped change because the basic numerals are often
viewed as a set of twelve rather than ten. The numeral for 15
in New Sinhalese on the other hand would have countered a
proscribed phonological pattern if changed to OV order; a
phonological constraint thus countered its syntactic change
(Ratajanoti 1976). Yet the extensive changes between Old
Sinhalese and New Sinhalese, even to the relatively inconse-
quential teen numerals, illustrates the cohesiveness of the
patterning of a language.

This cohesiveness may be demonstrated by examining change
in the languages of a family, such as the Indo-European, over
several millennia. Indo-European is the family best known to
us at present, because texts in the various languages have
been most thoroughly studied, and because these texts extend
through a period of almost four thousand years; eventually
the Afro-Asiatic and the Sino-Tibetan families may be known
as well, to the great advancement of linguistics. Even this
extent of time does not take us back to the parent language,
Proto-Indo-European, which, occupying the same relation to

the attested Indo-European languages as does Latin to the
Romance languages, must be posited no later than 3000 B.C.
Although the languages of the Indo-European subgroups have
been intensively studied for a century and a half, with the
aim of reconstructing the parent language, many problems
remain. Some of these have now been clarified with the help
of insights derived from typological studies. The following
are examples.

The early dialects differ in their relative clause markers,
some like Sanskrit and Greek deriving them from *yo-, others
like Hittite and Latin from *kʷi-. Moreover, the earliest
texts, especially in Hittite and Vedic Sanskrit, have a
majority of relative constructions preceding their nouns, as
in the following example from the Hittite Laws (Justus 1976:
234):

(8) a. Kuiš-   an āppa uwatezzi   nu-šše   6 GÍN
       Ptc.-Nom.-him back brings-3Sg. Ptc.-him 6 shekel(s)

       KUBABBAR pāi.
       silver   gives-3Sg.

       'They give six shekels of silver to the one who
         brings him back.'

Indo-Europeanists noted these facts, but were unable to
account for them; they selected one of the alternates,
typically *yo-, and posited it as the Proto-Indo-European
relative marker.

The early dialects also have postpositions rather than
prepositions, a situation which also was noted but not
accounted for.

Moreover, no reflexive pronoun could be reconstructed for
Proto-Indo-European. Even languages as recently attested as
the Germanic differ in these, as English myself, herself,
and so on compared with German mich, sich illustrate. On the

other hand, the early dialects contained a "reflexive verb,"
the so-called middle. This gradually was lost, while constructions including a reflexive pronoun replaced it, so that Greek
middle expressions like the following disappeared at some time
after the beginning of our era.

(8) b. Loúomai   tàs kheîras.
    I-wash (for myself) the hands
    'I wash my hands.'

Both the loss of the middle and the development of reflexive
pronouns are accounted for by comparing OV languages. In
these, verb forms indicating reflexivization with a suffix
like that of the Indo-European middle may be expected, and
also the absence of reflexive pronouns. A consideration of the
devices to indicate reflexivization in the Indo-European
languages, as well as the relative construction, postpositions, and many other characteristics then leads to the
conclusion that the early Indo-European languages were
developing from OV structure to VO. Proto-Indo-European itself
then may well have been a consistent OV language.

These conclusions clarify many of the changing constructions. If Proto-Indo-European had been OV, a relative pronoun
would not have been necessary, for relativization could have
been indicated by preposing of relative clauses as in Japanese.
But when the dialects were changing to VO structure, such a
pronoun was essential, it was developed from a topicalizer
in Hittite, as Justus has convincingly shown (1976: 213-245).
Moreover, the postpositions of the early dialects would be
explained, as would many other constructions. Among these
are survivals of OV comparatives, as in early Old English
poetry, such as the following line from a riddle (Williamson
1977: 92, Riddle 38.18).

(8) c. ond eofore   eom   æghwær   cenra.
    and boar-than I-am throughout bolder
    'and I am throughout bolder than a boar.'

Enumeration of all the OV characteristics in the early
dialects would require too much space in a general account,
yet the typical suffixation and absence of prefixation, the
large system of cases, the preposing of genitives and adjective modifiers might still be mentioned as well as the common
OV patterning of clauses in our earliest materials (for more
discussion see Lehmann 1974a). All of these constructions
changed, as the structure of the languages was modified
from OV to VO. The process and the time involved in the
change vary among the constructions. Problems having to do
with the interrelationships of such changes and the extent
of time involved in carrying them out require thorough study
like that devoted to the change of the English genitive by
Fries (1940; see also Traugott 1972). Eventually consistent
VO languages have emerged, such as French, Spanish, and
English.

The recognition of a drift toward consistency illuminates
many further constructions, such as complements in their
gradual development in the Germanic languages (Lehmann 1976b;
see also Ureland 1973). Early Germanic languages show a
variety of complementation patterns, including ACI (accusative
with infinitive): I expect him to go, and that-clauses: I
expect that he will go. There are also relics of preposed
complementation types to be expected in OV structure. The
patterning of Germanic dialects today developed only gradually;
for example, verbs of perception regularly used that-construc-
tions in the early period, and only later ACI as in I never
knew him to be late. The history of complementation in other
Indo-European dialects as well is clarified when one

recognizes that the patterns in each of them were replacements
for OV patterns, similar to those in Japanese. Even the that-
complementizer of Modern English still reflects its origin as
a nominalizer, as in:

(8) d. I know that they have arrived.

Compare this with:

(8) e. I know that. They have arrived.

f. They have arrived. That I know.

Similar observations can be made for early Greek; the typical
Classical Greek complementizer hóti originally — like NE
that — was a demonstrative pronoun which developed into a
conjunction.

Study of the syntactic changes in the Indo-European languages then indicates that when languages change, patterns of
the new type are introduced and gradually become established,
while the language becomes increasingly consistent. The
direction of change may encounter specific interferences, as
in the Indian linguistic area, illustrated above. In the
Indo-European family as a whole, especially in the Western
languages, the change from OV to VO represents an internal
drift. In the languages of India during the past two millennia,
on the other hand, syntactic change represents the results of
external influence. Yet in both groups consistency eventually
emerges. Syntactic change, whether in accordance with inter-
nally directed drift or external influences, can be accounted
for through use of the typological framework presented here.

8.4. German, an Example of an Inconsistent Language

A remarkable example of conflicting patterns is provided by
German. It illustrates how social forces may interfere with

development toward consistency. The simple clause pattern in German requires second position for the verb, so that clauses generally follow SVO order, though OVS is readily possible. By contrast, subordinate clauses require verb-final position, so they are SOV. It is illuminating to note the time and reason for introduction of the conflicting SOV pattern as well as its effects.

The OV pattern of subordinate clauses was adopted as the regular construction by learned writers around the beginning of the sixteenth century on the basis of Latin, though it was not wholly absent in earlier forms of German. Gradually the twofold patterning of VO order in independent clauses, OV in dependent, was installed, so that it is now regular in the standard written language. But it is not required in all dialects, nor in all spoken forms of the language.

Since adoption of OV subordinate clause order, various additional OV patterns have been introduced into standard German. Among these are postpositions. An example is wegen 'because', an old dative plural of Weg 'way', arising from expressions like von ... Wegen 'of ... ways' and first attested as a postposition in the seventeenth century. Another is entlang, comparable to New English along, first attested as a postposition in 1741.

A further OV characteristic is the use of preposed relative constructions, notorious in scientific German writing, as in the following sentence from Weizsäcker:

(9) Die Wasserstoff-energie enthält keinen uns
    hydrogen-   energy contains no   to-us

    bisher   bekannten Nebeneffekt.
    hitherto known   side-effect

    'Hydrogen energy contains no side-effect known to us
    up to the present.'

Like postpositions, this construction is widely found only
after introduction of OV order in subordinate clauses.

Other OV characteristics of Modern German can also, if
less surely, be associated with the newly observed order of
subordinate clauses. One is the postverbal negative.

(10) a. Ich weiss nicht.
     I   know   not
     'I don't know.'

In Middle High German a preposed verbal element was used to
indicate negation, in the VO pattern:

(10) b. Ih enweiz.
     I   not-know

Another is use of interrogatives medially:

(11) Das   hat wer getan?
     that has who done?
     'Who did that?'

Placing of interrogative in such positions is reminiscent of
Chinese, which also has OV characteristics, and of OV
languages like Japanese. OV patterning may also be evident
in constraints against ACI complements; one cannot translate
literally into German the example cited above: I never knew
him to be late.

In addition to studies of such patterns, investigations
should be undertaken to examine patterning of standard written
German in contrast with the spoken language and the dialects.
Some studies have determined that spoken language has more
notable VO structure than written language, as in the treatment of postpositions of the written language as prepositions.
Further, dialects preserve the Middle High German negative
with a twofold marker, as in the medieval *Song of Roland*,
line 8918:

(12) Da   ne was manne nehainer.
     there not was man   none
     'No one was there.'

But investigations are still far too limited, generally
dealing with only one area or one dialect, so that much
remains to be learned about the impact of the OV change on
standard written German.

These studies have broad theoretical implications. Among
the points to explore is existence of dual patterns in a
language. Many scholars examining German have declared it to
be OV in underlying structure, while others see it as VO,
with views varying in accordance with the criteria chosen as
decisive. If, for example, one assumes OV structure, the
independent clause pattern can be simply generated with a
transformational model. Yet a criterion frequently used to
classify languages, gapping of clauses containing objects and
verbs, is carried out in German as in English, leading to the
conclusion that German is VO:

(13) Marie fährt   ein Mercedes, und Hans ein VW.
     'Mary drives a   Mercedes, and Hans a   VW.'

A decision must be reached by identifying the primary constructions in the language, such as the principal clause,
especially if its type of government is prominently found in
adpositions and comparatives.

A further problem suggested by the German constructions
has to do with the importance of arrangement as a syntactic
device, notably with reference to syntactic change. To judge
by syntactic modifications following introduction of OV order
in subordinate clauses, arrangement is the central syntactic
device, in some sense determining all others.

German is also instructive for investigating relationships
between surface structures and underlying forms. Its recent

history supports the suggestion that surface arrangements, especially of clauses, closely reflects underlying form, even though patterns of selection may not.

All such questions need further investigation, and comparison with patterning in other languages. It would be highly interesting, for example, to determine why Japanese adopted a VO pattern for reflexivization alone but maintained all the other OV patterns. Similarly, study of Chinese dialects should illuminate our understanding of typological patterning, for southern dialects are more consistently VO than is the northern standard language, Putonghua. Aryan languages of India with their change toward OV order in the past two millennia will also provide insights into patterns modified under the influence of other languages. Such investigations will, moreover, provide data for statements of greater assurance about languages in change, supplementing observations made for Sinhalese and other languages so studied. Resulting conclusions will permit interpretation of many languages for which we have no lengthy series of materials.

8.5. Problems Resulting from Influence of Languages
    on Other Languages

Especially since Sandfeld's influential publication on Balkan languages (1930), attention has been given to characteristics of adjoining languages which may have been introduced by diffusion. While impressive for the extent of information about Greek, Albanian, Bulgarian, Rumanian, Serbo-Croatian, and Turkish of the present and past, their dialects, and further languages like Romany, Sandfeld's book illustrates that a great amount of further investigation needs to be carried out on areal influences. For even in the Balkan area, which has been studied more than a century and a half,

specific syntactic characteristics, as well as lexical items,
have been identified as due to diffusion, but not examined for
their cause of adoption nor their possible further implications
for individual languages.

For example, one such characteristic — the postposed article
in Albanian, Bulgarian, and Rumanian — has been ascribed to a
substratum, though not with general agreement (Sandfeld 1930:
165 - 172).

Other characteristics, such as the replacement of infinitives as verbal complements by subordinate clauses and the
formation of the future with auxiliary 'will', are ascribed
to the influence of Greek (Sandfeld 1930: 173 - 185); but their
origin in Greek has not been accounted for with general assent.
Found already in New Testament Greek, these constructions have
been ascribed to Semitic influence. It is now clear, however,
that use of auxiliaries like 'will' and preference for
subordinate clauses are VO characteristics. Accordingly, use
of an auxiliary to indicate future might have been expected
for internal reasons in Greek, which had long been developing
toward VO structure; even Homeric Greek includes many VO
characteristics. Adoption and use of such patterns in other
Balkan languages would be important to investigate, as well as
any additional syntactic modifications following their adoption. For, apart from Turkish, these languages are VO; the
adoption of specific VO patterns from Greek would not then
have such dramatic consequences for their structures as were
noted for Sinhalese or even for German. Nonetheless, study
of the Balkan linguistic area should illuminate diffusion of
syntactic characteristics in specific areas, in part because
many studies have already been carried out on its languages.

Effects of languages in given areas on others have been
observed, though reasons for the predominance of one language

type over another or for the adoption of one typological
pattern rather than another elude us. We can only speculate
on the predominance of the Dravidian OV pattern in the Indian
linguistic area: speakers of Dravidian languages most likely
outnumbered speakers of Indo-European and Munda languages.
Further, Indo-European languages had not yet eliminated all
OV characteristics when their speakers came into contact with
Dravidian speakers; while Classical Sanskrit has fewer OV
patterns than does Vedic Sanskrit, its structure is comparable
to those of Classical Greek and Latin, which also have OV
relics. Presence of maintained OV patterns may then have
eased adoption of Dravidian constructions.

Yet all linguistic areas should be examined, for the
questions involved have fascinated linguists as well as other
scholars, with no resolution of their views. One linguistic
area of wide concern is Western Europe. Its languages today
are so similar in structure that they seemed one in type to
Whorf, who called them SAE, Standard Average European (1956:
138). Origins of similar constructions in these languages,
such as compound tenses, are however disputed, as may be
illustrated by the differing viewpoints of the great linguists
Antoine Meillet and his student Emile Benveniste concerning
origin of the "perfect with 'to have' in Germanic" (Benveniste
1971: 178 - 179). Meillet ascribed it to "imitation of Latin
models." Benveniste on the other hand saw the solution of the
problem not in "historical grammar" but rather in "consideration of the system." On this basis he concluded that
"acquisition of a transitive perfect with 'to have' was an
autonomous development in Germanic and owes nothing to the
influence of Latin." For Benveniste nonautonomous development
would have been possible only after long Germano-Latin
bilingualism like the "Slavo-Turkish bilingualism that

circumstances imposed in Macedonia for five centuries" (1971:
179). Benveniste's argumentation is persuasive, based as it
is on "consideration of the system," that is, in accordance
with the aims discussed above of examining and accounting for
linguistic developments in terms of a typological framework.

Use of a framework is especially important when interrelationships between languages of a given area are poorly
known, or known only for very recent time-periods. Such areas
provide intriguing problems, as noted for Amerindian languages
by Franz Boas and Edward Sapir (Boas 1911: 36 - 37 et passim;
Sapir 1963: 205). Although information on these languages is
far less extensive than on long studied and well-documented
languages, it may lead to insights into the origin of
linguistic characteristics, such as use of person markers on
verbs. According to Ingram, "in a structurally balanced
system, a person marker will occur on the same side of a
verb as the NP to which it refers" (Ingram 1975; see also
Lehmann 1975b: 53). Representing person markers with lower-
case s = subject and o = object, one would expect an SOV
language with such markers to have the patterns SO (o-)s-V,
a VSO language the pattern V-s(-o) SO/V-o-s SO. Ingram's
principle is supported by forms like the Semitic perfective,
for example Classical Hebrew, a VSO language:

kātal	'he killed'	kətālō	'he killed him'
kātəlāh	'she killed'	kətālatū	'she killed him'
kātaltā	'thou killedst'	kətaltō	'thou killedst him'

If such a pattern, which had developed in a "structurally
balanced system," came under the influence of an SOV pattern,
these verb forms might be maintained, even though they no
longer agreed with the new pattern. Such aberrant forms might
then provide perspective on the language concerned, as well

as on dominant areal relationships. Ingram proposed such a
conclusion for some Salish languages. Parts of his argumentation have been disputed by Noonan, who points out the necessity
of taking clitics into consideration, and thus the need of
"great care" in "use of affixal morphology as a tool for
reconstructing earlier word order patterns" (Noonan 1976).
The importance of distinguishing between pronominal affixes
as concord markers and as person markers has also been indicated (Lehmann 1975b). To the present far too little is known
about person markers to propose hypotheses on their occurrence and origin. Besides Amerindian languages, investigations
are also being carried out on African languages (Givón 1971;
1975).

In spite of the lack of firm conclusions, person markers
have been discussed at some length here to illustrate how
further insights may be obtained from study of such characteristics, both for individual languages and for linguistic
areas. As further information is assembled, it may assist in
illuminating interrelationships among past linguistic areas,
such as the proposed Indo-European - Kartvelian area, or the
Mesopotamian area of the fourth and third millennia B.C.
Recent treatments of person markers are also instructive in
illustrating the usefulness of a typological framework in
disclosing further linguistic characteristics which may lead
to improved understanding of languages and their history.

8.6. Identification of Further Typological Characteristics

Through scrutiny of patterns in accordance with a typological
framework further characteristics of typological significance
will be identified and incorporated in the framework. An
additional pattern of interest is that of sentence-introducing
particles. Such particles might be expected for VSO languages,

since they are characterized by prefixation. Yet these
particles attracted attention in the study of Indo-European
languages, in which they have been treated quite independently
of typological structure. The attention resulted from the
observation that Irish and Hittite exhibit comparable particles. Irish, a VSO language, might well be assumed to
include them, but Hittite is OV. Accordingly the languages
in which they have been most thoroughly studied may seem to
indicate that any type of language might have sentence-
introductory particles as an indigenous characteristic.

   Hittite and other Anatolian languages have come to be
much better known since 1942, when Albrecht Goetze and
Myles Dillon made their initial observations about the
sentence-introductory particles (Dillon 1947). Of signal
importance in further information about Hittite is recognition
of a distinction between early texts and late texts, and
consequent assumption of two stages in the history of the
language: Old Hittite. and Late Hittite. It is noteworthy that
the particles are much more prominent in Late than in Old
Hittite. On the assumption that such particles would be
expected in VSO languages, we may ascribe their widespread
use in Anatolian languages to the influence of a VSO language;
Akkadian, widely used by the Hittite scribes, is the most
likely source of that syntactic influence. The particles can
therefore no longer be posited as a syntactic characteristic
of Proto-Indo-European, even though the morphological elements
can be related to particles like Sanskrit n̲u̲, Greek n̲ûn̲,
English n̲o̲w̲.

   A further complication, however, must be noted in dealing
with Anatolian languages. Akkadian — in contrast with other
Semitic and Afro-Asiatic languages in general, which are
strongly VSO — has many instances of verb-final sentences.

This characteristic may be ascribed to influence from Sumerian, which while OV in many characteristics exhibits VO features as well.

In short, the materials which have been used to understand the functioning of sentence-introductory particles are themselves in need of elucidation. Data for such elucidation may now be available in the finds at Ebla in Northern Syria; but they have not yet been made available. Until new data on the early period of Semitic languages illuminate their use of sentence connectives, or until material is provided from other languages, we must reserve judgment on their use.

Other features are similarly in need of investigation. Verbal qualifiers, as one set of examples, require considerable clarification. These are categories which have traditionally been treated in analyses of verbal systems, generally in relation to morphological markers. They are also studied by logicians, as in modal logic. In recent linguistic publications the nomenclature of logicians has often been preferred to that of traditional linguistics. Thus verbal qualifiers are labeled CAUSE rather than Causative, CHANGE rather than Inchoative, and the like. Moreover, many studies have indicated modal features by representing them with "higher sentences": He causes something. The child lies down. > He lays the child down. Further, there seem to be few bounds on the verbal features that are proposed in some studies. By contrast, with their basis in empirical observations, typological studies give precedence to verbal qualifiers that are widespread, if not universal, such as Interrogative, Negative, and others treated in patterns listed in section 1.3. As further languages are investigated these may need elaboration and closer definition, though such studies should be carried out with reference to a framework.

Only Indo-European languages have been thoroughly analyzed
for Q-features. Calbert, for example, has dealt in depth with
"modality," particularly in German. His conclusion illustrates
some of the difficulties involved in treating verbal features,
for he states that "modality is ... a matter of degree ...
Any act of saying (or any sentence) conveys a certain degree
of modality which goes from zero (or near zero) in neutral
reporting to the extremes of volition (will, command) and
absolute certainty" (Calbert and Vater 1975: 55). One could
thus scarcely expect systems using only binary characterization to represent fully nuances of utterances. Further,
languages may structure modal categories differently from the
patterning found in Indo-European languages. As noted above
in section 1.8, Q-features proposed here may be expanded when
additional typological investigations are carried out,
especially when these deal with languages differing in
structure from Indo-European.

Nominal constructions will also be explicated in further
study. Patterning in compound numerals, for example, has been
determined by Greenberg (1976). And the loose alignments of
apposition may in time be comprehended within a specific
structure (see Hauri 1976).

Besides constructions tied to central clause structure,
there are some that seem to be free of such relationship,
such as adverbial elements referring to time and place. In
English, adverbials referring to place precede those referring
to time, while in German the reverse order applies.

(14) a. We saw him there yesterday.

b. Wir haben ihn gestern dort gesehen.

Study of such free patterns is of great interest, for they

afford individuality to languages — in contrast with the
constructions regulated by types.

Typological investigations must be amplified, to examine
not only patterns discussed above in many further languages,
but also constructions and patterns which seem independent of
the central structures of language.

8.7. The Problem of Apparently Similar Patterns
     and Constructions in Different Languages

In the study of a wide range of languages problems result
from contrasts between apparently similar constructions.
The constructions labeled "passive" may serve as illustration.
Even in two closely related languages like German and English
the "passive" is not equivalent. German may use passive to
topicalize verbs as well as nouns, even intransitive verbs:

(15) Jetzt wird aber   geschlafen!
     now   is   however slept
     'Now we/you must really sleep!'

Although English uses passive only to topicalize nouns,
differences between the forms in the two languages are relatively minor, for in both, passive functions to indicate
topicalization.

By contrast, in Japanese and other languages of Southeast
Asia "passive" has totally different uses. It conveys the
connotation of an unfortunate occurrence, in the so-called
adversity passive (see section 2.3.7).

(16) John ga tuma ni sin-are-ta. (Kuno 1973: 23)
         wife by die-Pass.-Past
     'John suffered the death of his wife.'

It may also indicate potentiality, and then may carry honorific
meaning.

(17) Sensei   no iwareru   toori   desu.
     teacher   say-Pass. situation is   (Yamagiwa 1942: 181)
     'It is just as the teacher says.'

Besides these uses, the Japanese passive is also found without
such connotations, with an element other than the agent as
subject; this "normal" use of the passive has long been noted,
especially in embedded clauses, as Kuno has pointed out.

Comparison of the "passive" in languages without informed
understanding of its special uses would scarcely be illuminating. The difficulty is not simply brought about by application
of specific labels, for in Japanese and other Southeast Asian
languages the "normal" passive is comparable to the passive
of English and German. But each of these languages further
delimits the passive, associating additional characteristics
with it, in this way leading to uses which differ considerably
from language to language.

Characteristic delimitation or extension of widely found
patterns is by no means limited to languages cited here, nor
to the "passive." While the "passive" may provide a striking
example, all patterns must be examined with reference to the
language in which they are found, whether they seem clearly
identified, like causatives, or only vaguely, like subjunctives. The causative in Arabic, for example, is associated
with further modalities, such as volition. Modal categories
especially have been discussed at length by grammarians
dealing with intensively studied languages (Wackernagel 1926:
210 - 257). So have aspects and other categories, which have
been of especial interest to many scholars because of shifting
means of expression, as when the Indo-European inflectional
paradigms indicating tense and aspect are replaced by
compound expressions, and modal forms — subjunctive and
optative — are replaced by verbal phrases with auxiliaries

and by particles in various dialects. General linguistics will
profit greatly from such studies, especially if data are
analyzed in a more specific framework than that used in past
studies — a framework based on subsequent typological study.

8.8. Relations between Language Types and Other Cultural
Systems: Linguistic Relativity

The study of language has always been pursued to increase our
understanding of people and of cultural systems. Many linguists
concerned with typology have also maintained strong interest
in this aim. For example, Finck prefaced his eight published
lectures on "the German language as an expression of the
German world-view" with the following quotation from Wilhelm
von Humboldt (Finck 1899: my translation): "The characteristic
intellectual features and the linguistic structure of a
people stand in such intimacy of fusion with each other that
if the one were presented the other would have to be completely derivable from it." Finck's lectures then proceed to
illustrate the "fusion" for German. While one must respect
Finck's caution in proposing broad generalizations as well
as his extensive knowledge of many languages, his conclusions
have not been well received, in part because they were stated
in terms of medieval psychology, and of linguistics concerned
with surface structures.

  Comparable interest in the relations between a language
and the world-view of its speakers was manifested by Edward
Sapir and his contemporary Benjamin Whorf. Their work has
been so strongly identified with such a conception that the
proposed relationship between language and culture is often
referred to as the Sapir-Whorf hypothesis, alternatively as
linguistic relativity. Although the writings of Sapir and
Whorf aroused considerable interest, leading to attempts to

test the hypothesis in carefully designed experiments,
linguistic relativity is widely regarded with skepticism.
The esteem accorded it by typological linguists may also have
diminished regard for this approach to language.

Yet further advances in typology and in linguistics may
well provide guidelines for advantageous attention to
linguistic relativity. For example, patterns to be investigated must not be taken from deep structure, nor even from
those regulated by the principle stated above. Since deep
structure patterns are universal, they apply to all humanity,
and thus do not reflect possible specific influences of a
given language on the thinking and the world-view of its
speakers. Moreover, inferences drawn from such patterns must
be more than speculation.

An example of a particular pattern may be supplied from
Finck's concern with German. This pattern is the use of
endingless adjectives for adverbs as well as predicate adjectives (1899: 53).

(18) a. Sie ist schön.
        'She is beautiful.'

     b. Sie singt schön.
        'She sings beautifully.'

One may accept Finck's conclusion that the pattern tends to
give the copula a fuller meaning than it has in English and
the other Germanic languages because it is accompanied by the
same form of the adjective as are other verbs. With greater
reluctance one might also honor his interpretation that German
in this way tends not to ascribe permanent characteristics to
objects, but to view them as active and changing — a characteristic which he sees also in the maintenance of grammatical
gender in German. But the further interpretation relating

these linguistic patterns with the "strength of will and intellect" of their speakers strikes one as an imaginative flight.

In the same way, widely discussed proposals of Whorf relating cultural with linguistic characteristics in Amerindian languages, and their implications for English and SAE, have been regarded with skepticism; see especially Whorf 1956: 134 - 159. English has indeed a tense system in the verb, and SAE languages objectify time, speaking of "three hours" in the same way as of "three chairs." Moreover, western culture ascribes a great deal of weight to:

1. Records, diaries, bookkeeping, accounting, mathematics stimulated by accounting.
2. Interest in exact sequence, dating, calendars, chronology, clocks, time wages, time graphs, time as used in physics.
3. Annals, histories, the historical attitude, interest in the past, archeology, attitudes of introjection towards past periods, e.g., classicism, romanticism. (Whorf 1956: 153)

Yet Whorf's proposed "relation of habitual thought and behavior to language" scarcely rises above the level of speculation, even if poetic and intriguing. For when apparently comparable situations or comparable linguistic structures are examined, the relationships may not be the same as in the SAE area. Chinese culture, for example, exhibits similar attention to "records ... chronology ... histories," but Chinese does not have a tense system — though it does objectify time. Turkish on the other hand has a comprehensive tense system, but the accompanying culture does not assign the same importance to "records" and the like. Intuitively we may sympathize with Sapir's statement which Whorf cited as a foreword to this article "that the 'real world' is to a large extent unselfconsciously built up on [our] language habits" (Whorf 1956:

134). At the current stage of our knowledge of language and
of its role in society, however, we cannot declare such
statements confirmed. Their significance for understanding
ourselves, our culture, and other cultures, however, adds
additional weight to Whorf's subsequently stated plea: "We
must find out more about language! Already we know enough
about it to know it is not what the great majority of men,
lay or scientific, think it is" (1956: 250).

So much of linguistic activity consists in the attempt to
"assemble and arrange ... the whole body of linguistic
phenomena" that only a few linguists pursue Whitney's third
goal of "explaining" them, let alone relating language
systematically to other cultural matters (Whitney 1892: 6).
In this situation linguistic relativity must be viewed as an
intriguing hypothesis, to be confirmed, whether in part or
as a whole, or to be rejected or to be refined by scholars
of the future (Penn 1972).

8.9. Approaches to Language

Linguists assume as the goals of their discipline the three
tasks indicated by Whitney: assembling, arranging (i.e.,
describing), and explaining the phenomena of language. They
carry out this aim through the production of grammars accompanied by dictionaries. It is widely agreed that a grammar
is a theory of a language. A grammar should then have the
attributes of a theory, including predictive capability.

In seeking to meet these goals various approaches to the
study of language are proposed and maintained, often referred
to as "different 'theories'." But, as Dixon has stated
recently: "The term 'theory' is in fact, inappropriately used
in modern linguistics; many so-called 'theories' have no
predictive power and are little more than systems of notation,

'general plans' in terms of which the grammar of a language
may be formulated" (Dixon 1976: 75). While even the prominent
"theories" or "general plans" cannot be reviewed here without
undue expansion of this chapter, the contributions of
typological study to the aims of linguistics may be briefly
noted with reference to widely used approaches in the formal
study of language.

Typological study, like much other study of language, is
based on the view that linguistics is an empirical science.
Theory is formulated in accordance with the data of languages,
and tested by means of such data. In carrying out investigations, observation and description are certainly directed by
one's theory, which, whether transformational or other,
provides "discovery procedures." But the strength of a theory
lies in explanations it affords, or in understanding it
contributes.

In the nineteenth century, explanation was sought in
determining earlier forms. If a question was raised about an
element in the sound system, like the /r/ in were as opposed
to the /z/ in was, or about a specific form, like the past
tense sang as opposed to the present tense sing, attempts
were made to determine the situation in earlier stages of
the language and the conditions under which the concerned
elements arose. If these questions were solved, linguists
assumed that the elements were explained. Such "explanations"
are indeed satisfying, but they have their limitations. Even
for well-documented languages like English and its congeners,
explanations can be secured only for elements and events
subsequent to the so-called parent language, Proto-Indo-
European. Moreover, elements and events of languages with
little documentation, like those of America or Africa, can
be given only meager explanation with the historical approach.

Further, linguists found it impossible to explain the facts
of language as a phenomenon through its history; occasional
intrepid scholars indeed proposed deriving all the languages
of a continent from one, or all the languages of the world
from one, but the resulting views are very vague, and thus
are regarded largely as curiosities (e.g., Swadesh 1971). The
explanatory power of historical linguistics thus has severe
limitations.

Moreover, predictive possibilities of historical linguistics
are restricted to proposing hypothetical forms a given item
might have developed to in a certain language. For example,
if the cognate of Latin _equus_ and Greek _hĭppos_, Old English
eoh 'horse', had been maintained in Modern English it would
presumably be.ee, cf. OE _feoh_ > NE _fee_, OE _trēo_ > NE _tree_.
Further predictions could scarcely be ventured, as of the
loss of _eoh_. For similar monosyllables were maintained, such
as /ay/ _eye_, /ow/ _owe_, /ɔ/ _awe_. Possibilities of prediction
in historical linguistics, like its explanatory capabilities,
then provide only meager results among general expectations
for a theory.

The most prominent recent approach, transformational
grammar, seeks its explanations for the phenomena of language
in treatment of linguistic structures by the mind. In the
words of Chomsky: "The theory would suggest an explanation
for the linguistic intuition of native speakers as regards
John is _easy_ to _please_ and _John_ is _eager_ to _please_. This
explanation would rest on the assumption that the concepts
of grammatical structure and 'significant generalization' made
explicit in this theory constitute the set of tools used by
the learner in constructing an internal representation of
his language (i.e., a generative grammar), on the basis of

presented linguistic data" (Chomsky 1964: 928). Transformational grammar assumes that rules for complex syntactic
structures, the so-called transformational rules, differ from
those for relatively simple structures. Evidence for some of
the posited simple rules is indeed found in investigations of
child language learning, in the study of aphasia, in experi-
mental investigation of speakers, most spectacularly of
speakers with bisected brains. But in spite of extensive
psychological investigation, no psychological validity has
been found for transformational rules (Fodor et al 1974).
Accordingly, hopes of explanatory capabilities for transformational grammar have been severely reduced, especially since
treatment of simple structures in transformational grammar
differs little from that of traditional grammar. Moreover,
transformational grammar has never been demonstrated to have
predictive power. Many linguists are accordingly turning to
other approaches, none of which have been elaborated to the
extent of transformational grammar; discussion of them will
then be omitted here.

While transformational grammar has yielded only limited
gains, it is noteworthy that its chief proponent, Chomsky,
has recognized increasing kinship with linguistics of the past
(1975: 196 et passim). Such recognition supports the view
that linguistics is indeed a cumulative science. As some
findings of earlier linguists retain validity, so will some
contributions of transformational grammar. Among these is the
emphasis on abstract underlying structures. Such structures
are represented above in the universal rules of section 1.7,
and in the patterns exemplified throughout the book.

As these chapters illustrate, the typological approach
permits predictions for these patterns. If for example a
certain type of comparative construction is found in a

language, the prediction can be made that the language is OV
or VO; one needs little more, for example, than evidence of
the pattern in the Japanese sentence below to conclude that
it is an OV language (section 2.1.9, sentence 58a).

(19) Taroo wa Hanako yori zutto wakai.
                        than far   is-young
    'Taroo is far younger than Hanako.'

The other patterns listed in section 1.4 also permit such
prediction, whether they concern the simple clause or complex
structures involving embedding or complementation and the like.
OV languages, for example, include characteristic relative
constructions and other nominal modifiers, as well as characteristic verbal modifiers. A language including postverbal
interrogative markers, like Japanese ka, or postverbal negative
markers, like Japanese -nai, permits the prediction that it
is OV in clause structure. The identified patterns would be
used similarly in VO languages, as illustrated in Chapters 3,
4, and 6. When unmarked patterns of a language have been
recognized, their structure may also be determined.

The principles formulated in this book must then be incorporated in any theory of language. Besides permitting prediction, the principle in section 1.3 also yields an explanation
of its patterns once a language is determined as VO or OV.
For other constructions are so arranged that verb + object
sequences are not interrupted; and nominal modifiers are
placed nearest the noun (object) while verbal modifiers are
placed nearest the verb. By leading to such predictions and
explanations the approach presented in this book is demonstrated to be essential for an understanding of language as
well as fundamental for observation and description of specific
languages.

Besides these contributions, study undertaken with the typological approach has illustrated the immense complexity of language as a social system. Even the numerous patterns which have been singled out here fail to encompass its structures. Moreover, like any social system, language is subject to change. The elements, rules, and principles identified have then a statistical basis; they cannot be expected to apply in the rigorous sense used of elements and laws in the physical sciences. But even in change, languages of a given type are modified in accordance with the principles presented here. If, for example, a language changes from OV to VO structure, it will introduce characteristic VO patterns, such as prepositional constructions, preverbal devices for indicating interrogation, VO patterns of complementation, and so on. Such modifications have not been discussed at any length here. They have not yet been adequately investigated. Recent papers deal with some of the problems, such as those examining complementation in early Germanic and Greek (Kurzová 1968; Ureland 1973; Li, ed. 1975; 1976; Lehmann 1976b). The principles proposed above permit explanation of many phenomena attested in the languages investigated, but much remains to be done.

An illustration of explanatory contributions may be taken from reflexivization, which seems to be expressed by a bewildering variety of surface structures when treated simply from a morphological or lexical point of view. But the progression from an OV type of reflexive construction in the Proto-Indo-European middle to the lexical and morphological devices developed in Sanskrit, Greek, Germanic, and the other Indo-European dialects is clarified when reflexivization is viewed as a syntactic category accompanying verbs (Lehmann 1974a). Moreover, the diverse devices by which reciprocal and reflexive relationships are indicated in languages of the several types are readily interpreted when these are viewed as expressions of the middle category. Conclusions derived from the study of language as a phenomenon accordingly clarify syntactic change and reasons for different surface expressions for a given syntactic category.

Although such achievements have resulted from its application, the approach presented here and its findings need elaboration through study of many more languages. As such study is carried out, additional attention must be given to morphology and phonology, which partly for lack of space could not be treated at any length here. Moreover, patterns identified in recent treatments of discourse analysis must be examined with regard to language types (Grimes 1975; Longacre 1976). Further, while exploration of syntactic patterns discussed here has demonstrated remarkable interrelationships in the syntactic structure of language, fuller understanding of these interrelationships will result as other languages are investigated with the procedures illustrated here. Such investigations will also clarify the development of patterns which are produced to compensate for the rigidities, and for shortcomings of individual language types.

Linguists who like Saussure have thought deeply about language have come to be convinced of a "profound unity" underlying diversities apparent among the many languages used now and in the past. This book has been produced to demonstrate that such convictions are not illusory, and to encourage additional studies which will disclose more of that profound unity.

References

Abdullaev, Zapir G. 1971. Očerki po sintaksisu dafginskogo jazyka. Moscow: Nauka.

Adelung, Johann C. 1806 - 1816. Mithridates, vols 1 - 3. Berlin: Voss.

Aissen, Judith. 1974. Verb Raising. Linguistic Inquiry 5.325 - 366.

Akatsuka, N. 1972. A Study of Japanese Reflexivization. Urbana: University of Illinois dissertation.

Allen, William Sidney. 1956. Structure and System in the Abaza Verbal Complex. Transactions of the Philological Society 1956.117 - 176.

———. 1964. Transitivity and Possession. Language 40.337 - 343.

Altmann, Gabriel, and Werner Lehfelot. 1973. Allgemeine Sprachtypologie. Prinzipien und Messverfahren. Uni-Taschenbücher, 250. Munich: Fink.

Anderson, John M., and Charles Jones, eds. 1974. Historical Linguistics. Amsterdam: North-Holland.

Anderson, Stephen R. 1971. On the Role of Deep Structure in Semantic Interpretation. Foundations of Language 7.387 - 396.

———. 1976. On the Notion of Subject in Ergative Languages. Pp. 1 - 23 in Li, ed., 1976.

Aoki, Haruo. 1966. Nez Perce Vowel Harmony and Proto-Sahaptian
Vowels. Language 42.759 - 767.

Applegate, Richard B. 1972. Ineseño Chumash Grammar. Berkeley:
University of California dissertation.

Arms, David. 1974. Transitivity in Standard Fijian. Ann Arbor:
University of Michigan dissertation.

Bani, Ephraim, and Terry J. Klokeid. 1976. Ergative Switching
in Kala Lagau Langgus. In Languages of Cape York, edited
by P. Sutton. Canberra: Australian Institute of Aboriginal
Studies.

Baptista, Priscilla, and Ruth Wallin. 1967. Baure. In Bolivian
Indian Grammars: I. Norman, Okla.: Summer Institute of
Linguistics.

Bechert, Johannes. 1977. Zur funktionalen Erklärung des
Ergativsystems. Papiere zur Linguistik 12.57 - 86.

Benveniste, Emile. 1971. Problems in General Linguistics.
Translated by Mary Elizabeth Meek. Coral Gables: University
of Miami.

Bills, Garland D., Bernardo Vallejo C., and Rudolph C. Troike.
1969. An Introduction to Spoken Bolivian Quechua. Austin:
University of Texas Press.

Birnbaum, Henrik. 1970. Problems of Typological and Genetic
Linguistics Viewed in a Generative Framework. The Hague:
Mouton.

Blake, Barry J. 1976. On Ergativity and the Notion of Subject:
Some Australian Cases. Lingua 39.281 - 300.

Blixen, Olaf. 1973. Tradiciones Pascuenses II. Ure o Hei y
oes tres espíritus vengadores. — Tuapoi. — La veija del
brazo largo. — La niña de la Roto. Moana 1:b.1 - 11.

―――. 1974. Tradiciones Pascuenses III. Ure a Ohovehi.
Moana 1:7.1 - 12.

Bloomfield, Leonard. 1933. Language. New York: Holt.

Boas, Franz. 1911. Introduction to the Handbook of American Indian Languages. Washington: Georgetown University Press.

Brown, Penelope. Forthcoming. Tzeltal Grammar. Berkeley: University of California dissertation.

Calbert, Joseph P., and Heinz Vater. 1975. Aspekte der Modalität. Tübingen: Gunter Narr.

Capell, Arthur. 1969. A Survey of New Guinea Languages. Sydney: University Press.

Cardona, George. 1970. The Indo-Iranian Construction mana (mama) kṛtam. Language 46.1 - 12.

Carroll, Lewis. N.d. The Complete Works of Lewis Carroll. New York: Random House.

Chao, Yuen Ren. 1961. Mandarin Primer. Cambridge: Harvard University Press.

————. 1968. A Grammar of Spoken Chinese. Berkeley and Los Angeles: University of California Press.

Chapin, Paul G. 1974. Proto-Indonesian ai. Journal of the Polynesian Society 83.259 - 307.

Cheng, C. C. 1971. A Synchronic Phonology of Mandarin Chinese. Project on Linguistic Analysis, 14. University of California at Berkeley.

Cheung, H. N. 1973. A Comparative Study in Chinese Grammars: The ba-Construction. Journal of Chinese Linguistics 1.343 - 382.

Chi, Te-lee. 1974. Study of "Verb-Object" Compounds in Mandarin Chinese. In Thompson and Lord, eds., 1974.

Chomsky, Noam. 1964. The Logical Basis of Linguistic Theory. Pp. 914 - 978 in Proceedings of the Ninth International Congress of Linguists, edited by Horace G. Lunt. The Hague: Mouton.

————. 1965. Aspects of the Theory of Syntax. Cambridge, Mass.: MIT Press.

————. 1975. Questions of Form and Interpretation. Pp. 157 - 196 in The Scope of American Linguistics, edited by Robert Austerlitz. Lisse: deRidder.

Chung, Sandra. 1976. Case Marking and Grammatical Relations in Polynesian. Cambridge, Mass.: Harvard University dissertation. (To be published by University of Texas Press.)

Churchward, C. Maxwell. 1953. Tongan Grammar. London: Oxford University Press.

Cole, Peter, ed. 1976. Studies in Modern Hebrew Syntax and Semantics: The Transformational-Generative Approach. North-Holland Linguistics Ser., 32. Amsterdam: North-Holland.

Cole, Peter, and Jerry Sadock. 1973. Grammatical Relations. Syntax and Semantics, 9. New York: Academic Press.

Comrie, Bernard. 1973. The Ergative: Variations on a Theme. Lingua 32.239 - 253.

————. 1975. The Antiergative: Finland's Answer to Basque. Pp. 111 - 121 in Papers from the 11th Meeting of the Chicago Linguistic Society.

————. 1976a. Aspect: An Introduction to the Study of Verbal Aspect and Related Problems. Cambridge: Cambridge University Press.

————. 1976b. Review of Klimov (1973). Lingua 39.511 - 560.

————. 1976c. The Syntax of Actionan Nominals: A Cross-Language Study. Lingua 40.177 - 201.

————. Forthcoming. Definite and Animate Direct Objects: A Natural Class. Linguistic Silesiana 3.

Cowell. 1951. The Structure of Gilbertese. Beru, Gilbert Islands: Rongorongo Press.

Craig, Colette. 1976. Properties of Basic and Derived
    Subjects in Jacaltec. Pp. 99 - 123 in Li, ed., 1976.
————. 1977. The Structure of Jacaltec. Austin: University
    of Texas Press.
Crews, Frederick. 1977. The Random House Handbook. 2d ed.
    New York: Random House.
Danes, Frantisek. 1964. A Three-Level Approach to Syntax.
    Travaux Linguistiques de Prague 1.225 - 240.
de Laguna, Grace Andrews. 1927/1963. Speech: Its Function
    and Development. Bloomington: Indiana University Press.
Derbyshire, D. C. 1977. Word Order Universals and the
    Existence of OVS Languages. Linguistic Inquiry 8.590 - 599.
Dešeriev, Junus D. 1953. Bacbijskij jazyk. Moscow: Nauka.
Dillon, Myles. 1947. Celtic and the Other Indo-European
    Languages. Transactions of the Philological Society
    1947.15 - 24.
Dixon, Robert M. W. 1972. The Dyirbal Language of North
    Queensland. Cambridge: Cambridge University Press.
————. 1976. Review of Franz Boas (ed.), Handbook of American
    Indian Languages. Linguistics 152.75 - 77.
————. 1977a. A Grammar of Yidiɲ. Cambridge: Cambridge
    University Press.
————. 1977b. The Syntactic Development of Australian
    Languages. In Li, ed., 1977.
Dixon, Robert M. W., ed. 1976. Grammatical Categories in
    Australian Languages. Canberra: Australian Institute of
    Aboriginal Studies.
Ellegård, Alvar. 1974 [1975]. Rev. of Altmann and Lehfeldt,
    Allgemeine Sprachtypologie. Kratylos 19.11 - 14.
Englert, P. Sebastian. 1948. La tierra de Hotu Matu'a. Padre
    las Casas, Chile: Imprenta y Editorial "San Francisco."

Erguvanli, Eser. 1976. Pronominalization in Fijian.
    Unpublished paper, UCLA Department of Linguistics.

Finck, Franz Nikolaus. 1899. Der deutsche Sprachbau als
    Ausdruck deutscher Weltanschauung. Marburg: Elwert.

――――. 1909. Die Haupttypen des Sprachbaus. Leipzig and
    Berlin: Teubner.

Firbas, Jan. 1964. On Defining the Theme in Functional
    Sentence Analysis. Travaux Linguistiques de Prague
    1.267 - 280.

Fodor, Jerry A., T. G. Bever, and M. F. Garrett. 1974. The
    Psychology of Language. New York: McGraw-Hill.

Fries, Charles C. 1940. On the Development of the Structural
    Use of Word-Order in Modern English. Language 16.199 - 208.

Fuentes, Jordi. 1960. Dictionary and Grammar of the Easter
    Island Language. (Spanish and English versions bound into
    one volume.) Santiago de Chile: Editorial Andres Bello.

Gazzaniga, Michael S. 1970. The Bisected Brain. New York:
    Appleton-Century-Crofts.

Givón, Talmy. 1971. Historical Syntax and Synchronic
    Morphology: An Archeologist's Fieldtrip. Pp. 394 - 415
    in Papers from the 7th Regional Meeting, Chicago
    Linguistic Society.

――――. 1975. Serial Verbs and Syntactic Change. Pp. 47 - 112
    in Li, ed., 1975.

――――. 1976a. Topic, Pronoun and Grammatical Agreement.
    Pp. 149 - 188 in Li, ed., 1976.

――――. 1976b. On the VS Word Order in Israeli Hebrew:
    Pragmatics and Typological Change. In Cole, ed., 1976.

Gordon, Amnon. 1976. The Structure of the Relative Clause (in
    Fijian). Unpublished paper, UCLA Department of Linguistics.

Gordon, Lynn. 1976. Raising in Fijian. Unpublished paper,
    UCLA Department of Linguistics.

Greenberg, Joseph H. 1963/1966. Some Universals of Grammar
    with Particular Reference to the Order of Meaningful
    Elements. Pp. 73 - 113 in Universals of Language, edited
    by idem. Cambridge, Mass.: MIT Press.
———. 1976. On the Order of Numeral Components. Lecture.
Grimes, Joseph E. 1975. The Thread of Discourse. The Hague:
    Mouton.
Grjunberg, Alexandr L. 1972. Jazyki vostocnogo Gindukusa:
    Mundzanskij jazyk. Leningrad: Nauka.
Gukhman, Mira. 1977. On the Content and Aims of Historical
    Typology. Pp. 60 - 69 in Theoretical Aspects of Linguistics.
    Moscow: USSR Academy of Sciences.
Haarmann, Harald. 1976. Grundzüge der Sprachtypologie.
    Stuttgart: Kohlhammer.
Haig, John H. 1976. Shadow Pronoun Deletion in Japanese.
    Linguistic Inquiry 7.363 - 371.
Haiman, John. Forthcoming. Hua: A Papuan Language of New
    Guinea. In Variation among the Languages of the World,
    edited by Timothy Shopen.
Hale, Kenneth. 1967. Preliminary Remarks on Walbiri Grammar.
    Cambridge, Mass.: MIT manuscript.
———. 1973. Person Marking in Walbiri. In A Festschrift for
    Morris Halle. New York: Holt, Rinehart and Winston.
Hashimoto, Y. 1971. Mandarin Syntactic Structures. Unicorn,
    No. 8. Chinese Linguistics Project, Princeton University.
Hauri, Christoph. 1976. Typologie als Hilfsmittel der
    Syntax. Münchener Studien zur Sprachwissenschaft 35.33 - 46.
Hess, Harwood. 1968. The Syntactic Structure of Mezquital
    Otomi. The Hague: Mouton.
Hjelmslev, Louis. 1959. Essais linguistiques. Copenhagen:
    Nordisk Sprog-og Kulturforlag.

Hockett, Charles F. 1955. A Manual of Phonology. Baltimore:
   Waverly.

Hohepa, Patrick W. 1969. The Accusative-to-Ergative Drift in
   Polynesian Languages. Journal of the Polynesian Society
   78.295 - 329.

Horne, Kibbey M. 1966. Language Typology. Washington, D.C.:
   Georgetown University Press.

Humboldt, Wilhelm von. 1836/1968. Über die Verschiedenheit
   des menschlichen Sprachbaues und ihren Einfluss auf die
   geistige Entwicklung des Menschengeschlechts. Bonn:
   Dümmler.

Hyman, Larry M. 1975. On the Change from SOV to SVO: Evidence
   from Niger-Congo. Pp. 113 - 147 in Li, ed., 1975.

Ingram, David. 1975. A Note on Word Order in Proto-Salish.
   IJAL 41.165 - 168.

Jansky, Herbert. 1954. Lehrbuch der Türkischen Sprache.
   2d ed. Wiesbaden: Harrassowitz.

Jespersen, Otto. 1922. Language. London: Allen & Unwin.

———. 1924. The Philosophy of Grammar. London: Allen &
   Unwin.

———. 1949. A Modern English Grammar on Historical
   Principles. Vols. III, VII. Copenhagen: Munksgaard.

Josephs, L. 1972. Phenomena of Tense and Aspect in Japanese
   Relative Clauses. Language 48.109 - 133.

Justus, Carol. 1976. Relativization and Topicalization in
   Hittite. Pp. 213 - 245 in Li, ed., 1976.

Kaufman, E. S. 1974. Navajo Spatial Enclitics: A Case for
   Unbounded Rightward Movement. Linguistic Inquiry 5.507 -
   533.

Keenan, Edward L. 1976a. Remarkable Subjects in Malagasy. Pp.
   247 - 301 in Li, ed., 1976.

————. 1976b. Towards a Universal Definition of "Subject."
Pp. 303 - 333 in Li, ed., 1976.

————. Forthcoming. Some Logical Problems in Translation.
In Meaning and Translation: Philosophical and Linguistic
Approaches, edited by F. Guenthner and M. Guenthner.
London: Duckworth.

Keenan, Edward L., and Bernard Comrie. 1977. Noun Phrase
Accessibility and Universal Grammar. Linguistic Inquiry
9.63 - 101.

Kibrik, Aleksandr E., Sandro V. Kodzasov, and Irina P.
Olovjanonikona. 1972. Fragmenty grammatiki xinalugskogo
jazyka. Moscow: Izd-vo Moskovskogo Universiteta.

Kirsner, Robert. 1976. On the Subjectless "Pseudo-Passive"
in Standard Dutch and the Semantics of Background Agents.
Pp. 385 - 415 in Li, ed., 1976.

Klaeber, Friedrich, ed. 1950. Beowulf and the Fight at
Finnsburg. 3d ed. Boston: Heath.

Klimov, Georgi A. 1973. Očerk obščej teorii ergativnosti.
Moscow: Nauka.

————. 1977. On the Notion of Language Type. Pp. 70 - 77 in
Theoretical Aspects of Linguistics. Moscow: USSR Academy
of Sciences.

Kratochvil, P. 1968. The Chinese Language Today. London:
Hutchinson University Library.

Kuno, Susumu. 1971. The Position of Locatives in Existential
Sentences. Linguistic Inquiry 2.333 - 378.

————. 1972. Functional Sentence Perspective: A Case Study
from Japanese and English. Linguistic Inquiry 3.269 - 320.

————. 1973. The Structure of the Japanese Language.
Cambridge, Mass.: MIT Press.

————. 1974. The Position of Relative Clauses and Conjunctions. Linguistic Inquiry 5.117 - 136.

——. 1975. Three Perspectives in the Functional Approach
to Syntax. Pp. 276 – 336 in Papers from the Parasession on
Functionalism. Chicago Linguistic Society.

——. 1976a. Subject Raising. Pp. 17 – 49 in Shibatani,
ed., 1976b.

——. 1976b. Subject, Theme, and the Speaker's Empathy —
A Reexamination of Relativization Phenomena. Pp. 18 – 49 in
Li, ed., 1976.

——. 1976c. The Speaker's Empathy and its Effect on
Syntax — A Reexamination of Yaru and Kureru in Japanese.
Journal of the Association of Teachers of Japanese
11.249 – 271.

Kuno, Susumu, and E. Kaburaki. 1975. Empathy and Syntax. Pp.
1 – 73 in Harvard Studies in Syntax and Semantics 1, edited
by S. Kuno.

Kuroda, S.-Y. 1965. Generative Grammatical Studies in the
Japanese Language. Cambridge, Mass.: MIT dissertation.

——. 1972a. Anton Marty and the Transformational Theory of
Grammar. Foundations of Language 9.1 – 37.

——. 1972b. The Categorial and the Thetic Judgment:
Evidence from Japanese Syntax. Foundations of Language
9.153 – 185.

Kurzová, Helena. 1968. Zur syntaktischen Struktur des
griechischen Infinitiv und Nebensatz. Prague: Academia.
Amsterdam: Hakkert.

Lafitte, Pierre. 1962. Grammaire basque: Navarro-labourdin
littéraire. Rev. ed. Bayonne: Editions des "Amis du Musée
Basque" et "Ikas."

Lehmann, Winfred P. 1970. Definite Adjective Declensions
and Syntactic Types. In Donum Balticum, edited by Velta
Ruke-Dravina. Stockholm: Almqvist and Wiksell.

————. 1971. On the Rise of SOV Patterns in New High German.
Pp. 19 - 24 in Grammatik Kybernetik Kommunikation, edited
by K. G. Schweisthal. Bonn: Dümmler.

————. 1972a. Converging Theories in Linguistics. Language
48.266 - 275.

————. 1972b. Contemporary Linguistics and Indo-European
Studies. PMLA 87.976 - 993.

————. 1973a. A Structural Principle of Language and Its
Implications. Language 49.47 - 66.

————. 1973b. Historical Linguistics. New York: Holt,
Rinehart and Winston.

————. 1974a. Proto-Indo-European Syntax. Austin: University
of Texas Press.

————. 1974b. Japanese as a Consistent OV Language. Pp. 1 - 12
in Proceedings of a U.S.-Japanese Sociolinguistics
Meeting, edited by Bates Hoffer. San Antonio: Trinity
University.

————. 1975a. A Discussion of Compound and Word Order. Pp.
149 - 162 in Li, ed., 1975.

————. 1975b. The Challenge of History. Pp. 41 - 58 in The
Scope of American Linguistics, edited by Robert Austerlitz.
Lisse: deRidder.

————. 1976a. From Topic to Subject in Indo-European. Pp.
445 - 456 in Li, ed., 1976.

————. 1976b. On Complementation in the Early Germanic
Languages. Journal of the Linguistic Association of the
Southwest 1.1 - 7.

Lewy, Ernst. 1942. Der Bau der europäischen Sprachen. Dublin:
Hodges-Figgis. (Reprinted, Tübingen: Niemeyer, 1964.)

Li, Charles N. 1971. Semantics and the Structure of
Compounds in Chinese. Berkeley: University of California
dissertation.

Li, Charles N., ed. 1975. Word Order and Word Order Change. Austin: University of Texas Press.

———. 1976. Subject and Topic. New York: Academic Press.

———. 1977. Mechanisms of Syntactic Change. Austin: University of Texas Press.

Li, Charles N., and Sandra A. Thompson. 1974a. Historical Change of Word Order: A Case Study in Chinese and Its Implications. Pp. 199 - 217 in Anderson and Jones, eds., 1974.

———. 1974b. An Explanation of Word Order Change: SVO > SOV. Foundations of Language 12.201 - 214.

———. 1975. The Semantic Function of Word Order: A Case Study in Chinese. Pp. 163 - 195 in Li, ed., 1975.

———. 1976a. On the Issue of Word Order in a Synchronic Grammar: A Case against "Movement Transformations." Lingua 39.169 - 181.

———. 1976b. Subject and Topic: A New Typology of Language. Pp. 457 - 489 in Li, ed., 1976.

———. 1976c. Development of the Causative in Mandarin Chinese: Interaction of Diachronic Processes in Syntax. Pp. 477 - 492 in Shibatani, ed., 1976b.

———. Forthcoming a. The Semantics of the Descriptive Clause in Mandarin Chinese.

———. Forthcoming b. Constraints and Regularities on Zero-Pronominalization in Mandarin Chinese.

Li, Francis C. 1971. Case and Communicative Function in the Use of ba in Mandarin. Ithaca: Cornell University dissertation.

Light, Timothy. 1976. Word Order and Word Order Change in Mandarin Chinese. Paper presented at the Annual Meeting of the Linguistic Society of America.

Longacre, Robert E. 1976. An Anatomy of Speech Notions. Lisse: deRidder.

McCawley, Norika A. 1976. Reflexivization: A Transformational Approach. Pp. 511-516 in Shibatani, ed., 1976b.

McKay, Graham R. 1977. Are Australian Languages Syntactically Nominative-Ergative or Nominative-Accusative? Rembarnga. In Dixon, ed., 1976.

Malzac, R. P. 1926. Grammaire malgache. Paris: Société d'Editions Géographiques, Maritimes et Coloniales.

Martin, Samuel. 1975. A Reference Grammar of Japanese. New Haven: Yale University Press.

Mathesius, Vilém. 1964. On Linguistic Characterology with Illustrations from Modern English. Pp. 59-67 in A Prague School Reader in Linguistics, compiled by Josef Vachek. Bloomington: Indiana University Press.

Matteson, Esther. 1965. The Piro (Araawakan) Language. Berkeley and Los Angeles: University of California Publications in Linguistics.

Meillet, Antoine, and Marcel Cohen. 1952. Les Langues du monde. Paris: Champion.

Mikami, A. 1970. Zoo wa Hana Ga Nagai. Tokyo: Kurosio Syuppan.

Müller, Friedrich. 1876-1888. Grundriss der Sprachwissenschaft. Vienna.

Munro, Pam. 1974. Topics in Mojave Syntax. San Diego: University of California dissertation.

Noonan, Michael. 1976. On Proto-Salish Word Order: A Reply to Ingram. IJAL 42.363-366.

Ott, Willis G., and Rebecca H. Ott. 1967. "Ignaciano" in Bolivian Indian languages: One. Norman, Okla.: Summer Institute of Linguistics.

Panfilov, Vladimir. 1977. Linguistic Universals and Sentence Typology. Pp. 78-89 in Theoretical Aspects of Linguistics. Moscow: USSR Academy of Sciences.

Pawley, Andrew. 1966. Polynesian Languages: A Subgrouping
Based on Shared Innovations in Morphology. Journal of
the Polynesian Society 75.39 - 64.

––––––. 1967. The Relationships of Polynesian Outlier
Languages. Journal of the Polynesian Society 76.259 - 296.

Penn, Julia M. 1972. Linguistic Relativity versus Innate
Ideas. The Hague: Mouton.

Pickett, Velma. 1960. The Grammatical Hierarchy of Isthmus
Zapotec. Language Dissertation, 56. Baltimore: Linguistic
Society of America.

Pirejko, Lija A. 1968. Osnovnye voprosy ergativnosti na
materiale indoiranskix jazykov. Moscow: Nauka.

Pullum, Geoffrey. 1977. Word Order Universals and Grammatical
Relations. In Syntax and Semantics 8. New York: Academic
Press.

Ratanajoti, Hundirapola. 1975. The Syntactic Structure of
Sinhalese and Its Relation to That of the Other Indo-
Aryan Dialects. Austin: University of Texas dissertation.

––––––. 1976. The Sinhalese Numerals for the Teens. Indian
Linguistics 36.

Richards, Ivor Armstrong. 1943. Basic English and Its Uses.
New York: Norton.

Ross, John Robert. 1967. Constraints on Variables in Syntax.
Cambridge, Mass.: MIT dissertation.

Sandfeld, Kristian. 1930. Linguistique balkanique: Problemès
et résultats. Paris: Champion.

Sapir, Edward. 1921. Language. New York: Harcourt Brace.

––––––. 1963. Selected Writings in Language, Culture,
Personality, edited by David G. Mandelbaum. Berkeley and
Los Angeles: University of California Press.

Saussure, Ferdinand de. 1959. Course in General Linguistics.
Translated by Wade Baskin. New York: Philosophical Library.

Schachter, Paul, and F. Otanes. 1972. A Tagalog Reference
    Grammar. Los Angeles and Berkeley: University of California
    Press.

Schmidt, Pater Wilhelm. 1926. Die Sprachfamilien und Sprachen-
    kreise der Erde. Heidelberg: Winter.

Seiler, Hansjakob. 1975. Das linguistische Universalien-
    problem in neuer Sicht. Opladen: Westdeutscher Verlag.

Seuren, Pieter A. M. 1969. Operators and Nucleus. London:
    Cambridge University Press.

Sherzer, Joel. 1976. An Areal-Typological Study of American
    Indian Languages North of Mexico. Amsterdam: North-Holland.

Shibatani, Masayoshi. 1976. Grammatical Relations and Surface
    Cases. Unpublished paper, Department of Linguistics,
    University of Southern California.

Shibatani, Masayoshi, ed. 1976a. Japanese Generative Grammar.
    New York: Academic Press.

———. 1976b. The Grammar of Causative Constructions. New
    York: Academic Press.

Silitonga, Mangasa. 1973. Some Rules Reordering Constituents
    and Their Constraints in Batak. Urbana: University of
    Illinois dissertation.

Silverstein, Michael. 1976. Hierarchy of Features and
    Ergativity. In Dixon, ed., 1976.

Snell, Betty, and Mary Ruth Wise. 1963. Noncontingent
    Declarative Clauses in Macgiguenga (Arawak). In Peruvian
    Indian Languages: 1. Norman, Okla.: Summer Institute of
    Linguistics.

Steele, Susan. 1975. On Some Factors That Affect and Effect
    Word Order. Pp. 197-268 in Li, ed., 1975.

Steinthal, Heyman. 1850. Die Classification der Sprachen,
    dargestellt als die Entwicklung der Sprachidee. Berlin:
    Dümmler.

————. 1893. Charakteristik der hauptsächlichsten Typen des
Sprachbaues. 2d ed., revised by F. Misteli. Berlin.

Strunk, William, Jr., and E. B. White. 1972. The Elements
of Style. 2d ed. New York: Macmillan.

Swadesh, Morris. 1971. The Origin and Diversification of
Language. Chicago: Aldine, Atherton.

Tai, James H-Y. 1973a. A Derivational Constraint on Adverbial
Placement in Mandarin Chinese. Journal of Chinese
Linguistics 1.397 - 413.

————. 1973b. Chinese as a SOV Language. Pp. 659 - 671 in
Papers from the Ninth Annual Meeting of the Chicago
Linguistic Society.

Teng, Shou-Hsin. 1975. Semantic Study of Transitivity
Relations in Chinese. Berkeley and Los Angeles:
University of California Press.

Thompson, Sandra A. 1973a. Transitivity and Some Problems
with the ba Construction in Mandarin Chinese. Journal of
Chinese Linguistics 1.208 - 221.

————. 1973b. Resultative Verb Compounds in Mandarin Chinese:
A Case for Lexical Rules. Language 49.361 - 379.

Thompson, Sandra A., and C. Lord, eds. 1974. Approaches to
the Lexicon. UCLA Papers in Syntax, No. 6.

Timberlake, Alan. 1976. Subject Properties in the North
Russian Passive. Pp. 545 - 570 in Li, ed., 1976.

Traugott, Elizabeth Closs. 1972. A History of English Syntax.
New York: Holt, Rinehart and Winston.

Trubetzkoy, Nikolay S. 1969. Principles of Phonology.
Translated by Christiane A. M. Baltaxe. Berkeley and Los
Angeles: University of California Press.

Tung, T'ung-ho. 1964. A Descriptive Study of the Tsou
Language. Formosa Institute of History and Philology.

Academia Sinica Special Publications, No. 48. Taipei,
Taiwan.

Twaddell, W. Freeman. 1960. The English Verb Auxiliary.
Providence: Brown University Press.

Ureland, Sture. 1973. Verb Complementation in Swedish and
Other Germanic Languages. Stockholm: Skriptor.

Uspenskij, Boris P. 1968. Principles of Structural Typology.
The Hague: Mouton.

Vachek, Josef. 1966. The Linguistic School of Prague.
Bloomington: Indiana University Press.

Vattuone, Bartholomew. 1975. Notes on Genoese Syntax. London:
University College, unpublished paper.

Vennemann, Theo. 1974. Topics, Subjects and Word Order: From
SXV to SVX via TVS. Pp. 339 - 376 of Anderson and Jones,
eds., 1974.

————. 1975. An Explanation of Drift. Pp. 269 - 305 in Li,
ed., 1975.

Voegelin, Carl F., and F. M. Voegelin. 1973. Index of the
World's Languages. I - VII. Bloomington: Indiana University
(Office of Education: HEW).

von Gabain, A. 1974. Alttürkische Grammatik. 3d ed. Wiesbaden:
Harrassowitz.

von Humboldt, Wilhelm. *See* Humboldt, Wilhelm von.

Wackernagel, Jacob. 1926/1928. Vorlesungen über Syntax.
I, II. 2d ed. Basel: Birkhäuser.

Whitney, William Dwight. 1892. Language and the Study of
Language. New York: Scribner.

Whorf, Benjamin Lee. 1956. Language, Thought and Reality ...
Selected Writings, edited by John B. Carroll. Cambridge,
Mass.: MIT Press.

Williamson, Craig, ed. 1977. The Old English Riddles of the
Exeter Book. Chapel Hill: University of North Carolina Press.

Yamagiwa, Joseph K. 1942. Modern Conversational Japanese.
    New York: McGraw-Hill.
Yar-Shater, Ehsan. 1969. A Grammar of Southern Tati Dialects.
    The Hague: Mouton.
Yartseva, Victoria. 1977. Typology of Languages and the
    Problem of Universals. Pp. 90 - 99 in Theoretical Aspects
    of Linguistics. Moscow: USSR Academy of Sciences.
Zimmer, Karl. 1971. Some General Observations about Nominal
    Compounds. Working Papers on Language Universals, No. 5.
    Stanford University, Department of Linguistics.
————. 1972. Appropriateness Conditions for Nominal
    Compounds. Working Papers on Language Universals, No. 8.
    Stanford University, Department of Linguistics.

Index